NEW PERSPECTIVES ON
COMPUTER
CONCEPTS

Brief

by June Jamrich Parsons and Dan Oja **6th EDITION**

Includes an interactive
BookOnCD that contains the
entire contents of the textbook with figures that come
to life as videos, software
tours, and animations. Plus
labs, computer-scored
practice tests, and more!

**25 Thomson Place
Boston, MA 02210**

Australia • Canada • Denmark • Japan •
Mexico • New Zealand • Philippines •
Puerto Rico • Singapore • South Africa •
Spain • United Kingdom • United States

THOMSON

COURSE TECHNOLOGY

MANAGING EDITOR
Rachel Crapser

SENIOR PRODUCT MANAGER
Kathy Finnegan

TECHNOLOGY PRODUCT MANAGER
Amanda Shelton

PRODUCT MANAGER
Karen Stevens

EDITORIAL ASSISTANT
Emilie Perreault

MARKETING MANAGER
Rachel Valente

DEVELOPMENTAL EDITOR
Kathy Finnegan

PRODUCTION EDITOR
Debbie Masi

TEXT DESIGN AND COMPOSITION
MediaTechnics Corporation

PREPRESS PRODUCTION
GEX Publishing Services

MEDIA DEVELOPERS
Donna Schuch, Fatima Lockhart,
Keefe Crowley, Tensi Parsons

PHOTO AND VIDEO RESEARCHER
Abby Reip

PHOTOGRAPHERS
Greg Manis, Joe Bush

ILLUSTRATOR
Eric Murphy

NARRATORS
Chris Robbert and Michele Martinez

BOOKONCD DEVELOPMENT
MediaTechnics Corporation

CONTENTS AT A GLANCE

CHAPTER 1

2 COMPUTER, INTERNET, AND NETWORK BASICS

4 **Section A: Computer Basics**
14 Lab: Operating a Personal Computer

15 **Section B: Internet Basics**
25 LAB: Making a Dial-up Connection

26 **Section C: Web Basics**
35 LAB: Browsing and Searching

36 **Section D: E-mail Basics**
43 LAB: Using E-mail

44 **TechTalk: The Boot Process**

48 **Issue: How Private is E-mail?**

50 **Review Activities**

CHAPTER 2

56 COMPUTER HARDWARE

58 **Section A: Data Representation and Digital Electronics**
65 LAB: Working with Binary Numbers

66 **Section B: Microprocessors and Memory**
75 LAB: Benchmarking

76 **Section C: Storage Devices**

88 **Section D: Input and Output Devices**

98 **TechTalk: How a Microprocessor Executes Instructions**

102 **Issue: Why Recycle Computers?**

104 **Review Activities**

CHAPTER 3

110 COMPUTER SOFTWARE

112 **Section A: Software Basics**

118 **Section B: Personal Computer Operating Systems**
127 LAB: Using the Windows Interface

128 **Section C: Application Software**

148 **Section D: Software Installation and Copyrights**
156 LAB: Installing and Uninstalling Software

157 **TechTalk: The Windows Registry**

160 **Issue: Is Piracy a Problem?**

162 **Review Activities**

CHAPTER 4

168 FILE MANAGEMENT, VIRUS PROTECTION, AND BACKUP

170 **Section A: File Basics**

174 **Section B: File Management**
184 LAB: Working with Windows Explorer

185 **Section C: Computer Viruses**

193 **Section D: Data Backup**
202 LAB: Backing Up Your Computer

203 **TechTalk: File Formats**

208 **Issue: Is it a Crime?**

210 **Review Activities**

TABLE OF CONTENTS

CHAPTER 1

2 COMPUTER, INTERNET, AND NETWORK BASICS

4 **Section A: Computer Basics**
4 A Computer is...
6 Computer Categories
9 Personal Computer Systems
11 Data, Information, and Files
12 Application Software and Operating System Basics
13 QuickCheck A
14 LAB: Operating a Personal Computer

15 **Section B: Internet Basics**
15 Internet Resources
18 Internet Connections
20 Internet Service Providers
22 User IDs and Passwords
24 QuickCheck B
25 LAB: Making a Dial-up Connection

26 **Section C: Web Basics**
26 The World Wide Web
28 Browsers
31 Search Engines
34 QuickCheck C
35 LAB: Browsing and Searching

36 **Section D: E-mail Basics**
36 E-mail Overview
40 E-mail Technology
42 QuickCheck D
43 LAB: Using E-mail

44 **TechTalk: The Boot Process**
47 QuickCheck TechTalk

48 **Issue: How Private is E-mail?**

50 **Review Activities**
50 Interactive Summary
52 Interactive Key Terms
53 Interactive Situation Questions
54 Interactive Practice Tests
54 Study Tips
55 Projects
55 Additional Projects

CHAPTER 2

56 COMPUTER HARDWARE

58 **Section A: Data Representation and Digital Electronics**
58 Digital Data Representation
61 Quantifying Bits and Bytes
62 Digital Electronics
64 QuickCheck A
65 LAB: Working with Binary Numbers

66 **Section B: Microprocessors and Memory**
66 Microprocessor Basics
67 Microprocessor Performance Factors
69 Today's Microprocessors
70 Random Access Memory
72 Read-Only Memory
73 CMOS Memory
74 QuickCheck B
75 LAB: Benchmarking

76 **Section C: Storage Devices**
76 Storage Basics
79 Floppy Disk Technology
81 Hard Disk Technology
83 Tape Storage

84   CD Technology

86   DVD Technology

87   QuickCheck C

88   **Section D: Input and Output Devices**

88   Expansion Slots, Cards, and Ports

92   Installing Peripheral Devices

92   Display Devices

94   Printers

97   QuickCheck D

98   **TechTalk: How a Microprocessor Executes Instructions**

101   QuickCheck TechTalk

102   **Issue: Why Recycle Computers?**

104   **Review Activities**

104   Interactive Summary

106   Interactive Key Terms

107   Interactive Situation Questions

108   Interactive Practice Tests

108   Study Tips

109   Projects

109   Additional Projects

CHAPTER 3

110   COMPUTER SOFTWARE

112   **Section A: Software Basics**

114   Software, Programs, and Data Files

114   Programmers and Programming Languages

115   How Software Works

116   Application Software and System Software

117   QuickCheck A

118   **Section B: Personal Computer Operating Systems**

118   Operating System Overview

123   Windows, Mac OS, UNIX, and DOS

126   QuickCheck B

127   LAB: Using the Windows Interface

128   **Section C: Application Software**

128   Document Production Software

133   Spreadsheet Software

136   Accounting and Finance, Mathematical Modeling, and Statistical Software

137   Data Management Software

141   Graphics Software

143   Music Software

144   Video Editing Software

144   Educational and Reference Software

145   Entertainment Software

147   Business Software

147   QuickCheck C

148   **Section D: Software Installation and Copyrights**

148   Installation Basics

150   Installing From Distribution Disks or CDs

151   Installing Downloaded Software

152   Uninstalling Software

153   Software Copyrights

153   Software Licenses

155   QuickCheck D

153   LAB: Installing and Uninstalling Software

157   **TechTalk: The Windows Registry**

159   QuickCheck TechTalk

160   **Issue: Is Piracy a Problem?**

162   **Review Activities**

162   Interactive Summary

164   Interactive Key Terms

165   Software Key Terms

165   Interactive Situation Questions

166 Interactive Practice Tests
166 Study Tips
167 Projects
167 Additional Projects

CHAPTER 4

168 FILE MANAGEMENT, VIRUS PROTECTION, AND BACKUP

170 **Section A: File Basics**
170 Filenames, Extensions, and Formats
172 File Locations, Folders, and Paths
173 File Sizes and Dates
173 QuickCheck A

174 **Section B: File Management**
174 Application-Based File Management
176 File Management Utilities
177 File Management Metaphors
178 Windows Explorer
180 Physical File Storage
183 QuickCheck B
184 LAB: Working with Windows Explorer

185 **Section C: Computer Viruses**
185 Viruses, Trojan Horses, and Worms
189 Antivirus Software
191 Virus Hoaxes
192 QuickCheck C

193 **Section D: Data Backup**
193 Backup and Restore Procedures
198 Backup Equipment
200 Backup Software
201 QuickCheck D
202 LAB: Backing Up Your Computer

203 **TechTalk: File Formats**
207 QuickCheck TechTalk

208 **Issue: Is it a Crime?**

210 **Review Activities**
210 Interactive Summary
212 Interactive Key Terms

213 Interactive Situation Questions
214 Interactive Practice Tests
214 Study Tips
215 Projects
215 Additional Projects

PREFACE

FROM THE AUTHORS

Technology seems to be moving forward at an increasingly rapid pace. To help students and instructors stay in step with the march of technology, we've worked industriously to bring you *New Perspectives on Computer Concepts 6th Edition*—our first edition on an annual cycle. With this annual edition, we've retained the same organization for Chapters 1 through 4, and updated their content.

As an example of the updates for this edition, we have relegated Napster to history and replaced it with references to currently popular file-sharing sites, such as Kazaa, Morpheus, and Grokster. In addition, we have downplayed Web page frames because they are becoming less and less common. We have updated technical specifications, such as processing speed and memory capacity, for typical consumer computers. We also have included screenshots and information relevant to Windows XP, while still retaining examples from earlier versions of Windows. These and other updates—along with the InfoWebLinks—will keep you up-to-date on computer-related developments.

A year ago, we completed an extensive revision of this text, designed to meet the needs of today's students who typically have more practical experience with computers than their counterparts of 10 years ago. The goal of the 5th Edition was to take students beyond basic computer literacy and provide them with information that a college-educated person would be expected to know about computers. That goal remains in place for the 6th Edition. We hope that you enjoy the learning experience provided by our text-based and technology-based materials.

ACKNOWLEDGMENTS

Every edition of this text requires extraordinary effort by a dedicated and creative team. The content of every page is subjected to the scrutiny of professional educators, such as Beverly Amer, Ken Baldauf, Mary Caldwell, Becky Curtin, Ed Mott, Catherine Perlich, Martha J. Tilmann, and Mary Zayac. Student reviewers and testers, such as Kitty Edwards and Heather House, help us target our readers. Technical reviewers, such as Jeff Harrow, Barbra D. Letts, John Lucas, Ramachandran Bharath, and Karl Mulder, hold our feet to the fire when it comes to accuracy. We get additional help from professionals all over the world and are grateful to a number of Webmasters who have responded to our requests for additional information on topics of their specialties.

The book would not exist—and certainly would not arrive on schedule—were it not for the efforts of our media, editorial, and production teams. We thank Rachel Crapser and Kathy Finnegan for their tireless work on the entire New Perspectives series; Barbra D. Letts and Stephanie Low for their invaluable contributions to research and writing; Debbie Masi for managing production; Fatima Lockhart, Donna Schuch, Tensi Parsons, Keefe Crowley, Greg Manis, Joe Bush, and Eric Murphy for creating videos, screentours, interactive tests, photos, illustrations, and animations; Jean Insinga for her work on the Instuctor's Manual; Chris Robbert for his clear narrations; Sue Oja, Debora Elam, Deana Martinson, Karen Kangas, Jaclyn Kangas, and Kevin Lappi for checking and double-checking the alpha and beta CDs; Stacy Moran for making sure that every comma is in the right place; Keefe Crowley for designing and maintaining our Web site; Kathy Finnegan for her insightful developmental edit; and Abby Reip for photo research. We want to thank you all!

—June Parsons and Dan Oja

I am very impressed with this book. It is exceptionally well done and has clearly succeeded in talking TO, rather than AT readers. The integration of multimedia, "corrected" exercises, and live Web content exceeds anything I've previously seen in this genre.
—*Jeffrey R. Harrow, www.TheHarrowGroup.com*

THE STUDENT EXPERIENCE

STUDENT

CONNECT

Get customized notes from your instructor with the Instructor Annotations and Web Syllabus features, accessible directly from the BookOnCD. You can make sure your studies are on track by reading the extra notes and having a direct connection to the latest course syllabus.

READ

The comprehensive coverage of this textbook goes beyond basic computer literacy. Each chapter is divided into manageable sections, so you'll be able to plan your study time. And, with each section's QuickCheck questions, you'll be able to gauge when you're ready to learn more!

INTERACT

For those of you who want to go beyond the written word, the BookOnCD provides a structured environment to enhance your learning experience. Interact with the animations, experience simulated versions of software with the screentours, and watch videos of common tasks to make the experience come to life.

ENGAGE

And for those of you who want to "kick the tires" on the concepts you're learning, the labs present concepts through the use of step-by-step, interactive tutorials available on the BookOnCD. Each lab concludes with QuickCheck questions to help you evaluate your understanding of the material in the lab.

EXPLORE

Keep up with the latest trends and technologies. The InfoWebLinks allow you to get up-to-date information on important topics. While using the BookOnCD, you can click links to access www.infoweblinks.com—a collection of regularly updated Web pages that are directly related to what you're learning.

INVESTIGATE

Learn more than just how a computer works. The TechTalk sections present challenging technical topics in an easy-to-understand way. The Issues sections not only expose societal and sometimes controversial topics related to computing, they also give you the opportunity to express your opinions.

CHECK

When you're done with a chapter, you'll want to know "what you know" (before your next exam). Extensive end-of-chapter assignments and activities allow you to assess your progress using interactive summaries, key terms, situation questions, practice tests, study tips, and projects.

COMMUNICATE

Stay in touch. The WebTrack feature allows you to keep your instructor in the loop on your progress. With just a few mouse clicks, you can send the results of the interactive summaries, situation questions, practice tests, and lab QuickCheck questions directly to your instructor.

THE INSTRUCTOR EXPERIENCE

PLAN

Use the Web Syllabus feature to prepare and post a course syllabus. Your students can access the syllabus directly from the BookOnCD, allowing you to give them the most up-to-date course information quickly and easily.

CUSTOMIZE

With the Instructor Annotations feature, you can deliver additional educational content directly to your students—just when they need it! From the BookOnCD, students simply click a special Annotation button to link to a relevant video, audio clip, diagram, or note that you supply.

ORGANIZE

The variety of Instructor Supplements—including the Instructor's Manual and ExamView testing software—makes it easy for you to organize and enhance your teaching experience (see page xviii for more details).

PRESENT

Course Presenter, a CD-ROM-based presentation tool, gives you the choice of ready-made or custom presentations for use in class to complement your lectures.

CHALLENGE

Encourage your students to "go beyond" the topics at hand. Each chapter includes a TechTalk section that goes into greater detail and presents more challenging content. You can choose to assign these sections or skip them, depending on your students' progress and your specific goals for the course.

REINFORCE

The labs are highly interactive tutorials that your students can complete using the BookOnCD. Use the labs to reinforce material presented in the chapters and to give your students hands-on practice with important concepts and skills.

ASSESS

The end-of-chapter assignments and activities help you to evaluate your students' mastery of material:
- *Interactive Summaries* require students to fill in key terms and concepts.
- *Interactive Key Terms* work like electronic flashcards to help students remember important terms.
- *Interactive Situation Questions* help students apply their knowledge to realistic troubleshooting situations.
- *Interactive Practice Tests* generate computer-scored tests from a bank of over 100 questions per chapter.
- *Study Tips* provide activities students can complete for review or as pre-exam preparation.
- *Projects* encourage students to research and explore issues and technologies.

TRACK

WebTrack is an online delivery and reporting system that allows students to send you the results of the interactive assessment activities. You can download these results at your convenience and incorporate them into various reports.

INSTRUCTOR

LABS

Each lab offered in New Perspectives on Computer Concepts, 6th Edition is a highly interactive tutorial that presents important computer concepts through the use of concrete step-by-step examples. A lab is divided into sections. Each section has its own set of objectives and QuickCheck questions. Lab Assignments are printed in the text on the corresponding lab page.

CHAPTER 1:

Operating a Personal Computer
startup • sleep mode • screen savers • keyboarding • reset procedures • shutting down

Making a Dial-Up Connection
how to connect cables • subscribing to an ISP • installing ISP software • creating manual connections • disconnecting

Browsing and Searching
using the URL box, site list, history list, and navigation buttons • creating bookmarks • changing your home page • using search engines

Using E-Mail
working with Web-based e-mail • composing a message • replying to a message • printing and deleting mail • using the address book • working with attachments

CHAPTER 2:

Working with Binary Numbers
comparing binary and decimal number systems • counting in binary • manual conversions • using Windows Calculator

Benchmarking
computer performance factors • using benchmark software • interpreting and comparing benchmark results

CHAPTER 3:

Using the Windows Interface
common elements of Windows software • using ToolTips • menu conventions • working with dialog boxes and toolbars • screenshots

Installing and Uninstalling Software
installing software from a distribution CD • installing downloaded software • upgrades • uninstalling software applications

CHAPTER 4:

Working with Windows Explorer
expanding and collapsing the directory structure • locating files • renaming and deleting files and folders • creating a folder • working with groups of files

Backing Up Your Computer
creating a backup job • different types of backups • backing up the Registry • working with compressed backups • restoring an entire disk • restoring a single file

SUPPLEMENTS

BLACKBOARD AND WEBCT CONTENT

We offer a full range of content for use with BlackBoard and WebCT to simplify the use of New Perspectives in distance education settings.

MYCOURSE 2.0

MyCourse 2.0 is a powerful online course management and content delivery system. MyCourse 2.0 is maintained and hosted by Thomson, ensuring an online learning environment that is completely secure and delivers superior performance. With MyCourse 2.0, instructors can manage and customize courses with ease.

EXAMVIEW: OUR POWERFUL TESTING SOFTWARE PACKAGE

With ExamView, instructors can generate printed tests, create LAN-based tests, or test over the Internet.

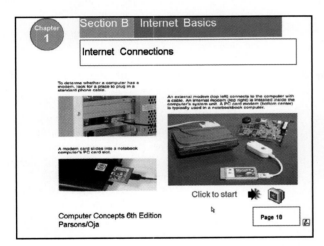

COURSE PRESENTER: READY-MADE OR CUSTOM-MADE PRESENTATIONS

Course Presenter is a CD-ROM-based presentation tool that provides instructors with a wealth of resources for use in the classroom, replacing traditional overhead transparencies with computer-generated presentations. Course Presenter includes a structured presentation along with videos, animations, labs, and more for each chapter of the textbook.

INSTRUCTOR'S MANUAL: HELP IS ONLY A FEW KEYSTROKES AWAY

This enhanced Instructor's Manual offers an outline for each chapter; suggestions for instruction on the chapter content, including how to effectively use and integrate the InfoWebLinks, the CD content, and the labs; answers to the end-of-chapter activities; and numerous teaching tips.

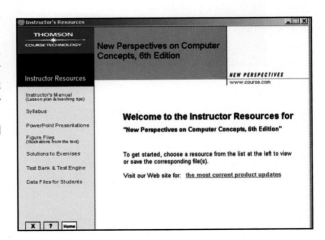

USING THE BookOnCD

Bring the concepts you've been reading about to life with the BookOnCD that accompanies the *New Perspectives on Computer Concepts, 6th Edition.* It's a snap to start the BookOnCD and use it on your computer.

The BookOnCD works on most computers that run Windows. The easiest way to find out if the BookOnCD works on your computer is to try it! Just follow the steps below to start the CD. If it works, you're all set. Otherwise, refer to the system requirements listed inside the front cover of this book, or contact your local technical support person.

STARTING THE BookOnCD

The BookOnCD is easy to use. Follow these simple steps to get started:

1. Make sure your computer is turned on.

2. Press the button on your computer's CD-ROM drive to open the drawer-like "tray," as shown in the photo below.

3. Place the BookOnCD into the tray with the label facing up.

4. Press the button on the CD-ROM drive to close the tray, then proceed with Step 5 on the next page.

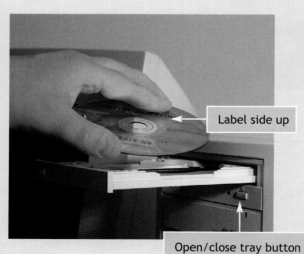

Label side up

Open/close tray button

FIGURE 1
To use the BookOnCD, your computer must have a CD-ROM drive. If you have any questions about its operation, check with your local technical support person.

5. Wait about 15 seconds. During this time, the light on your CD-ROM drive should flicker. Soon you should see a screen that displays the Computer Concepts menu. The first time you use the BookOnCD, your computer will check for several necessary Windows components. Any missing components will be installed automatically. When this process is complete, you might be prompted to reboot your computer, and then you can use any of the options on the Computer Concepts menu.

FIGURE 2
The Computer Concepts menu should appear on your computer screen after you insert the CD.

Click here to open the electronic book.

Click here when you're done to exit the program; then you can remove the BookOnCD from the CD-ROM drive.

FIGURE 3
Manual Start: Follow the instructions in this figure only if the Computer Concepts menu did not appear automatically in Step 5.

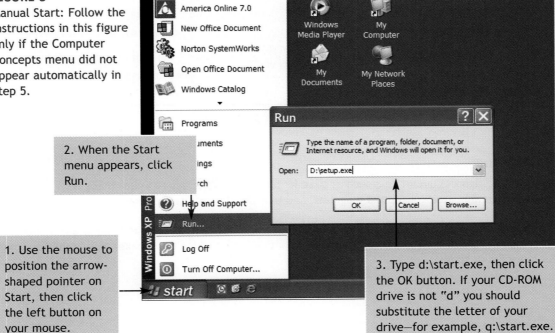

2. When the Start menu appears, click Run.

1. Use the mouse to position the arrow-shaped pointer on Start, then click the left button on your mouse.

3. Type d:\start.exe, then click the OK button. If your CD-ROM drive is not "d" you should substitute the letter of your drive—for example, q:\start.exe.

NAVIGATING THE BookOnCD

A menu bar, which stretches across the top of each page, provides all the options you need to move through and use the BookOnCD. Figure 4 describes each of these options.

FIGURE 4

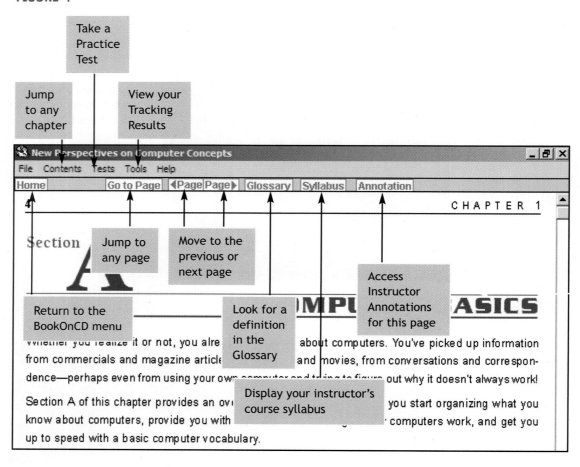

INTERACTING

Many of the figures contain links such as **click to start**. You can click these links to see video clips, watch animated conceptual diagrams, and tour popular software packages.

Note: If your computer is equipped for sound, you should hear audio during the videos and screentours. If you don't, check the volume control on your computer by clicking the speaker icon in the lower-right corner of your screen.

COMMUNICATING

Your instructor can communicate with you by using the Annotation feature. An Annotation button appears on your screen only if your instructor has provided a note for a page, and you are using a Tracking Disk. When you send Tracking Disk data to your instructor, the Annotation links are downloaded to your Tracking Disk.

EXPLORING

InfoWebLinks provide up-to-date links to Web sites where you will find additional information about important topics covered in each chapter. You can click any InfoWebLink to connect to a list of corresponding Web sites.

If you don't have antivirus software for your computer, you should get it. Use the **Antivirus Software** InfoWeb to link to Web sites where you can purchase and download antivirus software.

The InfoWebLinks work only if you have a browser and an Internet connection. When you click an InfoWebLink, the BookOnCD will automatically start your Web browser software and establish your connection.

When finished exploring an InfoWebLink, simply close your browser window and you will return to the BookOnCD.

EVALUATING

The BookOnCD includes a variety of activities that you can use to review the chapter material and evaluate your progress: QuickCheck questions at the end of each section, plus Interactive Summaries, Key Terms, Situations Questions, and Practice Tests at the end of each chapter. Simply follow the instructions for these activities to enter your answers. The computer automatically checks your responses and provides you with a score.

• For Interactive Practice Tests, you will also receive a study guide to help you find the answers to questions that you answered incorrectly.

• For Interactive Key Terms, your results are not scored or saved. This activity is for review only.

TRACKING

A Tracking Disk tracks your progress by saving your responses to the "What Do You Think?" questions on the Issues pages, as well as your scores on the labs, QuickChecks, and Interactive Summaries, Situation Questions, and Practice Tests. Follow these steps to create and work with a Tracking Disk:

1. The first time you want to save a score, click the Create button and insert a blank, formatted floppy disk. You only need to create a Tracking Disk one time.

2. When you complete an activity, such as a QuickCheck, a message is displayed asking if you want to save your score. Click the OK button, and then insert your Tracking Disk as instructed.

3. To view or print a summary report of all your scores, click the Tools menu on the Welcome screen.

NEED HELP?

Text Size: If the text appears small on your screen, your monitor is probably set at a high resolution. The type will appear larger if you reduce the resolution by completing the following steps:

1. Open the Control Panel (available from the Start menu).

2. Double-click the Display icon (or choose the Display option), and then click the Settings tab.

3. Move the Screen Area slider to 800 x 600 or 640 x 480. (This setting is optional; you can view the BookOnCD at most standard resolutions.)

Text Quality: If the text on your screen looks jumbled, your computer might be set to use Windows large fonts instead of standard fonts. Complete the following steps to change to standard fonts:

1. Open the Control Panel (available from the Start menu).

2. Double-click the Display icon (or choose the Display option), and then click the Appearance tab.

3. Click the Scheme list arrow, and then click Windows Standard.

Annotations: If you do not see the Annotation button on your screen, and your instructor has indicated that annotations have been provided, first use your Tracking Disk to send any results—the results from a QuickCheck, for example—to your instructor. If you still do not see annotations, check with your instructor.

Technical Support: For answers to technical questions, click the Get Technical Support link on the Computer Concepts BookOnCD menu or go to www.infoweblinks.com/np6/troubleshooting. Additional technical information is provided in the Readme.doc file on your BookOnCD.

NEW PERSPECTIVES ON

COMPUTER CONCEPTS

by June Jamrich Parsons and Dan Oja

6TH EDITION

1

COMPUTER, INTERNET, AND NETWORK BASICS

CONTENTS

➤※

SECTION A: COMPUTER BASICS
A Computer is...
Computer Categories
Personal Computer Systems
Data, Information, and Files
Application Software and
    Operating System Basics

➤

SECTION B: INTERNET BASICS
Internet Resources
Internet Connections
Internet Service Providers
User IDs and Passwords

➤※

SECTION C: WEB BASICS
The World Wide Web
Browsers
Search Engines

➤※

SECTION D: E-MAIL BASICS
E-mail Overview

➤※ E-mail Technology

TECHTALK: THE BOOT
➤※ **PROCESS**

ISSUE: HOW PRIVATE IS MY
➤※ **E-MAIL?**

REVIEW ACTIVITIES
Interactive Summary
Interactive Key Terms
Interactive Situation Questions
Interactive Practice Tests
Study Tips
Projects

➤※

➤※ **LABS**
➤※ Operating a Personal Computer
➤※ Making a Dial-Up Connection
    Browsing and Searching
    Using E-mail

InfoWebLinks

The InfoWebLinks, located in the margins of this chapter, show the way to a variety of Web sites that contain additional information and updates to the chapter topics. Your computer needs an Internet connection to access these links. You can connect to the Web links for this chapter by:

- clicking the InfoWeb links in the margins
- clicking this <u>underlined link</u>
- starting your browser and entering the URL
 www.infoweblinks.com/np6/chapter1.htm

 TIP

When using the **BookOnCD**, the ➤※ symbols are "clickable."

CHAPTER PREVIEW

1

The Net Generation has been the first to grow up in a world where "mouse" means a computer input device as well as a pesky white rodent. "Gen-N" is not, however, the only generation taking advantage of computer, network, and Internet technology. Members of the Great Generation that fought in World War II tote digital cameras on their annual pilgrimages to Florida. Grandparents and grandchildren exchange e-mail messages. Baby boomers mull over the latest technology innovation and its probable effects on their investment portfolios. Gen-Xers and Net-geners merrily trade music files on the Internet. Chapter 1 provides an overview of the technologies that have a major effect on people, regardless of their membership in one generation or another.

Section A begins by defining the basic characteristics of a computer system, and then provides a quick overview of data, information, and files. It concludes with an introduction to application software, operating systems, and platform compatibility. Section B introduces the Internet, a communications technology that's the "magic" behind e-mail, video conferencing, instant messaging, and e-commerce. Section C focuses on the Web—that seemingly bottomless ocean of information populated by "dot coms," connected by links, and accessed with a browser. Section D focuses on e-mail—how it works and how you use it. You'll get some tips on e-mail "netiquette," including the scoop on those flamboyant little symbols called "smileys."

When you complete this chapter you should be able to:

■ Define the term "computer" and identify the components of a personal computer system

■ Compare the computing capabilities of the following computer categories: personal computers, handheld computers, workstations, videogame consoles, mainframe computers, supercomputers, and servers

■ Explain how an operating system affects compatibility between computer platforms, such as PCs and Macs

■ Describe how data moves from point A to point B on the Internet, and list some of the most popular Internet resources

■ Evaluate various ways that you can connect a computer to the Internet and select an ISP

■ Describe how Web servers, URLs, HTML, HTTP, and browsers contribute to the Internet resource known as the Web

■ Demonstrate that you can use a search engine to locate information on the Web

■ List the features that you would expect to find in a typical e-mail software package

■ Explain how an e-mail system works, and the difference between POP mail and Web-based mail

 TIP   Click ▶ to access the Web for a complete list of learning objectives for Chapter 1.

Section A

COMPUTER BASICS

Whether you realize it or not, you already know a lot about computers. You've picked up information from commercials and magazine articles, from books and movies, from conversations and correspondence—perhaps even from using your own computer and trying to figure out why it doesn't always work!

Section A of this chapter provides an overview that's designed to help you start organizing what you know about computers, provide you with a basic understanding of how computers work, and get you up to speed with a basic computer vocabulary.

A COMPUTER IS...

How old is the word "computer"? The word "computer" has been part of the English language since 1646, but if you look in a dictionary printed before 1940, you might be surprised to find a computer defined as a *person* who performs calculations! Prior to 1940, machines that were designed to perform calculations were referred to as calculators and tabulators, not computers. The modern definition and use of the term "computer" emerged in the 1940s, when the first electronic computing devices were developed.

 When using the BookOnCD, click any boldface term to see its definition. You can also use the Glossary button at the top of each page to locate a definition for any term that was introduced in an earlier chapter.

What is a computer? Most people can formulate a mental picture of a computer, but computers do so many things and come in such a variety of shapes and sizes that it might seem difficult to distill their common characteristics into an all-purpose definition. At its core, a **computer** is a device that accepts input, processes data, stores data, and produces output, all according to a series of stored instructions.

Computer **input** is whatever is typed, submitted, or transmitted to a computer system. Input can be supplied by a person, by the environment, or by another computer. Examples of the kinds of input that a computer can accept include the words and symbols in a document, numbers for a calculation, pictures, temperatures from a thermostat, audio signals from a microphone, and instructions from a computer program. An input device, such as a keyboard or mouse, gathers input and transforms it into a series of electronic signals for the computer to store and manipulate.

In the context of computing, **data** refers to the symbols that represent facts, objects, and ideas. Computers manipulate data in many ways, and we call this manipulation **processing**. The series of instructions that tell a computer how to carry out processing tasks is referred to as a **computer program**, or simply a "program." These programs form the **software** that sets up a computer to do a specific task. Some of the ways that a computer can process data include performing calculations, sorting lists of words or numbers, modifying documents and pictures, and drawing graphs. In a computer, most processing takes place in a component called the **central processing unit** (CPU), which is sometimes described as the "brain" of the computer.

A computer stores data so that it will be available for processing. Most computers have more than one location for storing data, depending on how the data is being used. **Memory** is an area of a computer that *temporarily* holds data that is waiting to be processed, stored, or output. **Storage** is the area where data can be left on a *permanent* basis when it is not immediately needed for processing.

Output is the result produced by a computer. Some examples of computer output include reports, documents, music, graphs, and pictures. An output device displays, prints, or transmits the results of processing. Figure 1-1 helps you visualize the input, processing, storage, and output activities of a computer.

1

FIGURE 1-1

A computer can be defined by its ability to accept input, process data, store data, and produce output, all according to a set of instructions from a computer program.

Computers produce output on devices such as screens and printers.

A computer accepts input from an input device, such as a keyboard, mouse, scanner, or digital camera.

Data is processed in the CPU according to a set of instructions that was loaded into the computer's memory.

A computer uses disks and CDs to permanently store data.

What's so significant about a computer's ability to store instructions? Take a moment to think about the way that you use a simple hand-held calculator to balance your checkbook each month. You're forced to do the calculations in stages. And although you can store the data from one stage and use it in the next stage, you cannot store the sequence of formulas—the program—required to balance your checkbook. Every month, therefore, you have to perform a similar set of calculations. The process would be much simpler if your calculator remembered the set of calculations that you needed to perform, and simply asked you for this month's checkbook entries.

Early "computers" were really no more than calculating devices, designed to carry out a specific mathematical task. To use one of these devices for a different task, it was necessary to rewire its circuits—a task best left to an engineer. In a modern computer, the idea of a **stored program** means that a series of instructions for a computing task can be loaded into a computer's memory. These instructions can easily be replaced by a different set of instructions when it is time for the computer to perform a different task.

The stored program concept allows you to use your computer for one task, such as word processing, and then easily switch to a different type of computing task, such as editing a photo or sending an e-mail message. It is the single most important characteristic that distinguishes a computer from other simpler and less versatile devices, such as calculators and pocket-sized electronic dictionaries.

COMPUTER CATEGORIES

Why is it useful to categorize computers? Computers are versatile machines, which are able to perform a truly amazing assortment of tasks, but some types of computers are better suited to certain tasks than other types of computers. Categorizing computers is a way of grouping them according to criteria such as usage, cost, size, and capability. Knowing how a computer has been categorized provides an indication of its best potential use.

During the 1940s and 1950s, very few computers existed, and there was really no need to categorize them. Because the main circuitry was usually housed in a closet-sized metal frame, computer techies called these computers "mainframes." The term soon became synonymous with a category of large, expensive computers that were sold to big corporations and government agencies.

FIGURE 1-2

Personal computers are available in desktop and notebook configurations.

A desktop computer fits on a desk and runs on power from an electrical wall outlet. The main unit can be housed in either a vertical case (like the one shown) or a horizontal case.

A notebook computer is small and lightweight, giving it the advantage of portability. It can run on power supplied by an electrical outlet, or it can run on battery power.

In 1968, the term **minicomputer** was used to describe a second computer category. These computers were smaller, less expensive, and less powerful than mainframes, but were, nevertheless, able to provide adequate computing power for small businesses. In 1971, the first microcomputer appeared. A **microcomputer** could be clearly differentiated from computers in the other categories because its CPU consisted of a single "chip" called a **microprocessor**.

At one time, then, it was possible to define three distinct categories of computers: mainframes, minicomputers, and microcomputers. Technology has advanced rapidly since then. Today, just about every computer—no matter how large or small—uses one or more microprocessors as its CPU. Therefore, the use of a microprocessor is no longer a distinction between microcomputers and other computer categories. Furthermore, the term "minicomputer" has fallen into disuse. To reflect today's computer technology, the following categories might be more appropriate: personal computers, handheld computers, workstations, videogame consoles, mainframes, supercomputers, and servers.

What is a personal computer? A **personal computer** is a type of microcomputer designed to meet the computing needs of an individual. It typically provides access to a wide variety of computing applications, such as word processing, photo editing, e-mail, and Internet access. Personal computers are available as **desktop computers** or **notebook computers** (also called "laptop computers"), as illustrated in Figure 1-2. Basic personal computer prices start at $500, but most consumers select more powerful models that cost between $1,000 and $1,500.

Terminology note: The term "personal computer" is sometimes abbreviated as "PC." However, "PC" is often used for a specific type of personal computer that's descended from the original IBM PC and runs Windows software. In this book, "PC" is used for these IBM PC descendants, not as an abbreviation for the term "personal computer."

Learn more about the latest PDA models, prices, software, and accessories by visiting the PDA InfoWeb.

FIGURE 1-3

Many handheld computers accept handwriting input.

click to start

What is a handheld? A **handheld computer**, such as a Palm, iPAQ, PocketPC, or Visor, is one that is designed to fit into a pocket, run on batteries, and be used while you are holding it. Also called a **PDA** (Personal Digital Assistant), a computer in this category is typically used as an electronic appointment book, address book, calculator, and notepad. Inexpensive add-ons make it possible to send and receive e-mail, use maps and global positioning to get directions, maintain an expense account, and make voice calls using cellular service.

With its slow processing speed and small screen, a handheld computer is not powerful enough to handle many of the tasks that can be accomplished by desktop or notebook personal computers. A handheld computer is designed to be a computing accessory, rather than your primary computer. Happily, it is possible to synchronize information between a handheld and a personal computer. For example, suppose that while traveling you add an e-mail address to your PDA's address book. When you return home, you can use the synchronization feature to automatically update the address book on your desktop computer.

Some handheld computers accept input from a small—make that *tiny*—built-in keyboard. As Figure 1-3 illustrates, other handhelds accept handwriting input by means of a touch-sensitive screen.

What types of computers can be classified as workstations? The term "**workstation**" has two meanings. Computers advertised as workstations are usually powerful desktop computers designed for specialized tasks. A workstation can tackle tasks that require a lot of processing speed, such as medical imaging and computer-aided design. Some workstations contain more than one microprocessor, and most have circuitry specially designed for creating and displaying three-dimensional and animated graphics. Workstation prices range from $3,000 to $20,000. Because of its cost, a workstation is often dedicated to design tasks, and is not used for typical microcomputer applications, such as word processing, photo editing, and accessing the Web.

A second meaning of the term "workstation" applies to ordinary personal computers that are connected to a network. A **computer network** is two or more computers and other devices that are connected for the purpose of sharing data, programs, and hardware. A **LAN** (local area network) is simply a computer network that is located within a limited geographical area, such as a school computer lab or a small business.

Is a PlayStation a computer? A **videogame console**, such as Nintendo's® GameCube, Sony's PlayStation®, or Microsoft's XBox®, *is* a computer, but typically videogame consoles have not been considered a computer category because of their history as dedicated game devices that connect to a TV set and provide only a pair of joysticks for input. Today's videogame consoles contain microprocessors that are equivalent to any found in a fast personal computer, and they are equipped to produce graphics that rival those on sophisticated workstations. Add-ons, such as keyboards, DVD players, and Internet access, make it possible to use a videogame console to watch DVD movies, send and receive e-mail, and participate in online activities, such as multiplayer games. As with handheld computers, videogame consoles fill a specialized niche and are not considered a replacement for a personal computer—at least not yet.

FIGURE 1-4

This IBM S/390 mainframe computer weighs about 1,400 lbs. and is about 6.5 feet tall.

What's so special about a mainframe computer? A **mainframe computer** (or simply a "mainframe") is a large and expensive computer that is capable of simultaneously processing data for hundreds or thousands of users. Mainframes are generally used by businesses or governments to provide centralized storage, processing, and management for large amounts of data. Mainframes remain the computer of choice in situations where reliability, data security, and centralized control are necessary.

The price of a mainframe computer typically starts at several hundred thousand dollars and can easily exceed $1 million. Its main processing circuitry is housed in a closet-sized cabinet (Figure 1-4), but after additional large components are added for storage and output, a mainframe will fill a good-sized room.

How powerful is a supercomputer? A computer falls into the **supercomputer** category if it is, at the time of construction, one of the fastest computers in the world. Because of their speed, supercomputers can tackle complex tasks that just would not be practical for other computers. Typical uses for supercomputers include breaking codes, modeling worldwide weather systems, and simulating nuclear explosions. One impressive simulation designed to run on a supercomputer tracked the movement of thousands of dust particles as they were tossed about by a tornado.

What's the latest news about supercomputers? Visit the Supercomputer InfoWeb to learn more about these amazing machines.

At one time, supercomputer designers focused on building specialized, very fast, and very large CPUs. Today, a supercomputer CPU is constructed from thousands of microprocessors. As an example, a $100 million supercomputer scheduled for completion in 2005 is designed to use 1 million microprocessors, which will enable it to operate at speeds exceeding 1 quadrillion operations per second.

What makes a computer a "server"? In the computer industry, the term "server" has several meanings. It can refer to computer hardware, to a specific type of software, or to a combination of hardware and software. In any case, the purpose of a **server** is to "serve" the computers on a network (such as the Internet or a LAN) by supplying them with data. A personal computer, workstation, or software that requests data from a server is referred to as a **client**. For example, on a network, a server might respond to a client's request for a Web page. Another server might handle the steady stream of e-mail that travels among clients from all over the Internet. A server might also allow clients within a LAN to share files or access a centralized printer.

Remarkably, just about any personal computer, workstation, mainframe, or supercomputer can be configured to perform the work of a server. That fact should emphasize the concept that a server does not require a specific type of hardware. Nonetheless, computer manufacturers categorize some of their computers as "servers" because they are especially suited for storing and distributing data on a network. Despite impressive performance on server-related tasks, these machines do not include features, such as sound cards, DVD players, and other fun accessories that consumers expect on their desktop computers. Most consumers would not want to buy a server to replace a desktop computer.

PERSONAL COMPUTER SYSTEMS

What's a personal computer system? The term "computer system" usually refers to a computer and all of the input, output, and storage devices that are connected to it. At the core of a personal computer system is a desktop or notebook computer, which probably looks like one of those in Figure 1-5.

FIGURE 1-5

Personal computer designs run the gamut
from drab gray boxes to colorful curvy cases.

Despite cosmetic differences among personal computers, a personal computer system usually includes the following equipment:

- **Computer system unit.** The **system unit** is the case that holds the main circuit boards, microprocessor, power supply, and storage devices. The system unit for most notebook computers holds a built-in keyboard and speakers too.

- **Display device.** Most desktop computers use a separate **monitor** as a display device, whereas notebook computers use a flat panel **LCD screen** (liquid crystal display screen) that is attached to the system unit.

- **Keyboard.** Most computers are equipped with a keyboard as the primary input device.

- **Mouse.** A **mouse** is an alternative input device designed to manipulate on-screen graphical objects and controls.

- **Floppy disk drive.** A **floppy disk drive** is a storage device that reads data from and writes data to floppy disks (shown at right).

- **Hard disk drive.** A **hard disk drive** can store billions of characters of data. It is usually mounted inside the computer's system unit. A small external light indicates when the drive is reading or writing data.

- **CD-ROM or DVD drive.** A **CD-ROM drive** is a storage device that uses laser technology to read data that is permanently stored on computer or audio CDs. A **DVD drive** can read data from computer CDs, audio CDs, computer DVDs, or DVD movie disks. CD-ROM and DVD drives typically cannot be used to write data onto disks. "ROM" stands for "read-only memory," which means that the drive can read data from disks, but cannot be used to store new data on them.

- **CD-writer.** Many computers—especially desktop models—include a **CD-writer** that can be used to create and copy CDs.

- **Sound card and speakers.** Desktop computers have a rudimentary built-in speaker that's mostly limited to playing beeps. A small circuit board, called a **sound card**, is required for high-quality music, narration, and sound effects. A desktop computer's sound card sends signals to external speakers. A notebook's sound card sends signals to speakers that are built into the notebook system unit.

- **Modem.** Many personal computer systems include a built-in **modem** that can be used to establish an Internet connection using a standard telephone line.

- **Printer.** A computer printer is an output device that produces computer-generated text or graphical images on paper.

Figure 1-6 illustrates a typical personal computer system.

FIGURE 1-6

A typical personal computer system includes the system unit and a variety of storage, input, and output devices.

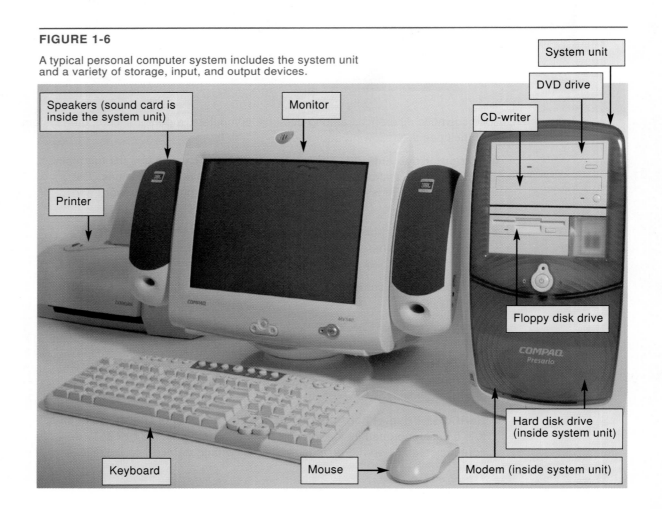

What's a peripheral device? The term **peripheral device** designates equipment that might be added to a computer system to enhance its functionality. A printer is a popular peripheral device, as is a digital camera, scanner, joystick, or graphics tablet.

Is a hard disk drive a peripheral device? The word "peripheral" is a relatively old part of computer jargon that dates back to the days of mainframes when the CPU was housed in a giant box and all input, output, and storage devices were housed separately. Technically, a peripheral is any device that is not housed within the CPU.

Although a hard disk drive seems to be an integral part of a computer, by the strictest technical definition, a hard disk drive would be classified as a peripheral device. The same goes for other storage devices and the keyboard, monitor, LCD screen, sound card, speakers, and modem. In the world of personal computers, however, the use of the term "peripheral" varies, and is often used to refer to any components that are not housed inside of the system unit.

DATA, INFORMATION, AND FILES

Is there a difference between data and information? In everyday conversation, people use the terms "data" and "information" interchangeably. Nevertheless, some computer professionals make a distinction between the two terms. They define **data** as the symbols that represent people, events, things, and ideas. Data becomes **information** when it is presented in a format that people can understand and use. Most computers store data in a **digital** format as a series of 1s and 0s. Each 1 or 0 is called a **bit**. Eight bits, called a **byte**, are used to represent one character—a letter, number, or punctuation mark.

As a rule of thumb, remember that (technically speaking) data is used by computers; information is used by humans. The bits and bytes that are stored by a computer are referred to as data. The words, numbers, and graphics displayed for people are referred to as information.

A computer stores data in files, right? A computer file, usually referred to simply as a **file**, is a named collection of data that exists on a storage medium, such as a hard disk, a floppy disk, or a CD. Although all files contain data, some files are classified as "data files," whereas other files are classified as "executable files." A **data file** might contain the text for a document, the numbers for a calculation, the specifications for a graph, the frames of a video, the contents of a Web page, or the notes of a musical passage. An **executable file** contains the programs or instructions that tell a computer how to perform a specific task. For example, the word processing program that tells your computer how to display and print text is stored as an executable file.

You can think of data files as passive—the data does not instruct the computer to do anything. Executable files, on the other hand, are active—the instructions stored in the file cause the computer to carry out some action.

Is there any way to tell what's in a file? Every file has a name, which often provides a clue to its contents. A file might also have a **filename extension**—usually referred to simply as an extension—that further describes a file's contents. For example, in Pbrush.exe, "Pbrush" is the filename and "exe" is the extension. As you can see, the filename is separated from the extension by a period called a "dot." To tell someone the name of this file, you would say, "Pbrush dot e-x-e."

Executable files typically have .exe extensions. Data files have a variety of extensions, such as .bmp or .tif for a graphic, .mid for synthesized music, or .htm for a Web page. Chapter 3 provides additional information on filenames and file types.

APPLICATION SOFTWARE AND OPERATING SYSTEM BASICS

What is application software? A computer can be "applied" to many tasks, such as writing, number crunching, video editing, and online shopping. **Application software** is a set of computer programs that helps a person carry out a task. Word processing software, for example, helps people create, edit, and print documents. Personal finance software helps people keep track of their money and investments. Video editing software helps people create and edit home movies—and even some professional films like the *Blair Witch Project*.

Is an operating system some type of application software? No. An **operating system** is essentially the master controller for all of the activities that take place within a computer. Operating systems are classified as **system software**, not application software, because their primary purpose is to help the computer system monitor itself in order to function efficiently.

Unlike application software, an operating system does not directly help people perform application-specific tasks, such as word processing. People do, however, interact with the operating system for certain operational and storage tasks, such as starting programs and locating data files.

What are the most popular operating systems? Popular personal computer operating systems include Microsoft Windows and Mac OS. Microsoft Windows CE and Palm OS control most handheld computers. Linux and UNIX are popular operating systems for servers.

Microsoft Windows (usually referred to simply as "Windows") is the most widely used operating system for personal computers. As shown in Figure 1-7, the Windows operating system displays menus and simulated on-screen controls, designed to be manipulated by a mouse.

FIGURE 1-7

The Windows operating system displays on-screen graphical controls designed to be manipulated by a mouse. Watch the video to learn more about using a mouse.

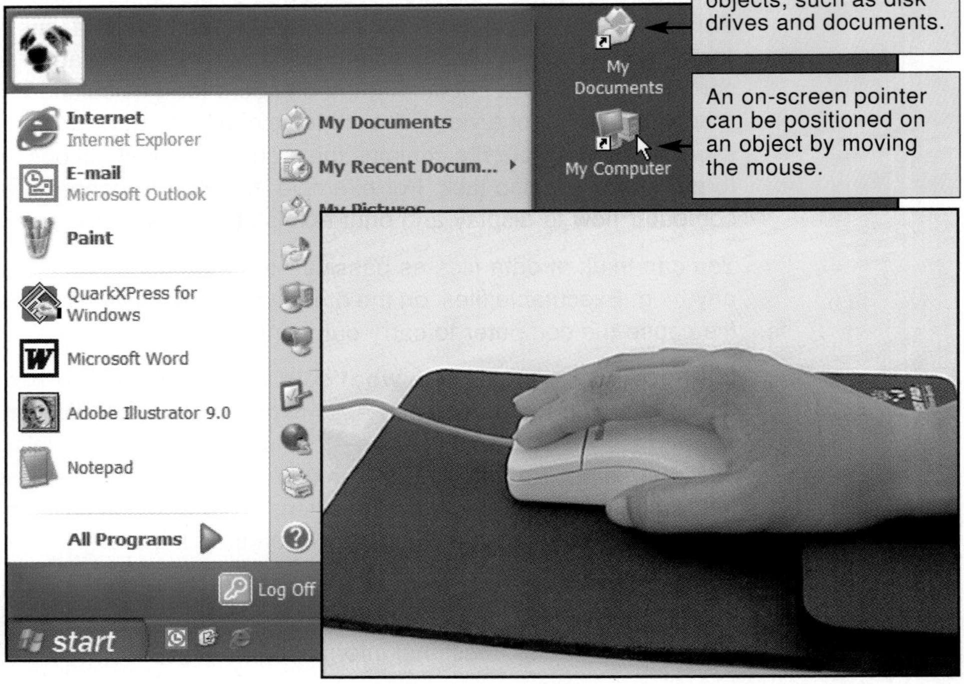

Small pictures called "icons" represent real objects, such as disk drives and documents.

An on-screen pointer can be positioned on an object by moving the mouse.

The Start button provides access to a menu of program, document, and customization options.

click to start ✳

Is Windows software the same thing as the Windows operating system? No. The term "Windows software" refers to any application software that is designed to run on computers that use Microsoft Windows as their operating system. A program called Microsoft Word for Windows is an example of a word processing program—an application program—that is referred to as "Windows software."

How does an operating system affect compatibility? Computers that operate in essentially the same way are said to be "compatible." Two of the most important factors that influence compatibility and define a computer's **platform** are the microprocessor and the operating system. Today, two of the most popular personal computer platforms are PCs and Macs.

PCs are based on the design for one of the first personal computer "superstars"—the IBM PC. The "great grandchildren" of the IBM PC are on computer store shelves today—a huge selection of personal computer brands and models manufactured by companies such as IBM, Hewlett-Packard, Toshiba, Dell, and Gateway. The Windows operating system was designed specifically for these personal computers and, therefore, the PC platform is sometimes called the "Windows platform." Most of the examples in this book pertain to PCs because they are so popular.

Apple Computer, Inc. is known for innovative computer design. You can learn about its newest computers by connecting to the Apple Computers InfoWeb.

└click ▪❋

Macs are based on a proprietary design for a personal computer called the Macintosh, manufactured almost exclusively by Apple Computer, Inc. The stylish iMac is one of Apple's most popular computers, and like other computers in the Mac platform, it uses Mac OS as its operating system.

The PC and Mac platforms are not compatible because their microprocessors and operating systems differ. Consequently, application software designed for Macs does not typically work with PCs. When shopping for new software, it is important to read the package to make sure that it is designed to work with your computer platform.

Can an operating system serve more than one platform? Different versions of some operating systems have been created to operate with more than one microprocessor. For example, a version of the Linux operating system exists for the PC platform, whereas another version exists for the Mac platform. Changing a computer's native operating system—thereby changing its platform—is not an exercise undertaken by most personal computer owners.

QUICKCheck Section A

1 A computer processes data in the [   ] processing unit.

2 The idea of a(n) [   ] program means that a series of instructions for a computing task can be loaded into a computer's memory.

3 The [   ] unit is the case that holds the main circuit boards, microprocessor, power supply, and storage devices for a personal computer system.

4 Data files usually have an .exe extension. True or false? [   ]

5 The term "microprocessor" is a synonym for the term "microcomputer." True or false? [   ]

6 A(n) [   ] system is the software that acts as the master controller for all of the activities that take place within a computer system.

check answers ▪❋

LAB 1-A
OPERATING A PERSONAL COMPUTER

Interactive**LAB**
Operating a
Personal Computer

└click to start ➤

In this lab, you'll learn:

■ How to start a Windows computer

■ What to do when a computer is in sleep mode

■ How to deactivate a screen saver

■ How to select a different screen saver

■ The terminology used for the four sections of a computer keyboard

■ How to use the Alt, Ctrl, Esc, Num Lock, Caps Lock, Windows, Fn, Backspace, Delete, and arrow keys

■ The difference between the forward and backward slashes

■ The location of the tilde

■ How to start and exit a program

■ How to close a program that is not responding

■ When to use the reset button

■ How to shut down Windows

> **TIP**
>
> The interactive labs are available on the BookOnCD.

LAB Assignments

1 Start the interactive part of the lab. Insert your Tracking Disk if you want to save your QuickCheck results. Perform each of the lab steps as directed, and answer all of the lab QuickCheck questions. When you exit the lab, your answers are automatically graded and your results are displayed.

2 Make a note of the brand and location of the computer that you're using to complete these lab assignments.

3 Use the Start button to access your computer's Control Panel folder. Describe the status of your computer's power saver settings.

4 Preview the screen savers that are available on the computer that you use most frequently. Select the screen saver that you like the best and describe it in a few sentences.

5 What is the purpose of an Fn key? Does your computer keyboard include an Fn key? Explain why or why not.

6 In your own words, describe what happens when you (a) click the Close button, (b) hold down the Ctrl, Alt, and Del keys, (c) press the reset button, and (d) select the Shut Down option.

Section **B**

INTERNET BASICS

The term "cyberspace" was coined by science-fiction writer William Gibson, who might be alarmed at the way it is currently used. Visit the Cyberspace InfoWeb for additional background and links to books for sci-fi afficionados.

click

Sometimes referred to as "cyberspace," the **Internet** is a collection of local, regional, national, and international computer networks that is linked together to exchange data and distribute processing tasks. Most people are familiar with its capability to carry e-mail messages, store all sorts of useful information, and provide access to online shopping. Section B provides a basic overview of the Internet, with an emphasis on how you can connect to it and use it.

INTERNET RESOURCES

How does the Internet work? You can think of the Internet as a network of interconnected communications lines that creates a sort of highway system for transporting data. The main routes of the Internet—analogous to interstate highways—are referred to as the **Internet backbone**. Constructed and maintained by major telecommunications companies, such as AT&T and Sprint, these telecommunications links can move huge amounts of data at incredible speeds. Data traveling from the U.S. can arrive in England in less than 60 ms—60 thousandths of a second.

In addition to the backbone, the Internet encompasses an intricate collection of regional and local communications links. These links can include local telephone systems, cable television lines, cellular telephone systems, and personal satellite dishes.

The Internet's communications system (Figure 1-8) transports data to and from millions of computers and other electronic devices. Amazingly, this data transport works seamlessly between all kinds of platforms—between PCs and Macs, and even between personal computers and mainframes. Communication between all of the different devices on the Internet is made possible by **TCP/IP** (Transmission Control Protocol/Internet Protocol), a standard set of rules for electronically addressing and transmitting data.

FIGURE 1-8

Personal computers are connected to regional and local communications links, which in turn connect to the Internet backbone.

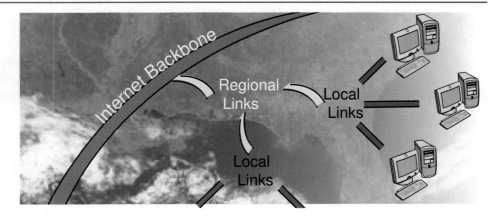

Where is all of the Internet data stored? The Internet provides access to an amazing volume of data, including corporate Web pages, merchandise catalogs, software, music, tutorials on all manner of subjects, school science projects, telephone directories, library card catalogs, and so on. Although difficult to pin down exact figures, it is estimated that the Internet provides access to more data than is stored in all of the academic research libraries in the U.S.

Most of the "stuff" that's accessible on the Internet is stored on servers, which are owned and maintained by government agencies, corporations, small businesses, schools, organizations, and even individuals. These servers use special server software to locate and distribute data requested by Internet users.

How does data get from point A to point B on the Internet? Every device that's connected to the Internet is assigned a unique number, called an **IP address**, that pinpoints its location in cyberspace. To prepare data for transport, a computer divides the data into small chunks, called **packets**. Each packet is labeled with the IP address of its destination and then transmitted. When a packet reaches an intersection in the Internet's communications links, a device called a **router** examines the packet's address. The router checks the address in a routing table and then sends the packet along the appropriate link towards its destination. As packets arrive at their destinations, they are reassembled into a replica of the original file.

What sort of resources does the Internet provide? If you're looking for information, if you want to communicate with someone, or if you want to buy something, the Internet offers a good set of resources. Here is a quick overview of Internet resources.

Web sites. Most people envision **Web sites** as various locations in cyberspace that correspond to a corporation's headquarters, a store, a magazine, or a library. A Web site can provide information, or it can provide access to other resources, such as search engines and e-mail.

Search engines. Without search engines, using the Internet would be like trying to find a book in the Library of Congress by wandering around the stacks. **Search engines** help catalog a huge portion of the data stored on servers that are connected to the Internet.

> www.
> InfoWebLinks.
> com
>
> If you'd like to check out some of the resources described in this section, connect to the <u>Internet Resources</u> InfoWeb. There you'll find links to examples and to the software that you need to access these useful Internet resources.
>
> ⌐click ➧

E-commerce. The Internet is revolutionizing business by directly linking consumers with retailers, manufacturers, and distributors. **E-commerce**, or "electronic commerce," includes activities such as online shopping, electronic auctions, and online stock trading.

E-mail. Also known as "electronic mail," **e-mail** allows one person to send an electronic message to another person or to a group of people listed in a personal address book. A variation of e-mail called a **mailing list server**, or "listserv," maintains a public list of people who are interested in a particular topic. Messages sent to the list server are automatically distributed to everyone on the mailing list.

Bulletin boards. Usenet is a worldwide bulletin board system that contains more than 15,000 discussion forums called **newsgroups**. Newsgroup members post messages to the bulletin board, which can be read and responded to by other group members.

Downloads and uploads. Internet servers store all sorts of useful files containing documents, music, software, videos, animations, and photos. The process of transferring one of these files from a remote computer, such as a server, to a local computer, such as your personal computer, is called **downloading**. Sending a file from a local computer to a remote computer is called **uploading** (Figure 1-9).

FIGURE 1-9

Many Web sites provide files that the public can download to personal computers. Uploads, on the other hand, are limited to people who have password access to the site.

For a demonstration of how to download a file, click the Start icon.

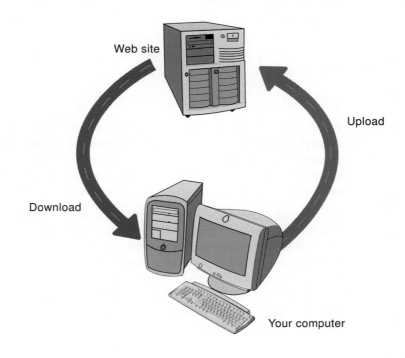

Web site

Upload

Download

Your computer

click to start ➧

Chat groups and instant messaging. A **chat group** consists of several people who connect to the Internet and communicate by typing comments to each other using their computer keyboards. A private version of a chat room, called **instant messaging**, allows two or more people to send typed messages back and forth.

Internet telephony. Although it is not as simple as picking up the telephone, **Internet telephony** allows telephone-style conversations to travel over the Internet to virtually anywhere in the world. Internet telephony requires special software at both ends of the conversation and, instead of a telephone, it uses a microphone connected to a computer. When using Internet telephony, the sound quality is sometimes worse than a cellular phone, but the price—free—is right.

Broadcasting. The Internet carries radio shows and teleconferences that can be broadcast worldwide. Internet radio is popular because broadcasts aren't limited to a small local region, but instead can be heard by listeners all over the world. Internet broadcasting technology, referred to as multicasting technology, has the potential to further increase the use and popularity of Internet broadcasts.

Remote access and control. With the right software and a valid password, the Internet can link two computers together and allow one computer to control another. Commands entered on one computer are actually executed on the other computer. One version of this process is referred to as **Telnet**. An example of remote control is when a technical support person located in a manufacturer's service center takes remote control of your computer to fix a problem.

P2P. A technology known as **peer-to-peer**, recently rechristened "P2P," makes it possible for one person's computer to directly access the content of another person's hard disk—with permission, of course. This technology is the basis for popular music and file exchange Web sites, which use the Internet to give individuals access to one another's files.

INTERNET CONNECTIONS

What are my options for Internet connections? To take advantage of everything that the Internet has to offer, you'll have to establish some sort of communications link between your computer and the Internet. Possibilities include using your existing telephone line, a cable television line, a personal satellite link, wireless or cell phone service, or special high-speed telephone services.

What's the easiest, cheapest way to access the Internet? Many people literally dial-up the Internet using an existing telephone line. This type of connection—often referred to as a **dial-up connection**—is relatively simple and inexpensive because the necessary equipment and software are preinstalled on most new computers. A dial-up connection requires a device called a **voice band modem** (often simply called a "modem"), which converts your computer's digital signals into a type of signal that can travel over telephone lines. Figure 1-10 will help you determine whether or not a computer has a modem.

FIGURE 1-10

To determine whether a computer has a modem, look for a place to plug in a standard phone cable.

An external modem (top left) connects to the computer with a cable. An internal modem (top right) is installed inside the computer's system unit. A PC card modem (bottom center) is typically used in a notebook computer.

A modem card slides into a notebook computer's PC card slot.

click to start ✱

To establish a dial-up connection, your computer's modem dials a special access number, which is answered by an Internet modem. Once the connection is established, your computer is "on the Internet." When you complete an Internet session, your modem "hangs up" and the connection is discontinued until the next time you dial in.

Theoretically, the top speed of a dial-up connection is 56 Kbps, meaning that 56,000 bits of data are transmitted per second. Actual speed is usually reduced by distance, interference, and other technical problems, however, so the speed of most 56 Kbps dial-up connections is more like 45 Kbps. This speed is useable for e-mail, e-commerce, and chat. It is not, however, optimal for applications that require large amounts of data to be quickly transferred over the Internet. Watching an Internet-based video or participating in a teleconference over a 56 Kbps dial-up connection can be like watching a badly organized parade—the sound can be out of sync with the image, and the "show" can be interrupted by lengthy pauses as your computer waits for the next set of video frames to arrive.

Does a cable modem provide a faster Internet connection? Many cable TV companies offer Internet access in addition to the traditional roster of movie channels, network television, and specialty channels. This type of Internet access, often referred to as "cable modem service," is offered to a cable company's customers for an additional monthly charge. Cable modem service usually requires two pieces of equipment: a network card and a cable modem. A **network card** is a device that's designed to connect a personal computer to a local area network—when you get cable modem service, this card allows you to join a computer network that provides Internet access. Many of today's computers come equipped with a preinstalled network card. If not, one can be added for less than $50. A **cable modem** is a device that changes a computer's signals into a form that can travel over cable TV links (Figure 1-11.) Cable modems can be installed by consumers or installed (sometimes for a fee) by the "cable guy," and typically remain the property of the cable company.

FIGURE 1-11

A cable modem can be a standalone device, or it can be integrated with the other electronic components of a cable TV set-top box.
A standalone cable modem is usually set up close to a computer, whereas a set-top box is usually set up right next to a television.

Cable modem access is referred to as an **always-on connection**, because your computer is, in effect, always connected to the Internet, unlike a dial-up connection that is established only when the dialing sequence is completed. An always-on connection is convenient because you don't have to wait 30–40 seconds for the dial/answer sequence to be completed. A cable modem receives data at about 1.5 Mbps (1.5 million bits per second), which is more than 25 times faster than a dial-up connection. This speed is suitable for most Internet activities, including real-time video and teleconferencing.

What about access provided by a school or business network? The computers in a school lab or business are usually connected to a local area network that is connected to the Internet. These computers offer an always-on connection, similar to cable modem service, which does not require a dial/answer sequence to establish an Internet connection. School and business networks do not, however, typically access the Internet via a cable company. Instead they use a high-speed telecommunications link dedicated solely to Internet access.

What other high-speed Internet access options are available? Many telephone and independent telecommunications companies offer high-speed Internet access over ISDN and DSL lines. **ISDN** (Integrated Services Digital Network) provides data transfer speeds of either 64 Kbps or 128 Kbps. Given data transfer speeds that are only marginally better than a free 56 Kbps dial-up connection, and substantial monthly fees, ISDN ranks low on the list of high-speed Internet options for most consumers.

If you want a really "hot" Internet connection, consider DSL. **DSL** (Digital Subscriber Line) and xDSL are generic names for a family of high-speed Internet links, including ADSL, SDSL, and DSL lite. Each type of DSL provides different maximum speeds—from twice as fast to approximately 125 times faster than a 56 Kbps dial-up connection. The faster types of DSL require professional installation, but DSL lite can be installed by consumers.

Both ISDN and DSL connections require proximity to a telephone switching station, which can be a problem for speed-hungry consumers in rural areas. Satellite dishes to the rescue! Once limited to only receiving Internet data (data flowing out of your personal computer had to travel over a dial-up connection), **DSS** (Digital Satellite Service) today offers two-way Internet access at an average speed of about 500 Kbps. Monthly fees for a DSS connection are typically less than DSL, but more than cable modem service. Consumers are required to rent or purchase a satellite dish and pay for its installation.

INTERNET SERVICE PROVIDERS

What's an ISP? To access the Internet, you do not typically connect your computer directly to the backbone. Instead, you connect it to an ISP, which in turn connects to the backbone. An **ISP** (Internet Service Provider) is a company that maintains Internet computers and telecommunications equipment in order to provide Internet access to businesses, organizations, and individuals. An ISP that offers dial-up connections, for example, maintains a bank of modems, which communicates with the modems in customers' computers.

An ISP, such as AOL (America Online), works in much the same way as a local telephone company. Just as a telephone company provides a point of access to telephones all over the world, an ISP is a point of access to the Internet. ISP customers arrange for service—in this case for Internet access—for which they pay a monthly fee. In addition to a monthly fee, an ISP might also charge an installation fee. Subscribers may also be required to pay per-minute fees for long-distance access.

What's the difference between a local ISP and a national ISP? A local ISP usually supplies Internet access within a limited geographical area, such as within a particular area code. A national ISP supplies access for customers spread throughout a large geographical area. A local ISP is a good choice unless you want to use your computer outside of your local dialing area. To access a local ISP while away from home, you'll probably have to dial long distance and pay minute-by-minute long-distance charges for the duration of your connect time. A national ISP, on the other hand, offers access in many different area codes. AT&T WorldNet, for example, offers access num-

1

bers in more than 500 cities. Customers who live in or travel to any of these cities can use the access numbers without additional long-distance fees. National ISPs usually also offer an 800 number for nationwide access. The 800 prefix can be misleading, however, because it is not a toll-free number. This 800-number access usually costs about a dime per minute. A national ISP is probably better than a local ISP for people who travel frequently, for retirees who migrate to warmer climates for the winter months, and for students who spend part of the year away at school.

How can I find a list of ISPs that provide service in my area? The Yellow Pages typically list ISPs under "Internet." Also check newspaper ads for new services that are being offered in your area. Your computer might include a directory of national ISPs. Look for an Internet Connection icon on your desktop, or browse through the options on the Start menu to find the Internet Connection Wizard.

How do I choose an ISP? Selecting an ISP depends on a variety of factors, such as where service is provided; the speed of data transfer; and the cost of equipment, installation, and monthly service.

☑ **Geographical coverage.** The ISP that you select should provide service in the places that you typically use your computer. If your work takes you on the road a lot, you'll want to consider a national ISP that provides local access numbers in the cities that you visit. Retirees and students who migrate between locations might also consider a national ISP. For homebodies, a local ISP is usually a very acceptable option. With cable modem or DSL service, your computer must remain tethered to your service provider's network, which does not provide Internet access while traveling.

☑ **Type of service.** An ISP usually specializes in one type of service, so a company that offers dial-up connections is not likely to also offer cable connections. If your heart is set on a particular type of service—cable modem service, for example—you might not have a choice of providers.

☑ **Quality of service.** The quality of dial-up and cable modem services tends to decrease as the number of customers increases. In the case of dial-up connections, too many customers clamoring for modem connections can result in busy signals when you try to connect to your ISP. Cable modem service works sort of like a lawn sprinkler system that's connected to a small water pump. With only one sprinkler, the water gushes out. Connect 100 sprinklers to the system and the gushing turns into a trickle. Because all of the subscribers in your neighborhood use the same data "pipe," as more and more of your neighbors go online, the effective speed of your cable connection can deteriorate. Ask an ISP's current customers what they think of the access speed. Is it consistent, or does it deteriorate during peak usage hours?

☑ **Cost of monthly service.** In the U.S. and Canada, monthly service fees vary from about $15 per month for dial-up service to $50 per month for basic DSL service. ISP rate plans may offer unlimited access for a flat monthly fee. Other rate plans include a limited number of hours; if you're online for additional hours, you'll pay by the hour. Outside of the U.S. and Canada, many ISPs charge by the minute for Internet access.

☑ **Cost of equipment and installation.** When considering the cost of Internet service, it is important to factor in the cost of equipment and installation. Whereas a modem is relatively inexpensive, a satellite dish costs several hundred dollars. Installation can also be costly—sometimes exceeding $100.

☑**Extra services.** An ISP typically provides a connection to the Internet and an e-mail account. It might also offer useful extra services, such as multiple e-mail accounts so that all of the members of your family can send and receive their own e-mail messages. Some ISPs, such as America Online, offer a host of **proprietary services** that are available only to subscribers. These services might include content channels with substantive articles on health, hobbies, investing, and sports; activities specially designed for kids and teens; online shops that comply with high standards for security and customer satisfaction; a variety of voice and text messaging services; and collections of free (and virus-free) software. To find out if proprietary features should influence your ISP choice, talk to subscribers who have similar computer experience; ask them if these features are useful.

☑**Customer service.** Most ISPs are prepared to answer customers' questions over the phone or via e-mail. The critical customer service question is, "How long will it take to get a response?" Some national ISPs are notorious for keeping customers on hold for hours, and an e-mail reply can take days. Given a choice, most customers prefer an ISP that can respond quickly. To get an idea of the response time and expertise of an ISP, talk to current customers.

USER IDS AND PASSWORDS

Is access to the Internet restricted in any way? Although the Internet is a public network, access to the Internet, or to some parts of the Internet, can be restricted in various ways. For example, an ISP usually limits Internet access to its subscribers. Some parts of the Internet—such as military computers—are off limits to the general public. Other parts of the Internet—such as the *New York Times* archives—limit access to paid members. Many parts of the Internet encourage memberships and offer additional perks if you sign up.

User IDs and passwords are designed to provide access to authorized users and to prevent unauthorized access. A **user ID** is a series of characters—letters and possibly numbers—that becomes a person's unique identifier, similar to a social security number. A **password** is a different series of characters that verifies the user ID, similar to the way a PIN (personal identification number) verifies your identity at an ATM machine. Typically, your ISP provides you with a user ID and password that you use to connect to the Internet. You will accumulate additional user IDs and passwords from other sources for specific Internet activities, such as reading *New York Time*s articles, or participating in an online auction. The process of entering a user ID and password is usually referred to as "logging in" or "logging on" (Figure 1-12).

FIGURE 1-12

Typically, when you log in and enter your password, a series of asterisks appears on the screen to prevent someone from looking over your shoulder to discover your password.

Can I choose my own user ID? In some cases, you will be allowed to select your user ID, but in other cases, it might be assigned to you by your service provider. Often a user ID is a variation of your name. Brunhilde Jefferson's user ID might be bjeffe, bjefferson, brunhilde_jefferson, or bjeff0918445. The rules for creating a user ID are not consistent throughout the Internet, so it is important to carefully read all of the instructions provided before finalizing your ID. For example, spaces might not be allowed in a user ID. Hence, the underline in brunhilde_jefferson is used instead of a space. There might be a length limitation, so Ms. Jefferson might have to choose a short user ID, such as bjeffe. Some Internet computers don't differentiate between uppercase and lowercase letters, so the user IDs B_Jefferson and b_jefferson are the same. Other computers are **case sensitive** and differentiate between uppercase and lowercase. On such a computer, if Ms. Jefferson selected Brun_Jeff as her user ID, she would not be able to gain access by typing brun_jeff. To avoid such problems, most people stick to lowercase letters for their user IDs.

Can I choose my own password? Even when you are assigned a "starter" password, you should select a new password immediately, and then change it periodically. Don't share your password with anyone or write it down where it could be found. If your password is discovered, someone could log on and pretend to be you—sending inflammatory e-mail under your name, and signing up for memberships at various unsavory Web sites.

Your password should be a sequence of characters that is easy for you to remember, but would be difficult for someone else to guess. After all, your password only provides protection if it is secret (Figure 1-13).

FIGURE 1-13

Use these tips to select a secure password.

DO:
- Select a password that is at least five characters long
- Try to use both numbers and letters in your password
- Select a password that you can remember
- Consider making a password by combining two or more words, or the first letters of a poem or phrase
- Change your password if you think that someone discovered it

DON'T:
- Select a password that can be found in a dictionary
- Use your name, nickname, social security number, birth date, or name of a close relative
- Write your password where it is easy to find—under the keyboard is the first place that a password thief will look

How do I remember my passwords? When you use the Internet, you'll accumulate a batch of passwords—from your ISP, from online shopping sites, from your online travel agent, and maybe even from your favorite news and information sites. The problem is not remembering *one* password, it's remembering lots of different passwords and their corresponding user IDs.

Your passwords provide the most protection if they are unique, but if you want access to 40 different Internet sites that require passwords, you'll need a really good memory to remember 40 unique passwords and 40 user IDs. You can, of course, resort to writing them down. That practice, however, makes them much more susceptible to thievery.

Instead of using 40 different user IDs and passwords, you need some way to reduce the number of things that you'll have to memorize. First, strive to use the same user ID whenever possible. Remember that people before you with the same name might have already taken the obvious user IDs. So that you can use the same ID everywhere, try to select a user ID that is not likely to be used by others. For example, if your name is John Smith, you can bet that other people have already used johnsmith, jsmith, and john_smith. To keep his user ID unique, John might instead select jsw2bam (the first letters in "John Smith wants 2 be a millionaire").

Next, select two passwords—one for high security and one for low security. Use your high-security password to protect critical data—for online banking, for managing an online stock portfolio, or for your account at an online bookstore that stores a copy of your billing and credit card information. Change your high-security password periodically in all of the places that you use it.

Use your low-security password in situations where you don't really care if your security is compromised. Some places on the Internet want you to establish an account with a user ID and password just to collect basic contact information and put your name on a mailing list. At other sites, your user ID and password provide access to information, but none of your own data (a credit card number, for example) is stored there. It is not necessary to change your low-security password very often.

QUICKCheck Section B

1 The main routes of the Internet are referred to as the Internet [＿＿＿＿＿＿].

2 Communication between all of the different devices on the Internet is made possible by [＿＿＿＿＿＿] /IP.

3 Most of the "stuff" that's accessible on the Internet is stored on [＿＿＿＿＿＿] that are maintained by various businesses and organizations.

4 A dial-up connection requires a device called a(n) [＿＿＿＿＿＿] band modem.

5 You can use the same modem for a dial-up service as for cable modem service. True or false? [＿＿＿＿＿＿]

6 Dial-up, cable modem, and DSL service are examples of always-on connections. True or false? [＿＿＿＿＿＿]

7 People who want to access the Internet while traveling should probably select a(n) [＿＿＿＿＿＿] ISP.

8 Most ISPs provide customers with a choice of dial-up, cable, DSL, or ISDN service. True or false? [＿＿＿＿＿＿]

9 The process of entering a user ID and password is referred to as [＿＿＿＿＿＿].

10 A low-security password must be changed frequently. True or false? [＿＿＿＿＿＿]

check answers ➤

LAB 1-B
MAKING A DIAL-UP CONNECTION

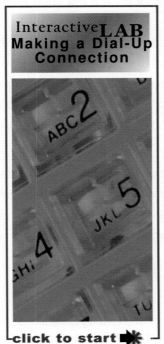

Interactive **LAB**
Making a Dial-Up Connection

click to start ▶

In this lab, you'll learn:

- How to connect a computer to your telephone line
- How to connect your computer and your phone to the same wall plug
- How to find an ISP with the Windows Internet Connection Wizard
- The general procedure for subscribing to an ISP
- How to connect to the Internet using ISP-provided software
- Why you might need to manually create a dial-up connection
- What information is necessary in order to create a dial-up connection
- How to create your own customized dial-up icon
- How to use a dial-up icon to connect to your ISP
- How to disconnect at the end of an Internet session

LAB Assignments

1 Start the interactive part of the lab. Insert your Tracking Disk if you want to save your QuickCheck results. Perform each of the lab steps as directed, and answer all of the lab QuickCheck questions. When you exit the lab, your answers are automatically graded and your results are displayed.

2 Make a list of at least five ISPs that are available in your area. If possible, include both local and national ISPs in your list.

3 Suppose that you intend to manually create a dial-up connection icon for AT&T WorldNet. What's missing from the following information?

- AT&T's dial-in telephone number and country
- AT&T's IP address
- Your password

4 Provide the following information about the Internet connection that you typically use: name of ISP, type of Internet connection (dial-up, DSL, cable modem, ISDN, DSS, school network, or business network), connection speed, and monthly fee. (If you don't currently have Internet access, describe the type of connection that you would like to use.)

Section C

WEB BASICS

In the 1960s, long before personal computers or the Internet existed, a Harvard student named Ted Nelson wrote a term paper in which he described a set of documents, called a **hypertext**, that would be stored on a computer. While reading a document in the hypertext, a person could use a set of "links" to view related documents. A revolutionary idea for its time, today hypertext is the foundation for a part of the Internet that's fondly called "the Web" by the millions of people who use it every day.

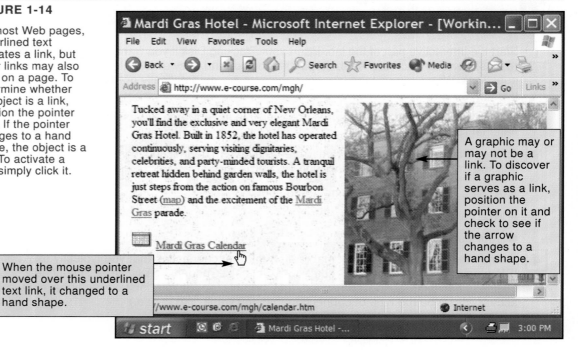

www.InfoWebLinks.com

Although Ted Nelson is credited with coining the term "hypertext," the basic concept of linked documents has its roots farther back in time. Visit the Hypertext InfoWeb for the more complete story of hypertext.

⌐click ➹

If you're familiar with the Web, Section C may give you a better understanding of how it works. For those of you who are just embarking into cyberspace, this section provides you with tools and techniques to get started. The Lab provides some hands-on experience with a Web browser and a search engine.

THE WORLD WIDE WEB

What is the Web? One of the Internet's most captivating attractions, the **Web** (short for "World Wide Web") is a collection of files organized as a giant hypertext. Many of these files produce documents called **Web pages**. Other files contain photos, videos, animations, and sounds that can be incorporated into specific Web pages. Most Web pages contain **links** (sometimes called "hyperlinks") to related documents and media files (Figure 1-14).

FIGURE 1-14

On most Web pages, underlined text indicates a link, but other links may also exist on a page. To determine whether an object is a link, position the pointer on it. If the pointer changes to a hand shape, the object is a link. To activate a link, simply click it.

Mardi Gras Hotel - Microsoft Internet Explorer - [Workin...

File   Edit   View   Favorites   Tools   Help

Back   Search   Favorites   Media

Address http://www.e-course.com/mgh/   Go   Links

Tucked away in a quiet corner of New Orleans, you'll find the exclusive and very elegant Mardi Gras Hotel. Built in 1852, the hotel has operated continuously, serving visiting dignitaries, celebrities, and party-minded tourists. A tranquil retreat hidden behind garden walls, the hotel is just steps from the action on famous Bourbon Street (map) and the excitement of the Mardi Gras parade.

Mardi Gras Calendar

A graphic may or may not be a link. To discover if a graphic serves as a link, position the pointer on it and check to see if the arrow changes to a hand shape.

When the mouse pointer moved over this underlined text link, it changed to a hand shape.

/www.e-course.com/mgh/calendar.htm   Internet

start   Mardi Gras Hotel -...   3:00 PM

What is a Web site? A series of Web pages can be grouped into a **Web site**—a sort of virtual "place" in cyberspace. Every day, thousands of people shop at Nordstrom's Web site, an online department store featuring clothing, shoes, and jewelry. Thousands of people visit the Webopedia Web site to look up the meaning of computer terms. At the ABC News Web site, people not only read about the latest news, sports, and weather, but also discuss current issues with other readers. The Web encompasses these and hundreds of thousands of other sites.

Web sites are hosted by corporate, government, college, and private computers all over the world. The computers and software that store and distribute Web pages are called **Web servers**.

What is a URL? Every Web page has a unique address called a **URL** (uniform resource locator, pronounced "You Are ELL"). For example, the URL for the Cable News Network Web site is http://www.cnn.com. Most URLs begin with *http://*. **HTTP** (Hypertext Transfer Protocol) is the communications standard that's instrumental in ferrying Web documents to all corners of the Internet. When typing a URL, the *http://* can usually be omitted, so *www.cnn.com* works just as well as *http://www.cnn.com*.

Most Web sites have a main page that acts as a "doorway" to the rest of the pages at the site. This main page is sometimes referred to as a "home page," although this term also has another meaning that will be presented later in the chapter. The URL for a Web site's main page is typically short and to the point, like *www.cnn.com*. The site might then be divided into topic areas, which are reflected in the URL. For example, the CNN site might include a weather center *www.cnn.com/weather/* and an entertainment desk *www.cnn.com/showbiz/*. A series of Web pages will then be grouped under the appropriate topic. For example, you might find a page about hurricanes at the URL *www.cnn.com/weather/hurricanes.html* and you could find a page about el niño at *www.cnn.com/weather/elnino.html*. The filename of a specific Web page always appears last in the URL—*hurricanes.html* and *elnino.html* are the names of two Web pages. Web page filenames usually have an .htm or .html extension, indicating that the page was created with **HTML** (Hyptertext Markup Language), a standard format for Web documents. Figure 1-15 identifies the parts of a URL.

FIGURE 1-15

The URL for a Web page indicates the computer on which it is stored, its location on the Web server, its filename, and its extension.

http://www.cnn.com/showbiz/movies.htm

| Web protocol standard | Web server name | Folder name | Document name and filename extension |

What are the rules for correctly typing a URL? A URL never contains a space, even after a punctuation mark, so do not type any spaces within a URL. An underline character is sometimes used to give the appearance of a space between words, as in the URL *www.detroit.com/best_restaurants.html.* Be sure to use the correct type of slash—always a forward slash (/)—and duplicate the URL's capitalization exactly. The servers that run some Web sites are case sensitive, which means that an uppercase letter is not the same as a lowercase letter. On these servers, typing *www.cmu.edu/Overview.html* (with an uppercase "O") will not locate the page that's actually stored as *www.cmu.edu/overview.html* (with a lowercase "o").

BROWSERS

What is a browser? A Web browser—usually referred to simply as a **browser**—is a software program that runs on your computer and helps you access Web pages. Two of today's most popular browsers are Microsoft Internet Explorer® (IE) and Netscape Navigator® (Navigator). Browser software provides a set of tools for viewing Web pages and navigating from one Web page to another (Figure 1-16).

InfoWebLinks.com

The best-selling browsers are updated on a regular basis, and occasionally new browsers challenge the old standbys. For up-to-the-minute information on these important Web tools, tune into the Browser InfoWeb.

click ►

FIGURE 1-16

A browser provides a sort of "window" in which it displays a Web page. The border of the window contains a set of menus and controls to help you navigate from one Web page to another.

The title bar contains the name of the Web page that is currently displayed, and the name of the browser.

The menu bar displays the titles of pull-down menus that provide options for commands such as saving, printing, copying, navigating, and configuring the browser's settings.

The toolbar provides a series of buttons for frequently used tasks.

The Address bar provides a space for you to enter URLs.

A Web page might not fit within the browser window; the scroll bars allow you to move the page up and down or right and left.

The status bar displays information about Web pages and links. For example, here it displays the URL of the link on which the pointer is positioned.

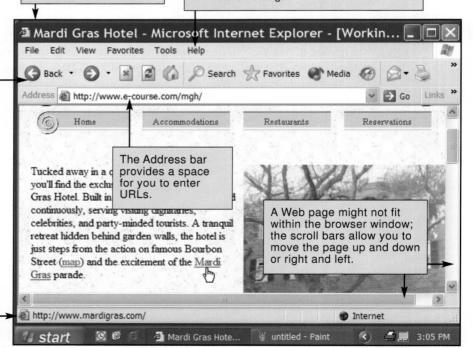

Exactly what does a browser do? A browser fetches and displays Web pages. Suppose that you want to view the Web page located at *www.dogs.com/boxer.html*. You enter the URL into a special Address box that's provided by your browser. When you press the Enter key, the browser contacts the Web server at *www.dogs.com* and requests the *boxer.html* page. The server sends your computer the data that's stored in *boxer.html*. This data includes two things: the information that you want to view, and embedded codes, called **HTML tags**, that tell your browser how to display it. The tags specify details such as the color of the background, the text color and size, and the placement of graphics. Figure 1-17 shows that a browser assembles a document on your computer screen according to the specifications contained in the tags.

FIGURE 1-17

A browser uses HTML tags embedded in a document to correctly display text, titles, colors, links, and graphics.

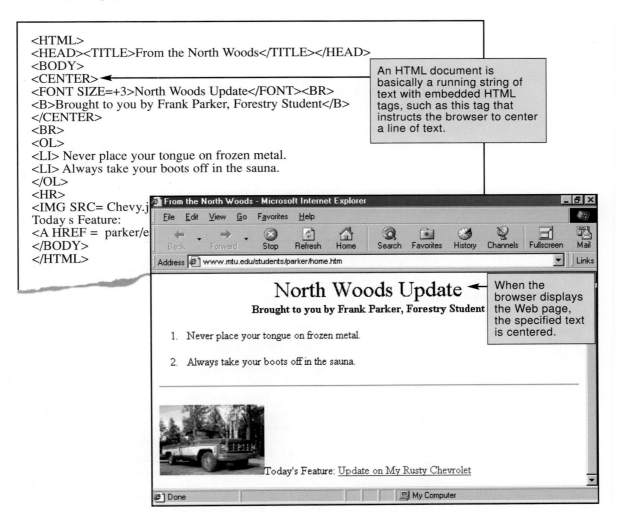

Which features are common to most browsers? Despite small cosmetic differences and some variations in terminology, Web browsers offer a remarkably similar set of features and capabilities. Lab 1-C shows you how to use them:

URL box. Whether it's called a "URL box," an "Address box," a "Location box," or a "Netsite box," most browsers provide a space for entering URLs.

Navigation buttons. After you look at a sequence of pages, the browser's Back button lets you retrace your steps to view pages that you've seen previously. Most browsers also have a Forward button, which—contrary to what you might expect—does not take you to new pages that you haven't yet viewed. Instead, the Forward button simply shows you the page that you were viewing before you pressed the Back button.

Home button. Your browser lets you select a **home page**, which is the Web page that appears every time you start your browser. The idea is that you'll select a home page that contains links or information that you use often, such as a news site, or a search engine. Whenever you click the Home button, your browser displays your home page, providing access to all of the "goodies" that it contains.

Print. Typically, a browser provides access to a print option from a button or a menu, allowing you to print the contents of a Web page.

Save. Most browsers let you save a copy of a Web page and place it at the storage location of your choice—usually your computer's hard disk. Look for a Save button, or check the menus for a Save option. Many browsers also allow you to save a copy of a graphic or sound that you find on a Web page.

Copy. Most browsers provide a Copy command that allows you to copy a section of text from a Web page, which you can then paste into one of your own documents (Figure 1-18). This browser feature provides a handy way to compile notes for a paper. To keep track of the source for each note, you can also use the Copy command to record the Web page's URL from the Address box, and then paste the URL into your document.

FIGURE 1-18

To copy a passage of text from a Web page, highlight the text, click the Edit menu, then select Copy. Next, switch to your own document and use the Paste option.

For a demonstration of this process, click the Start icon.

click to start ➡️✳

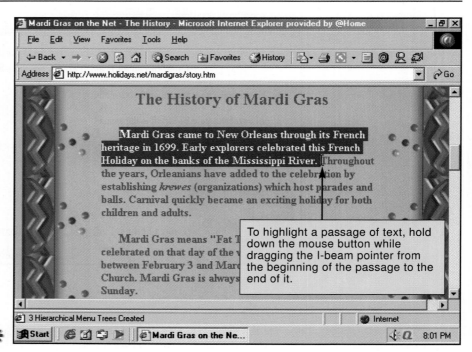

To highlight a passage of text, hold down the mouse button while dragging the I-beam pointer from the beginning of the passage to the end of it.

History List. The Forward and Back buttons keep track of only the pages that you visited since you started your browser; however, they won't help you locate pages that you visited in previous sessions. To help you revisit sites from previous sessions, your browser provides a History list. You can display this list by clicking a button or menu option provided by your browser. To revisit any site in the History list, click its URL. Many browsers allow you to specify how long a URL will remain in the History list. Two or three weeks is usually sufficient.

Favorites or Bookmarks. Suppose that you found a great Web site and you suspect that you'll want to revisit it sometime in the future. Instead of writing down its URL, you can add the URL to a list, typically called "Favorites" or "Bookmarks." After adding a site to this list, you can simply click its URL to display it.

Stop button. Sometimes a Web page takes a very long time to appear on your screen. If you don't want to wait for a page, click the Stop button.

Find. A Web page is not necessarily the length of a standard piece of paper. Instead, some Web "pages" can be equivalent to 10 or even 100 typed pages. If you're looking for specific information on a "long" Web page, you can save yourself a lot of reading by using the Find option on your browser's Edit menu to locate a particular word or phrase.

SEARCH ENGINES

What is a search engine? The term **search engine** popularly refers to a Web site that provides a variety of tools to help you find information. They are an indispensible tool when it comes to finding information on the Web. Depending on the search engine that you use, you may be able to find information by entering a description, filling out a form, or clicking a series of links to drill down through a list of topics and subtopics. Based on your input, the search engine provides a list of Web pages like the one shown in Figure 1-19.

FIGURE 1-19

In response to your query, a search engine produces a list of relevant Web pages, along with a brief description of each page and a link to it.

The search engine displays the total number of relevant pages.

The search was for railroad cars.

Search results are typically arranged in order of relevancy, so that the most promising Web pages should be at the top of the list. A brief description of the page helps you determine whether you want to view it.

Underlined links make it easy to quickly connect to any of the Web pages in the list.

Exactly what is a query? A **query** describes the information that you want to find. It includes one or more keywords and may also include search operators. A **keyword** (sometimes called a "search term") is any word that describes the information that you're trying to find. For example, *gorp* could be used as a keyword in a query for information about tasty trail mixes. You can enter more than one search term. Separate each term with a space or a search operator.

Search engines change at an astonishing rate. Visit the **Search Engine** InfoWeb for a list of popular search engines and their URLs, some comparative statistics, and tips on finding the search engine that's right for you.

Search engines have a tendency to inundate you with possibilities—often finding thousands of potentially relevant Web pages. To receive a more manageable list of results, you need to formulate a more specific search. A **search operator** is a word or symbol that describes a relationship between keywords and thereby helps you create a more focused query. The search operators that you can use with each search engine vary slightly. To discover exactly how to formulate a query for a particular search engine, refer to its Help pages. Most search engines allow you to formulate queries with the search operators described below.

AND. When two search terms are joined by AND, both terms must appear on a Web page before it can be included in the search results. The query *railroad AND cars* will locate pages that contain both the words "railroad" and "cars." Your search results might include pages containing information about old railroad cars, about railroad car construction, and even about railroads that haul automobiles ("cars"). Some search engines use the Plus symbol (+) instead of the word AND.

OR. When two search terms are joined by OR, either one or both of the search words could appear on a page. Entering the query *railroad OR cars* produces information about railroad fares, railroad routes, railroad cars, automobile safety records, and even car ferries.

NOT. The keyword following NOT must not appear on any of the pages found by the search engine. Entering *railroad NOT cars* would tell the search engine to look for pages that include "railroad" but not the keyword "cars." In some search engines, the minus sign (-) can be used instead of the word NOT.

Quotation marks. Surrounding a series of keywords with quotation marks indicates that the search engine must treat the words as a phrase. The complete phrase must exist on a Web page for it to be included in the list of results. Entering *"green card"* would indicate that you are looking for information on immigration, not information on the color green, on golf greens, or greeting cards.

NEAR. The NEAR operator tells a search engine that you want documents in which one of the keywords is located close to but not necessarily next to the other keyword. The query *library NEAR/15 congress* means that the words "library" and "congress" must appear within 15 words of each other. Successful searches could include documents containing phrases such as "Library of Congress" or "Congress funds special library research."

Wildcards. The asterisk (*) is sometimes referred to as a "wildcard character." It allows a search engine to find pages with any derivation of a basic word. For example, the query *medic** would not only produce pages containing the word "medic," but also "medics," "medicine," "medical," "medication," and "medicinal."

Field searches. Some search engines allow you to search for a Web page by its title, or by any part of its URL. The query *T:Backcountry Recipe Book* indicates that you want to find a specific Web page titled "Backcountry Recipe Book." In this search, the *T:* tells the search engine to look at Web page titles and the information following the colon identifies the name of the title.

How do I use a topic directory? A **topic directory** is a list of topics and subtopics, such as Arts, Business, Computers, and so on, which are arranged in a hierarchy (Figure 1-20). The top level of the hierarchy contains general topics. Each successive level of the hierarchy contains more and more specific subtopics. A topic directory might also be referred to as a "category list," "index," or "directory."

FIGURE 1-20

To use a topic directory, simply click a general topic. When a list of subtopics appears, click the one that's most relevant to the information you are trying to locate. If your selection results in another list of subtopics, continue to select the most relevant one until the search engine presents a list of Web pages. You can then link to these pages just as if you had used a keyword query.

click to start ➡

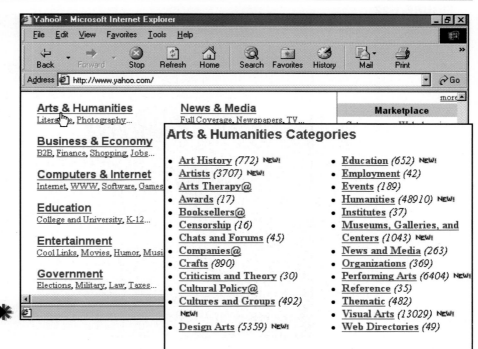

How do I use a form to find information? Many search engines provide an advanced search form that helps you formulate a very targeted search. A search form, like the one shown in Figure 1-21, typically helps you enter complex queries. It also might allow you to search for pages that are written in a particular language, located on a specific Web server, or created within a limited range of dates.

FIGURE 1-21

Many search engines provide forms that are designed to simplify the search process. These forms are usually accessible by clicking an Advanced Search link, which often is located on the main page of the search engine Web site.

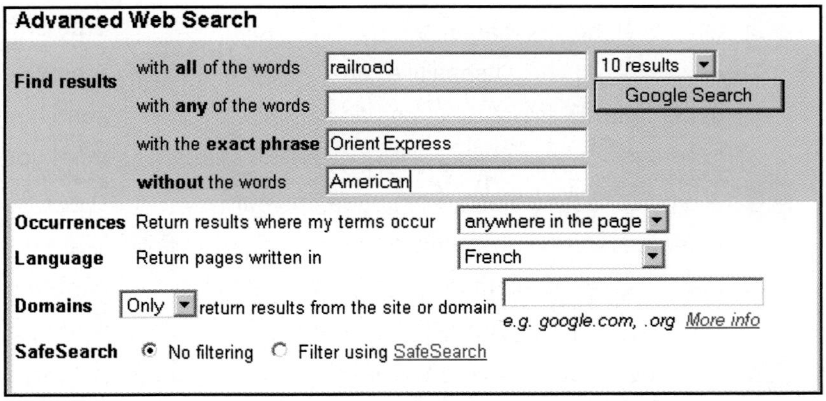

Can't I just ask a simple question and get an answer? Instead of entering a cryptic query such as *movie+review+"The Matrix"* wouldn't it be nice to enter a more straightforward question like *Where can I find a review of The Matrix?* A few search engines specialize in natural language queries, which accept questions written in plain English (Figure 1-22).

FIGURE 1-22

Some search engines accept natural language queries.

QUICK Check C
Section

1 Every Web page has a unique address called a(n) _____ .

2 On a Web server that is _____ sensitive, an uppercase "E" is not the same as a lowercase "e".

3 A browser assembles a Web page on your computer screen according to the specifications contained in _____ tags.

4 Whenever you start your browser, it displays your _____ page.

5 Most browsers provide a way to save a copy of a Web page or media element. True or false? _____

6 A browser helps you find information by searching the Web for any pages that meet your specifications. True or false? _____

7 The _____ *railroad AND cars* will locate pages that contain both the words "railroad" and "cars."

8 A search engine's topic _____ helps you drill down through a hierarchy of topics and subtopics.

check answers ▸▸▸

LAB 1-C
BROWSING AND SEARCHING

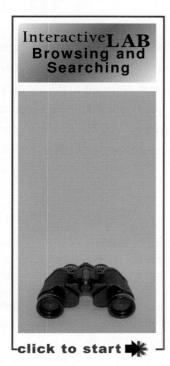

Interactive **LAB**
Browsing and Searching

click to start ➡

In this lab, you'll learn:

■ How to start a browser

■ How to work with the URL box, site list, and History list

■ How to use links and navigation buttons

■ How to work with Bookmarks and Favorites lists

■ What to do if you encounter a "page not found" message

■ How to change your home page

■ How to access a search engine

■ Where to get help about using a search engine

■ How to enter a keyword search query

■ How to use a topic directory

■ How to use the results list provided by a search engine

LAB Assignments

1   Start the interactive part of the lab. Insert your Tracking Disk if you want to save your QuickCheck results. Perform each of the lab steps as directed, and answer all of the lab QuickCheck questions. When you exit the lab, your answers are automatically graded and your results are displayed.

2   Make a note of the brand and location of the computer that you're using to complete these lab assignments.

3   Examine the Favorites or Bookmarks list. How many pages are included in this list? Link to three of the pages, and provide their URLs and a brief description of their contents.

4   Suppose that you want to make your own trail mix, but you need a recipe. Enter the query *"trail mix" AND recipe* in three different search engines. (Refer to the Search Engines InfoWeb for a list of popular search engines.) Describe the similarities and differences in the results lists produced by each of the three search engines.

5   Use the search engine of your choice to determine whether the query:

   "Blue book price" Taurus -"used car" provides the same results as the query:

   Blue book price Taurus -"used car"

   Make sure that you enter each query exactly as specified, including the quotation marks (no space after the hyphen). Explain the similarities and differences in the query results.

Section D

E-MAIL BASICS

The Internet really took off when people discovered electronic mail. More than 15 billion e-mail messages speed over the Internet each year. **Electronic mail** (usually abbreviated as "e-mail" or "email") can refer to a single electronic message or to the entire system of computers and software that transmits, receives, and stores e-mail messages. In this section of the chapter, you'll get some background information about how e-mail works—in particular, the difference between "free" Web-based e-mail and "traditional" store-and-forward e-mail. The Lab for this section provides a hands-on overview of how to read, compose, send, and reply to e-mail messages.

E-MAIL OVERVIEW

Who can use e-mail? Any person with an e-mail account can send and receive e-mail. An **e-mail account** provides the rights to a storage area, or "mailbox," supplied by an e-mail provider, such as an ISP. Each mailbox has a unique address, which typically consists of a user ID, an @ symbol, and the name of the computer that maintains the mailbox. For example, suppose that a university student named Dee Greene has an electronic mailbox on a computer called rutgers.edu. If her user ID is "dee_greene," her e-mail address would be *dee_greene@rutgers.edu*.

Exactly what is an e-mail message? An **e-mail message** is a document that is composed on a computer and remains in digital, or "electronic," form so that it can be transmitted to another computer. Every message includes a **message header** and the body of the message, usually displayed in a form, as shown in Figure 1-23.

FIGURE 1-23

When you compose an e-mail message, you'll begin by entering the address of one or more recipients and the subject of the message. You can also specify one or more files to attach to the message. The body of the e-mail message contains the message itself.

When the message is sent, your e-mail software adds the date and your e-mail address to identify you as the sender.

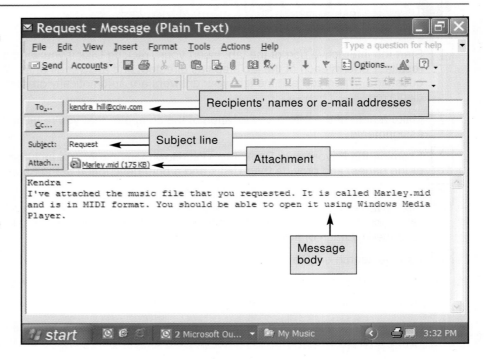

What can I do with basic e-mail? Basic e-mail activities consist of writing, reading, replying to (Figure 1-24), and forwarding messages. Messages can be printed, kept for later reference, or deleted.

FIGURE 1-24

The Reply button creates a new e-mail message and automatically addresses it to the person who sent the original message. Most e-mail systems also copy the text of the original message into the reply so that everyone has a complete transcript of the messages exchanged.

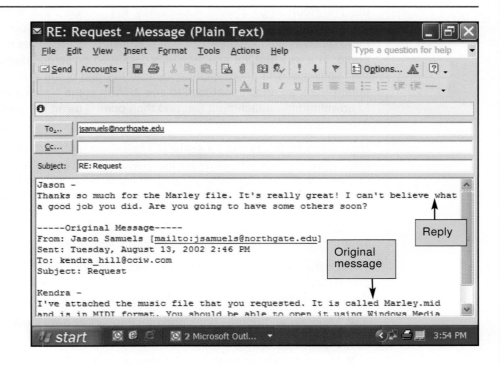

How does forwarding work? After you receive an e-mail message, you can use the Forward feature to pass it on to other people. You might, for example, forward a message that was sent to you, but that should be handled by someone else. When you initiate the forward process, the original e-mail message is copied into a new message window, complete with the address of the original sender. You can then enter the address of the person to whom you are forwarding the message. You can also add a note about why you are passing the message along.

Some e-mail systems allow you to alter the text of the original message before you forward it. If you do so, include a note explaining your changes, especially if they alter the intent of the original message. You should not forward messages that were intended to be confidential. If you think that such a message needs to be shared with other people, obtain permission from the author of the original message.

What's an e-mail attachment? Originally, e-mail messages were stored in a plain and simple format called "ASCII text." No fancy formatting was allowed—no variation in font type or color, no underlining or boldface, and of course, no pictures or sounds. Although you cannot insert a digital photo or sound file into a plain ASCII e-mail message, you can send these kinds of files as e-mail attachments. Any file that travels with an e-mail message is called an **e-mail attachment**. A conversion process called **MIME** (multi-purpose Internet mail extensions) provides a clever way of disguising digital photos, sounds, and other media as plain ASCII text that can travel over the Internet as e-mail attachments. An electronic message incorporated in the e-mail header provides your e-mail software with the information that allows it to reconstruct the attachment into its original form.

Suppose you want to e-mail a photo of your high school reunion to your mom. The photo is stored in a file called *Reunion.gif*. You can address an e-mail message to your mom, write a short note ("I can't believe that it's been five years since I graduated"), and then use the Attachment option provided by your e-mail software to specify that the file *Reunion.gif* should accompany the e-mail. Your e-mail software converts *Reunion.gif* into a MIME format and sends it along with your message. When your mom receives the message, her e-mail software reconstitutes the file into your reunion photo. The way that the attachment is displayed on screen depends on your mom's e-mail software. The photo might appear at the end of the e-mail, or she might have to double-click an attachment icon to see it. With some e-mail systems, she might have to download the attachment file, and then open it using the same software with which it was created.

How does HTML relate to e-mail? Most e-mail software allows you to create e-mail messages in HTML format. Why use HTML format for your mail? HTML messages can contain lots of fancy formatting that's just not possible with plain ASCII text. By selecting your e-mail software's HTML option, you enter a world of colored text, bold, italic, underlining, fancy fonts, embedded graphics, and various font sizes. The only limitation is that your e-mail recipients must have HTML-compliant e-mail software. Otherwise, your message will be delivered as plain old ASCII text.

What other advanced e-mail features are available? In addition to attachments and HTML formatting, today's sophisticated e-mail systems typically allow you to do the following tasks. Check your e-mail system to see if these are available:

- Maintain an address book and use it to select e-mail addresses instead of entering them every time you compose a message.

- Use the address book to send mail to a "group" that consists of several e-mail addresses.

- Send a "carbon copy" (Cc:) of a message to one or more recipients.

- Send a "blind carbon copy" (Bcc:), which hides the addresses in the Bcc: field from other recipients of the message.

- Assign a priority to a message—high priority is usually indicated by an exclamation point or red color.

- Find a particular message in your list of old mail.

- Enlarge text size for easier reading.

- Sort messages by date received, sender's name, subject, or priority.

- Refuse to accept messages that arrive from a particular e-mail address.

- Automate replies to messages that you receive while on vacation, or when you will not be responding to e-mail messages for a few days.

- Automatically fetch mail at specified intervals.

- Check spelling before sending a message.

Is e-mail different than other types of communication? In some respects, e-mail is similar to an old-fashioned letter, whose message is conveyed without benefit of the facial expressions, voice inflections, and body gestures that accompany face-to-face conversations. E-mail is faster than the post office, but lacks the immediacy of a telephone conversation. Although e-mail is delivered quickly, when composing a message, it is important to take enough time to carefully consider the message that you want to convey.

By understanding netiquette, you can avoid some of the pitfalls and problems of e-mail communications. **Netiquette** is online jargon for "Internet etiquette." It is a series of customs or guidelines for maintaining civilized and effective communications in online discussions and e-mail exchanges.

☑ **Put a meaningful title on the subject line.** The subject line of your message should clearly describe the content of your e-mail message.

☑ **Use uppercase and lowercase letters.** An e-mail message that's typed in all uppercase means that you're shouting.

☑ **Check spelling.** Most e-mail software offers a Check Spelling command. Use it.

☑ **Be careful what you send.** E-mail is not private, nor is it secure. Treat your messages as if they are postcards that can be read by anyone. Remember that all laws governing copyright, slander, and discrimination apply to e-mail.

☑ **Be polite.** Avoid wording that makes your messages sound inflammatory or argumentative. If you would not say it face-to-face, don't say it in e-mail.

☑ **Be concise.** People are busy and tend to receive lots of e-mail. Make your point and then stop.

☑ **Be cautious when using sarcasm and humor.** The words in your e-mail arrive without facial expressions or voice intonations, so a sarcastic comment can easily be misinterpreted.

☑ **Use smileys cautiously. Smileys** are symbols that represent emotions (see margin). They can help convey the intent behind your words, but should be used only in correspondence with people who understand them.

☑ **Use the Bcc function for group mailings.** By placing your list of e-mail addresses in the Bcc box, the recipients of your message won't have to scroll through a long list of addresses before reaching the "meat" of your message.

☑ **Don't send replies to "all recipients."** Use the Reply All command only when there is a very specific need for everyone listed in the To, Cc, and Bcc boxes to receive the message.

☑ **Don't send huge attachments.** Try to limit the size of attachments to 50 KB or less. If necessary, use a compression program, such as WinZip, to shrink the attachment.

☑ **Explain all attachments.** Attachments can harbor computer viruses. To determine if an attachment is legitimate, your correspondents will want to know the filename of the attachment, what the attachment contains, and the name of the software that you used to create it.

☑ **Stay alert for viruses.** Because viruses can tag along with e-mail attachments, don't open an attachment unless it was sent from a reliable source, its purpose is clearly explained in the body of the e-mail, and it was scanned using anitvirus software (see Chapter 4).

☑ **Notify recipients of viruses.** If you discover that your computer sent out infected attachments, notify anyone who might have received one.

"Don't take offense."

"Just kidding!"

"I'm not happy about that."

"I'm perplexed."

8-)
"I'm amazed."

www.
InfoWebLinks.
com

Read more about effective e-mail communications and smileys at the Netiquette InfoWeb.

click ►

1

E-MAIL TECHNOLOGY

What is an e-mail system? An **e-mail system** is the equipment and software that carries and manipulates e-mail messages. It includes computers and software called **e-mail servers** that sort, store, and route mail. An e-mail system also includes the personal computers that belong to individuals who send and receive mail. E-mail is based on **store-and-forward technology**—a communications method in which data that cannot be sent directly to its destination will be temporarily stored until transmission is possible. This technology allows e-mail messages to be routed to a server and held until they are forwarded to the next server or to a personal mailbox.

Three types of e-mail systems are widely used today: POP, IMAP, and Web-based mail. **POP** (Post Office Protocol) temporarily stores new messages in your mailbox on an e-mail server. When you connect to your ISP and request your mail, it is downloaded and stored on your computer. **IMAP** (Internet Messaging Access Protocol) is similar to POP, except that you have the option of downloading your mail or leaving it on the server. **Web-based e-mail** keeps your mail at a Web site, rather than transferring it to your computer.

> **www.InfoWebLinks.com**
>
> One of the biggest advantages of a Web-based e-mail account is that it's free. For descriptions and addresses of the most popular e-mail Web sites, hop over to the <u>Web-based E-mail</u> InfoWeb.
>
> ⬛click ➡

How do I use Web-based e-mail? Before you can use Web-based e-mail, you'll need an e-mail account with a Web-based e-mail provider. To obtain one, simply connect to the Web-based e-mail provider's Web site and enter the information required to obtain an e-mail address, a user ID, and password. Armed with these identifiers, you can connect to the e-mail Web site from any computer that has access to the Internet (Figure 1-25). At the Web site, you can write, read, reply to, forward, and delete e-mail messages. Because most Web-based e-mail providers allocate a limited amount of space to each account, it is important to delete messages when you no longer need them. You don't want your electronic mailbox to overflow and cause some messages to be returned to the person who sent them.

FIGURE 1-25

If you have a Web-based e-mail account, you can use a browser to access e-mail messages. Writing, reading, replying to, deleting, and forwarding messages is accomplished by interacting with a series of Web pages that lists your mail.

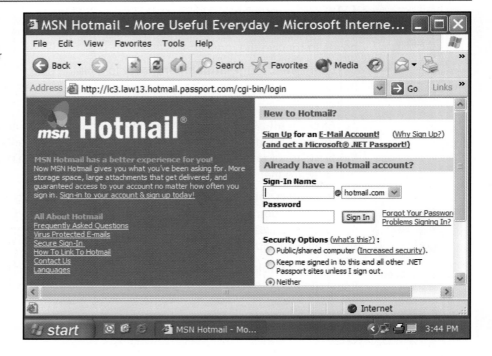

What's the latest news about e-mail client software? You'll find descriptions, reviews, and links at the <u>E-mail Client Software</u> InfoWeb.

How do POP and IMAP work? Although you can choose to use Web-based mail, you usually don't have much choice about whether you'll use POP or IMAP—you'll use the one that's offered by your ISP. Of the two, POP is currently most typical, so let's look at how it works. Most people who use POP have obtained an e-mail account from an ISP. Such an account provides a mailbox on the ISP's **POP server**—a computer that stores your incoming messages until they can be transferred to your hard disk. Using POP requires **e-mail client software**. This software, which is installed on your computer, provides an Inbox and an Outbox that allow you to work with your mail, even while your computer is not online.

An Inbox holds incoming messages. When you ask the e-mail server to deliver your mail, all of the messages stored in your mailbox on the server are transferred to your computer, stored on your computer's disk drive, and listed as new mail in your Inbox. You can then disconnect from the Internet, if you like, and read the new mail at your leisure.

An Outbox temporarily holds messages that you composed and completed, but that haven't been transmitted over the Internet. Suppose you want to compose several e-mail messages. You can fire up your e-mail client software, but remain offline while you work on the messages. The ability to compose mail offline is especially useful if you access the Internet over a dial-up connection because the phone line isn't tied up while you compose mail. As you complete a message, it is stored on your computer and listed in the Outbox. When you go online, you can send all of the mail that's being held in your Outbox. Outgoing mail is routed by an **SMTP server** (Simple Mail Transfer Protocol server), instead of by the POP server, as Figure 1-26 illustrates.

FIGURE 1-26

Outgoing mail can be stored in your Outbox until you connect to the Internet and send it. Incoming mail can be stored on a POP server until it is downloaded to the Inbox on your hard disk.

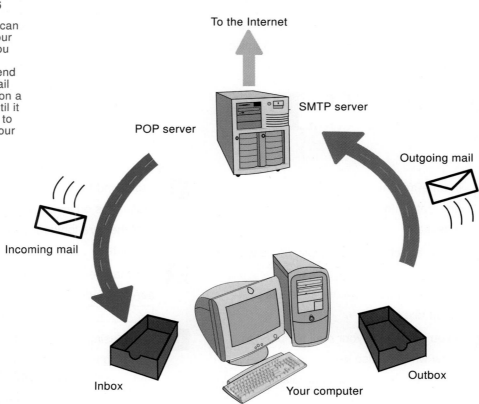

Does e-mail client software work only for offline e-mail tasks? No. Although you can use your e-mail client software to compose, read, and reply to messages while you're offline, you can also use it while you are online. In fact, this software often provides a setting that bypasses the Outbox and immediately sends messages out over the Internet.

Is POP mail better than Web-based e-mail? Before answering this question, let's review the important distinctions between the two types of e-mail. First, POP mail requires you to install e-mail client software on your own computer, whereas Web-based e-mail allows you to use a browser as e-mail client software. Second, POP transfers your messages to the hard disk drive of your computer, whereas a Web-based e-mail system retains your messages on its server. For the most part, both e-mail systems provide similar features, allowing you to read, compose, reply to, delete, and forward e-mail messages; maintain an address book; and send attachments. Each system does, however, have unique advantages. A user's individual needs determine which system is better.

Control. POP mail provides you with more control over your messages because they are transferred to your computer's hard disk drive, where you can control access to them. Web-based e-mail maintains your messages on its server, where you have less control over who can access them.

Security. When messages are stored on your computer, a hard disk drive malfunction could wipe out all of your correspondence (along with the rest of your files). Your Web-based e-mail provider is very rigorous about safeguarding its data, so your mail might be safer than if it was stored on your hard disk.

Travel. The major advantage of Web-based e-mail is that you can access your messages from any computer that's connected to the Internet. Therefore, you can get your e-mail when you travel without taking your computer. In contrast, with POP, your computer contains your old mail, your address book, and your e-mail software. Therefore, to use your familiar e-mail tools on the road, you really have to carry your computer with you.

QUICK Check Section D

1 In an e-mail message, To, From, Subject, and Date information is stored in the message [＿＿＿＿＿].

2 E-mail attachments are typically converted using [＿＿＿＿＿], which disguises media and other files as plain ASCII text.

3 If you don't want your mail recipient to know who will also get a copy of a message, use Bcc. True or false? [＿＿＿＿＿]

4 Store-and-forward technology stores messages on an e-mail [＿＿＿＿＿] until they are forwarded to an individual's computer.

5 For many e-mail systems, a(n) [＿＿＿＿＿] server handles incoming mail, and a(n) [＿＿＿＿＿] server handles outgoing mail.

6 When using e-mail client software, incoming mail is stored in a(n) [＿＿＿＿＿] and outgoing mail is stored in a(n) [＿＿＿＿＿] on your computer.

 **check answers**

LAB 1-D
USING E-MAIL

Interactive**LAB**
Using E-mail

click to start ➡❋

In this lab, you'll learn:

- How to open a Web-based e-mail account
- How to compose an e-mail message
- How to reply to a message
- How to intersperse your reply within the text of the original message
- How to delete a message
- How to print a message
- How to add a name to your address book
- How to create a group in your address book
- How to use your address book
- How to add an attachment to an e-mail message
- How to view an e-mail attachment

1

LAB Assignments

1   Start the interactive part of the lab. Insert your Tracking Disk if you want to save your QuickCheck results. Perform each of the lab steps as directed, and answer all of the lab QuickCheck questions. When you exit the lab, your answers are automatically graded and your results are displayed.

2   Using the e-mail software of your choice, send an e-mail message to kendra_hill@cciw.com. In the body of your message, ask for a copy of the "Most Influential Person Survey."

3   Wait a few minutes after sending the message to Kendra Hill, then check your mail. You should receive a survey from Kendra Hill. Reply to this message and Cc: your instructor. In your reply, answer each question in the survey, interspersing your answers with the original text. Send the reply, following the procedures required by your e-mail provider.

4   Examine the address book offered by your e-mail software. Describe how much information (name, home address, business address, birth date, telephone number, fax number, etc.) you can enter for each person. In your opinion, would this address book be suitable for a business person to use for storing contact information? Why or why not? Send the descriptions and answers to these questions to your instructor in an e-mail.

TechTalk

THE BOOT PROCESS

The sequence of events that occurs between the time that you turn on a computer and the time that it is ready for you to issue commands is referred to as the **boot process** or "booting" your computer. The term "boot" comes from the word "bootstrap," which describes a small loop on the back of a boot. Just as you can pull on a big boot using a small bootstrap, your computer boots up by first loading a small program into memory, then it uses that small program to load a large operating system. Your computer's small bootstrap program is built into special ROM (read-only memory) circuitry that's housed in the computer's system unit. When you turn on a computer, the ROM circuitry receives power and it begins the boot process.

With a Windows computer, the boot process usually proceeds smoothly and, in a short time, you can begin working with your application software. Sometimes, however, the boot process encounters a problem that must be fixed before you can begin a computing session. You can fix many of the problems that a computer might encounter during the boot process—a valuable skill for keeping your own computer up and running. Make sure, however, that you follow the guidelines provided by your school or employer if you encounter equipment problems with computers in school labs or your workplace.

What is the purpose of the boot process? The boot process involves a lot of flashing lights, whirring noises, and beeping as your computer performs a set of diagnostic tests called the **power-on self-test** (POST). The good news is that these tests can warn you if certain crucial components of your computer system are out of wack. The bad news is that these tests cannot warn you of impending failures. Also, problems identified during the boot process usually must be fixed before you can start a computing session.

The boot process serves an additional purpose—loading the operating system from the hard disk and into memory so that it can help the computer carry out basic operations. Without the operating system, a computer's CPU is pretty much unable to communicate with any input, output, or storage devices. It can't display information, accept commands, store data, or run any application software. Therefore, loading the operating system is a crucial step in the boot process.

Why doesn't a computer simply leave the operating system in memory? Most of a computer's memory is "volatile" random access memory (RAM), which cannot hold any data when the power is off. Although a copy of the operating system is housed in RAM while the computer is in operation, this copy is erased as soon as the power is turned off.

In addition to RAM, computers have non-volatile memory circuitry, such as ROM and CMOS, which can store data even when the power is off. Typically, ROM and CMOS are not nearly large enough to store an entire operating system.

Given the volatility of RAM and the insufficient size of ROM and CMOS, computer designers decided to store the operating system on a computer's hard disk. During the boot process, a copy of the operating system is copied into RAM where it can be accessed quickly whenever the computer needs to carry out an input, output, or storage operation. The operating system remains in RAM until the computer is turned off.

What is the order of events during the boot process? Six major events happen during the boot process:

1. **Power up.** When you turn on the power switch, the power light is illuminated, and power is distributed to the computer circuitry.

2. **Start boot program.** The microprocessor begins to execute the bootstrap program that is stored in ROM.

3. **Power-on self-test.** The computer performs diagnostic tests of several crucial system components.

4. **Identify peripheral devices.** The operating system identifies the peripheral devices that are connected to the computer and checks their settings.

5. **Load operating system.** The operating system is copied from the hard disk to RAM.

6. **Check configuration and customization.** The microprocessor reads configuration data and executes any customized startup routines specified by the user.

What if I turn on a computer and nothing happens? The first step in the boot process is the power-up stage. Power from a wall outlet or battery activates a small power light. If the power light does not come on when you flip the "on" switch, refer to the checklist in Figure 1-27.

FIGURE 1-27

Power Up Checklist

- ☑ Make sure that the power cable is plugged into the wall and into the back of the computer.

- ☑ Check batteries if you're using a notebook computer.

- ☑ Try to plug your notebook into a wall outlet.

- ☑ Make sure that the wall outlet is supplying power (plug a lamp into it and make sure that you can turn it on).

- ☑ If the computer is plugged into a surge strip, extension cord, or uninterruptible power supply, make sure that it is turned on and functioning correctly.

- ☑ Can you hear the fan in your desktop computer? If not, the computer's power supply mechanism might have failed.

What kinds of problems are likely to show up during the power-on self-test? The POST checks your computer's main circuitry, screen display, memory, and keyboard. It can identify when one of these devices has failed, but it cannot identify intermittent problems or impending failures.

The POST notifies you of a hardware problem by displaying an error message on the screen, or by emitting a series of beeps. A POST error message can help you pinpoint the source of a problem. Unfortunately, many computers display these error messages as numeric codes, such as "1790 Disk 0 Error." You can check the documentation or Web site for your computer to find the specific meaning of numeric error codes.

A **beep code** provides your computer with a way to signal a problem, even if the screen is not functioning. Two short beeps might mean a problem with the keyboard. Three long beeps might mean a problem with the screen display. Beep codes differ from one computer to another, depending on the ROM bootstrap program. The printed or online reference manual for a computer usually explains the meaning of each beep code.

Should I try to fix these problems myself? If a computer displays error messages, emits beep codes, or seems to "freeze up" during the boot process, you can take some simple steps that might fix it. First, turn the computer off, wait five seconds, then try to start the computer again and hope that the boot process proceeds smoothly. If the boot problem reoccurs, turn the computer off again and check all of the cables that run between your computer and peripheral devices, such as the keyboard, mouse, and monitor. After checking the cables, try to boot again. If you still encounter a boot error, contact a technical support person.

What's the long list of stuff that appears on my screen during the boot process? After the POST, the bootstrap program tries to identify all of the devices that are connected to the computer. Depending on the make and model of your computer, the settings for each device may appear on the screen, creating a list of rather esoteric information, as shown in Figure 1-28.

FIGURE 1-28

During the boot process, your computer tries to identify its storage devices, display devices, and other peripheral devices.

```
Award Medallion BIOS v6.0
Copyright (C) 1984-98, Award Software, Inc.

Copyright 1999 by Hewlett Packard, Inc
    Rev. 1.01

Intel(R) Pentium(R) III 500MHz Processor
Memory Test : 1310725 OK

Award Plug and Play BIOS Extension v1.0A
Initialize Plug and Play Cards . . .
PNP Init Completed

Detecting Primary Master        Maxtor 53073H6
Detecting Primary Slave         IOMEGA ZIP 100    ATAPI
Detecting Secondary Master      R/RW 4x4x24
Detecting Secondary Slave       FX482IT
```

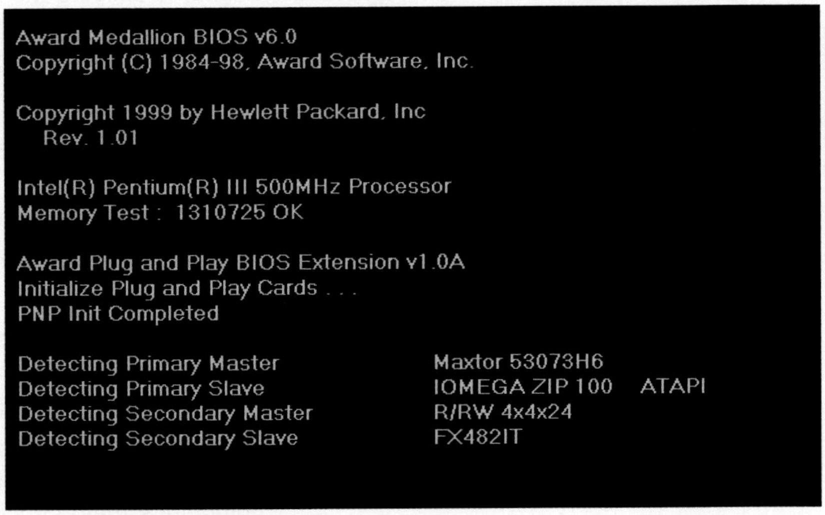

On occasion, a device gets skipped or misidentified during the boot process. An error message is not produced, but the device won't seem to work properly. To resolve this problem, shut down the computer and reboot it again. If a device is causing persistent problems, you may need to check the manufacturer's Web site to see if a new software "patch" will improve its operation.

Do computers have trouble loading the operating system or applying customization settings? Problems during the last stages of the boot process are rare, except when a disk has been inadvertently left in the floppy disk drive. Before computers were equipped with hard disk drives, floppy disks were used to store the operating system and application software. As a legacy from these early machines, today's computers first check the floppy disk drive for a disk containing the operating system. If it doesn't find a disk in the drive, it merrily proceeds to look for the operating system on the hard disk. However, if a floppy disk happens to be hanging around in drive A, the computer will assume that you want to boot from it and will look for the operating system on that disk. The error message "Non-system disk or disk error" is the clue to this problem. Remove the floppy disk and press any key to resume the boot process.

How do I know when the boot process is finished? The boot process is complete when the computer is ready to accept your commands. Usually, the computer displays an operating system prompt or main screen. The Windows operating system, for example, displays the Windows desktop when the boot process is complete.

If Windows cannot complete the boot process, you are likely to see a menu that contains an option for Safe Mode. **Safe Mode** is a limited version of Windows that allows you to use your mouse, monitor, and keyboard, but not other peripheral devices. This mode is designed for troubleshooting, not for real computing tasks. If your computer enters Safe Mode at the end of the boot process (Figure 1-29 on the next page), you should use the Shut Down command on the Start menu to properly shut down and turn off your computer. You can then turn on your computer again. It should complete the boot process in regular Windows mode. If your computer enters Safe Mode again, consult a technician.

FIGURE 1-29

Windows enters Safe Mode as a response to a problem—usually to problems caused by the device driver software that controls a particular piece of peripheral equipment. You can also force a computer into Safe Mode by pressing the F8 key during the boot sequence.

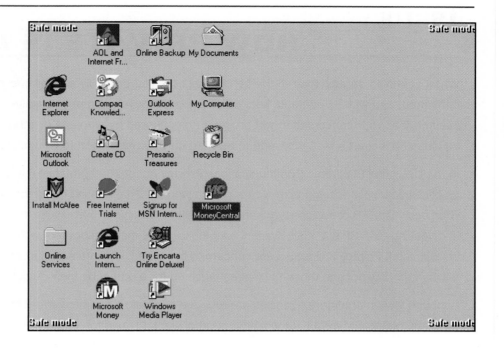

1

---

www. InfoWebLinks.com

Safe Mode can help technically savvy computer owners identify and fix a number of problems caused by installing new hardware devices. To learn more, check out the **Safe Mode** InfoWeb.

click ➡✳

When a computer is behaving erratically, does rebooting help? Sometimes—especially if a computer has been left on for a few weeks straight—the operating system seems to forget how to handle part of its job. Such problems can be caused by transient, "soft errors" in the memory circuits that are supposed to hold the operating system instructions. In other cases, areas of memory that are supposed to be reserved for the operating system somehow get overwritten by snippets of application programs. The end effect is the same—parts of the operating system are missing and can't control a particular input, output, or storage function. As a result, a computer might begin to behave erratically. The remedy for this problem is to restore the operating system back to full functionality. Usually, rebooting does the trick. If not, consider the possibility that your computer might have contracted a virus. (More information on the topic of viruses can be found in Chapter 4.)

QUICK Check
TechTalk

1 The boot process loads the [_____] from the hard disk into memory.

2 During the boot process, the [_____] checks your computer's main circuitry, screen display, memory, and keyboard.

3 Windows [_____] mode provides a limited version of Windows that allows you to troubleshoot, but not use most peripheral devices.

4 If a computer is behaving erratically, rebooting might restore functionality. True or false? [_____]

check answers ➡✳

ISSUE
HOW PRIVATE IS E-MAIL?

When you drop an envelope in the corner mailbox, you probably expect it to arrive at its destination unopened, and with its contents kept safe from prying eyes. When you make a phone call, you might assume that your conversation will proceed unmonitored by wiretaps or other listening devices. Can you also expect an e-mail message to be read only by the person to whom it is addressed?

In the U.S., The Electronic Communications Privacy Act of 2000 prohibits the use of intercepted e-mail as evidence unless a judge approved a search warrant. That doesn't mean the government isn't reading your mail. The FBI developed a technology called Carnivore that scans through messages entering and leaving an ISP's e-mail system and looks for e-mail associated with a person who is under investigation. Privacy advocates are concerned because Carnivore scans all of the messages that pass through an ISP, not just those messages destined for a particular individual.

Although law enforcement agencies are required to obtain a search warrant before intercepting e-mail, no such restriction exists for employers who want to monitor employee e-mail. According to the American Management Association, 27 percent of U.S. businesses monitor employee e-mail. But this intentional eavesdropping is only one way in which the contents of your e-mail messages might become public. The recipient of your e-mail can forward it to one or more people—people you never intended for it to reach. Your e-mail messages could pop up on a technician's screen in the course of system maintenance or repairs. Also, keep in mind that e-mail messages—including those that you delete from your own PC—can be stored on backups of your ISP's e-mail server. You might wonder if such open access to your e-mail is legal. The answer in most cases is yes.

The United States Omnibus Crime Control and Safe Streets Act of 1968 and the Electronic Communications Privacy Act of 1986 prohibit public and private employers from engaging in surreptitious surveillance of employee activity through the use of electronic devices. However, two exceptions to these privacy statutes exist. The first exception permits an employer to monitor e-mail if one party to the communication consents to the monitoring. An employer must inform employees of this policy before undertaking any monitoring. The second exception permits employers to monitor their employees' e-mail if a legitimate business need exists, and the monitoring takes place within the business-owned e-mail system.

Employees have not been successful in defending their rights to e-mail privacy. For example, in 1996, a Pillsbury employee was fired from his job for making unprofessional comments in an e-mail to his supervisor. The employee sued because he claimed that the company repeatedly assured its employees that e-mail was private. The court ruled that the employee's right to privacy did not outweigh the interests of the company. Although it would seem that the company violated the requirement to inform employees according to the first exception to the privacy statutes, the fact that the company owned the e-mail system gave it the right to monitor any correspondence carried out over that system. In more recent cases, Dow Chemical fired more than 90 people for sending pornographic e-mail, and the New York Times fired 23 people for sending offensive e-mail.

Like employees of a business, students who use a school's e-mail system cannot be assured of e-mail privacy. When a CalTech student was accused of sexually harassing a female student by sending lewd e-mail to her and her boyfriend, investigators retrieved all of the student's e-mail from the archives of the e-mail server. The student was expelled from the university even though he claimed that the e-mail had been "spoofed" to make it look as though he had sent it, when it had actually been sent by someone else.

InfoWebLinks.com

You'll find lots more information about e-mail privacy (and lack of it) at the **E-mail Privacy** InfoWeb.

click

Why would an employer want to know the contents of employee e-mail? Why would a school be concerned with the correspondence of its students? It is probably true that some organizations simply snoop on the off chance that important information might be discovered. Other organizations have more legitimate reasons for monitoring e-mail. An organization that owns an e-mail system can be held responsible for the consequences of actions related to the contents of e-mail messages on that system. For example, a school has a responsibility to protect students from harassment. If it fails to do so, it can be sued along with the author of the offending e-mail message. Organizations also recognize a need to protect themselves from false rumors and industrial espionage. For example, a business wants to know if an employee is supplying its competitor with information on product research and development.

Many schools and businesses have established e-mail privacy policies, which explain the conditions under which you can and cannot expect your e-mail to remain private. Court decisions, however, seem to support the notion that because an organization owns and operates its e-mail system, the organization owns the e-mail messages that are generated on its system. The individual who authors an e-mail message does not own it and therefore has no rights related to it. A company can, therefore, legally monitor your e-mail. You should use your e-mail account with the expectation that some of your mail will be read from time to time. Think of your e-mail as a postcard, rather than a letter, and save your controversial comments for face-to-face conversations.

─ WHAT DO YOU THINK? ─

1. Do you think most people believe that their e-mail is private?   ○ Yes   ○ No   ○ Not sure

2. Do you agree with CalTech's decision to expel the student who was accused of sending harassing e-mail to another student?   ○ Yes   ○ No   ○ Not sure

3. Should the laws be changed to make it illegal for employers to monitor e-mail without court approval?   ○ Yes   ○ No   ○ Not sure

4. Would you have different privacy expectations regarding an e-mail account at your place of work as opposed to an account that you purchase from an e-mail service provider?   ○ Yes   ○ No   ○ Not sure

click to save your responses ►

INTERACTIVE SUMMARY

The Interactive Summary helps you review important concepts from this chapter. Fill in the blanks to best complete each sentence. When using the NP6 BookOnCD, you can click the Check Answers buttons to automatically score your answers. Place your Tracking Disk in the floppy disk drive if you want to save your scores.

A computer is a device that accepts input, [_____] data, stores data, and produces output according to a series of stored instructions. Before a computer processes data, it is temporarily held in [_____]. This data is then processed in the [_____] (CPU). The idea of a [_____] program means that a series of instructions for a computing task can be loaded into a computer's memory.

Computers are grouped into categories, such as personal computers, handhelds, mainframes, supercomputers, servers, workstations, and videogame consoles. A [_____] computer is a type of microcomputer that is designed to meet the needs of an individual. Computers process, store, and transmit data in [_____] format as a series of 1s and 0s. Each 1 or 0 is called a [_____]. Eight bits, called a [_____], represent one character—a letter, number, or punctuation mark. Data becomes [_____] when it is presented in a format that people can understand and use.

An [_____] system, such as Windows, UNIX, or Mac OS, is essentially the master controller for all of the activities that take place within a computer. [_____] software is any set of computer programs that helps a person carry out a task. Although "Windows" is the name of an operating system, the term "Windows software" refers to application software that is designed for computers that run the Windows operating system.

check answers ➧✳

The Internet is a collection of local, regional, national, and international computer [_____] that are linked together to exchange data and distribute processing tasks. The main routes of the Internet are referred to as the Internet [_____]. Communications between all of the devices on the Internet is made possible by a standard set of rules called [_____]. To transmit data, files are divided into small chunks called [_____] and sent to the IP address of their destination. The Internet hosts a wide variety of activities, such as Web browsing, e-commerce, e-mail, bulletin boards, chat groups, instant messaging, Internet telephony, digital broadcasts, remote access, downloads, uploads, and peer-to-peer connections.

Most people access the Internet using a dial-up connection that simply requires a telephone line and a [_____]. Faster access methods include cable modem service, ISDN, DSL, and satellite service. Regardless of the access method, individuals cannot typically connect directly to the Internet backbone and, therefore, need to use an [_____] as an intermediary. Both national ISPs and local ISPs have advantages that cater to different computing lifestyles.

Access to the Internet is not restricted, but access to some areas requires a [_____] and password. Passwords are most secure when they consist of two non-related words, or a word and a number. Managing multiple passwords can be simplified by selecting a low-security password and a high-security password, then applying them as necessary.

check answers ➧✳

Composed of millions of files that are stored on Web [＿＿＿＿] all over the world, the Web is one of the most popular aspects of the Internet. Many of these Web-based files are documents that a browser displays as Web [＿＿＿＿]. Other files contain photos, videos, animations, and sound clips that can be incorporated into specific Web pages. Web pages also contain text or graphics [＿＿＿＿] to related documents and media files. Every Web page has a unique address called a [＿＿＿＿]. Most of them begin with "http", which stands for Hypertext [＿＿＿＿] Protocol, the communications standard that's instrumental in ferrying Web documents to all corners of the Internet. A group of Web pages is usually referred to as a Web [＿＿＿＿].

A [＿＿＿＿] is a software program that runs on your computer and helps you access Web pages. It fetches Web pages and interprets HTML [＿＿＿＿] in order to properly display the page on your computer screen. Current browsers simply fetch information from a given URL, but they do not have the capability to search for specific information based on your search specifications. A search [＿＿＿＿] provides the tools that you need to search for specific information on the Web. These tools include keyword search input areas, advanced search forms, category lists, and "agents" that understand queries entered as simple questions.

check answers

E-mail, short for "electronic mail," can refer to a single electronic message, or to the entire system of computers and software that transmits, receives, and stores digital e-mail messages. Any person with an e-mail [＿＿＿＿] can send and receive electronic mail. Basic e-mail activities include composing, reading, replying to, sending, forwarding, and deleting messages. More advanced activities include adding attachments, using HTML format, and maintaining an address book. Most e-mail messages are created in a plain and simple format called [＿＿＿＿] text. It is also possible to create messages in [＿＿＿＿] format, which includes underlining, fancy fonts, colored text, and embedded graphics.

E-mail has similarities and differences from other forms of communications, but it is the differences that spawned a collection of online communications guidelines called [＿＿＿＿].

An e-mail system consists of e-mail servers, which are accessible to e-mail account holders. Today, consumers can choose between three types of e-mail. [＿＿＿＿] mail holds your incoming mail on an e-mail server until you download it to your computer using e-mail [＿＿＿＿] software. [＿＿＿＿] mail gives you the option of downloading your mail or storing it on the e-mail server. Web-based e-mail operates exclusively from the Web. [＿＿＿＿]-based mail allows you to use a browser as e-mail client software.

check answers

INTERACTIVE
KEY TERMS

Make sure that you understand all of the boldfaced key terms presented in this chapter. If you're using the NP6 BookOnCD, you can use this list of terms as an interactive study activity. First, try to define a term in your own words, then click the term to compare your definition with the definition that is presented in the chapter.

Always-on connection, 19
Application software, 12
Beep code, 45
Bit, 11
Boot process, 44
Browser, 28
Byte, 11
Cable modem, 19
Case sensitive, 23
CD-ROM drive, 10
CD-writer, 10
Central processing unit (CPU), 4
Chat group, 17
Client , 8
Computer, 4
Computer network, 7
Computer program, 4
Data, 4, 11
Data file, 11
Desktop computer, 6
Dial-up connection, 18
Digital, 11
Downloading, 17
DSL, 20
DSS, 20
DVD drive, 10
E-commerce, 16
Electronic mail, 36
E-mail, 16
E-mail account, 36
E-mail attachment, 37
E-mail client software, 41
E-mail message, 36
E-mail servers, 40
E-mail system, 40
Executable file, 11
File, 11
Filename extension, 11
Floppy disk drive, 9
Handheld computer, 7
Hard disk drive, 9
Home page, 30
HTML, 27
HTML tags, 29

HTTP, 27
Hypertext, 26
IMAP, 40
Information, 11
Input, 4
Instant messaging, 17
Internet, 15
Internet backbone, 15
Internet telephony, 17
IP address, 16
ISDN, 20
ISP, 20
Keyword, 32
LCD screen, 9
Links, 26
Local area network (LAN), 7
Macs, 13
Mailing list server, 16
Mainframe computer, 8
Memory, 5
Message header, 36
Microcomputer, 6
Microprocessor, 6
MIME, 37
Minicomputer, 6
Modem, 10
Monitor, 9
Mouse, 9
Netiquette, 39
Network card, 19
Newsgroups, 16
Notebook computer, 6
Operating system, 12
Output, 5
Packets, 16
Password, 22
PCs, 13
PDA, 7
Peer-to-peer, 18
Peripheral device, 11
Personal computer, 6
Platform, 13
POP, 40
POP server, 41

Power-on self-test (POST), 44
Processing, 4
Proprietary services, 22
Query, 32
Router, 16
Safe Mode, 46
Search engines, 16, 31
Search operator, 32
Server, 8
Smileys, 39
SMTP server, 41
Software, 4
Sound card, 10
Storage, 5
Store-and-forward technology, 40
Stored program, 5
Supercomputer, 8
System software, 12
System unit, 9
TCP/IP, 15
Telnet, 18
Topic directory, 33
Uploading, 17
URL, 27
Usenet, 16
User ID, 22
Videogame console, 7
Voice band modem, 18
Web, 26
Web pages, 26
Web servers, 27
Web site, 27
Web sites, 16
Web-based e-mail, 40
Workstation, 7

INTERACTIVE
SITUATION QUESTIONS

Apply what you've learned to some typical computing situations. When using the NP6 BookOnCD, you can type your answers, then use the Check Answers button to automatically score your responses. Place your Tracking Disk in the floppy disk drive if you want to save your scores.

1 You walk into an office and see the computer pictured to the right. You would probably assume that it would be categorized as a(n) _____ computer, but it might also be a(n) _____ or a server.

2 You receive a floppy disk from a friend and it contains a file called *Quake.exe*. Because of the filename extension, you assume that the disk contains a(n) _____ file that is some type of computer program, rather than a data file.

3 You are a musician and you use your Gateway PC to compose music. Your friend, who has an iMac computer, wants to try your software. If you loan the composition software to your friend, can she use it on her iMac? Yes or no? _____

4 You are a computer technician hired by Ben and Jerry's Ice Cream to set up a Web server. You know that your server will need a unique _____ address that pinpoints its location in cyberspace, and your server will need to use _____, the standard Internet protocol that transports data between all sorts of computer platforms over the Internet.

5 You want the cheapest Internet connection. You don't mind if the connection is limited to speeds under 56 Kbps and doesn't provide very good video performance. You would probably select an ISP that provides a(n) _____ connection.

6 You need to select a password for your online bank account. Which of the following passwords would be the LEAST secure: hddtmrutc, gargantuan, brickcloset, high348? _____

7 You want to look at the latest Nike athletic shoes. The URL that will probably get you to Nike's home page is _____.

8 You want to find some Web pages that contain information about snowboarding competitions. You know that your _____ can only fetch and display Web pages, so you'll need to connect to a(n) _____ site and enter a query, such as "snowboard competition."

9 If your ISP does not supply you with an e-mail account, you can get a free _____ e-mail account from a site such as Hotmail or Excite.

10 You receive an e-mail message that contains colored text and underlining. You assume that the person who sent the message had his mail software set for _____ format.

check answers ➧

1

INTERACTIVE
PRACTICE TESTS

When you use the NP6 BookOnCD, you can take Practice Tests that consist of 10 multiple-choice, true/false, and fill-in-the-blank questions. The questions are selected at random from a large test bank, so each time you take a test, you'll receive a different set of questions. Your tests are scored immediately, and you can print study guides that help you find the correct answers for any questions that you missed. If you are using a Tracking Disk, insert it in the floppy disk drive to save your test scores.   **click to start** ▸✱

STUDY
TIPS

Study Tips help you to organize and consolidate the information in a chapter by making lists, outlines, charts, and sketches. You can use paper and pencil or word processing software to complete most of the Study Tips activities.

1 Make sure that you can use your own words to correctly answer each of the green focus questions that appear throughout the chapter.

2 Explain how a computer makes use of input, processing, storage, memory, output, and the stored program concept.

3 List, briefly describe, and rank (in terms of computing capacity) the characteristics of each computer category described in Section A of this chapter.

4 Identify, list, and describe each of the components of a basic personal computer system.

5 Describe the difference between a data file and an executable file.

6 Describe the difference between an operating system and application software.

7 Discuss what makes two computer platforms compatible or incompatible.

8 Describe the significance of packets, IP addresses, TCP/IP, and routers on the Internet.

9 List at least five resources that are provided by the Internet, and identify those that are most popular.

10 Explain why so many people need the services of an ISP.

11 Make a list of the Internet connections presented in this chapter, and specify typical data transport speeds for each.

12 Describe how to select a password that is secure, yet easy to remember.

13 Describe the similarities and differences between a URL and an e-mail address.

14 Make sure that you can explain the difference between HTML, HTTP, and hypertext.

15 Make a list of the rules that you should follow when typing a URL.

16 Describe the difference between a browser and a search engine.

17 Explain the role of MIME as it relates to e-mail attachments.

18 Describe how e-mail is stored and transmitted by POP and SMTP servers.

PROJECTS

An NP6 Project is an open-ended activity that will help you apply the concepts you have learned. Many projects require resources in addition to your textbook, such as current magazines, library materials, or Web access. When you tackle a project, be prepared to use your critical thinking skills, logical analysis skills, and your creativity.

1 **Issue Research: E-Mail Privacy** The Issue section of this chapter focused on how much—or how little—privacy you can expect when using an e-mail account. For this project, you will write a two–five page paper about e-mail privacy based on information that you gather from the Internet. To begin this project, consult the E-mail Privacy InfoWeb (see page 49) and link to the recommended Web pages to get an in-depth overview of the issue. Next, determine the viewpoint that you will present in your paper. You might, for example, decide to present the viewpoint of a student who believes that e-mail should be afforded the same privacy rights as a sealed letter. Or, you might present the viewpoint of an employer who wants to explain why your business believes that it is necessary to monitor employee e-mail. Whatever viewpoint you decide to present, make sure that you can back it up with facts and references to authoritative articles and Web pages. You can place citations to these pages (including the author's name, article title, date of publication, and URL) at the end of your paper as endnotes, on each page as footnotes, or along with the appropriate paragraphs using parentheses. Follow your professor's instructions for submitting your paper via e-mail or as a printed document.

2 **Describe Your Personal Computer Using Key Terms** Chapter 1 presented you with many computer terms that describe computer equipment. For this project, write a one-page paper that describes the computer that you use most frequently. Refer to the Interactive Key Terms list on page 52 and use as many of the terms as possible. In your final draft, underline each Key Term that you used in your paper. Follow your professor's instructions for submitting your paper as an e-mail attachment or as a printed document.

3 **Who Wants to be a Millionaire** Suppose that producers for the television show *Who Wants to be a Millionaire* ask you to help them create a set of computer-related questions for the next show. Each question should be in multiple-choice format with four possible answers. They need 10 questions: two very simple questions, five questions of medium difficulty, and three difficult questions. Compose a set of 10 questions based on the information provided in Chapter 1. For each question, indicate the correct answer and the page in this book on which the answer can be found.

4 **Get Creative** A new ISP is getting ready to open in your area, and the president of the company asks you to design its new logo. Before starting on the design, imagine that you interview the company president to find out the company name, the type of services offered (dial-up, cable modem, etc.), the speed of service, the geographical coverage, price, and special or proprietary services. For this project, design a logo for the company using a computer or freehand tools. Submit your logo design along with a short written summary that describes how this logo reflects the name of the ISP and the services that it offers.

ADDITIONAL
PROJECTS

Click ➡✳ to access the Web for additional projects.

2

COMPUTER HARDWARE

CONTENTS

➤✴ **SECTION A: DATA REPRESENTATION AND DIGITAL ELECTRONICS**
Digital Data Representation
Quantifying Bits and Bytes
Digital Electronics

➤✴ **SECTION B: MICROPROCESSORS AND MEMORY**
Microprocessor Basics
Microprocessor Performance Factors
Today's Microprocessors
Random Access Memory
Read-only Memory
CMOS Memory

➤✴ **SECTION C: STORAGE DEVICES**
Storage Basics
Floppy Disk Technology
Hard Disk Technology
Tape Storage
CD Technology
DVD Technology

➤✴ **SECTION D: INPUT AND OUTPUT DEVICES**
Expansion Slots, Cards, and Ports
Installing Peripherals
Display Devices
Printers

➤✴ **TECHTALK: HOW A MICROPROCESSOR EXECUTES INSTRUCTIONS**

➤✴ **ISSUE: WHY RECYCLE COMPUTERS?**

➤✴ **REVIEW ACTIVITIES**
Interactive Summary
Interactive Key Terms
Interactive Situation Questions
Interactive Practice Tests
Study Tips
Projects

LABS
➤✴ Working with Binary Numbers
➤✴ Benchmarking

InfoWebLinks

The InfoWebLinks, located in the margins of this chapter, show the way to a variety of Web sites that contain additional information and updates to the chapter topics. Your computer needs an Internet connection to access these links. You can connect to the Web links for this chapter by:

- clicking the InfoWeb links in the margins
- clicking this <u>underlined link</u>
- starting your browser and entering the URL *www.infoweblinks.com/np6/chapter2.htm*

TIP

When using the **BookOnCD**, the symbols are "clickable."

CHAPTER PREVIEW

2

In 1969, Apollo 11 astronauts blasted off for the moon carrying a "state-of-the-art" computer called the AGC (Apollo Guidance Computer). With only 2 K of random access memory, 34 programmed operations, an 18-key keyboard, and a processor that poked along at 1 MHz, the AGC provided less computing capability than one of today's $29 hand-held scientific calculators, and certainly far less capability than your average desktop PC. In Chapter 2, you'll learn more about the capabilities of today's computers, find out how various components work, and learn how to decipher a typical computer ad.

Section A jumps right into data representation and digital electronics—the two major elements that make computers "tick." With this background, you can begin to make sense out of the bits, bytes, and megabytes that enter into just about every discussion about computers. Section B helps you answer questions like "How fast?" and "How much capacity?" in reference to microprocessors and computer memory. Section C focuses on computer storage so that you can understand storage technology and make decisions about storage devices for your computer. Section D explains how to use the expansion bus to add devices to a computer, and then looks at a variety of popular printer and display technologies. The TechTalk section delves into the details of how a microprocessor executes instructions.

When you complete this chapter you should be able to:

- Explain why most computers are digital, and how that relates to representing numbers by using 0 and 1 bits

- Describe the role of a microprocessor's ALU, control unit, registers, and instruction set

- List the factors that affect microprocessor performance

- Explain how RAM works, and how it differs from disk storage

- List facts about RAM that are important to computer buyers and owners

- Describe the difference between magnetic storage and optical storage

- Use criteria such as versatility, durability, capacity, access time, and data transfer rate to compare storage technologies such as floppy disks, hard disks, tapes, CDs, and DVDs

- Describe the components of a computer's expansion bus, including various types of expansion slots and cables

- Explain the hardware compatibility considerations, device drivers, and procedures that are involved in installing a peripheral device

- Explain the factors that might help a shopper decide whether to purchase a CRT or an LCD monitor

- Compare and contrast the technologies and applications for ink jet, solid ink, thermal, dye sublimation, laser, and dot matrix printers

 TIP Click ➤ to access the Web for a complete list of learning objectives for Chapter 2.

Section

A

DATA REPRESENTATION AND DIGITAL ELECTRONICS

Understanding what makes a computer "tick" can come in handy in today's information age. It can help you decipher computer ads, troubleshoot equipment problems, and make software work. Although scientists are tinkering with exotic technologies such as quantum computers and molecular computers, just about every computer today is an electronic, digital device based on a concept that's as simple as a basic light switch.

Obviously, letters, numbers, musical notes, and pictures don't squirt from the keyboard through the circuitry of a computer, and then jump out onto the screen or printer. So how is it that a computer can work with documents, photos, videos, and sound recordings? The answer to that question is what data representation and digital electronics are all about. **Data representation** makes it possible to convert letters, sounds, and images into electrical signals. **Digital electronics** makes it possible for a computer to manipulate simple "on" and "off" signals to perform complex tasks.

FIGURE 2-1

A computer is a digital device, more like a standard light switch than a dimmer switch.

DIGITAL DATA REPRESENTATION

Why are computers digital? Most computers are digital, as opposed to analog, devices. A **digital device** works with discrete—distinct or separate—data or digits, such as 1 and 0. An **analog device** works with continuous data. As an analogy, a traditional light switch has two discrete states—on and off, so it is a digital device. A dimmer switch, on the other hand, has a rotating dial that controls a continuous range of brightness. It is, therefore, an analog device (Figure 2-1).

Computers are digital primarily because computer designers have found it to be a relatively simple, dependable, and adaptable technology. Just as a standard light switch is a simpler technology than a dimmer switch, a digital computer is a simpler technology than an analog computer. In fact, most computers use the simplest type of digital technology—their circuits have only two possible states. For convenience, let's say that one of those states is "on" and the other state is "off." When discussing these states, we usually indicate the "on" state with 1 and the "off" state with 0. So, the sequence "on" "on" "off" "off" would be written 1100. These 1s and 0s are referred to as **binary digits**. It is from this term that we get the word "bit"—*bi*nary digi*t*. Computers use sequences of bits to represent numbers, letters, punctuation marks, music, pictures, and videos.

How can a computer represent numbers using bits? Numeric data consists of numbers that might be used in arithmetic operations. For example, your annual income is numeric data, as is your age. The price of a Razor scooter is numeric data. So is your car's average gas mileage. Computers represent numeric data—like 24 (your car's average gas mileage)—using the **binary number system**, also called "base 2."

The binary number system has only two digits: 0 and 1. No "squiggle" like "2" exists in this system, so the number "two" is represented in binary as "10" (pronounced "one zero"). You'll recognize the similarity to what happens when you're counting from 1 to 10 in the familiar decimal system. After you reach 9, you run out of digits. For "ten," you have to use "10"—zero is a placeholder and the "1" indicates "one group of tens." In binary, you just run out of digits sooner—right after you count to 1. To get to the next number, you have to use the zero as a placeholder and the "1" indicates "one group of 2s." In binary then, you count 0 ("zero"), 1 ("one"), 10 ("one zero"), instead of counting 0, 1, 2 in decimal. If you need to brush up on binary numbers, refer to Figure 2-2 and to the lab at the end of Section A.

The important point to understand is that the binary number system allows computers to represent virtually any number simply by using 0s and 1s, which conveniently translate into electrical "on" and "off" signals. Your average gas mileage (24) is 11000 in binary, and can be represented by "on" "on" "off" "off" "off."

2

FIGURE 2-2

The decimal system uses ten symbols to represent numbers: 0, 1, 2, 3, 4, 5, 6, 7, 8, and 9. The binary number system uses only two symbols: 0 and 1.

DECIMAL (BASE 10)	BINARY (BASE 2)
0	0
1	1
2	10
3	11
4	100
5	101
6	110
7	111
8	1000
9	1001
10	1010
11	1011
1000	1111101000

01001000　　01001001　00100001

How can a computer represent words and letters using bits? Character data is composed of letters, symbols, and numerals that will not be used in arithmetic operations. Examples of character data include your name, address, and hair color. Just as Morse code uses dashes and dots to represent the letters of the alphabet, a digital computer uses a series of bits to represent letters, characters, and numerals. (See "HI!" at left, along with the bits that a computer can use to represent each character.)

Computers employ several types of codes to represent character data, including ASCII, EBCDIC, and Unicode. **ASCII** (American Standard Code for Information Interchange, pronounced "ASK ee") requires only seven bits for each character. For example, the ASCII code for an uppercase "A" is 1000001. ASCII provides codes for 128 characters, including uppercase letters, lowercase letters, punctuation symbols, and numerals. A superset of ASCII, called **Extended ASCII**, uses eight bits to represent each character. The eighth bit provides codes for 128 additional characters, which are usually boxes, circles, and other graphical symbols. **EBCDIC** (Extended Binary-Coded Decimal Interchange Code, pronounced "EB seh dick") is an alternative 8-bit code, usually used by older, IBM mainframe computers. **Unicode** (pronounced "YOU ni code") uses 16 bits and provides codes for 65,000 characters—a real bonus for representing the alphabets of multiple languages. Most personal computers use Extended ASCII code (shown in Figure 2-3), although Unicode is becoming increasingly popular.

FIGURE 2-3

The extended ASCII code uses a series of eight 1s and 0s to represent 256 characters, including lowercase letters, uppercase letters, symbols, and numerals. The first 63 ASCII characters are not shown in this table because they represent special control sequences that cannot be printed. The two "blank" entries are space characters.

☐ 00100000	> 00111110	\ 01011100	z 01111010	ÿ 10011000	╢ 10110110	╘ 11010100	≥ 11110010
! 00100001	? 00111111	] 01011101	{ 01111011	Ö 10011001	╖ 10110111	╒ 11010101	≤ 11110011
" 00100010	@ 01000000	^ 01011110	| 01111100	Ü 10011010	╕ 10111000	╓ 11010110	⌠ 11110100
# 00100011	A 01000001	_ 01011111	} 01111101	¢ 10011011	╣ 10111001	╫ 11010111	⌡ 11110101
$ 00100100	B 01000010	` 01100000	~ 01111110	£ 10011100	║ 10111010	╪ 11011000	÷ 11110110
% 00100101	C 01000011	a 01100001	⌂ 01111111	¥ 10011101	╗ 10111011	┘ 11011001	≈ 11110111
& 00100110	D 01000100	b 01100010	Ç 10000000	₧ 10011110	╝ 10111100	┌ 11011010	° 11111000
' 00100111	E 01000101	c 01100011	ü 10000001	ƒ 10011111	╜ 10111101	█ 11011011	· 11111001
(00101000	F 01000110	d 01100100	é 10000010	á 10100000	╛ 10111110	▄ 11011100	· 11111010
) 00101001	G 01000111	e 01100101	â 10000011	í 10100001	┐ 10111111	▌ 11011101	√ 11111011
* 00101010	H 01001000	f 01100110	ä 10000100	ó 10100010	└ 11000000	▐ 11011110	ⁿ 11111100
+ 00101011	I 01001001	g 01100111	à 10000101	ú 10100011	┴ 11000001	▀ 11011111	² 11111101
, 00101100	J 01001010	h 01101000	å 10000110	ñ 10100100	┬ 11000010	α 11100000	■ 11111110
- 00101101	K 01001011	i 01101001	ç 10000111	Ñ 10100101	├ 11000011	ß 11100001	11111111
. 00101110	L 01001100	j 01101010	ê 10001000	ª 10100110	─ 11000100	Γ 11100010	
/ 00101111	M 01001101	k 01101011	ë 10001001	º 10100111	┼ 11000101	π 11100011	
0 00110000	N 01001110	l 01101100	è 10001010	¿ 10101000	╞ 11000110	Σ 11100100	
1 00110001	O 01001111	m 01101101	ï 10001011	⌐ 10101001	╟ 11000111	σ 11100101	
2 00110010	P 01010000	n 01101110	î 10001100	¬ 10101010	╚ 11001000	µ 11100110	
3 00110011	Q 01010001	o 01101111	ì 10001101	½ 10101011	╔ 11001001	τ 11100111	
4 00110100	R 01010010	p 01110000	Ä 10001110	¼ 10101100	╩ 11001010	Φ 11101000	
5 00110101	S 01010011	q 01110001	Å 10001111	¡ 10101101	╦ 11001011	Θ 11101001	
6 00110110	T 01010100	r 01110010	É 10010000	« 10101110	╠ 11001100	Ω 11101010	
7 00110111	U 01010101	s 01110011	æ 10010001	» 10101111	═ 11001101	δ 11101011	
8 00111000	V 01010110	t 01110100	Æ 10010010	░ 10110000	╬ 11001110	∞ 11101100	
9 00111001	W 01010111	u 01110101	ô 10010011	▒ 10110001	╧ 11001111	φ 11101101	
: 00111010	X 01011000	v 01110110	ö 10010100	▓ 10110010	╨ 11010000	ε 11101110	
; 00111011	Y 01011001	w 01110111	ò 10010101	│ 10110011	╤ 11010001	∩ 11101111	
< 00111100	Z 01011010	x 01111000	û 10010110	┤ 10110100	╥ 11010010	≡ 11110000	
= 00111101	[01011011	y 01111001	ù 10010111	╡ 10110101	╙ 11010011	± 11110001	

Why does ASCII provide codes for 0, 1, 2, 3, 4, 5, 6, 7, 8, and 9? Computers represent numeric data with binary equivalents, so it might seem as if there would be no need for ASCII codes that represent numbers. Computers, however, sometimes distinguish between numeric data and numerals. For example, you don't typically use your social security "number" in calculations, so a computer typically considers it character data, composed of *numerals*, not numbers. Likewise, the "numbers" in your street address are treated as character data, not numeric data. A computer uses the ASCII code numerals for your social security number and street address, whereas it uses a binary number to code numeric data such as your age.

How does a computer convert sounds and pictures into codes? Sounds and pictures are not small, discrete objects like numbers or the letters of the alphabet. To work with sounds and pictures, a computer must somehow **digitize** colors, notes, and instrument sounds into 1s and 0s. Computers convert colors and sounds into numbers, which can be represented by bits. For example, a red dot on your computer screen might be represented by 1100, a green dot by 0010.

When a computer works with a series of 1s and 0s, how does it know which code to use? All of the "stuff" that your computer works with is stored in files as a long—make that really long—series of 1s and 0s. Your computer needs to know whether to interpret those 1s and 0s as ASCII code, binary numbers, or the code for a picture or sound. Imagine the mess if your computer thought that your term paper, stored as ASCII, was an accounting file that contained a series of numbers stored in binary format. It would never be able to reconstruct the words and sentences of your term paper.

To avoid confusion, most computer files contain a **file header** with information on the code that was used to represent the file data. A file header is stored along with the file and can be read by the computer, but never appears on the screen. By reading the header information, a computer can tell how a file's contents were coded.

QUANTIFYING BITS AND BYTES

How can I tell the difference between bits and bytes? Computer ads include lots of abbreviations relating to bits and bytes. A few key concepts will help you understand what these abbreviations mean. Even though the word "bit" is an abbreviation for "binary digit," it can be further abbreviated, usually as a lowercase "b." A byte, on the other hand, is composed of eight bits and is usually abbreviated as an uppercase "B." By the way, halfway between a little "bit" and a big "byte" is a thing called a nibble (four bits).

Transmission speeds are usually expressed in bits, whereas storage space is usually expressed in bytes. In Chapter 1, for example, you learned that the speed of most voice band modems is 56 Kbps—56 kilo*bits* per second. In a computer ad, you might see the capacity of a hard disk drive described as 8 GB—8 giga*bytes*.

What do the prefixes kilo- mega- and giga- mean? "Kilo" is usually a prefix that means 1,000. For example, $50 K means $50,000. When it refers to bits or bytes, a "kilo" is 1,024 because computer engineers measure everything in base 2, and 2^{10} turns out to be 1,024, not 1,000. So a **kilobit** (abbreviated Kb or Kbit) is 1,024 bits and a **kilobyte** (abbreviated KB or Kbyte) is 1,024 bytes.

The prefix "mega" refers to a million, or in the context of bits and bytes, precisely 1,048,576 (the equivalent of 2^{20}). Mb or Mbit is the abbreviation for **megabit**. MB or Mbyte is the abbreviation for **megabyte**. The prefixes **giga-** (billion), **tera-** (trillion), and **exa-** (quintillion) work the same way.

DIGITAL ELECTRONICS

How does a computer store and transport all of those bits? Because most computers are electronic devices, bits take the form of electrical pulses that can travel over circuits, much in the same way that electricity flows over a wire when you turn on a light switch. All of the circuits, chips, and mechanical components that form a computer are designed to work with bits. Most of these essential components are housed within the computer's system unit.

Does a typical computer owner need to mess around inside the system unit? If it weren't for the miniaturization made possible by digital electronic technology, computers would be huge, and the inside of a computer's system unit would contain a complex jumble of wires and other electronic gizmos. Instead, today's computers contain relatively few parts. Desktop computers are designed with the expectation that owners will forage around inside the system unit to add or replace various components. Notebook computers, on the other hand, usually provide access for expansion and replacement from outside of the case. In Figure 2-4, you can see what's inside a typical desktop computer.

FIGURE 2-4

A computer's system unit typically contains circuit boards, storage devices, and a power supply that converts current from an AC wall outlet into the DC current used by computer circuitry.

Power supply and fan

CD-ROM drive

Floppy disk drive

Hard disk drive

Microprocessor located under cooling fan

Cables that transfer data from storage devices to motherboard

Expansion cards

Main circuit board (motherboard)

FIGURE 2-5

Chips are classified by the number of miniaturized components they contain—from small-scale integration (SSI) of less than 100 components per chip to "ultra large-scale integration" (ULSI) of more than 1 million components per chip.

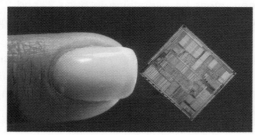

What's a computer chip? The terms "computer chip," "microchip," and "chip" originated as technical jargon for "integrated circuit." An **integrated circuit** (IC), such as the one pictured in Figure 2-5, is a super thin slice of semiconducting material packed with microscopic circuit elements such as wires, transistors, capacitors, logic gates, and resistors.

Semiconducting materials (or "semiconductors"), such as silicon and germanium, are substances with properties between those of a conductor (like copper) and an insulator (like wood). To fabricate a chip, the conductive properties of selective parts of the semiconducting material can be enhanced to essentially create miniature electronic pathways and components, such as transistors.

COMPUTER HARDWARE   **63**

Find out how thousands
of miles of wires and
millions of components
can be miniaturized to
the size of a baby's
fingernail at the
Integrated Circuits
InfoWeb.

click ▶︎✳

The assortment of chips inside of a computer includes the microprocessor, memory modules, and support circuitry. These chips are packaged in a protective carrier that also provides connectors to other computer components. Chip carriers vary in shape and size—including small rectangular **DIPs** (dual in-line package) with caterpillar-like legs protruding from a black, rectangular "body;" long, slim **DIMMs** (dual in-line memory modules); pin-cushion-like **PGAs** (pin-grid arrays); and cassette-like **SEC cartridges** (single edge contact cartridges). Terms like DIMM and PGA frequently appear in computer ads. Figure 2-6 helps you visualize these components.

2

FIGURE 2-6

Integrated circuits can be used for microprocessors, memory, and support circuitry. They are housed within a ceramic carrier. These carriers exist in several configurations, or "chip packages," such as DIPs, DIMMs, PGAs, and SECs.

A DIP has two rows of pins that connect the IC circuitry to a circuit board.

A DIMM is a small circuit board containing several chips, typically used for memory.

A PGA is a square chip package with pins arranged in concentric squares, typically used for microprocessors.

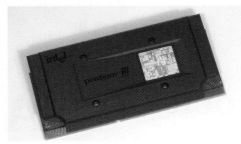

An SEC cartridge is a popular chip package for microprocessors.

How do chips fit together to make a computer? The computer's main circuit board, called a **motherboard** or "main board," houses all essential chips and provides connecting circuitry between them. If you look carefully at a motherboard, you'll see that some chips are permanently soldered in place. Other chips are plugged into special sockets and connectors, which allow chips to be removed for repairs or upgrades. When multiple chips are required for a single function, such as generating stereo-quality sound, the chips might be gathered together on a separate small circuit board, which can then be plugged into a special slot-like connector. Figure 2-7 on the next page provides a handy guide that can help you identify the components on your computer's motherboard. You will learn more about the components of a motherboard in this and subsequent chapters.

FIGURE 2-7

A computer motherboard provides sockets for chips, slots for small circuit boards, and the circuitry that connects all of these components.

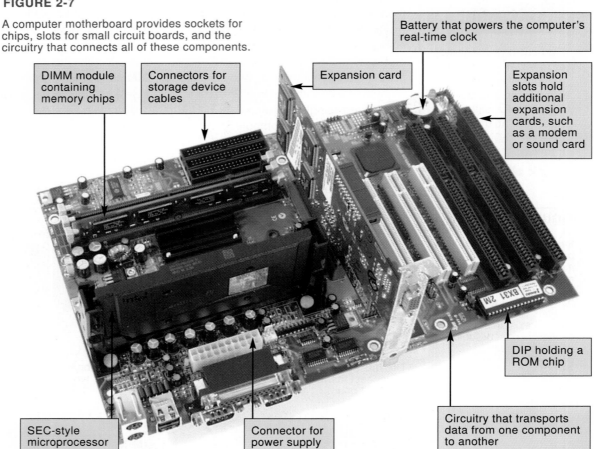

DIMM module containing memory chips

Connectors for storage device cables

Expansion card

Battery that powers the computer's real-time clock

Expansion slots hold additional expansion cards, such as a modem or sound card

DIP holding a ROM chip

SEC-style microprocessor

Connector for power supply

Circuitry that transports data from one component to another

QUICK^{Check} Section A

1 A(n) [_____] device works with discrete numbers, whereas a(n) [_____] device works with continuous data.

2 The [_____] number system represents numeric data as a series of 0s and 1s.

3 ASCII provides codes for numerals 0 through 9. True or false? [_____]

4 Most personal computers use the [_____] code to represent character data.

5 A computer uses [_____] code numerals for your social security number and street address, whereas it uses a(n) [_____] number to code numeric data such as your age.

6 100 MB is larger than 100 Mbit. True or false? [_____]

7 A(n) [_____] contains microscopic circuit elements, such as wires, transistors, and capacitors, that are packed onto a very small square of semiconducting material.

check answers ▶✳

LAB 2-A
WORKING WITH BINARY NUMBERS

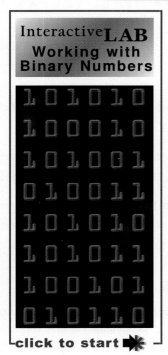

Interactive **LAB**
Working with Binary Numbers

└ click to start ➡ ┘

In this lab, you'll review and learn:

- The difference between the binary number system and the decimal number system
- How to count in binary
- How to convert decimal numbers into binary numbers
- How to convert binary numbers into decimal numbers
- How to use the Windows Calculator to convert numbers
- How to work with "powers of two"

2

LAB Assignments

1 Start the interactive part of the lab. Insert your Tracking Disk if you want to save your QuickCheck results. Perform each of the lab steps as directed, and answer all of the lab QuickCheck questions. When you exit the lab, your answers are automatically graded and your results are displayed.

2 Using paper and pencil, manually convert the following decimal numbers into binary numbers. Your instructor might ask you to show the process that you used for each conversion.

    a. 100   b. 1,000   c. 256   d. 27

    e. 48   f. 112   g. 96   h. 1,024

3 Using paper and pencil, manually convert the following binary numbers into decimal numbers. Your instructor might ask you to show the process that you used for each conversion.

    a. 100   b. 101   c. 1100   d. 10101

    e. 1111   f. 10000   g. 1111000   h. 110110

4 Describe what is wrong with the following sequence:

    10 100 110 1000 1001 1100 1110 10000

5 What is the decimal equivalent of 2^0? 2^1? 2^8?

Section B

MICROPROCESSORS AND MEMORY

A typical computer ad contains a long list of specifications that describe a computer's components and capabilities (Figure 2-8.) Savvy shoppers must have a good understanding of these specifications, including their effect on the price of a computer system. Most computer specifications begin with the microprocessor type and speed. Computer manufacturers want consumers to think that faster is better, but is there a point at which you can pay for speed that you won't need?

Computer ads also contain information about a computer's memory capacity. Lots of memory can add hundreds of dollars to the cost of a computer. Consumers are right to ask, "How much RAM is enough?"

The microprocessor and memory are two of the most important components in a computer. To understand how they affect computer performance and price, it is handy to know a little bit about how they work. Along the way, you'll learn to decipher computer ad terminology, such as MHz, SDRAM, and cache.

FIGURE 2-8

A typical computer ad is sprinkled liberally with acronyms and computer jargon. In this section of the chapter, you'll learn how to decipher the microprocessor and memory specifications highlighted in yellow.

- Intel Pentium 4 processor 2.53 GHz
- 1 GB RDRAM (max. 2 GB)
- 8 K L1 cache, 512 K L2 cache
- 80 GB UltraATA-100 HD (5400 rpm)
- 48 X Max CD-RW
- 3½" 1.44 MB floppy disk drive
- 19" (18.0" vis.) 26 dp. monitor
- 64 MB AGP graphics card
- Sound Blaster Live! PCI sound card
- Altec Lansing speakers
- U.S. Robotics 56 Kbps modem
- Mouse & keyboard
- Windows XP Home Edition
- External drive bays: 3 5.25" bays for diskette, tape, or CD drives; 1 3.5" bay for a floppy drive
- Internal drive bays: 2 HDD bays
- 4 USB ports
- 1 serial, 1 parallel port, and 1 video port
- 1 network port (RJ45 connector)
- 5 PCI slots and 1 AGP slot
- Home/small business software bundle
- 3-year limited warranty

MICROPROCESSOR BASICS

Exactly what is a microprocessor? A **microprocessor** (sometimes simply referred to as a "processor") is an integrated circuit designed to process instructions. It is the most important component of a computer, and usually the most expensive single component. Although a microprocessor is sometimes mistakenly referred to as "a computer on a chip," it can be more accurately described as "a CPU on a chip" because it contains—on a single chip—circuitry that performs essentially the same tasks as the central processing unit of a classic mainframe computer.

What does it look like? Looking inside a computer, you can usually identify the microprocessor because it is the largest chip on the motherboard, although it might be hidden under a cooling fan. Depending on the brand and model, a microprocessor might be housed in an SEC cartridge or in a square PGA, like those shown in Figure 2-6, earlier in the chapter on page 63.

Inside the chip carrier, a microprocessor is a very complex integrated circuit, containing as many as 300 million miniaturized electronic components. Some of these components are only 30 nanometers thick. A **nanometer** is one billionth of a meter. Thirty nanometers are about the thickness of three atoms. You could stack 5,000 of them, one on top of another, and they would be only the thickness of a single sheet of notebook paper! The miniaturized circuitry in a microprocessor is grouped into important functional areas, such as the ALU and the control unit.

The **ALU** (arithmetic logic unit) performs arithmetic operations, such as addition and subtraction. It also performs logical operations, such as comparing two numbers to see if they are the same. The ALU uses **registers** to hold data that is being processed, just as you use a mixing bowl to hold the ingredients for a batch of brownies. The microprocessor's **control unit** fetches each instruction, just as you get each ingredient out of a cupboard or the refrigerator. The computer loads data into the ALU's registers, just as you add all of the ingredients to the mixing bowl. Finally, the control unit gives the ALU the green light to begin processing, just as you flip the switch to your electric mixer to begin blending all of the brownie ingredients.

Where does the microprocessor get its instructions? The simple answer is that a microprocessor executes instructions that are provided by a computer program. However, a microprocessor can't follow just any instructions. A program that contains an instruction to "self destruct" won't have much effect because a microprocessor can perform only a limited list of instructions—"self destruct" isn't one of them.

The list of instructions that a microprocessor can perform is called its **instruction set**. These instructions are hard-wired into the processor's circuitry and include basic arithmetic and logical operations, fetching data, and clearing registers. A computer can perform very complex tasks, but it does so by performing a combination of simple tasks from its instruction set.

MICROPROCESSOR PERFORMANCE FACTORS

What makes one microprocessor perform better than another? The performance of a microprocessor is affected by several factors, including clock speed, word size, cache size, instruction set, and processing techniques.

What do MHz and GHz have to do with computer performance? The speed specifications that you see in a computer ad indicate the speed of the **microprocessor clock**—a timing device that sets the pace for executing instructions. Most computer ads specify the speed of a microprocessor in megahertz (MHz) or gigahertz (GHz). **Megahertz** means a million cycles per second. **Gigahertz** means a billion cycles per second.

A cycle is the smallest unit of time in a microprocessor's universe. Every action that a processor performs is measured by these cycles. It is important, however, to understand that the clock speed is not equal to the number of instructions that a processor can execute in one second. In many computers, some instructions occur within one cycle, but other instructions might require multiple cycles. Some processors can even execute several instructions in a single clock cycle.

A specification such as 2.53 GHz means that the microprocessor's clock operates at a speed of 2.53 billion cycles per second. All other things being equal, a computer with a 2.53 GHz processor is faster than a computer with a 1.5 GHz processor or a 933 MHz processor.

Which is faster, an 8-bit processor or a 64-bit processor? Word size refers to the number of bits that a microprocessor can manipulate at one time. Word size is based on the size of the registers in the ALU, and the capacity of circuits that lead to those registers. A microprocessor with an 8-bit word size, for example, has 8-bit registers, processes eight bits at a time, and is referred to as an "8-bit processor." Processors with a larger word size can process more data during each processor cycle, a factor that leads to increased computer performance. Today's personal computers typically contain 32-bit or 64-bit processors.

How does the cache size affect performance? **Cache** (pronounced "cash") is sometimes called "RAM cache" or "cache memory." It is special high-speed memory that allows a microprocessor to access data more rapidly than from memory located elsewhere on the motherboard. Some computer ads specify cache type and capacity. A **Level 1 cache** (L1) is built into the processor chip, whereas a **Level 2 cache** (L2) is located on a separate chip and takes a little more time to get data to the processor. Cache capacity is usually measured in kilobytes.

In theory, a large cache increases processing speed. In today's computers, however, cache size is usually tied to a particular processor brand and model. It is not of particular significance to consumers because cache is not configurable. For example, you can't add more L1 cache to your computer without replacing the microprocessor.

What's the difference between CISC and RISC? As chip designers developed various instruction sets for microprocessors, they tended to add increasingly more complex instructions that each required several clock cycles for execution. A microprocessor with such an instruction set uses **CISC** (complex instruction set computer) technology. A microprocessor with a limited set of simple instructions uses **RISC** (reduced instruction set computer) technology. A RISC processor performs most instructions faster than a CISC processor. It might, however, require more of these simple instructions to complete a task than a CISC processor requires for the same task.

In theory, a RISC processor should be faster than a CISC processor. In practice, CISC processors excel at some processing tasks, while RISC processors excel at others. Most of the processors in today's Macs use RISC technology; most PCs use CISC technology. In fact, it is the availability of specialized, multiple clock-cycle graphics processing instructions in your PC's microprocessor that makes computer games perform at dizzying speeds.

Can a microprocessor execute more than one instruction at a time? Some processors execute instructions "serially"—that is, one instruction at a time. With **serial processing**, the processor must complete all of the steps in the instruction cycle before it begins to execute the next instruction. However, using a technology called **pipelining**, a processor can begin executing an instruction before it completes the previous instruction. Many of today's microprocessors also perform **parallel processing**, in which multiple instructions are executed at the same time. Pipelining and parallel processing enhance processor performance.

To get a clearer picture of serial, pipelining, and parallel processing techniques, consider an analogy in which computer instructions are pizzas. Serial processing executes only one instruction at a time, just like a pizzeria with one oven that holds only one pizza.

Test your own computer's performance by trying some of the tests at the <u>Benchmark</u> InfoWeb.

click ✳

Pipelining is similar to a pizza conveyor belt. A pizza (instruction) starts moving along the conveyor belt, but before it reaches the end, another pizza starts moving along the belt. Parallel processing is similar to a pizzeria with many ovens. Just as these ovens can bake more than one pizza at a time, a parallel processor can execute more than one instruction at a time.

With so many factors to consider, how can I compare various microprocessors? Various testing laboratories run a series of tests to gauge the overall speed of a microprocessor. The results of these tests—called **benchmarks**—can then be compared to the results for other microprocessors. The results of benchmark tests are usually available on the Web, and are published in computer magazine articles.

TODAY'S MICROPROCESSORS

Which companies produce most of today's popular microprocessors? The specifications for a computer usually include the company that produced the microprocessor. Intel is the world's largest chipmaker and supplies a sizeable percentage of the microprocessors that power PCs. In 1971, Intel introduced the world's first microprocessor—the 4004. The company has produced a steady stream of new processor models, beginning with the 8088 processor that powered the original IBM PC.

AMD (Advanced Micro Devices) is Intel's chief rival in the PC chip market. It produces microprocessors that work just like Intel's chips, but at a lower price. AMD and a few other chipmakers provide consumers with chip choices in the PC marketplace. Motorola is the main chip supplier for Apple computers.

To learn about the latest microprocessor models from Intel and AMD, visit the **Microprocessor Update** InfoWeb.

└**click** ▶

Which microprocessor is best for my PC? Microprocessor models and enhancements seem to appear much more frequently than new car models. Intel is continually upgrading its line of Pentium processors. After introducing the original Pentium in 1993, the Pentium II was unveiled in 1997, the Pentium III in 1999, the Pentium 4 in 2000, the Itanium in 2001, and the Itanium2 in 2002. Intel's "budget" Celeron processors are not quite as powerful as the Pentiums, but they do a fine job of running software, and might mean a savings of $100 to $300 on the price of a computer.

AMD's Athlon and Opteron processors are direct competitors to Intel's Pentium and Itanium lines, and have a slight performance advantage according to some benchmarks. The Duron processor is AMD's "budget" model.

The microprocessor that's "best" for you depends on your budget and the type of work and play that you plan to do. The microprocessors that are marketed with the current crop of computers will handle most business, educational, and entertainment applications. You'll want to consider the fastest processor offerings from Intel or AMD if you typically engage in processing-hungry activities such as 3-D animated computer games, desktop publishing, or video editing. A little research on the Web or in computer magazines will help you to decide which of the current microprocessor offerings would be most suitable for your computing needs.

Can I replace my computer's microprocessor with a faster one? It is technically possible to upgrade your computer's microprocessor, but computer owners rarely do so. One reason is the cost. The price of the latest, greatest microprocessor can often get you more than half way to buying an entirely new computer system. Technical factors also discourage microprocessor upgrades. A microprocessor can operate at full efficiency only if all of the components in the computer also can handle the faster speeds. In many cases, installing a new processor in an old computer can be like attaching a huge outboard engine to a canoe. Safety issues aside, a canoe is not designed to handle all that power, so you can't expect it to go as fast as a high-performance speedboat.

If you are considering a microprocessor upgrade, you can consult your computer manufacturer's Web site to determine your upgrade options. Your computer's motherboard contains a processor socket for some type of PGA or SEC chip package. Several variations of each socket exist, including Slot 1, Slot 2, Slot A, Socket 7, and Socket 370. When you upgrade, you must purchase a microprocessor that will fit into the socket provided by your computer's motherboard. You can find information about your current microprocessor and socket type in the documentation for your computer. To find out whether an upgrade would be worth the cost, you might look for relevant articles in printed or Web-based computer magazines.

2

RANDOM ACCESS MEMORY

What is RAM? RAM (random access memory) is a temporary holding area for data, application program instructions, and the operating system. In a personal computer, RAM is usually several chips or small circuit boards that plug into the motherboard within the computer's system unit.

A computer's RAM capacity is invariably included in the list of specifications in a computer ad. The amount of RAM in a computer can affect the overall price of a computer system. To understand how much RAM your computer needs, and to understand computer ad terminology, it is handy to have a little background on how RAM works and what it does.

Why is RAM so important? RAM is the "waiting room" for the computer's processor. It holds raw data that is waiting to be processed, as well as the program instructions for processing that data. In addition, RAM holds the results of processing until they can be stored more permanently on disk or tape. Let's look at an example. When you use personal finance software to balance your checkbook, you enter raw data for check amounts, which is held in RAM. The personal finance software sends the instructions for processing this data to RAM. The processor uses these instructions to calculate your checkbook balance and sends the results back to RAM. From RAM, your checkbook balance can be stored on disk, displayed, or printed (Figure 2-9).

FIGURE 2-9

RAM is the computer equivalent of the waiting room at an airport or train station. It holds data that is waiting to be processed, stored, displayed, or printed.

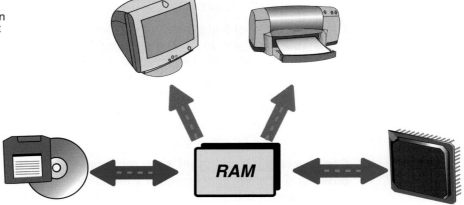

In addition to data and application software instructions, RAM also holds operating system instructions that control the basic functions of a computer system. These instructions are loaded into RAM every time you start your computer, and they remain there until you turn off your computer.

How does RAM differ from hard-disk storage? People who are new to computers sometimes tend to confuse RAM and hard-disk storage, maybe because both of these components hold data, because they typically are "hidden" inside the system unit, or because they can both be measured in gigabytes. To differentiate between RAM and hard-disk storage, remember that RAM holds data in circuitry, whereas hard-disk storage places data on magnetic media. RAM is temporary storage, whereas hard-disk storage is more permanent. In addition, RAM usually has less storage capacity than that of hard-disk storage.

How does RAM work? In RAM, microscopic electronic parts called **capacitors** hold the bits that represent data. You can visualize the capacitors as microscopic lights that can be turned on or off. A charged capacitor is "turned on" and represents a "1" bit. A discharged capacitor is "turned off" and represents a "0" bit.

Each bank of capacitors holds eight bits—one byte—of data. A RAM address on each bank helps the computer locate data, as needed, for processing (Figure 2-10).

FIGURE 2-10

Each RAM location has an address and holds one byte of data by using eight capacitors to represent the eight bits in a byte.

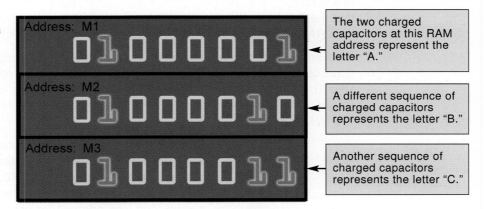

Address: M1 — The two charged capacitors at this RAM address represent the letter "A."

Address: M2 — A different sequence of charged capacitors represents the letter "B."

Address: M3 — Another sequence of charged capacitors represents the letter "C."

In some respects, RAM is similar to a chalkboard. You can use a chalkboard to write mathematical formulas, erase them, and then write an outline for a report. In a similar way, RAM can hold numbers and formulas when you balance your checkbook, then hold the text of your English essay when you use word processing software. The contents of RAM can be changed just by changing the charge of the capacitors. Unlike disk storage, most RAM is **volatile**, which means that it requires electrical power to hold data. If the computer is turned off, or if the power goes out, all data stored in RAM instantly and permanently disappears. When someone exclaims, "Rats! I just lost my document," it often means that the person was entering the text of a document (which was being held in RAM) and the power went out before the data was saved on disk.

How much RAM does my computer need? The capacity of RAM is usually expressed in megabytes (MB) or gigabytes (GB). Today's personal computers typically feature between 128 MB and 2 GB of RAM. The amount of RAM needed by your computer depends on the software that you use. RAM requirements are routinely specified on the outside of a software package. If you need more RAM, you can purchase and install additional memory up to the limit set by the computer manufacturer. The computer ad in Figure 2-8 specified 1 GB RDRAM (max. 2 GB), meaning that the computer is shipped with 1 GB of RAM, but can be expanded up to 2 GB.

It might seem logical that the more you do with your computer, the more memory it needs. For example, what happens if you want to work with word processing software that requires 32 MB of RAM, and you want to work with several other programs and large graphics at the same time? Will your computer eventually run out of memory? The answer is "probably not." Today's personal computer operating systems are quite adept at allocating RAM space to multiple programs. If a program exceeds the allocated space, the operating system uses an area of the hard disk, called **virtual memory**, to store parts of a program or data file until they are needed. By selectively exchanging the data in RAM with the data in virtual memory, your computer effectively gains almost unlimited memory capacity. Too much dependence on virtual memory can have a negative affect on your computer's performance, however, because getting data from a mechanical device, such as a hard disk, is much slower than getting data from an electronic device, such as RAM. Loading up your computer with as much RAM as possible will help your computer speed through all of its tasks.

Do all computers use the same type of RAM? No. RAM components vary in speed, technology, and configuration. Many computer ads provide information on all three aspects of RAM, but consumers have to wade through a thicket of acronyms and technical jargon to understand what it all means. To unlock the meaning of technical specifications, such as "1 GB 10 ns RDRAM," you need an understanding of a few more acronyms and abbreviations.

RAM speed is often expressed in nanoseconds. One **nanosecond** (ns) is 1 billionth of a second. In the context of RAM speed, lower numbers are better because it means that the RAM circuitry can react faster to update the data that it holds. For example, 8 ns RAM is faster than 10 ns RAM.

RAM speed can also be expressed in MHz (millions of cycles per second). Just the opposite of nanoseconds, higher MHz ratings mean faster speeds. For example, 100 MHz RAM is faster than 80 MHz RAM. If you're trying to compare computers with RAM speeds expressed on different scales, 83 MHz = 12 ns, 100 MHz = 10 ns, and 115 MHz = 8 ns.

FIGURE 2-11

SDRAM is the most popular type of RAM in today's computers.

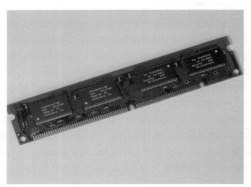

Most of today's personal computers use SDRAM (Figure 2-11) or RDRAM. **SDRAM** (synchronous dynamic RAM) is fast and relatively inexpensive. **RDRAM** (Rambus dynamic RAM) was first developed for the popular Nintendo 64® game system, and was adapted for use in personal computers in 1999. Although more expensive than SDRAM, RDRAM is usually paired with microprocessors that run at speeds faster than 1 GHz because it can somewhat increase overall system performance.

RAM is usually configured as a series of DIPs soldered onto a small circuit board called a DIMM (dual in-line memory module), **RIMM** (Rambus in-line memory module), or **SO-RIMM** (small outline Rambus in-line memory module). DIMMs contain SDRAM, whereas RIMMs and SO-RIMMs contain RDRAM.

READ-ONLY MEMORY

How is ROM different from RAM? **ROM** (read-only memory) is a type of memory circuitry that holds the computer's startup routine. ROM is housed in a single integrated circuit—usually a fairly large, caterpillar-like DIP package—which is plugged into the motherboard.

Whereas RAM is temporary and volatile, ROM is permanent and non-volatile. ROM circuitry holds "hard-wired" instructions that are a permanent part of the circuitry and remain in place even when the computer power is turned off. This is a familiar concept to anyone who has used a hand calculator that includes various "hard-wired" routines for calculating square roots, cosines, and other functions. The instructions in ROM are permanent, and the only way to change them is to replace the ROM chip.

If a computer has RAM, why does it need ROM too? When you turn on your computer, the microprocessor receives electrical power and is ready to begin executing instructions. But, as a result of the power being off, RAM is empty and it doesn't contain any instructions for the microprocessor to execute. Now ROM plays its part. ROM contains a small set of instructions called the **ROM BIOS** (basic input/output system). These instructions tell the computer how to access the hard disk, find the operating system, and load it into RAM. Once the operating system is loaded, the computer can understand your input, display output, run software, and access your data.

CMOS MEMORY

Where does a computer store its basic hardware settings? In order to operate correctly, a computer must have some basic information about storage, memory, and display configurations. For example, your computer needs to know how much memory is available so that it can allocate space for all of the programs that you want to run. RAM goes blank when the computer power is turned off, so configuration information cannot be stored there. ROM would not be a good place for this information either because it holds data on a permanent basis. If, for example, your computer stored the memory size in ROM, you could never add more memory—well, you might be able to add it, but you couldn't change the size specification in ROM. To store some basic system information, your computer needs a type of memory that's more permanent than RAM, but less permanent than ROM. CMOS is just the ticket.

CMOS memory (complementary metal oxide semiconductor memory), pronounced "SEE moss," is a type of chip that requires very little power to hold data. It can be powered by a small battery that's integrated into the motherboard and automatically recharges while your computer power is on. The battery trickles power to the CMOS chip so that it can retain vital data about your computer system configuration even when your computer is turned off.

When you change the configuration of your computer system—by adding RAM, for example—the data in CMOS must be updated. Some operating systems recognize such changes and automatically perform the update. You can manually change CMOS settings by running the CMOS setup program, as described in Figure 2-12.

FIGURE 2-12

CMOS holds computer configuration settings, such as the date and time, hard disk capacity, number of floppy disk drives, and RAM capacity. To access the CMOS setup program, hold down the F1 key as your computer boots. But be careful! If you make a mistake with these settings, your computer might not be able to start.

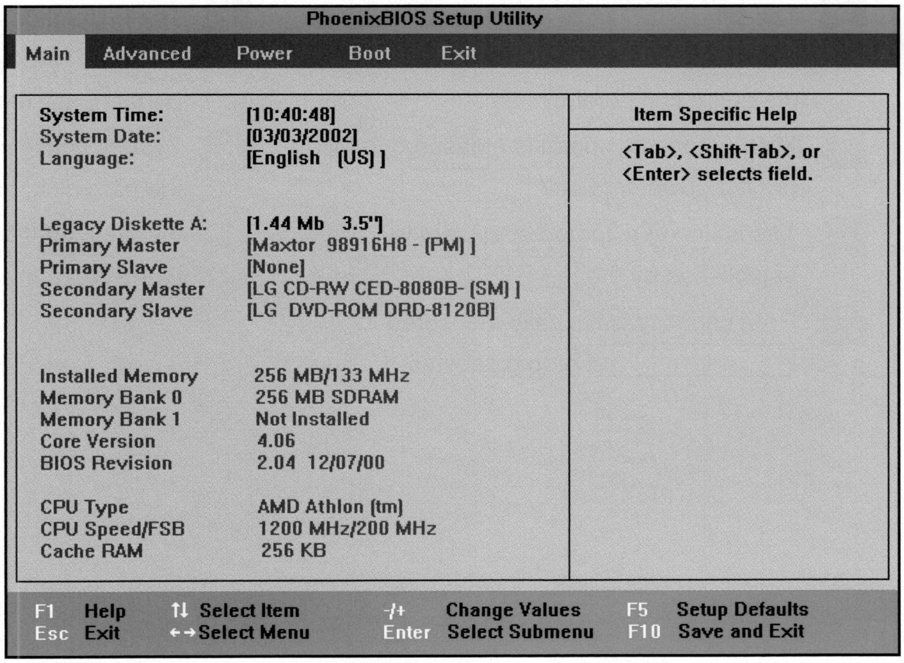

```
                    PhoenixBIOS Setup Utility

  Main    Advanced    Power    Boot    Exit

  System Time:          [10:40:48]              Item Specific Help
  System Date:          [03/03/2002]
  Language:             [English  [US] ]       <Tab>, <Shift-Tab>, or
                                               <Enter> selects field.

  Legacy Diskette A:    [1.44 Mb  3.5"]
  Primary Master        [Maxtor  98916H8 - [PM] ]
  Primary Slave         [None]
  Secondary Master      [LG CD-RW CED-8080B- [SM] ]
  Secondary Slave       [LG  DVD-ROM DRD-8120B]

  Installed Memory      256 MB/133 MHz
  Memory Bank 0         256 MB SDRAM
  Memory Bank 1         Not Installed
  Core Version          4.06
  BIOS Revision         2.04  12/07/00

  CPU Type              AMD Athlon [tm]
  CPU Speed/FSB         1200 MHz/200 MHz
  Cache RAM             256 KB

  F1   Help      ↑↓ Select Item     -/+    Change Values   F5    Setup Defaults
  Esc  Exit      ←→ Select Menu     Enter  Select Submenu  F10   Save and Exit
```

If you mistakenly enter the Setup program, follow the on-screen instructions to exit and proceed with the boot process. In Figure 2-12, the Esc (Escape) key allows you to exit the Setup program without making any changes to the CMOS settings.

What's the most important information about memory provided by computer ads?
Even though ROM and CMOS have important roles in the operation of a computer, it is really RAM capacity that makes a difference you can notice. The more data and programs that can fit into RAM, the less time your computer will spend moving data to and from virtual memory. With lots of RAM, you'll find that documents scroll faster, games respond more quickly, and many graphics operations take less time than with a computer that has a skimpy RAM capacity.

Most ads specify RAM capacity, speed, and type. Now when you see the specification "1 GB 8 ns RDRAM (max. 2 GB)" in a computer ad, you'll know that the computer's RAM capacity is 1 gigabyte (plenty to run most of today's software), that it operates at 8 nanoseconds (fairly fast), and that it uses RDRAM (a little faster and more expensive than SDRAM). You'll also have important information about the maximum amount of RAM that can be installed in the computer—2 GB, which is more than enough for the typical computer owner who does a bit of word processing, surfs the Web, and plays computer games.

QUICK Check Section B

1 The _____ in the microprocessor performs arithmetic and logical operations.

2 The _____ in the CPU directs and coordinates the operation of the entire computer system.

3 Microprocessor speed is measured in MHz or GHz. True or false? _____

4 The timing in a computer system is established by the _____ .

5 RAM capacity is typically measured in _____ or in gigabytes.

6 In RAM, microscopic electronic parts called _____ hold the electrical signals that represent data.

7 The instructions that your computer performs when it is first turned on are permanently stored in _____ .

8 System configuration information about the hard disk, date, and RAM capacity is stored in battery-powered _____ memory.

check answers ✳

COMPUTER HARDWARE   **75**

LAB 2-B
BENCHMARKING

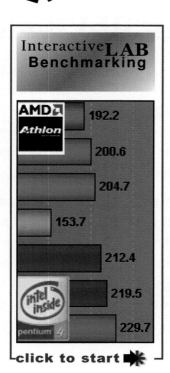

‐click to start ➡

In this lab, you'll learn:

■ Which computer performance factors can be measured by benchmark tests

■ How to run a test that identifies a computer's processor type, RAM capacity, and graphics card type

■ How to run benchmarking software that analyzes a computer's processor speed and graphics processing speed

■ How to interpret the results of a benchmark test

■ How to compare the results from benchmark tests that were performed on different system configurations

■ When benchmark tests might not provide accurate information on computer performance

2

Processor Benchmarks		
Processor	**Quake 3 Arena**	**Sysmark2000**
Athlon 1.466 MHz	204.7	267
Pentium 4 1.5 GHz	219.5	210

LAB Assignments

1. Start the interactive part of the lab. Insert your Tracking Disk if you want to save your QuickCheck results. Perform each of the lab steps as directed, and answer all of the lab QuickCheck questions. When you exit the lab, your answers are automatically graded and your results are displayed.

2. If Microsoft Word is available, use the System Info button to analyze the computer that you typically use. Provide the results of the analysis along with a brief description of the computer that you tested and its location (at home, at work, in a computer lab, etc.).

3. From the Processor Benchmarks table above, which processor appears to be faster at graphics processing? Which processor appears to be better at overall processing tasks?

4. Explain why you might perform a benchmark test on your own computer, but get different results from those that you read about in a computer magazine, which tested the same computer with the same benchmark test.

5. Use a search engine on the Web to find benchmark ratings for Intel's Pentium 4 processors. What do these ratings show about the relative performance for 1.36 GHz, 1.5 GHz, and 1.7 GHz Pentium 4s?

Section

STORAGE DEVICES

Computer manufacturers typically try to entice consumers by configuring computers with a variety of storage devices, such as a floppy disk drive, hard disk drive, and some sort of CD or DVD drive. What's the point of having so many storage devices? As it turns out, none of today's storage technologies is perfect. While one technology might provide really fast access to data, it might also be susceptible to problems that could potentially wipe out all of your data. A different technology might be more dependable, but it might have the disadvantage of providing relatively slow access to data.

Smart shoppers make sure that their new computers are equipped with a variety of storage devices. Informed computer owners understand the strengths and weaknesses of each storage technology so that they can use these devices with maximum effectiveness. In this section of the chapter, you'll learn many of the secrets that will make you a smart storage technology buyer and owner. The storage technologies that you'll learn about are now used in a variety of devices—from digital cameras to player pianos—so an understanding of storage technology can be useful outside the boundaries of personal computing.

STORAGE BASICS

What are the basic components of a data storage system? A data storage system has two main components: a storage medium and a storage device. A **storage medium** (storage media is the plural) is the disk, tape, CD, DVD, paper, or other substance that contains data. A **storage device** is the mechanical apparatus that records and retrieves data from a storage medium. Storage devices include floppy disk drives, Zip drives, hard disk drives, tape drives, CD drives, and DVD drives. The term "storage technology" refers to a storage device and the media it uses.

How does a storage system interact with other computer components? You can think of your computer's storage devices as having a direct pipeline to RAM. Data gets copied from a storage device into RAM, where it waits to be processed. After data is processed, it is held temporarily in RAM, but it is usually copied to a storage medium for more permanent safekeeping.

The process of storing data is often referred to as "writing data" or "saving a file" because the storage device writes the data on the storage medium to save it for later use. The process of retrieving data is often referred to as "reading data," "loading data," or "opening a file." The terms "writing" and "reading" make sense if you imagine that you are the computer. As the computer, you write a note and save it for later. You retrieve the note and read it when you need the information it contains. The terms "reading data" and "writing data" are often associated with mainframe applications. The terms "saving" and "opening" are standard personal computer terminology.

As you know, a computer works with data that has been coded into bits that can be represented by 1s and 0s. When data is stored, these 1s and 0s must be converted into some kind of signal or mark that's fairly permanent, but can be changed when necessary.

Obviously, the data is not literally written as "1" or "0". Instead, the 1s and 0s must be transformed into changes in the surface of a storage medium. Exactly how this transformation happens depends on the storage technology. For example, floppy disks store data in a different way than CD-ROMs. Two types of storage technologies are commonly used for personal computers: magnetic and optical.

What's the difference between magnetic and optical storage technologies?
Hard disk, floppy disk, and tape storage technologies can be classified as **magnetic storage**, which stores data by magnetizing microscopic particles on the disk or tape surface. The particles retain their magnetic orientation until that orientation is changed, thereby making disks and tapes fairly permanent but modifiable storage media. A **read-write head** mechanism in the disk drive reads and writes the magnetized particles that represent data. Figure 2-13 shows how a computer stores data on magnetic media.

2

FIGURE 2-13

Before data is stored, the particles on the surface of the disk are scattered in random patterns. The disk drive's read-write head magnetizes the particles, and orients them in either a positive (north) or negative (south) direction. These patterns of magnetized particles represent 0 and 1 bits.

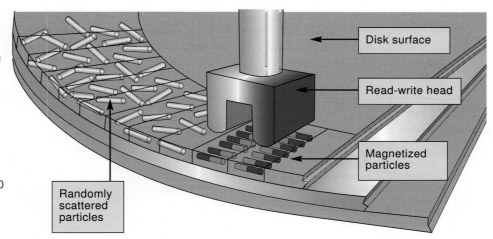

Disk surface

Read-write head

Magnetized particles

Randomly scattered particles

Data stored magnetically can be easily changed or deleted simply by changing the magnetic orientation of the appropriate particles on the disk surface. This feature of magnetic storage provides lots of flexibility for editing data and reusing areas of a storage medium that contains unneeded data.

Data stored on magnetic media such as floppy disks can be altered by magnetic fields, dust, mold, smoke particles, heat, and mechanical problems with a storage device. Placing a magnet on a floppy disk, for example, is a sure way of losing data.

Magnetic media gradually lose their magnetic charge, resulting in lost data. Some experts estimate that the reliable life span of data stored on magnetic media is about three years. They recommend that you refresh your data every two years by recopying it.

FIGURE 2-14

As seen through an electron microscope, the pits on an optical storage disk look like small craters. Each pit is less than 1 micron (one millionth of a meter) in diameter—1,500 pits lined up side by side are about as wide as the head of a pin.

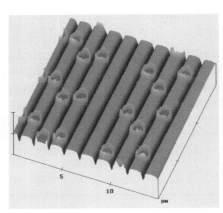

CD and DVD storage technologies can be classified as **optical storage**, which stores data as microscopic light and dark spots on the disk surface. The dark spots, which are shown in Figure 2-14, are called **pits**. The lighter, non-pitted surface areas of the disk are called **lands**.

Optical storage gets its name because data is read using a laser light, and it is possible to see the data using a high-powered microscope. The transition between pits and lands is interpreted as the 1s and 0s that represent data. An optical storage device uses a low-power laser light to read the data stored on an optical disk. Data recorded on optical media is generally considered to be less susceptible to environmental damage than data recorded on magnetic media.

Can I add storage devices to my computer? Usually you can. The system unit case for a desktop computer contains several storage device "parking spaces" called **drive bays**. If you have an empty bay of the right type and size, you can add a storage device. Bays come in two widths—5¼" and 3½". CD and DVD drives require 5¼" bays; a floppy disk drive fits in a 3½" bay. Some drive bays provide access from the outside of the system unit—a necessity for a storage device with removable media, such as floppy disks, CDs, tapes, and DVDs. Internal drive bays are located deep inside the system unit and are designed for hard disk drives, which don't use removable storage media (Figure 2-15).

FIGURE 2-15

Most desktop computers have several drive bays, some accessible from outside of the case, and others—designed for hard disk drives—without any external access. Most notebook computers provide bays for one floppy disk drive, one hard disk drive, and one CD or DVD drive. If you run out of bays, you can purchase stand-alone, external drives that sit outside of the computer case and are connected to the computer by a cable.

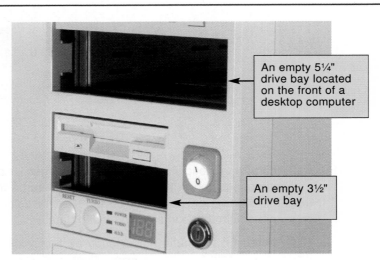

An empty 5¼" drive bay located on the front of a desktop computer

An empty 3½" drive bay

click to start ✳

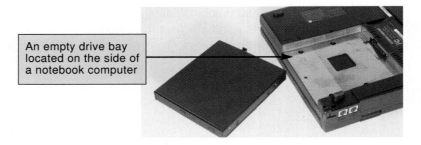

An empty drive bay located on the side of a notebook computer

Which storage technology is best? Each storage technology has its advantages and disadvantages. If one storage system was perfect, we wouldn't need so many disk and tape drives connected to our computers! To compare storage devices, it is useful to apply four criteria: versatility, durability, speed, and capacity.

- **Versatility.** Some storage devices can access data from only one type of medium. More versatile devices can access data from several different media. A floppy disk drive, for example, can access only floppy disks, whereas a DVD drive can access computer DVDs, DVD movies, audio CDs, computer CDs, and CD-Rs.

- **Durability.** Most storage technologies are susceptible to damage from mishandling or other environmental factors, such as heat and moisture. Some technologies are less susceptible than others. Optical technologies tend to be less susceptible than magnetic technologies to damage that could cause data loss.

- **Speed.** Quick access to data is important, so fast storage devices are preferred over slower devices. **Access time** is the average time it takes a computer to locate data on the storage medium and read it. Access time for a personal computer storage device, such as a disk drive, is measured in milliseconds (thousandths of a second). One millisecond (ms) is one-thousandth of a second. Lower numbers indicate faster access times. For example, a drive with a 6 ms access time is faster than a drive with an access time of 11 ms. Access time is best for random-access devices. **Random access** (also called "direct access") is the ability of a device to "jump" directly to the requested data. Floppy disk, hard disk, CD, and DVD drives are random-access devices. A tape drive, on the other hand, must use slower **sequential access** by reading through the data from the beginning of the tape. The advantage of random access becomes clear when you consider how much faster and easier it is to locate a song on a CD (random access) than on a cassette tape (sequential access).

Data transfer rate is the amount of data that a storage device can move from the storage medium to the computer per second. Higher numbers indicate faster transfer rates. For example, a CD-ROM drive with a 600 KBps (kilobytes per second) data transfer rate is faster than one with a 300 KBps transfer rate.

- **Capacity.** In today's computing environment, higher capacity is almost always preferred. Storage capacity is the maximum amount of data that can be stored on a storage medium, and it is usually measured in kilobytes, megabytes, gigabytes, or terabytes.

FLOPPY DISK TECHNOLOGY

Why is it called a "floppy disk?" A **floppy disk** (Figure 2-16) is a round piece of flexible mylar plastic covered with a thin layer of magnetic oxide and sealed inside a protective casing. If you break open the disk casing (something you should never do unless you want to ruin the disk), you would see that the mylar disk inside is thin and literally floppy. Floppy disks are also referred to as "floppies" or "diskettes." It is not correct to call them "hard disks" even though they seem to have a "hard" or rigid plastic casing. The term "hard disk" refers to an entirely different storage technology.

FIGURE 2-16

The storage device that records and retrieves data on a floppy disk is a floppy disk drive, shown here with a 3½" floppy disk.

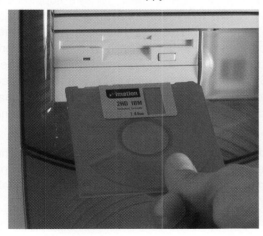

What's the capacity of a floppy disk? Floppy disks come in many sizes and capacities. The floppies most commonly used on today's personal computers are 3½" disks with a capacity of 1.44 MB, which means they can store 1,440,000 bytes of data.

Two additional storage systems use floppy disk technology. Zip disks, manufactured by Iomega, are available in 100 MB, 250 MB, and 750 MB versions. Superdisks, manufactured by Imation, have a capacity of 120 or 240 MB. Although the increased storage capacity is attractive, a standard floppy disk drive will not read them. They require special disk drives, shown in Figure 2-17.

FIGURE 2-17

A Zip disk (left) requires special disk drives, but is transportable and provides more storage capacity than a floppy disk. A Superdisk (right) provides an alternative high-capacity, transportable storage option. Superdisk drives can read standard floppy disks, but a Superdisk cannot be used in a standard floppy disk drive.

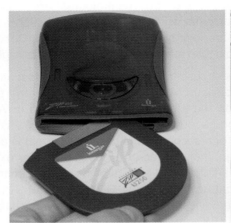

How can Zip disks and Superdisks store so much more data than a standard floppy on the same size disk? The amount of data that a disk stores depends on its density. **Disk density** refers to the closeness and size of the magnetic particles on the disk surface. The higher the disk density, the smaller the magnetic particles on the disk surface, and the more data it can store. Think of it this way: just as you can put more lemons than grapefruit in a basket, you can store more data on a disk coated with smaller particles than one with larger particles. Zip disks and Superdisks store data at a higher density than a standard 3½" floppy disk.

Get an update on the latest computer storage technologies and prices at the Storage Frontiers InfoWeb.

What does "HD DS" mean? When you see "HD DS" on a box of floppy disks, it means "high-density double-sided." Although the storage capacity of a standard floppy disk pales beside that of Zip disks and Superdisks, there was a time when floppies stored even less. Today's floppies are "high-density disks" (HD or HDD), which store considerably more data than older "single-density" and "double-density" floppies. At one time, floppy disks stored data only on one side. Today, however, most store data on both sides. As you might guess, a double-sided disk (sometimes abbreviated as DSD or DS) stores twice as much data as a single-sided disk. Read-write heads above and below the disk read both sides so that you don't have to turn the disk over. Today, standard floppy disks are high-density and double-sided. To purchase these disks, look for "HD DS" on the disk label or box.

What are the advantages and disadvantages of floppy disk technology? The major advantage of floppy disks is their portability. Floppies are still used in many school computer labs so that students can transport their data to different lab machines or to their personal computers.

Unfortunately, a floppy disk drive is not a particularly speedy device. It takes about half a second for the drive to spin the disk up to maximum speed, and then find a specific sector that contains data. A Zip drive is about 20 times faster, but both are real turtles compared to the speed of a hard disk drive.

FIGURE 2-18

When the write-protect window is open, the disk drive cannot add, modify, or delete data from a disk.

Write-protect window

The limited storage capacity of floppy disks makes them less attractive as a distribution medium. In the past, software was distributed on floppy disks. Today, most software vendors use CD-ROM or DVD-ROM disks instead. Local computer networks and the Internet have made it easy to share data files, so floppy disks are shipped less frequently.

Can I protect the data on a floppy disk? A floppy disk features a **write-protect window** (shown in Figure 2-18). When you open the window, the disk is "write-protected," which means that a computer cannot write data on the disk. Although it sounds like a potentially useful feature, the write-protect window doesn't do much to protect your data from accidental erasures or changes. The reason: with the write-protect window open, all you can do is look at the files on a disk. But typically when you use a disk, you want to save a new file or modify the data in an existing file. To do so, you must close the write-protect window and the disk is no longer protected. Therefore, when you use a disk and the chance of mistakenly deleting data is highest, you're not likely to have the write protection feature turned on.

HARD DISK TECHNOLOGY

Why are hard disk drives so popular? Hard disk technology is the preferred type of main storage for most computer systems for three reasons. First, it provides lots of storage capacity. Second, it provides faster access to files than provided by floppy disk drives. Third, a hard disk is economical. Incredibly, a hard disk typically stores millions of times more data than a floppy disk, but a hard disk drive might cost only three times as much as a floppy disk drive.

How does a hard disk work? A hard disk is one or more platters and their associated read-write heads. A **hard disk platter** is a flat, rigid disk made of aluminum or glass and coated with magnetic iron oxide particles. You will frequently see the terms "hard disk" and "hard disk drive" used interchangeably. You might also hear the term "fixed disk" used to refer to hard disks.

Personal computer hard disk platters are typically 3½" in diameter—the same size as the circular mylar disk in a floppy. However, the density of the surface particles and the data storage capacity of a hard disk far exceed those of a floppy disk. Also, the access time for a hard disk is significantly faster than that for a floppy disk. Hard disk storage capacities of 80 GB and access times of 6 to 11 ms are not uncommon. Hard disk drive speed is sometimes measured in revolutions per minute (rpm). The faster that a drive spins, the more rapidly it can position the read-write head over specific data. For example, a 7,200 rpm drive is able to access data faster than a 5,400 rpm drive.

Computer ads typically specify the capacity and access time of a hard disk drive. So "80 GB 8 ms HD" means a hard disk drive with 80 gigabyte capacity, and an access time of 8 milliseconds.

You might guess that a hard disk drive would fill one platter before storing data on a second platter. However, it is more efficient to store data at the same locations on all platters before moving the read-write heads to the next location. A vertical stack of storage locations is called a "cylinder"—the basic storage bin for a hard disk drive. Figure 2-19 provides more information on how a hard disk drive works.

FIGURE 2-19

Hard disk platters are sealed inside the drive case or cartridge to prevent dust and other contaminants from interfering with the read-write heads.

The drive spindle supports one or more hard disk platters. Both sides of the platter are used for data storage. More platters mean more data storage capacity. Hard disk platters rotate as a unit on the spindle to position read-write heads over specific data. The platters spin continuously, making thousands of rotations per minute.

click to start ➡️

Each data storage surface has its own read-write head, which moves in and out from the center of the disk to locate data. The head hovers only a few microinches above the disk surface, so the magnetic field is much more compact than on a floppy disk. As a result, more data is packed into a smaller area on a hard disk platter.

What's all this business about Ultra ATA, EIDE, SCSI, and DMA? Computer ads use these acronyms to describe hard disk drive technology. A hard drive mechanism includes a circuit board called a **controller** that positions the disk and read-write heads to locate data. Disk drives are classified according to the type of controller. Popular drive controllers include Ultra ATA, EIDE, and SCSI. **Ultra ATA** (AT attachment) and **EIDE** (enhanced integrated drive electronics) use essentially the same basic drive technology. Both feature high storage capacity and fast data transfer. Ultra ATA drives, which are commonly found in today's PCs, are twice as fast as their EIDE counterparts. **SCSI** (small computer system interface) drives provide a slight performance advantage over EIDE drives, and are typically found in high-performance workstations and servers.

The storage technology used on many PCs transfers data from a disk, through the controller, to the processor, and finally to RAM before it is actually processed. **DMA** (direct memory access) technology allows a computer to transfer data directly from a drive into RAM, without intervention from the processor. This architecture relieves the processor of data-transfer duties and frees up processing cycles for other tasks. **UDMA** (ultra DMA) is a faster version of DMA technology. DMA and Ultra ATA are companion technologies. A common storage configuration for PCs pairs an Ultra ATA drive that implements UDMA data transfer.

What's the downside of hard disk storage? Hard disks are not as durable as many other storage technologies. The read-write heads in a hard disk hover a microscopic distance above the disk surface. If a read-write head runs into a dust particle or some other contaminant on the disk, it might cause what is called a **head crash**. A head crash damages some of the data on the disk. To help eliminate contaminants from contacting the platters and causing head crashes, a hard disk is sealed in its case. A head crash can also be triggered by jarring the hard disk while it is in use. Although hard disks have become considerably more rugged in recent years, you should still handle and transport them with care.

Can I use a second hard disk drive as a backup? Yes. Because of the ever-present possibility of a head crash, it is a good idea to make a backup copy of the data stored on your hard disk. One strategy is to use a second hard disk, which can be installed internally or connected externally. A more typical strategy is to use a removable hard disk, tape drive, or CD-writer. Other supplementary storage devices, such as RAID, are used in situations where data is critical.

Removable hard disks or hard disk cartridges contain platters and read-write heads that can be inserted and removed from the drive much like a floppy disk. Removable hard disks increase the potential storage capacity of your computer system, although the data is available on only one disk at a time. Removable hard disks also provide security for data by allowing you to remove the hard disk cartridge and store it separately from the computer.

A **RAID** (redundant array of independent disks) storage device contains many disk platters, provides redundancy, and achieves faster data access than conventional hard disks. The redundancy feature of RAID technology protects data from media failures by recording the same data on more than one disk platter. RAID is a popular option for mainframe and server storage, but is less popular for personal computers.

TAPE STORAGE

What's the purpose of a tape drive? New computers are rarely outfitted with a tape drive, which is a bit puzzling considering the fact that many experts consider it the best device for backing up data.

As you have learned in this chapter, hard disk data can be easily destroyed as a result of a head crash. Protecting the data on the hard disk is of particular concern because it contains so much data—data that would be difficult and time-consuming to reconstruct. A **tape backup** is a copy of the data on a hard disk, which is stored on magnetic tape and used to restore lost data. A tape backup is relatively inexpensive and can rescue you from the overwhelming task of trying to reconstruct lost data. If you have a tape backup of your hard disk, you can copy the data from the tape to any functional hard disk.

Despite its value as a backup device, a tape drive is not suitable for everyday storage tasks. To find out why, you need to understand how a tape drive works.

How does a tape drive work? A tape is a sequential, rather than a random-access, storage medium. Essentially, data is arranged as a long sequence of bits that begins at one end of the tape and stretches to the other end. The beginning and end of each file are marked with special "header labels." To locate a file, the tape drive must start at one end of the tape and read through all of the data until it finds the right header label. A tape may contain hundreds or—in the case of a mainframe—thousands of feet of tape. Access time is measured in slow seconds, not in milliseconds as for a hard disk drive.

Tape is simply too slow to be practical as your computer's main storage device. Its pokey nature doesn't, however, diminish its effectiveness as a backup device. When you make a backup, you're simply copying lots of data onto the tape. You don't need to locate specific data, or jump back and forth between different files. For a backup device, access time is less important than the time it takes to copy data from your hard disk to tape. Manufacturers do not always supply such performance specifications, but most users can expect a tape drive to back up 1 GB in 15-20 minutes. Chapter 4 provides more details on the process and equipment for making backups.

Is it easy to install a tape drive? Yes, and you should consider adding one to your computer system if it doesn't already include one. Tape drives are available in either internal or external models. An internal tape drive fits into a standard drive bay. An external model is a standalone device that you can tether to your computer with a cable. This model is preferred by notebook owners because it can be left at home and connected only when it is time to make a backup. Figure 2-20 shows several different kinds of tape used with personal computer tape drivers.

FIGURE 2-20

A tape cartridge is a removable magnetic tape module similar to a cassette tape. The most popular types of tape drives for personal computers use tape cartridges, but there are several tape specifications and cartridge sizes, including (from top to bottom) ADR (advanced digital recording), Ditto, Travan, and DDS (digital data storage). Check the tape drive manual to make sure that you purchase the correct type of tape for your tape drive.

CD TECHNOLOGY

Why would I want a CD-ROM drive in addition to a hard disk drive? Today, most computers come equipped with some type of optical drive—often a CD-ROM drive (sometimes called a "CD player"). CD-ROM (compact disc read-only memory, pronounced "cee dee rom") is based on the same technology as the audio CDs that contain your favorite music. A computer CD-ROM disk, like its audio counterpart, contains data that was stamped on the disk surface when it was manufactured.

Before CD-ROM drives became popular, and before software programs required megabytes of storage space, software manufacturers distributed software on floppy disks. Today, when you purchase software from a computer store, the box typically contains CDs. Therefore, unless you plan to download all of your new software from the Internet, your computer should have a CD drive so that you can install new software.

Furthermore, some software—particularly reference CDs and games—requires you to place the CD in the drive and leave it there while you use it. Without a CD drive, you would not be able to use this type of software.

What's the capacity and speed of a CD? CD-ROM technology provides storage capacity that far exceeds that of a floppy or Zip disk. A single CD-ROM disk holds up to 680 MB—equivalent to more than 300,000 pages of text. The surface of the disk is coated with a clear plastic, making the disk quite durable. Unlike magnetic media, a CD-ROM is not susceptible to humidity, fingerprints, dust, or magnets. If you spill coffee on a CD-ROM disk, you can just rinse it off and it will be as good as new. The useful life of a CD-ROM disk is estimated to exceed 500 years. Wow!

Although a CD-ROM disk provides pretty good storage capacity, you can't store any of your own data on one. The "RO" in ROM means "read only." Your computer can read data from a CD-ROM, but cannot record or store data on it.

The original CD-ROM drives were able to access 150 KB of data per second. The next generation of drives doubled the data transfer rate and were consequently dubbed "2X" drives. Transfer rates seem to be continually increasing. A 24X CD-ROM drive, for example, would transfer data at a rate of 24 X 150 KB, or 3,600 KB per second. Refer to the CD & DVD InfoWeb for the latest specifications.

What's the difference between CD-ROM and ROM BIOS? Even though both contain the word "ROM," they refer to quite different technologies. As you should recall from earlier in the chapter, ROM BIOS refers to a chip on the motherboard that contains permanent instructions for the computer's boot sequence. A CD-ROM drive is an optical storage device that's usually installed in one of the system unit's drive bays. (See Figure 2-21.) To avoid confusion, a CD-ROM probably should have been called a "CD-ROS" for "read-only storage."

www.InfoWebLinks.com

For additional information about current CD and DVD technology, plus tips on how to handle and clean your CDs, connect to the **CD & DVD** InfoWeb.

◄click ➧

2

FIGURE 2-21

A CD-ROM drive is similar to a floppy disk drive, but uses a laser to read data, instead of a magnetized read-write head.

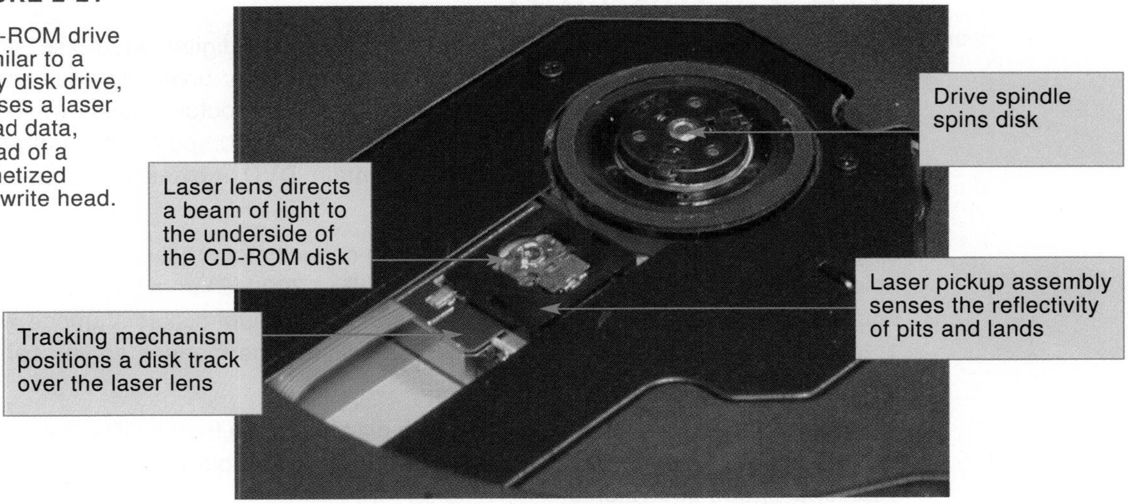

Drive spindle spins disk

Laser lens directs a beam of light to the underside of the CD-ROM disk

Laser pickup assembly senses the reflectivity of pits and lands

Tracking mechanism positions a disk track over the laser lens

Can I create my own CDs? Two CD-writer technologies called CD-R and CD-RW allow you to create your own CDs. A **CD-R** (compact disc recordable) drive records data on a special CD-R disk. The drive mechanism includes a laser that changes the reflectivity of a dye layer on a blank CD-R disk. As a result, the data on the disk is not actually stored in pits. Dark spots in the dye layer, however, play the same role as pits to represent data and allow the disks that you create to be read by not only a CD-R drive, but also by a standard CD-ROM drive or a DVD drive.

As with regular CD-ROM disks, the data on a CD-R cannot be erased or modified once you record it. However, most CD-R drives allow you to record your data in multiple sessions. For example, you can store two files on a CD-R disk today, then add the data for a few more files to the disk tomorrow.

CD-RW (compact disc rewritable) technology allows you to write data on a CD, then change that data at a later time. The process requires special CD-RW disks and a CD-RW drive, which uses **phase change technology** to alter the crystal structure on the disk surface. Altering the crystal structure creates patterns of light and dark spots similar to the pits and lands on a CD-ROM disk. The crystal structure can be changed from light to dark and back again many times, making it possible to record and modify data much like on a hard disk.

Is CD-RW a viable replacement for a hard disk? Unfortunately, the process of accessing, saving, and modifying data on a CD-RW disk is relatively slow compared to the speed of hard disk access. Therefore, CD-RW is a fine addition to a computer system, but is not a good replacement for a hard disk drive. Both CD-R and CD-RW technologies are quite useful for creating music CDs, storing graphics files, making backups, archiving data, and distributing large files. **Archiving** refers to the process of moving data off a primary storage device when that data is not accessed frequently. For example, a business might archive its accounting data for previous years, or a hospital might archive billing records once the accounts are paid. Archived data does not generally change, so even a CD-R is suitable. If you have some large files, such as photos or videos that you want to send to friends, clients, or colleagues, you can create a CD using either a CD-R or CD-RW drive. You might have a little better luck with a CD-R drive, however, because some optical devices tend to have trouble reading the data that's been stored on a CD-RW disk.

DVD TECHNOLOGY

How is DVD different from CD technology? **DVD** ("digital video disc" or "digital versatile disk") is a variation of CD technology that was originally designed as an alternative to VCRs, but was quickly adopted by the computer industry to store data. A computer's DVD drive can read disks that contain computer data (often called **DVD-ROM** disks), as well as disks that contain DVD movies (sometimes called **DVD-Video** disks).

Originally designed to provide enough storage capacity for a full-length movie, a DVD holds much more data than a CD—about 4.7 GB (4,700 MB) on a DVD compared with 680 MB on a CD-ROM. Like a CD-ROM disk, a DVD-ROM disk is stamped with data at the time of manufacture. The data on these disks is permanent, so you cannot add or change data.

The speed of a DVD drive is measured on a different scale than a CD drive. A 1X DVD drive is about the same speed as a 9X CD drive. The table in Figure 2-22 provides additional speed equivalents.

FIGURE 2-22	DVD and CD Drive Speed Comparison	
DVD Drive Speed	**Data Transfer Rate**	**CD Speed**
1X	11.08 Mbps	9X
2X	22.16 Mbps	18X
4X	44.32 Mbps	36X
5X	55.40 Mbps	46X

Is my computer DVD drive the same as the one that's connected to my television set? Not exactly. Even with the large storage capacity of a DVD, movie files are much too large to fit on a disk unless they are compressed, or shrunk, using a special type of data coding called MPEG-2. The DVD player that you connect to your television includes MPEG decoding circuitry, which is not included on your computer's DVD drive. When you play DVD movies on your computer, it uses the CPU as an MPEG decoder. The necessary decoder software is included with Windows, or can be located on the DVD itself.

Are CDs and DVDs interchangeable? If you have to choose between a CD-ROM drive and a DVD drive, go with DVD. You cannot play DVDs on your CD-ROM drive, but you can play CD-ROM, most CD-R, and most CD-RW disks on your DVD drive.

Is there a DVD equivalent to CD-RW? DVD manufacturers have introduced several competing technologies that make it possible to write data on DVD disks. All of these technologies can read DVD-ROM and DVD-Video discs, but each uses a different type of disk for recording. DVD-R can record data once, uses a disk medium that's very similar to CD-R technology, and can be read by most DVD drives and players. Read/write formats include **DVD-RAM**, **DVD-RW**, and **DVD+RW**, which can be rewritten hundreds of times. Disks written with these devices can always be read by the same type of device that created them. Reading them with other devices might sometimes be a problem, however. Most experts predict that eventually today's multiple CD and DVD devices will be replaced by a single DVD device that reads CDs and DVD-ROMs, plays DVD movies, and writes DVDs that can be read by any other DVD device.

QUICK Check **C**
Section

1 Data on an optical storage medium is stored as _____ and lands.

2 _____ time is the average time that it takes a computer to locate data on a storage medium and read it.

3 A computer can move directly to any file on a(n) _____ access device, but must start at the beginning and read through all of the data on a(n) _____ access device.

4 Higher disk _____ provides increased storage capacity.

5 "HD DS" means "hard disk double-sided." True or false? _____

6 EIDE, Ultra ATA, and SCSI refer to the type of _____ used by a hard disk drive.

7 CD-R technology allows you to write data on a disk, then change that data. True or false? _____

8 A(n) _____ drive stores 4.7 GB on a disk, but does not allow you to change the data once it has been stored.

check answers ➤✴

Section

INPUT AND OUTPUT DEVICES

Some computer manufacturers and retailers bundle a monitor, printer, and other peripheral devices with new computers. Are these bundles a good value? Typically, the cost of the bundle is less than purchasing everything separately, but the real value of the bundle depends on your computing needs.

Even after you purchase a computer, you can be fairly certain that you will want to add more equipment to expand or update its capabilities. How can you tell which peripheral devices are compatible with your computer? How do you install them and get them to work?

In this part of the chapter, you'll get a general overview of the computer's expansion bus—the components in a computer that carry data to peripheral devices. With that knowledge in hand, you'll be able to select, install, and use all kinds of peripherals. The section ends with a look at two of the most popular categories of peripherals: display devices and printers. You'll learn about other peripherals as they fit into the topics discussed in later chapters.

EXPANSION SLOTS, CARDS, AND PORTS

How does a computer get data from RAM to a peripheral device? Within a computer, data travels from one component to another over circuits called a **data bus**. One part of the data bus runs between RAM and the microprocessor. Another part of the data bus runs between RAM and various storage devices. The segment of the data bus that extends between RAM and peripheral devices is called the **expansion bus**. As data moves along the expansion bus, it may travel through expansion slots, cards, ports, and cables.

FIGURE 2-23

An expansion card simply slides into an expansion slot, then it can be secured with a small screw.

click to start ▪✦

What's an expansion slot? An **expansion slot** is a long, narrow socket on the motherboard into which you can plug an expansion card. An **expansion card** is a small circuit board that provides a computer with the ability to control a storage device, an input device, or an output device. Expansion cards are also called "expansion boards," "controller cards," or "adapters." Figure 2-23 shows how to plug an expansion card into an expansion slot.

Most desktop computers have four to eight expansion slots, but some of the slots usually contain expansion cards. A graphics card (sometimes called a "video card") provides a path for data traveling to the monitor. A modem provides a way to transmit data over phone lines or cable television lines. A sound card carries data out to speakers and headphones, or back from a microphone. A network card allows you to connect your computer to a local area network. You might add other expansion cards if you want to connect a scanner or download videos from a camera or VCR.

What are the major types of expansion slots? A desktop computer may have up to three types of expansion slots:

- **ISA** (industry standard architecture) slots are an old technology, used today only for some modems and other relatively slow devices. Many new computers have few or no ISA slots.

- **PCI** (peripheral component interconnect) slots offer fast transfer speeds and a 32-bit or 64-bit data bus. These slots typically house a graphics card, sound card, video capture card, modem, or network interface card.

- **AGP** (accelerated graphics port) slots provide a high-speed data pathway that is primarily used for graphics cards.

Expansion cards are built for only one type of slot. If you plan to add or upgrade a card in your computer, you must make sure that the right type of slot is available on the motherboard. For example, suppose that you want to replace your computer's modem with a faster one. Before making your purchase, take a look inside of your computer's system unit to see which type of slot holds the current modem. As you shop, you can read the connection information on the modem boxes to make sure that you select a modem that fits in the same type of slot as your old modem. Figure 2-24 shows you how to identify AGP, PCI, and ISA slots.

FIGURE 2-24

AGP, PCI, and ISA slots are different lengths, so you can easily identify them by opening your computer's system unit and looking at the motherboard.

FIGURE 2-25

Notebooks typically use PC cards for expansion.

PC card

What is an expansion port? An **expansion port** is any connector that passes data in and out of a computer or peripheral device. Ports are sometimes called "jacks" or "connectors"—the terminology is inconsistent.

An expansion port is often housed on an expansion card so that it is accessible through an opening in the back of the computer's system unit. A port might also be built into the system unit case of a desktop or notebook computer. The built-in ports that are supplied with a computer usually include a mouse port, keyboard port, serial port, and USB port. Ports that have been added with expansion cards usually protrude through rectangular cutouts in the back of the case. Figure 2-26 illustrates the major types of expansion ports on a typical desktop computer.

What are the major types of expansion cables? With so many types of ports, you can expect a corresponding variety of cables. If a cable is supplied with a peripheral device, you can usually figure out where to plug it in by matching the shape of the cable connector to the port. If you have to purchase a cable, you'll need to know the correct type and designation.

Do notebook computers also contain expansion slots? Most notebook computers are equipped with a special type of external slot called a **PCMCIA slot** (personal computer memory card international association). Typically, a notebook computer has only one of these slots, but the slot can hold more than one **PC card** (also called "PCMCIA expansion cards" or "Card Bus cards"). PCMCIA slots are classified according to their thickness. Type I slots accept only the thinnest PC cards, such as memory expansion cards. Type II slots accept most of the popular PC cards—those that contain modems, sound cards, and network cards. Type III slots—commonly included with today's notebook computers—accept the thickest PC cards, which contain devices such as hard disk drives. A Type III slot can also hold two Type I cards, two Type II cards, or a Type I and Type II card. Figure 2-25 illustrates PCMCIA slots and PC cards.

FIGURE 2-26

Expansion ports

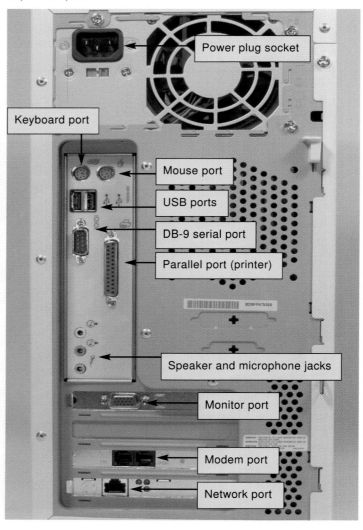

Power plug socket

Keyboard port

Mouse port

USB ports

DB-9 serial port

Parallel port (printer)

Speaker and microphone jacks

Monitor port

Modem port

Network port

Most connectors have a shape-and-pin designation such as DB-9 or C-50. The first part of the designation indicates the shape of the connector. For example, DB and C connectors are trapezoidal, whereas DIN connectors are round. The second part of the designation indicates the number of pins. A DB-9 connector has nine pins. Most types of connectors have male and female versions. The male version has pins that stick out, whereas the female version has holes. Figure 2-27 describes the cable connectors you might need to connect peripheral devices to your PC.

FIGURE 2-27	Personal Computer Cables and Connectors		
	Connector	Description	Devices
	Serial DB-9	Connects to serial port, which sends data over a single data line one bit at a time at speeds of 56 Kbps.	Mouse or modem
	Parallel DB-25M	Connects to parallel port, which sends data simultaneously over 8 data lines at speeds of 12,000 Kbps.	Printer, external CD-ROM drive, Zip drive, external hard disk drive, or tape backup device
	USB	Connects to universal serial bus (USB), which sends data over a single data line and can support up to 127 devices. USB-1 carries data at speeds up to 12,000 Kbps; USB-2 at 480,000 Kbps.	Modem, keyboard, joystick, scanner, mouse, external hard disk drive, MP3 player
	SCSI C-50F	Connects to SCSI ("scuzzy") port, which sends data simultaneously over 8 or 16 data lines at speeds between 40,000 Kbps and 640,000 Kbps; supports up to 16 devices.	Internal or external hard disk drive, scanner, CD-ROM drive, tape backup device
	IEEE 1394	Connects to the "FireWire" port, which sends data at 400,000 Kbps.	Video camera, DVD player
	VGA HDB-15	Connects to the video port.	Monitor

What's the best port to use for connecting peripheral devices? USB ports are probably the most popular ports for connecting peripheral devices. Most computers feature two USB ports, and on many computer models these ports are conveniently located on the front of the system unit, so that peripherals can be easily connected and disconnected. Many kinds of peripheral devices—including mice, scanners, and joysticks—are available with USB connections. Windows automatically recognizes most USB devices, which makes installation simple.

INSTALLING PERIPHERAL DEVICES

Is it difficult to install a new peripheral device? The basic qualifications for installing peripheral devices are an ability to use a screwdriver and read directions. If you own a desktop computer, you might have to open the system unit. Before doing so, make sure that you unplug the computer and ground yourself—that's technical jargon for releasing static electricity by using a special grounding wristband, or by touching both hands to a metal object. Simply follow the directions to install any necessary expansion cards and plug in the required cables.

Why do some peripheral devices include a disk or CD? Some devices require software, called a **device driver**, to set up communication between your computer and the device. The directions supplied with your new peripheral device will include instructions on how to install the device driver. Typically, you'll use the device driver disk or CD one time to get everything set up, then you can put the disk away in a safe place.

Long-time computer techies probably remember the days when installing a peripheral device meant messing around with little electronic components called dip switches, and a host of complex software settings called IRQs. Fortunately, today's PCs include a feature called **Plug and Play** (also known as PnP) that automatically takes care of these technical details. Although it took several years to refine Plug and Play technology, it works quite well for just about every popular peripheral device. If PnP doesn't work, your computer simply won't recognize the device and won't be able to transmit data to it or receive data from it. If you've got a stubborn peripheral device, check the manufacturer's Web site for a device driver update, or call the manufacturer's technical support department.

DISPLAY DEVICES

What are the components of a typical computer display system? The two key components of a computer display system include a graphics card and a display device, such as a monitor or LCD screen. A **graphics card** (also called a "graphics board" or a "video card") contains circuitry that generates the signals for displaying an image on the screen. It also contains special video memory, which stores screen images as they are processed, before they are displayed. Today's fastest graphics cards fit in an AGP expansion slot. PCI graphics cards typically take a bit longer to update the screen. Many graphics cards contain special graphics accelerator technology to boost performance for 3-D graphics applications, including computer games.

For up-to-the-minute information on the latest and greatest graphics cards, monitors, and LCDs, check out the **Display Devices** InfoWeb.

click ➤

What's the difference between a CRT and an LCD? CRT monitors were once the only game in town for desktop computer displays. **CRT** (cathode ray tube) technology uses gun-like mechanisms to direct beams of electrons toward the screen and activate individual dots of color that form an image. CRTs offer an inexpensive and dependable computer display. As an alternative to a CRT monitor, an **LCD** (liquid crystal display) produces an image by manipulating light within a layer of liquid crystal cells. Modern LCD technology is compact in size, lightweight, and provides an easy-to-read display. LCDs are standard equipment on notebook computers. Stand-alone LCDs, referred to as "LCD monitors" or "flat panel displays," have also become available for desktop computers, as a replacement for CRT monitors.

The advantages of an LCD monitor include display clarity, low radiation emission, portability, and compactness. Unfortunately, an LCD monitor can be triple the price of an equivalent CRT monitor, so most people consider one to be a luxury item. In addition to their high cost, LCD monitors have a limited viewing angle. The brightness and color tones that you see depend on the angle from which you view the screen because of the way that light reflects off the LCD elements. For this reason, graphic artists prefer CRT technology, which displays uniform color from any viewing angle.

Which display device produces the best image? Image quality is a factor of screen size, dot pitch, resolution, and color depth. Screen size is the measurement in inches from one corner of the screen diagonally across to the opposite corner. Typical monitor screen sizes range from 13" to 21". On most monitors, the viewable image does not stretch to the edge of the screen. Instead, a black border makes the image smaller than the size specified. Many computer ads now include a measurement of the **viewable image size** (vis). A 15" monitor has an approximately 13.9" vis. **Dot pitch** (dp) is a measure of image clarity. A smaller dot pitch means a crisper image. Technically, dot pitch is the distance in millimeters between like-colored **pixels**—the small dots of light that form an image. A dot pitch between .26 and .23 is typical for today's monitors.

Your computer's graphics card sends an image to the monitor at a specific **resolution**, defined as the maximum number of horizontal and vertical pixels that are displayed on the screen. The standard for many of the earliest PC graphics cards was called **VGA** (Video Graphics Array), which provided a resolution of 640 x 480. A succession of graphics card standards allowed higher resolutions. **SVGA** (Super VGA) provides 800 x 600 resolution, **XGA** (eXtended Graphics Array) provides 1024 x 768 resolution, **SXGA** (super XGA) provides 1280 x 1024 resolution, and **UXGA** (Ultra XGA) provides up to 1600 x 1200 resolution.

At higher resolutions, text and other objects appear smaller, but the computer can display a larger work area, such as an entire page of a document. The two screen shots in Figure 2-28 help you compare a display set at 640 x 480 resolution with a display set at 1024 x 768 resolution.

FIGURE 2-28

The upper-left screen shows a computer display set at 1024 x 768 resolution. Notice the size of text and other screen-based objects. The lower-right screen shows 640 x 480 resolution. Text and other objects appear larger than on the high-resolution screen, but you see a smaller portion of the screen-based desktop.

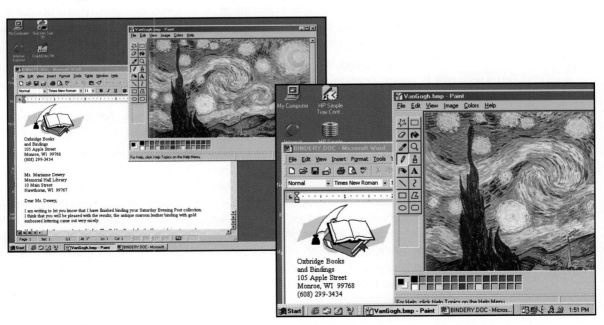

The number of colors that a monitor and graphics card can display is referred to as **color depth** or "bit depth." Most PCs have the capability to display millions of colors. When set at 24-bit color depth (sometimes called "True Color") your PC can display more than 16 million colors—and produce what are considered to be photographic-quality images. Windows allows you to select resolution and color depth. Most desktop owners choose 24-bit color at 1024 x 768 resolution.

What about notebook computer display systems? Many older notebooks had passive matrix screens, sometimes referred to as "dual-scan." A **passive matrix screen** relies on timing to make sure the liquid crystal cells are illuminated. As a result, the process of updating the screen image does not always keep up with moving images, and the display can appear blurred. Newer notebooks feature an **active matrix screen**, sometimes referred to as "TFT" (thin film transistor), which updates rapidly and is essential for a crisp display of animations and video.

Although you can set the color depth and resolution of your notebook computer display, you might not have as many options as with a desktop computer. LCD displays look their best at their "native resolution"—the resolution that is set by the computer's manufacturer. While a notebook might allow you to change to a different resolution, images and characters tend to appear grainy or blurry.

Typically, graphics card circuitry is built into the motherboard of a notebook computer, making it difficult to upgrade and gain more video memory for additional resolution and color depth. Inexpensive notebook computers, which feature VGA displays, provide a maximum resolution of 640 x 480. Mid-priced notebooks typically feature SVGA displays. More expensive notebooks feature XGA, SXGA, or UXGA displays.

PRINTERS

What features should I look for in a printer? Today's printer technologies include ink jet, solid ink, thermal transfer, dye sublimation, laser, and dot matrix. These printers differ in resolution and speed, which affect the print quality and price.

Resolution. The quality or sharpness of printed images and text depends on the printer's resolution—the density of the gridwork of dots that create an image. Printer resolution is measured by the number of dots it can print per linear inch, abbreviated as dpi. At normal reading distance, a resolution of about 900 dots per inch appears solid to the human eye, but a close examination of color sections will reveal a dot pattern. Although 900 dpi might be considered sufficient for some magazines, expensive coffee-table books are typically produced on printers with 2,400 dpi or higher.

Before you shop for a printer, take a look at the buying tips listed at the <u>Printer Buyer's Guide</u> InfoWeb.

 click

Print speed. Printer speeds are measured either by pages per minute (ppm) or characters per second (cps). Color printouts typically take longer than black-and-white printouts. Pages that contain mostly text tend to print more rapidly than pages that contain graphics. Ten pages per minute is a typical speed for a personal computer printer.

What's the most popular type of printer? Ink jet printers outsell all of the others because they print in color and they are inexpensive. An **ink jet printer** has a nozzle-like print head that sprays ink onto paper to form characters and graphics. Today's most popular printer technology, ink jet printers produce low-cost color or black-and-white printouts. The print head in a color ink jet printer consists of a series of nozzles, each with its own ink cartridge. Most ink jet printers use CMYK color, which requires only cyan (blue), magenta (pink), yellow, and black inks to create a printout that appears to have thousands of colors. Alternatively, some printers use six ink colors to print midtone shades that create slightly more realistic photographic images.

Operating costs for an ink jet printer are reasonable. You must periodically replace the black ink cartridge and a second cartridge that carries the colored inks. Each replacement ink cartridge costs between $25 and $35. Under realistic use, the cost for color printing will be between 5 and 15 cents per page. A potential hidden cost of operating an ink jet printer is special paper. Although you can satisfactorily print documents with small graphics and line art on the same type of inexpensive paper that you might use in a photocopier, photo printouts look best on special paper that can cost between $0.08 and $1.50 per sheet. Typically, this special paper has a super-smooth finish that prevents the ink from bleeding and creating dull colors.

Today's ink jet printers (Figure 2-29) have excellent resolution, which can range from 600 dpi to 2,880 dpi, depending on the model. If you want camera-store quality when printing photographic images, you need a printer with high resolution. Some ink jet printers can produce ultra-high resolution by making multiple passes over the paper. Although it might seem logical that this technique would slow down the printing process, multiple-pass ink jet printers produce a respectable five pages per minute.

FIGURE 2-29

Most ink jet printers are small, lightweight, and inexpensive, yet produce very good quality color output.

What's the difference between an ink jet printer and a solid ink printer? A **solid ink printer** melts sticks of crayon-like ink and then sprays the liquefied ink through the print head's tiny nozzles. The ink solidifies before it can be absorbed by the paper, and a pair of rollers finishes fusing the ink onto the paper. A solid ink printer produces vibrant colors on most types of paper, so unlike an ink jet printer, it does not require special, expensive paper to produce photographic-quality images.

What about thermal wax transfer and dye sublimation printers? A **thermal transfer printer** uses a page-sized ribbon that is coated with cyan, magenta, yellow, and black wax. The print head consists of thousands of tiny heating elements that melt the wax onto specially coated paper or transparency film (the kind that's used for overhead projectors). This type of printer excels at printing colorful transparencies for presentations, but the fairly expensive per-page costs and the requirement for special paper make this a niche market printer used mainly by businesses.

A **dye sublimation printer** uses technology similar to wax transfer. The difference is that the page-sized ribbon contains dye instead of colored wax. Heating elements in the print head diffuse the dye onto the surface of specially coated paper. Dye sublimation printers produce excellent color quality—perhaps the best of any printer technology. At $3 to $4 per page, however, these printers are a bit pricey for most personal computer owners.

Is a laser better than an ink jet? A **laser printer** uses the same technology as a photocopier to paint dots of light on a light-sensitive drum. Electrostatically charged ink is applied to the drum, then transferred to paper.

As with other printer technologies, print speed and resolution will be key factors in your purchase decision. Personal laser printers produce six to eight ppm (pages per minute) at a resolution of 600 dpi. Professional models pump out 15 to 25 ppm at 1,200 dpi. A personal laser printer has a duty cycle of about 3,000 pages per month—that means roughly 100 pages per day. You wouldn't want to use it to produce 5,000 campaign brochures for next Monday, but you would find it quite suitable for printing 10 copies of a five-page outline for a meeting tomorrow.

FIGURE 2-30

Laser printers are a popular technology for situations that require high-volume output or good quality printouts.

click to start ▶✹

Some people are surprised to discover that laser printers are less expensive to operate than ink jet printers. On average, you can expect to pay about 2 cents per page for black-and-white laser printing. This per-page cost includes periodically replacing the toner cartridge and drum.

Laser printers (Figure 2-30) accept print commands from a personal computer, but use their own printer language to construct a page before printing it. **Printer Control Language** (PCL) is the most widely used printer language, but some printers use the **PostScript** language, which is preferred by many publishing professionals. Printer languages require memory, and most laser printers have between 2 MB and 8 MB. A large memory capacity is required to print color images and graphics-intensive documents. A laser printer comes equipped with enough memory for typical print jobs. If you find that you need more memory, check the printer documentation for information.

Why would anyone want a dot matrix printer? When PCs first began to appear in the late 1970s, dot matrix printers were the technology of choice, and they are still available today. A **dot matrix printer** produces characters and graphics by using a grid of fine wires. As the print head noisily clatters across the paper, the wires strike the ribbon and paper in a pattern prescribed by your PC. Dot matrix printers can print text and graphics—some even print in color using a multicolored ribbon.

With a resolution of 140 dpi, a dot matrix printer produces low-quality output with clearly discernible dots forming letters and graphics. Dot matrix speed is typically measured in characters per second (cps). A fast dot matrix device can print at speeds up to 455 cps—about five pages per minute. Today, dot matrix printers, like the one in Figure 2-31, are used primarily for "back-office" applications that demand low operating cost and dependability, but not high print quality. A $4 ribbon can print more than 3 million characters before it must be replaced.

FIGURE 2-31

A dot matrix printer uses a grid of thin wires to strike a ribbon and create an image on paper. Unlike laser and ink jet technologies, a dot matrix printer actually strikes the paper and, therefore, can print multipart carbon forms.

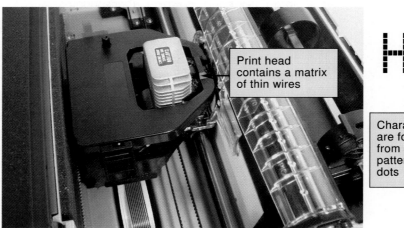

Print head contains a matrix of thin wires

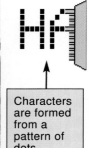

Characters are formed from a pattern of dots

COMPUTER HARDWARE   97

Is it easy to install a printer? Most printers include a cable that connects to one of your computer's ports. Most consumers typically use a parallel or USB port to connect a printer to a computer, although some printers can be connected to a serial port. When buying a printer, it is a good idea to check what kind of connection is required.

Many printers come packaged with device driver software, which must be installed on your computer. If you are connecting a USB printer, Windows should automatically initiate the installation process when you plug in the printer and turn it on. Otherwise, you can use the Printers window, shown in Figure 2-32, to install a printer and select it as the "default printer"—the one you will use regularly.

FIGURE 2-32

After you connect a new printer to your PC, you might be required to manually install the device driver. You can initiate the installation process by inserting the Setup disk supplied by the printer manufacturer, or by accessing the Printers window from the Start button.

click to start ➡✳

QUICKCheck D
Section

1 The _____ bus carries data from RAM to peripheral devices.

2 AGP, PCI, and ISA are types of expansion _____, which are part of a personal computer's motherboard.

3 Many peripheral devices come packaged with device _____ software.

4 640 x 480 and 1024 x 768 refer to the _____ of a monitor or graphics card.

5 The number of colors that a monitor can display is referred to as bit _____.

6 The best notebook computer displays use XGA passive matrix screens. True or false? _____

7 The most popular printers for personal computers are _____, which are inexpensive and produce good quality color printouts.

check answers ➡✳

TechTalk
HOW A MICROPROCESSOR EXECUTES INSTRUCTIONS

Remarkable advances in microprocessor technology have produced exponential increases in computer speed and power. In 1965, Gordon Moore, co-founder of chip-production giant Intel Corporation, predicted that the number of transistors on a chip would double every year. Much to the surprise of engineers and Moore himself, "Moore's law" accurately predicted 30 years of chip development. In 1958, the first integrated circuit contained two transistors. The Pentium III Xeon processor, introduced in 1999, had 9.5 million transistors. The Pentium 4 processor, introduced only a year later, featured 42 million transistors.

What's really fascinating, though, is how these chips perform complex tasks simply by manipulating those ubiquitous bits. How can pushing around 1s and 0s result in professional-quality documents, exciting action games, animated graphics, cool music, street maps, and e-commerce Web sites? To satisfy your curiosity about what happens deep in the heart of a microprocessor, you'll need to venture into the realm of instruction sets, fetch cycles, accumulators, and pointers.

Exactly what kind of instructions does a computer execute? A computer accomplishes a complex task by performing a series of very simple steps, referred to as instructions. An instruction tells the computer to perform a specific arithmetic, logical, or control operation.

To be executed by a computer, an instruction must be in the form of electrical signals—those now familiar 1s and 0s that represent "ons" and "offs." In this form, instructions are referred to as **machine code**. They are, of course, very difficult for people to read, so typically when discussing them, we use more understandable mnemonics, such as JMP, MI, and REG1.

An instruction has two parts: the op code and the operands. An **op code**, which is short for "operation code," is a command word for an operation such as add, compare, or jump. The **operands** for an instruction specify the data, or the address of the data, for the operation. Let's look at an example of an instruction from a hypothetical instruction set:

In the instruction JMP M1, the op code is JMP and the operand is M1. The op code JMP means jump or go to a different instruction. The operand M1 stands for the RAM address of the instruction to which the computer is supposed to go. The instruction JMP M1 has only one operand, but some instructions have more than one operand. For example, the instruction ADD REG1 REG2 has two operands: REG1 and REG2.

The list of instructions that a microprocessor is able to execute is known as its instruction set. This instruction set is built into the microprocessor when it is manufactured. Every task that a computer performs is determined by the list of instructions in its instruction set. As you look at the instruction set in Figure 2-33 on the next page, consider that the computer must use instructions such as these for all of the tasks it helps you perform—from database management to word processing.

FIGURE 2-33	A Simple Microprocessor Instruction Set	
Op Code	**Operation**	**Example**
INP	Input the given value into the specified memory address	INP 7 M1
CLA	Clear the accumulator to 0	CLA
MAM	Move the value from the accumulator to the specified memory location	MAM M1
MMR	Move the value from the specified memory location to the specified register	MMR M1 REG1
MRA	Move the value from the specified register to the accumulator	MRA REG1
MAR	Move the value from the accumulator to the specified register	MAR REG1
ADD	Add the values in two registers, place the result in the accumulator	ADD REG1 REG2
SUB	Subtract the value in the second register from the value in the first register, place the result in the accumulator	SUB REG1 REG2
MUL	Multiply values in two registers, place the result in the accumulator	MUL REG1 REG2
DIV	Divide the value in the first register by the value in the second register, place the result in the accumulator	DIV REG 1 REG2
INC	Increment (increase) the value in the register by 1	INC REG1
DEC	Decrement (decrease) the value in the register by 1	DEC REG1
CMP	Compare the values in two registers; if values are equal, put 1 in the accumulator, otherwise put 0 in the accumulator	CMP REG1 REG2
JMP	Jump to the instruction at the specified memory address	JMP P2
JPZ	Jump to the specified address if the accumulator holds 0	JPZ P3
JPN	Jump to the specified address if the accumulator does not hold 0	JPN P2
HLT	Halt program execution	HLT

What happens when a computer executes an instruction? The term **instruction cycle** refers to the process in which a computer executes a single instruction. Some parts of the instruction cycle are performed by the microprocessor's control unit; other parts of the cycle are performed by the ALU. The steps in this cycle are summarized in Figure 2-34.

FIGURE 2-34

The instruction cycle includes four activities.

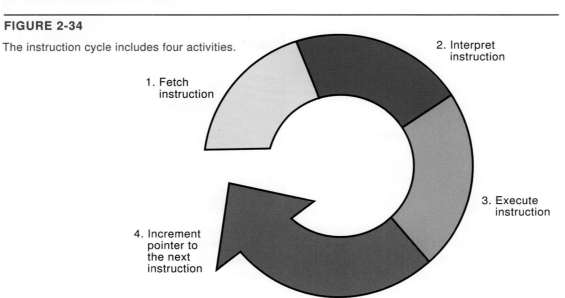

1. Fetch instruction

2. Interpret instruction

3. Execute instruction

4. Increment pointer to the next instruction

What role does the control unit play? The instructions that a computer is supposed to process for a particular program are held in RAM. When the program begins, the RAM address of the first instruction is placed in a part of the microprocessor's control unit called an instruction pointer. The control unit can then fetch the instruction by copying data from that address into its instruction register. From there, the control unit can interpret the instruction, gather the specified data, or tell the ALU to begin processing. Figure 2-35 helps you visualize the control unit's role in processing an instruction.

FIGURE 2-35

The control unit fetches instructions, interprets them, fetches data, and tells the ALU which processing operations to perform.

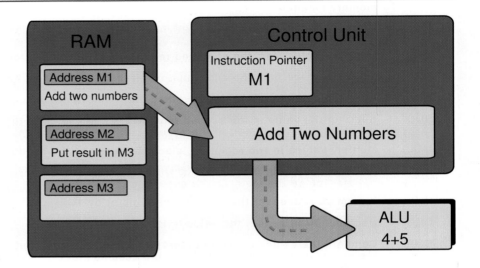

When does the ALU swing into action? The ALU is responsible for performing arithmetic and logical operations. It uses registers to hold data ready to be processed. When it gets the go-ahead signal from the control unit, the ALU processes the data and places the result in an accumulator. From the accumulator, the data can be sent to RAM, or used for further processing. Figure 2-36 helps you visualize what happens in the ALU as the computer processes data.

FIGURE 2-36

The ALU uses data from its registers to perform arithmetic and logical operations. The results are placed in another register, called the accumulator.

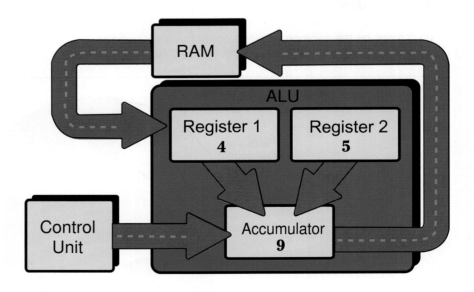

What happens after an instruction is executed? When the computer completes an instruction, the control unit "increments" the instruction pointer to the RAM address of the next instruction and the instruction cycle begins again. So how does this all fit together? Figure 2-37 on the next page explains how the ALU, control unit, and RAM work together to process instructions.

FIGURE 2-37 The ALU, control unit, and RAM each have a part to play in the processing of instructions.

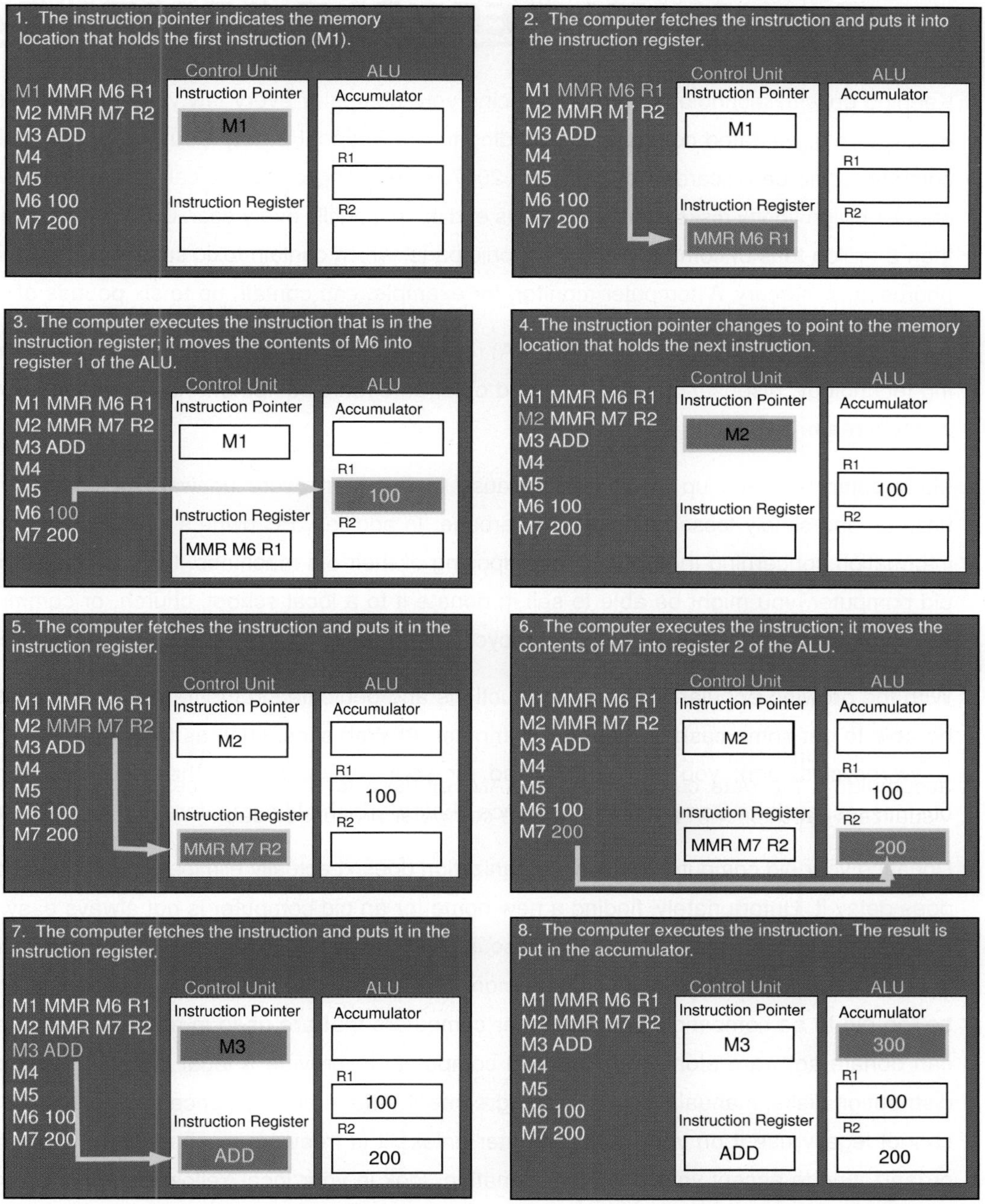

1. The instruction pointer indicates the memory location that holds the first instruction (M1).

| Control Unit | ALU |

M1 MMR M6 R1
M2 MMR M7 R2
M3 ADD
M4
M5
M6 100
M7 200

Instruction Pointer: **M1**
Accumulator
R1
Instruction Register
R2

2. The computer fetches the instruction and puts it into the instruction register.

M1 MMR M6 R1
M2 MMR M7 R2
M3 ADD
M4
M5
M6 100
M7 200

Instruction Pointer: **M1**
Accumulator
R1
Instruction Register: MMR M6 R1
R2

3. The computer executes the instruction that is in the instruction register; it moves the contents of M6 into register 1 of the ALU.

M1 MMR M6 R1
M2 MMR M7 R2
M3 ADD
M4
M5
M6 100
M7 200

Instruction Pointer: **M1**
Accumulator
R1: **100**
Instruction Register: MMR M6 R1
R2

4. The instruction pointer changes to point to the memory location that holds the next instruction.

M1 MMR M6 R1
M2 MMR M7 R2
M3 ADD
M4
M5
M6 100
M7 200

Instruction Pointer: **M2**
Accumulator
R1: **100**
Instruction Register
R2

5. The computer fetches the instruction and puts it in the instruction register.

M1 MMR M6 R1
M2 MMR M7 R2
M3 ADD
M4
M5
M6 100
M7 200

Instruction Pointer: **M2**
Accumulator
R1: **100**
Instruction Register: MMR M7 R2
R2

6. The computer executes the instruction; it moves the contents of M7 into register 2 of the ALU.

M1 MMR M6 R1
M2 MMR M7 R2
M3 ADD
M4
M5
M6 100
M7 200

Instruction Pointer: **M2**
Accumulator
R1: **100**
Instruction Register: MMR M7 R2
R2: **200**

7. The computer fetches the instruction and puts it in the instruction register.

M1 MMR M6 R1
M2 MMR M7 R2
M3 ADD
M4
M5
M6 100
M7 200

Instruction Pointer: **M3**
Accumulator
R1: **100**
Instruction Register: ADD
R2: **200**

8. The computer executes the instruction. The result is put in the accumulator.

M1 MMR M6 R1
M2 MMR M7 R2
M3 ADD
M4
M5
M6 100
M7 200

Instruction Pointer: **M3**
Accumulator: **300**
R1: **100**
Instruction Register: ADD
R2: **200**

QUICKCheck TechTalk

1 _____ code instructions are in the form of 0s and 1s.

2 JMP is an example of a(n) _____ code.

3 An instruction _____ indicates the instruction that is to be executed.

4 The results of processing are held in a(n) _____.

check answers

Issue
WHY RECYCLE COMPUTERS?

Keeping up with technology means replacing your computer every few years, but what should you do with your old, outdated computer? According to the National Safety Council, an estimated 250 million computers will be discarded by the year 2007. A recycling company called GreenDisk estimates that about 1 billion floppy disks, CDs, and DVDs end up in landfills every year. U.S. landfills already hold more than 2 million tons of computer and electronic parts, which contain toxic substances such as lead, phosphorus, and mercury. A computer monitor, for example, can contain up to six pounds of lead.

An Environmental Protection Agency (EPA) report sums up the situation: "In this world of rapidly changing technology, disposal of computers and other electronic equipment has created a new and growing waste stream."

Many computers end up in landfills because their owners were unaware of potential environmental hazards and simply tossed them in the garbage. In addition, PC owners typically are not provided with information concerning the options for disposing of their old machines. Instead of throwing away your old computer, you might be able to sell it; donate it to a local school, church, or community program; have it hauled away by a professional recycling firm; or send it back to the manufacturer.

With the growing popularity of Internet auctions and dedicated computer reclamation sites, you might be able to get some cash for your old computer. At Web sites, such as the Computer Recycle Center (www.recycles.com), you can post an ad for your "old stuff." Off the Web, you can find several businesses, such as Computer Renaissance, that refurbish old computers and sell them in retail stores.

Donating your old computer to a local organization doesn't actually eliminate the disposal problem, but it does delay it. Unfortunately, finding a new home for an old computer is not always easy. Most schools and community organizations have few resources for repairing broken equipment, so if your old computer is not in good working order, it could be more of a burden than a gift. In addition, your computer might be too old to be compatible with the other computers that are used in an organization. It helps if you can donate software along with your old computer. To provide a legal transfer, include the software distribution disks, manuals, and license agreement. And remember, once you donate the software, you cannot legally use it on your new computer unless it is freeware or shareware. If you cannot find an organization to accept your computer donation, look in your local Yellow Pages or on the Internet for an electronics recycling firm, which will haul away your computer and recycle any usable materials.

Despite the private sector options for selling, donating, or recycling old computers, many governments are worried that these "voluntary" efforts will not be enough to prevent massive dumping of an ever-growing population of obsolete computers. Many lawmakers in the United States, Japan, and the European Union believe that legislation is necessary, but they can't agree on an implementation plan. Basic to the issue is the question of "Who pays?" Should it be the taxpayer, the individual consumer, or the computer manufacturer?

Currently, taxpayers pick up the tab for electronic waste disposal through municipal trash pick-up fees or local taxes. But is this approach fair to individual taxpayers who generate very little electronic waste?

To make consumers responsible for the cost of recycling the products that they buy, some lawmakers suggest adding a special recycling tax to computers and other electronic devices. A proposal in South Carolina, for example, would impose a $5 fee on the sale of each piece of electronic equipment containing a CRT, and require the state treasurer to deposit the fees into a recycling fund for electronic equipment.

Other lawmakers propose to make manufacturers responsible for recycling costs and logistics. "Extended producer responsibility" refers to the idea of holding manufacturers responsible for the environmental effects of their products through the entire product life cycle, which includes taking them back, recycling them, or disposing of them. Proposed legislation in Europe would require manufacturers

You'll find much more information about how you can recycle an old computer at the **Computer Recycling** InfoWeb.

└click ▶✳

to accept returns of their old equipment free of charge, then take appropriate steps to recycle it. The economics of a mandatory take-back program are likely to increase the costs of products because manufacturers would typically pass on recycling costs to consumers.

Some companies currently participate in voluntary extended producer responsibility programs. Hewlett-Packard, Dell, 3M, Apple, Nokia, IBM, Sony, Gateway, and Xerox, for example, provide recycling options for some products and components. Sony recently implemented a takeback program in Minnesota that allows residents to recycle all Sony products at no cost for the next five years. Using IBM's PC Recycling Service you can ship any make of computer including system units, monitors, printers, and optional attachments, to a recycling center for $29.99. Such programs are important steps in the effort to keep our planet green.

┌ WHAT DO YOU THINK? ─────────────────

1. Have you ever thrown away an old computer or other electronic device?   ○ Yes   ○ No   ○ Not sure

2. Are you aware of any options for recycling electronic equipment in your local area?   ○ Yes   ○ No   ○ Not sure

3. Would it be fair for consumers to pay a recycling tax on any electronic equipment that they purchase?   ○ Yes   ○ No   ○ Not sure

───────────────────**click to save your responses** ▶✳ ─┘

INTERACTIVE SUMMARY

The Interactive Summary helps you to review important concepts from this chapter. Fill in the blanks to best complete each sentence. When using the NP6 BookOnCD, you can click the Check Answers buttons to automatically score your answers. Place your Tracking Disk in the floppy disk drive if you want to save your scores.

Most of today's computers are electronic, digital devices that work with data coded as binary digits, also known as [_____]. To represent numeric data, a computer can use the [_____] number system. To represent character data, a computer uses [_____], EBCDIC, or Unicode. These codes also provide digital representations for the numerals 0 through 9 that are distinguished from numbers by the fact that they are not typically used in mathematical operations. Computers also [_____] sounds, pictures, and videos into 1s and 0s.

A [_____] is a single 1 or 0, whereas a [_____] is a sequence of eight 1s and 0s. Transmission speeds are usually measured in [_____], but storage space is usually measured in [_____] or gigabytes. In the context of computing, the prefix "kilo" means exactly 1,024. Kb stands for [_____], while the abbreviation KB stands for [_____]. The prefix [_____] means precisely 1,048,576, or about 1 million. The prefix "giga" means about 1 billion; "tera" means about 1 trillion; and "exa" means about 1 quintillion.

The terms "computer chip," "microchip," and "chip" originated as techie jargon for [_____] circuits. These chips are made from a super-thin slice of semiconducting material and are packed with millions of microscopic circuit elements. In a computer, these chips include the [_____], memory modules, and other support circuitry. They are housed on a large circuit board inside of the computer's system unit called the [_____].   **check answers** ✳

The microprocessor and memory are two of the most important components in a computer. The microprocessor is an [_____] circuit, which is designed to process data, based on a set of instructions. Its miniaturized circuitry is grouped into important functional areas. The [_____] unit performs arithmetic and logical operations. The [_____] unit fetches each instruction, interprets it, loads data into the ALU's registers, and directs all of the processing activities within the microprocessor. In computer ads, microprocessor performance is usually measured in megahertz or [_____]—the number of cycles per second, or clock rate. Other factors affecting overall processing speed include word size, cache size, instruction set complexity, parallel processing, and pipelining.

RAM is a special holding area for data, program instructions, and the [_____] system. It stores data on a temporary basis while it waits to be processed. In most computers, RAM is composed of integrated circuits called [_____] or RDRAM. The speed of RAM circuitry is measured in [_____] or in megahertz (MHz). RAM is different from disk storage because it is [_____], which means that it can only hold data when the computer power is turned on. Computers also contain [_____], which is a type of memory that provides a set of "hard-wired" instructions that a computer uses to boot up. A third type of memory, called [_____], is battery powered and contains configuration settings.

check answers ✳

Today's personal computers use a variety of storage technologies, including floppy disks, hard disks, CD-ROMs, CD-Rs, CD-RWs, DVDs, and tapes. Each storage device essentially has a direct pipeline to a computer's [   ], so that data and instructions can move from a more permanent storage area to a temporary holding area and vice versa. The process of storing data is often referred to as "[   ] data" or "saving a file." The process of retrieving data is often referred to as "[   ] data" or "opening a file."

Magnetic storage technology stores data by magnetizing microscopic particles on the surface of a disk or tape. Optical storage technologies store data as a series of [   ] and lands on the surface of a CD or DVD. A standard 3½" floppy disk stores [   ] MB of data. Two variations of floppy disk technology—Zip disks and Superdisks—provide higher storage [   ] and are able to store more data on a 3½" disk.

A hard disk provides multiple platters for data storage, and these platters are sealed inside of the drive case or cartridge to prevent airborne contaminants from interfering with the read-write heads. These disks are less durable than floppy disks, so it is important to make a [   ] of the data they contain. Computer ads usually contain information about a hard disk's capacity and its [   ] card type: EIDE, UltraATA, or SCSI.

Optical storage technologies, such as CD- and DVD-[   ], provide good storage capacity, but do not allow you to write data on the disks. The [   ] technology allows you to write data on a CD once, while [   ] technology allows you to write and rewrite data on a CD.

check answers ➤❋

Within a computer, data travels from one component to another over circuitry called the data bus. The part of the bus that runs between [   ] and peripheral devices is called the expansion bus. When you add new devices to a computer system, you connect them to this expansion bus by plugging an expansion card into an expansion slot, or by connecting a cable to an expansion [   ]. Most of today's personal computers include three types of expansion slots: ISA, PCI, and [   ]. Before purchasing a device that has its own expansion card, it is important to check inside the computer to make sure that the right type of expansion slot is available. Instead of slots on the motherboard, a notebook computer typically uses an external [   ] slot, which can accept one or more Type I, Type II, or Type III cards.

A computer's display system consists of a display device and a [   ] card. Desktop computers tend to use [   ] technology, whereas notebook computers tend to use [   ] technology for the display device. The quality of a display device relates to its screen size, resolution, color depth, and dot pitch. Most of today's display devices are used at [   ] of 640 x 480, 800 x 600, or 1024 x 768. Personal computer printer technologies include ink jet, solid ink, thermal wax, laser, dot matrix, and dye sublimation. [   ] printers tend to be most popular for home computers, whereas [   ] printers tend to be favored by businesses that need speed and a duty cycle of hundreds of pages per day.

check answers ➤❋

INTERACTIVE
KEY TERMS

Make sure that you understand all of the boldfaced key terms presented in this chapter. If you're using the NP6 BookOnCD, you can use this list of terms as an interactive study activity. First, try to define a term in your own words, then click the term to compare your definition with the definition that is presented in the chapter.

Access time, 79	Expansion bus, 88	Pipelining, 68
Active matrix screen, 94	Expansion card, 88	Pits, 78
AGP, 89	Expansion port, 90	Pixels, 93
ALU, 67	Expansion slot, 88	Plug and Play, 92
Analog device, 58	Extended ASCII, 60	PostScript, 96
Archiving, 86	File header, 61	Printer control language (PCL), 96
ASCII, 60	Floppy disk, 79	RAID, 83
Benchmarks, 68	Giga-, 61	RAM, 70
Binary digits, 58	Gigahertz (GHz), 67	Random access, 79
Binary number system, 59	Graphics card, 92	RDRAM, 72
Cache, 68	Hard disk platter, 81	Read-write head, 77
Capacitors, 71	Head crash, 83	Registers, 67
CD-R, 85	Ink jet printer, 94	Resolution, 93
CD-RW, 86	Instruction cycle, 99	RIMM, 72
Character data, 59	Instruction set, 67	RISC, 68
CISC, 68	Integrated circuit (IC), 62	ROM BIOS, 72
CMOS memory, 73	ISA, 89	ROM, 72
Color depth, 94	Kilobit, 61	SCSI, 82
Controller, 82	Kilobyte, 61	SDRAM, 72
Control unit, 67	Lands, 78	SEC cartridges, 63
CRT, 92	Laser printer, 95	Semiconducting materials, 62
Data bus, 88	LCD, 92	Sequential access, 79
Data representation, 58	Level 1 cache, 68	Serial processing, 68
Data transfer rate, 79	Level 2 cache, 68	Solid ink printer, 95
Device driver, 92	Machine code, 98	SO-RIMM, 72
Digital device, 58	Magnetic storage, 77	Storage device, 76
Digital electronics, 58	Megabit, 61	Storage medium, 76
Digitize, 61	Megabyte, 61	SVGA, 93
DIMMs, 63	Megahertz (MHz), 67	SXGA, 93
DIPs, 63	Microprocessor, 66	Tape backup, 83
Disk density, 80	Microprocessor clock, 67	Tera-, 61
DMA, 82	Motherboard, 63	Thermal transfer printer, 95
Dot matrix printer, 96	Nanometer, 66	UDMA, 82
Dot pitch, 93	Nanosecond, 72	Ultra ATA, 82
Drive bays, 78	Numeric data, 59	Unicode, 60
DVD, 86	Op code, 98	UXGA, 93
DVD+RW, 87	Operands, 98	VGA, 93
DVD-RAM, 87	Optical storage, 78	Viewable image size, 93
DVD-ROM, 86	Parallel processing, 68	Virtual memory, 71
DVD-RW, 87	Passive matrix screen, 94	Volatile, 71
DVD-Video, 86	PCI, 89	Word size, 67
Dye sublimation printer, 95	PC card, 90	Write-protect window, 81
EBCDIC, 60	PCMCIA slot, 90	XGA, 93
EIDE, 82	PGAs, 63	
Exa-, 61	Phase change technology, 86	

INTERACTIVE
SITUATION QUESTIONS

Apply what you've learned to some typical computing situations. When using the NP6 BookOnCD, you can type your answers, then use the Check Answers button to automatically score your responses. Place your Tracking Disk in the floppy disk drive if you want to save your scores.

1 Suppose that you're reading a computer magazine and you come across the ad pictured to the right. By looking at the specs, you can tell that the microprocessor was manufactured by which company? ☐

2 The capacity of the hard disk drive in the ad is ☐ and the memory capacity is ☐.

3 The computer in the ad appears to have a(n) ☐ controller card for the hard disk drive.

4 You are thinking about upgrading the microprocessor in your three-year-old computer, which has a 733 MHz Pentium microprocessor and 16 MB of RAM. Would it be worthwhile to spend $500 to install a 1.3 GHz Pentium processor? ☐ (Yes or no?)

5 You're in the process of booting up your computer and suddenly the screen contains an assortment of settings for date and time, hard disk drive, and memory capacity. From what you've learned in this chapter, you can surmise that these are settings stored in the ☐ memory, and that they are best left unmodified.

6 You want to add a storage device to your computer that reads CD-ROMs, DVD-ROMs, DVD-Videos, and CD-Rs. You should select a(n) ☐ drive.

7 You're planning to archive some old photos that you digitized. You decide to use a(n) ☐ disk to store the archive copies because they are durable and can be read by most optical drives.

HOME/SMALL BUSINESS DESKTOP MODEL XP2002

- Pentium 4 1.5 GHz
- 128 MB 8 ns RDRAM
- 60 GB UltraATA HD (5400 rpm)
- 32 X Max CD-RW
- 3½" 1.44 MB FDD
- 21" 24 dp monitor
- 64 MB AGP graphics card
- Sound Blaster 64v PCI sound card
- Altec Lansing speakers
- U.S. Robotics 56 Kbps modem
- 3-year limited warranty*

$ 899

---

8 Your hard disk contains at least 30 GB of programs, data, and games that you don't want to lose. A(n) ☐ backup would be an inexpensive way to keep a copy of your data in case your hard disk crashes.

9 You are a graphics designer. To select a display device that will give you the best colors from all viewing angles, you prefer ☐ technology, rather than a(n) ☐ screen.

10 Suppose that you want the very best type of personal computer printer for photographic images, and price is not a factor. You should select a(n) ☐ printer.

check answers

2

INTERACTIVE
PRACTICE TESTS

When you use the NP6 BookOnCD, you can take Practice Tests that consist of 10 multiple-choice, true/false, and fill-in-the-blank questions. The questions are selected at random from a large test bank, so each time you take a test, you'll receive a different set of questions. Your tests are scored immediately, and you can print study guides that help you find the correct answers for any questions that you missed. If you are using a Tracking Disk, insert it in the floppy disk drive to save your test scores.

click to start ➡✳

STUDY
TIPS

Study Tips help you to organize and consolidate the information in a chapter by making lists, outlines, charts, and sketches. You can use paper and pencil or word processing software to complete most of the Study Tips activities.

1 Make sure that you can use your own words to correctly answer each of the green focus questions that appear throughout the chapter.

2 Explain the difference between an analog and a digital device. Provide a few examples of your own in addition to the example in the chapter.

3 Describe how the binary number system and binary coded decimals can use only 1s and 0s to represent numbers.

4 List and briefly describe the four codes that computers typically use for character data.

5 Describe the difference between numeric data, character data, and numerals.

6 Make sure that you understand the meaning of the following measurement terms, and indicate what aspects of a computer system they are used to measure: KB, Kb, MB, Mb, GB, KBps, Kbps, MHz, GHz, ms, ns.

7 Create your own diagram of a computer motherboard, indicating the approximate location of the microprocessor, RAM, and expansion slots.

8 Describe the appearance (or draw a sketch) of a DIP, DIMM, PGA, and SEC.

9 Describe how the ALU and the control unit interact to process data.

10 List and describe the factors that affect microprocessor performance.

11 Name two companies that produce microprocessors, and list some of the models that each company produces.

12 List four types of memory and briefly describe how each one works.

13 Describe the advantages and disadvantages of magnetic storage and optical storage.

14 Create a table that compares the storage capacity of floppy disks, Zip disks, hard disks, CDs, and DVDs.

15 Create a grid with each type of storage device written across the top. Make a list of the corresponding media down the left side of the grid. Working down from the top, place an X in cells for any of the media that can be read by the device listed at the top of the column.

16 Summarize the most important uses for each type of storage technology.

17 Create your own diagram to illustrate how the data bus connects RAM, the microprocessor, and peripheral devices.

18 Summarize what you know about how a graphics card can affect a monitor's resolution.

19 Create a table to summarize what you know about the printer technologies that were discussed in this chapter.

PROJECTS

An NP6 Project is an open-ended activity that will help you apply the concepts you have learned. Many projects require resources in addition to your textbook, such as current magazines, library materials, or Web access. When you tackle a project, be prepared to use your critical thinking skills, logical analysis skills, and creativity.

1   **Issue Research: Why Recycle Computers?** The Issue section of this chapter focused on the potential for discarded computers and other electronic devices to become a significant environmental problem. For this project, you will write a two–five page paper about recycling computers, based on information that you gather from the Internet. To begin this project, consult the Computer Recycling InfoWeb (see page 103) and link to the recommended Web pages to get an in-depth overview of the issue. Next, determine the specific aspect of the issue that you will present in your paper. You might, for example, decide to focus on the toxic materials that are contained in computers that end up in landfills. Or, you might tackle the barriers that discourage the shipment of old computers across national borders. Whatever aspect of the issue you decide to present, make sure that you can back up your discussion with facts and references to authoritative articles and Web pages. You can place citations to these pages (including the author's name, article title, date of publication, and URL) at the end of your paper as endnotes, on each page as footnotes, or along with the appropriate paragraphs using parentheses. Follow your professor's instructions for submitting your paper via e-mail or as a printed document.

2   **Buying a New Computer** Chapter 2 presented you with many computer terms that are used in computer ads and at online shopping sites to describe computer systems. For this project, suppose that you are going to purchase a new computer and you have a budget of $2,000 for everything—computer, display device, printer, storage devices, and software. Go to the Computer Buyer's Guide InfoWeb and fill out the Needs Assessment worksheet. Next, fill out the Peripherals and Accessories worksheet. Finally, using the shopping links, find three computers that meet your needs and fit within your budget (don't forget to save some money for the accessories and peripherals that you need!). Fill out the Comparison worksheet with the specifications for these computers. After filling out all of the worksheets, write a short description of your final equipment selection, indicating how well you managed to stay within your budget. Follow your professor's instructions for submitting your materials via e-mail or as a printed document.

The **Computer Buyer's Guide** InfoWeb contains all kinds of tips about how to be a savvy computer shopper. Plus, you'll find worksheets to help you assess your needs, compare different computers, and shop for accessories.

└click ▪►

3   **The Jargon of Computer Ads** You know that you're really a tech wizard when you can decipher every term and acronym in a computer ad. But even the most knowledgeable computer gurus sometimes need a dictionary for new terms. Let's see how you fare. For this project, photocopy a full page from a current computer magazine that contains an ad for a computer system. On the copy of the ad, use a colored pen to circle each descriptive term and acronym. On a separate sheet of paper, or using a word processor, list all of the terms that you circled and write a definition for each term. If you encounter a term that was not defined in the chapter, use a computer dictionary, or refer to the Webopedia Web site (*www.webopedia.com*) to locate the correct definition.

ADDITIONAL
PROJECTS

 TIP

Click ▪► to access the Web for additional projects.

3 ⚙ COMPUTER SOFTWARE

CONTENTS

➡✳ **SECTION A: SOFTWARE BASICS**
Software, Programs, and Data Files
Programmers and Programming
  Languages
How Software Works
Application Software and System
  Software

➡✳ **SECTION B: PERSONAL COMPUTER
OPERATING SYSTEMS**
Operating System Overview
Windows, Mac OS, UNIX, Linux,
  and DOS

➡✳ **SECTION C: APPLICATION
SOFTWARE**
Document Production Software
Spreadsheet Software
Accounting and Finance,
  Mathematical Modeling, and
  Statistical Software
Data Management Software
Graphics Software
Music Software
Video Editing Software
Educational and Reference
  Software
Entertainment Software
Business Software

➡✳ **SECTION D: SOFTWARE
INSTALLATION AND COPYRIGHTS**
Installation Basics
Installing From a Distribution Disk
  or CD
Installing Downloaded Software
Uninstalling Software
Software Copyrights
Software Licenses

➡✳ **TECHTALK: THE WINDOWS
REGISTRY**

➡✳ **ISSUE: IS PIRACY A PROBLEM?**

➡✳ **REVIEW ACTIVITIES**
Interactive Summary
Interactive Key Terms
Interactive Situation Questions
Interactive Practice Tests
Study Tips
Projects

LABS
➡✳ Using the Windows Interface
➡✳ Installing and Uninstalling
  Software

InfoWebLinks

The InfoWebLinks, located in the margins of this chapter, show
the way to a variety of Web sites that contain additional
information and updates to the chapter topics. Your computer
needs an Internet connection to access these links. You can
connect to the Web links for this chapter by:

- clicking the InfoWeb links in the margins
- clicking this underlined link
- starting your browser and entering the URL
  www.infoweblinks.com/np6/chapter3.htm

 TIP

When using the **BookOnCD**,
the ➡✳ symbols are "clickable."

CHAPTER PREVIEW

Transformer toys are fascinating. By twisting one part, folding up another part, and deftly maneuvering several other levers and gears, transformers morph into something totally different—action figures transform into animals; dragons and other exotic animals transform into robots, jets, tanks, motorcycles, or helicopters.

In a sense, computers have a transformer-like quality too. For example, a computer can transform from one kind of machine to another—from a drafting station to a typesetting machine, from a flight simulator to a calculator, from a filing system to a video editing studio. A computer's versatility is possible because of software—the set of instructions that tells a computer how to perform a specific type of task. But how does software work? What can it do? How do you add it to your computer? The answers to those questions are the focus of this chapter.

Section A begins with a look at the components of a typical software package and explains how these components work together. Section B focuses on a computer's most important system software—its operating system. Section C presents an overview of software applications, including document production, spreadsheets, data management, graphics, music, video editing, and games. Section D wraps up with important practical information about installing software, uninstalling software, and software copyrights.

When you complete this chapter you should be able to:

■ Describe the software components of a typical software package, including executable files, support modules, and data modules

■ Trace the development of a computer program from its inception as a set of high-level language instructions through the interpretation process into machine language

■ Describe the way an operating system manages each computer resource

■ Identify personal computer operating systems, such as Windows, Mac OS, Linux, UNIX, and DOS

■ Describe the differences between system software and application software

■ Explain the key features and uses for word processing, desktop publishing, and Web authoring software

■ Describe the major features of spreadsheet software

■ Compare the features and uses of file management software to those of database software

■ List the types of software that are available in the following software categories: graphics, music, educational and reference, entertainment, and business

■ Explain how to install and uninstall software, whether it is supplied on CDs or as a Web download

■ Describe the rights granted by: copyright law, a typical commercial software license, a shareware license, a freeware license, an open source license, and public domain software.

3

 TIP   Click ➧✳ to access the Web for a complete list of learning objectives for Chapter 3.

Section

A

SOFTWARE BASICS

In common practice, the term "software" is typically used to describe a commercial product, such as the one shown in Figure 3-1. Computer software determines the types of tasks that a computer can help you accomplish. Some software helps you create documents, while other software helps you create presentations, prepare your tax return, or design the floor plan for a new house. But how does software transform your computer into a machine that can help with so many tasks? Section A delves into the characteristics of computer software and explains how it works.

FIGURE 3-1

In popular usage, the term "software" usually refers to one or more computer programs and any additional files that are provided to carry out a specific type of task.

SOFTWARE, PROGRAMS, AND DATA FILES

What is software? Software consists of computer programs and data files that work together to provide a computer with the instructions and data necessary for carrying out a specific type of task, such as document production, video editing, graphic design, or Web browsing.

A **computer program**, or "program," is a detailed set of instructions that tells a computer how to solve a problem or carry out a task. Some computer programs supplied with a software package are designed to be launched, or started, by users. These programs are stored in files that typically have .exe filename extensions, and are sometimes referred to as "executable files" or "user-executable files." When using a Windows PC, you can start a program by clicking its icon, selecting it from the Start menu, or entering its name in the Run dialog box.

Other computer programs supplied with a software package are not designed to be run by users. These programs, sometimes referred to as "support modules," contain instructions for the computer to use in conjunction with the main user-executable file. Each support module is stored in its own file. The main executable file can "call," or activate, a support program as needed. In the context of Windows software, support modules often have filename extensions such as .dll and .ocx. To understand how these programs work, suppose that you want to edit some video footage with the VideoFactory software. You run the executable file, *Vidfact.exe*, to start the program and display the main screen. When it comes time to capture the video footage from your camera and transfer it to your PC, you select the Capture command. Your selection requires program instructions that are not included in the *Vidfact.exe* executable file, so the .exe file starts a support program called *Sftrans1.dll* to assist with this task.

As you might expect, the data files included with a software package contain any data that is necessary for a task, but not supplied by the user. These files might contain the text of a software package's Help file or license agreement, word lists for a dictionary or thesaurus, or graphics for the software's toolbar icons. The data files supplied with a software package sport filename extensions such as .txt, .bmp, and .hlp.

Is the data that I create classified as software? "Software" is a slippery term. In the early days of the computer industry, it became popular to use the term "software" for all non-hardware components of a computer. In this context, software referred to computer programs and to the data used by the programs. It could also refer to any data that existed in digital format, such as documents or photos. Using today's terminology, however, the documents and photos that you create are usually classified as "data" rather than as "software."

Why does software require so many files? You might be surprised by the number of files that are necessary to make software work. Most software packages, like the one in Figure 3-2, include at least one user-executable program plus several support programs and data files.

FIGURE 3-2

The files required by the VideoFactory software contain user-executable programs, support programs, and data.

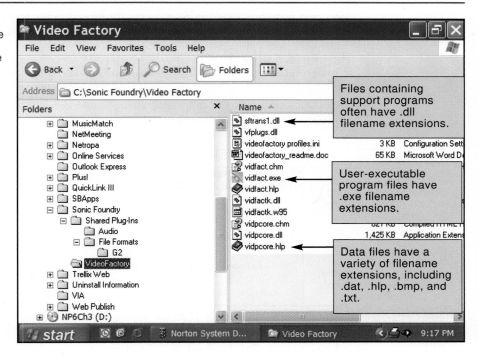

The use of a main user-executable file plus several support programs and data files provides a great deal of flexibility and efficiency for programmers. Support programs and data files can usually be modified without changing the main executable file. This modular approach can save programmers many hours of programming and testing within the main executable file, which is usually long and fairly complex. The modular approach also allows programmers to reuse their support programs and adapt pre-programmed support modules for use in their own software.

Modular programming techniques would be of only passing interest to people who use computer programs, except for the fact that such techniques affect the process of installing and uninstalling software, discussed later in this section. It is important, therefore, to remember that computer software typically consists of many files that contain user-executable programs, support programs, and data.

PROGRAMMERS AND PROGRAMMING LANGUAGES

Who creates computer software? Computer programmers write the instructions for the computer programs that become the components of a computer software product. The finished software product is then distributed by the programmers themselves, or by **software publishers**—companies that specialize in packaging, marketing, and selling commercial software.

At one time, businesses, organizations, and individuals had to write most of the software that they wanted to use. Today, however, most businesses and organizations purchase commercial software (sometimes referred to as "off-the-shelf software") to avoid the time and expense of writing their own. Individuals rarely write software for their personal computers, preferring to select from thousands of software titles available in stores, from catalogs, and on the Internet. Although most computer owners do not write their own software, working as a computer programmer and writing software for a government agency, business, or software publisher can be a challenging career.

How does a programmer "write" software? Most software is designed to provide a task-related environment, which includes a screen display, a means of collecting commands and data from the user, the specifications for processing data, and a method for displaying or outputting data. Figure 3-3 illustrates a very simple software environment that converts a Fahrenheit temperature to Celsius and displays the result.

FIGURE 3-3

Today's graphical software environments include menus, buttons, and other control objects. These controls are defined by a programmer, who designates their properties. For example, one of the properties of the Convert button specifies how to convert Fahrenheit temperatures to Celsius.

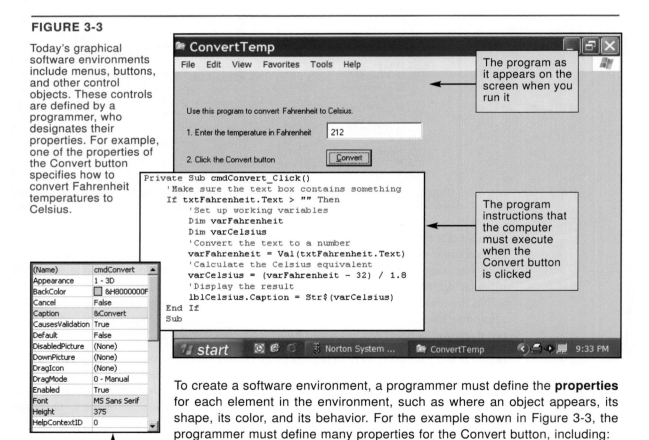

Properties associated with the Convert button

```
Private Sub cmdConvert_Click()
    'Make sure the text box contains something
    If txtFahrenheit.Text > "" Then
        'Set up working variables
        Dim varFahrenheit
        Dim varCelsius
        'Convert the text to a number
        varFahrenheit = Val(txtFahrenheit.Text)
        'Calculate the Celsius equivalent
        varCelsius = (varFahrenheit - 32) / 1.8
        'Display the result
        lblCelsius.Caption = Str$(varCelsius)
    End If
Sub
```

To create a software environment, a programmer must define the **properties** for each element in the environment, such as where an object appears, its shape, its color, and its behavior. For the example shown in Figure 3-3, the programmer must define many properties for the Convert button, including:

■ **Its height:** 375

■ **Its label (caption):** Convert

■ **What happens when you click it:** Subtract 32 from Fahrenheit, divide by 1.8, and then display the answer

A **programming language** (sometimes referred to as a "computer language") provides the tools that a programmer uses to create software and produce a lengthy list of instructions, called **source code**, that defines the software environment in every detail—how it looks, how the user enters commands, and how it manipulates data. Most programmers today prefer to use **high-level languages**, such as C++, Java, COBOL, and Visual Basic, which have some similarities to human languages, and produce programs that are fairly easy to test and modify.

HOW SOFTWARE WORKS

How does a high-level language relate to the microprocessor's instruction set? A computer's microprocessor only understands **machine language**—the instruction set that is "hard wired" within the microprocessor's circuits. Therefore, instructions written in a high-level language must be translated into machine language before a computer can use them. Figure 3-4 gives you an idea of what happens to a high-level instruction when it is converted into machine language instructions.

FIGURE 3-4

High-level Language Instruction	Machine Language Equivalent	Description of Machine Language Instructions
Answer = FirstNumber + SecondNumber	10001000 00011000 010000000	Load FirstNumber into Register 1
	10001000 00010000 00100000	Load SecondNumber into Register 2
	00000000 00011000 00010000	Perform ADD operation
	10100010 00111000	Move the number from the accumulator to the RAM location called Answer

The process of translating instructions from a high-level language into machine language can be accomplished by two special types of programs: compilers and interpreters. A **compiler** translates all of the instructions in a program as a single batch, and the resulting machine language instructions, called **object code**, are placed in a new file (see Figure 3-5). Most of the program files that you receive on the distribution CD for commercial software are compiled so that they contain machine language instructions that are ready for the processor to execute.

FIGURE 3-5

A compiler converts high-level instructions into a new file containing machine language instructions.

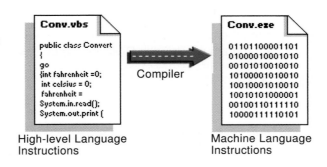

High-level Language Instructions — Compiler — Machine Language Instructions

As an alternative to a compiler, an **interpreter** converts one instruction at a time while the program is running. This method of converting high-level instructions into machine language is more common with Web-based programs called **scripts**, written in languages such as JavaScript and VBScript. These scripts contain high-level instructions, which arrive as part of a Web page. An interpreter reads the first instruction in a script, converts it into machine language, and then sends it to the microprocessor. After the instruction is executed, the interpreter converts the next instruction, and so on (see Figure 3-6).

FIGURE 3-6

An interpreter converts high-level instructions into machine language instructions while the program is running.

An interpreted program runs more slowly than a compiled program because the translation process happens while the program is running.

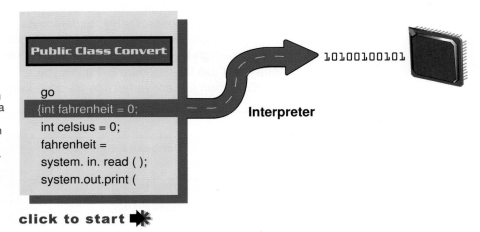

```
Public Class Convert

go
{int fahrenheit = 0;
int celsius = 0;
fahrenheit =
system. in. read ( );
system.out.print (
```

Interpreter

10100100101

click to start ▄▶✳

To run a script, your computer must have the corresponding interpreter program. These programs are typically supplied with Web browser software, or are available as downloads from the Web.

So how does software work? Let's assume that a video editing program, such as VideoFactory, was installed on your computer, which is running Windows. You click the Start button, then select VideoFactory from the Programs menu. Your selection activates the main executable file called *Vidfact.exe*, which exists in compiled format on your computer's hard disk. The instructions for this program are loaded into RAM and then sent to the microprocessor. As processing begins, the VideoFactory window opens and the graphical controls for video editing tasks appear. The program waits for you to select a control by clicking it with the mouse. Based on your selection, the program follows its instructions and performs a specified action. Many of the instructions for these actions are included in the main executable file, but it might be necessary to call a support program in order to access its instructions. The program continues to respond to the controls that you select until you click the Close button, which halts execution of the program instructions, closes the program window, and releases the space that the program occupied in RAM for use by other programs or data.

APPLICATION SOFTWARE AND SYSTEM SOFTWARE

How is software categorized? Software is categorized as either application software or system software. When you hear the word "application," your first reaction might be to envision a financial aid application, or some other form that you would fill out to apply for a job, a club membership, or a driver's license. The word "application" has other meanings, however. One of them is a synonym for the word "use." A computer certainly has many uses, such as creating documents, crunching numbers, drawing

COMPUTER SOFTWARE   117

designs, and editing photographs. Each of these uses is considered an "application," and the software that provides the computer with instructions for each of these uses is called **application software**, or simply an "application." The primary purpose of application software is to help people carry out tasks using a computer.

In contrast, the primary purpose of **system software**—your computer's operating system, device drivers, and utilities—is to help the computer carry out its basic operating functions. Figure 3-7 illustrates the division between system software and application software. You'll learn more about these software categories in Sections B and C.

FIGURE 3-7

Software can be classified into categories.

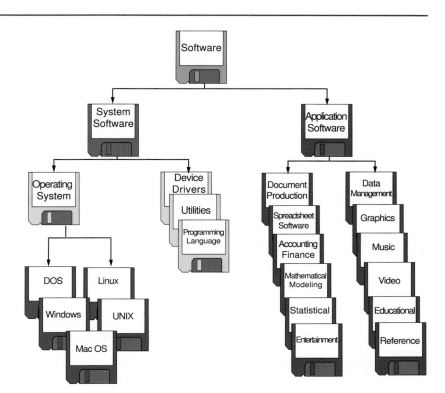

QUICK**Check** **A**
Section

1 Software usually contains support programs and data files, in addition to a user-[_____] file that you run to start the software.

2 To create a software environment, a programmer must define the [_____] for each element in the environment.

3 Instructions that are written in a [_____]-level language must

be translated into [_____] language before a computer can use them.

4 A(n) [_____] translates all of the instructions in a program as a single batch, and the resulting machine language instructions are placed in a new file.

5 Software can be divided into two major categories: application software and [_____] software.

check answers ✳

118   CHAPTER 3

Section **B**

PERSONAL COMPUTER
OPERATING SYSTEMS

Chapter 1 provided a quick introduction to operating systems, such as Windows, Mac OS, Linux, UNIX, and DOS. It explained that an operating system is one of the factors that determines a computer's platform and compatibility. The term **operating system** (abbreviated OS) is defined as system software, which acts as the master controller for all of the activities that take place within a computer system.

An operating system is an integral part of virtually every computer system, including supercomputers, mainframes, servers, workstations, video game systems, handhelds, and personal computers. It fundamentally affects how you can use your computer. Can you run two programs at the same time? Can you connect your computer to a network? Will your computer run dependably? Will all of your software have a similar "look and feel," or will you have to learn a different set of controls and commands for each new program that you acquire?

To answer questions like these, it is helpful to have a clear idea about what an operating system is and what it does. In this section of the chapter, you'll get an overview of operating systems, and compare some of the most popular operating systems for personal computers.

OPERATING SYSTEM OVERVIEW

What does an operating system do? A computer's software is similar to the chain of command in an army. You issue a command using application software. Application software tells the operating system what to do. The operating system tells the device drivers, device drivers tell the hardware, and the hardware actually does the work. Figure 3-8 illustrates this chain of command for printing a document or photo.

FIGURE 3-8

Your command to print a document is relayed through various levels of software, including the operating system, until it reaches the printer.

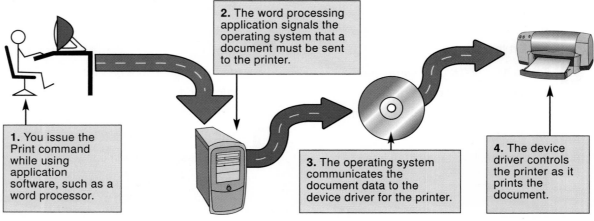

2. The word processing application signals the operating system that a document must be sent to the printer.

1. You issue the Print command while using application software, such as a word processor.

3. The operating system communicates the document data to the device driver for the printer.

4. The device driver controls the printer as it prints the document.

COMPUTER SOFTWARE   **119**

The operating system interacts with application software, device drivers, and hardware to manage a computer's resources. In the context of a computer system, the term **resource** refers to any component that is required to perform work. For example, the processor is a resource. RAM, storage space, and peripherals are also resources. While you interact with application software, your computer's operating system is busy behind the scenes with tasks such as identifying storage space, allocating memory, and communicating with your printer.

Many operating systems also influence the "look and feel" of your software—what kinds of menus and controls are displayed on the screen, and how they react to your input. Let's take a closer look at how an operating system manages resources and affects "look and feel."

How does the OS manage processor resources? Chapter 2 explained how the control unit directs activities within the microprocessor. The operating system also controls the microprocessor—just at a slightly higher level. Every cycle of a computer's microprocessor is a resource for accomplishing tasks. Many activities—called "processes"—compete for the attention of your computer's microprocessor. Commands are arriving from programs that you're using, while input is arriving from the keyboard and mouse. At the same time, data must be sent to the display device or printer, and Web pages are arriving from your Internet connection. To manage all of these competing processes, your computer's operating system must ensure that each one receives its share of microprocessor cycles. Ideally, the operating system should be able to help the microprocessor switch tasks so that, from the user's vantage point, everything seems to be happening at the same time. The operating system also must ensure that the microprocessor doesn't "spin its wheels" waiting for input, while it could be working on some other processing task.

Why does an operating system need to manage memory? A microprocessor works with data and executes instructions that are stored in RAM—one of your computer's most important resources. When you want to run more than one program at a time, the operating system has to allocate specific areas of memory for each program, as shown in Figure 3-9. While multiple programs are running, the OS must ensure that instructions and data from one area of memory don't "leak" into an area allocated to another program. If an OS falls down on the job and fails to protect each program's memory area, data can get corrupted, programs can "crash," and your computer will display error messages, such as "General Protection Fault." Your PC can sometimes recover from memory leak problems if you use the Ctrl-Alt-Del key sequence to close the corrupted program.

FIGURE 3-9

The operating system allocates a specific area of RAM for each program that is open and running.

The operating system is itself a program, and so it requires RAM space, too.

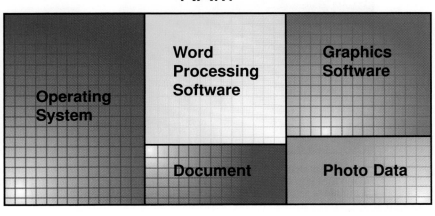

RAM

Operating System

Word Processing Software

Graphics Software

Document

Photo Data

How does the OS keep track of storage resources? Behind the scenes, an operating system acts as a filing clerk that stores and retrieves files from your disks and CDs. It remembers the names and locations of all your files, and keeps track of empty spaces where new files can be stored. Chapter 4 explores file storage in more depth because this aspect of the operating system directly affects the way that you create, name, save, and retrieve files.

Why does the operating system get involved with peripheral devices? Every device that's connected to a computer is regarded as a resource. Your computer's operating system communicates with device driver software so that data can travel smoothly between the computer and these peripheral resources. If a peripheral device or driver is not performing correctly, the operating system makes a decision about what to do—usually it displays an on-screen message to warn you of the problem.

Your computer's operating system ensures that input and output proceed in an orderly manner, using "queues" and "buffers" to collect and hold data while the computer is busy with other tasks. By using a keyboard buffer, for example, your computer never misses one of your keystrokes, regardless of how fast you type, or what else is happening within your computer system at the same time.

How does the operating system affect the "look and feel" of application software? A **user interface** can be defined as the combination of hardware and software that helps people and computers communicate with each other. Your computer's user interface includes the mouse and keyboard that accept your input and carry out your commands, as well as the display device that provides cues to help you use software, and displays error messages that alert you to problems. An operating system typically provides user interface tools, such as menus and toolbar buttons, that define the "look and feel" for all of its compatible software.

Most computers today feature a graphical user interface. Sometimes abbreviated "GUI" and referred to as a "gooey," a **graphical user interface** provides a way to point and click a mouse to select menu options and manipulate graphical objects that are displayed on the screen. The original GUI concept was conceived at the prestigious Xerox PARC research facility. A few years later, in 1984, Apple Computer turned the idea into a commercial success with the launch of its popular Macintosh computer, which featured a GUI operating system and applications. GUIs didn't really catch on in the PC market until 1992 when Windows 3.1 became standard issue on most PCs, replacing a **command-line interface**, which requires users to type various memorized commands to run programs and accomplish tasks (see Figure 3-10).

FIGURE 3-10

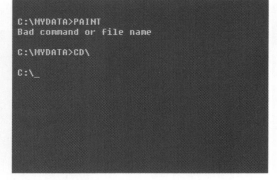

A graphical user interface features menus and icons that you can manipulate with the click of a mouse.

A command-line interface requires you to memorize and type commands.

HOME GO TO CHAPTER GLOSSARY ◀ PAGE PAGE▶   PRACTICE TRACKING

COMPUTER SOFTWARE   **121**

Where is the operating system? In some computers—typically handhelds and video game consoles—the entire operating system is small enough to be stored in ROM. For nearly all personal computers, servers, workstations, mainframes, and supercomputers, the operating system program is quite large, so most of it is stored on a hard disk. The operating system's small **bootstrap program** is stored in ROM, and provides the instructions needed to load the core parts into memory when the system boots. This core part of the operating system, called the **kernel**, provides the most essential operating system services, such as memory management and file access. The kernel stays in memory all the time your computer is on. Other parts of the operating system, such as customization utilities, are loaded into memory as they are needed.

Do I ever interact directly with the OS? Although its main purpose is to control what happens "behind the scenes" of a computer system, many operating systems provide helpful tools, called **utilities**, that you can use to control and customize your computer equipment and work environment. Utilities, like those listed below, are typically accessed by using a graphical user interface, such as the familiar Windows desktop.

- **Launch programs.** When you start your computer, Windows displays graphical objects, such as icons, the Start button, and the Programs menu, which you can manipulate to start programs.

- **Manage files.** Another useful utility, called Windows Explorer, allows you to view a list of files, move them to different storage devices, copy them, rename them, and delete them.

- **Get help.** Windows provides a Help system that you can use to find out how various commands work.

- **Customize the user interface.** The Control Panel, accessible from the Start menu, provides utilities that help you customize your screen display and work environment.

- **Configure equipment.** The Windows Control Panel also provides access to utilities that help you set up and configure your computer's hardware and peripheral devices. (See Figure 3-11.)

FIGURE 3-11

Many Windows utilities can be accessed from the Control Panel. You'll find it by clicking the Start button. If it does not appear on the Start menu, select Settings, then select Control Panel.

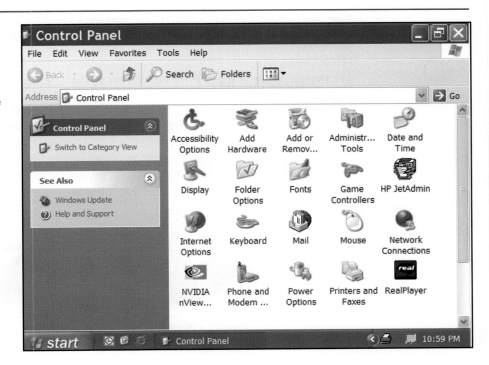

Are different operating systems needed for different computing tasks? One operating system might be better suited to some computing tasks than others. To provide clues to their strengths and weaknesses, operating systems are informally categorized and characterized using one or more of the following terms:

A **single-user operating system** expects to deal with one set of input devices—those that can be controlled by one user at a time. Operating systems for handheld computers and many personal computers fit into the single-user category.

A **multiuser operating system** allows a single computer—often a mainframe—to deal with simultaneous input, output, and processing requests from many users. One of its most difficult responsibilities is to schedule all of the processing requests that must be performed by a centralized computer. Terminology note: The word "multiuser" appears in many contexts in which it means simply "multiple users" and has nothing to do with multiuser operating systems. For example, a "multiuser" game can be played by more than one person at a time. It doesn't necessarily require a multiuser operating system.

A **network operating system** (also referred to as a "server operating system") provides communications and routing services that allow computers to share data, programs, and peripheral devices. Novell Netware, for example, is almost always referred to as a network operating system. The difference between network services and multiuser services can seem a little hazy—especially because operating systems such as UNIX and Linux offer both. The main difference, however, is that multiuser operating systems schedule requests for processing on a centralized computer, whereas a network operating system simply routes data and programs to each user's local computer, where the actual processing takes place.

A **multitasking operating system** provides process and memory management services that allow two or more programs to run simultaneously. Most of today's operating systems, including the OS on your personal computer, offer multitasking services.

A **desktop operating system** is one that's designed for a personal computer—either a desktop or notebook computer. The computer that you typically use at home, at school, or at work is most likely configured with a desktop operating system, such as Windows or Mac OS. Typically, these operating systems are designed to accommodate a single user, but may also provide networking capability. Today's desktop operating systems invariably provide multitasking capabilities.

WINDOWS, MAC OS, LINUX, UNIX, AND DOS

What's the best-selling operating system? **Microsoft Windows** is installed on over 80 percent of the world's personal computers. The number and variety of programs that run on Windows are unmatched by any other operating system, a fact that contributes to its dominant position as the most widely used desktop operating system. Since its introduction in 1985, Windows has evolved through several versions, as listed in Figure 3-12.

FIGURE 3-12

Windows timeline

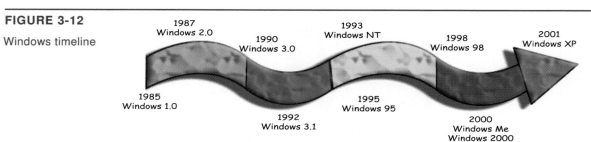

1987 Windows 2.0
1990 Windows 3.0
1993 Windows NT
1998 Windows 98
2001 Windows XP

1985 Windows 1.0
1992 Windows 3.1
1995 Windows 95
2000 Windows Me Windows 2000

COMPUTER SOFTWARE   123

www.InfoWebLinks.com

You'll find lots of current information about Windows at the **Microsoft Windows** InfoWeb.

◄click ▪◀

The first versions of Windows, including Windows 3.1, were sometimes referred to as "operating environments" rather than operating systems, because they ran in addition to DOS, which supplied the operating system services. Windows operating environments were primarily responsible for supplying a point and click user interface, complete with graphical screen displays and mouse input. Early versions of Windows evolved into today's true operating systems, such as Windows 2000 and Windows XP.

The Windows operating system gets its name from the rectangular work areas that appear on the screen-based desktop. Each work area can display a different document or program, providing a visual model of the operating system's multitasking capabilities (Figure 3-13).

FIGURE 3-13

If you find a Start button sporting the Windows logo in the lower-left corner of the screen, it is a good bet that the computer is running some version of Windows.

The graphical interface for Windows NT, 98, 2000, and Me (shown at right) features many similarities and some differences when compared to the interface for Windows XP (shown below)

When set for the classic menu style, the left side of the Start menu displays the version of the Windows OS that is in use.

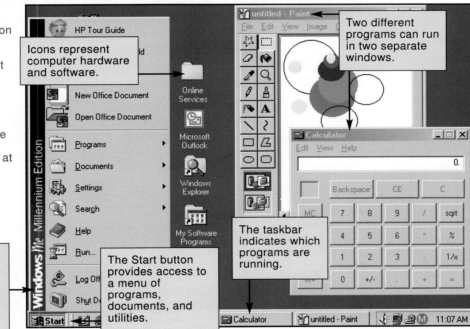

Icons represent computer hardware and software.

Two different programs can run in two separate windows.

The taskbar indicates which programs are running.

The Start button provides access to a menu of programs, documents, and utilities.

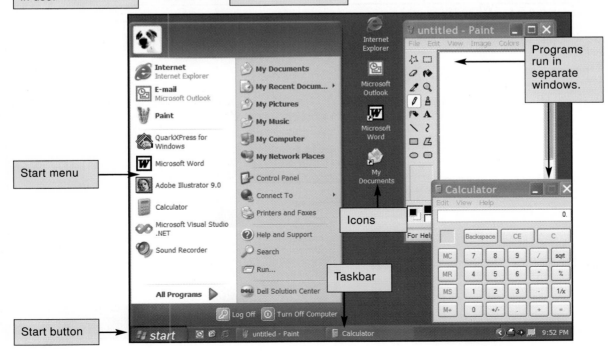

Programs run in separate windows.

Start menu

Icons

Taskbar

Start button

3

Windows 95, Windows 98, Windows Me, and Windows XP provide basic networking capabilities, making them suitable for small networks in homes and businesses. Despite this capability, they are classified as desktop operating systems, whereas Windows NT and Windows 2000 are typically classified as server operating systems because they're designed to handle the security and management demands of medium-size to large-size networks. Windows 95, Windows 98, and Windows Me use a different kernel than the NT, 2000, and XP versions of Windows, so even though their user interfaces appear similar, they are technically different and offer different upgrade paths.

Microsoft provides operating system upgrades that automate the process of changing from an older version of Windows to a newer version. These upgrades provide all of the features, but typically cost less than the "full" version. Currently, you can easily upgrade only within your Windows "track." For example, you can upgrade Windows 95 and 98 to Windows Me, but not to Windows NT or Windows 2000. You can also upgrade easily from Windows NT to Windows 2000, but not to Windows Me. Just be aware that once you install a Windows upgrade, it can be difficult to go back to the previous version if some of your software doesn't seem to work properly. Make sure that your hard disk is backed up before you upgrade.

Is Mac OS similar to Windows? Although **Mac OS** was developed several years before Windows, both operating systems base their user interfaces on the graphical model that was pioneered at Xerox PARC. Like Windows, Mac OS has been through a number of revisions, including OS X (X meaning version 10), which made its debut in 2001.

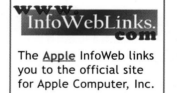

The Apple InfoWeb links you to the official site for Apple Computer, Inc.

click ▶❋

A quick comparison of Figure 3-13 and Figure 3-14 shows that both Mac and Windows interfaces use a mouse to point and click various icons and menus. Both interfaces feature rectangular work areas to reflect multitasking capabilities. Both operating systems provide basic networking services. A decent collection of software is available for computers that run Mac OS, though the selection is not as vast as the collection for Windows. Many of the most prolific software publishers produce one version of their software for Windows and another, similar version for Mac OS.

FIGURE 3-14

The Apple logo at the top of the screen is your clue that a computer is running Mac OS.

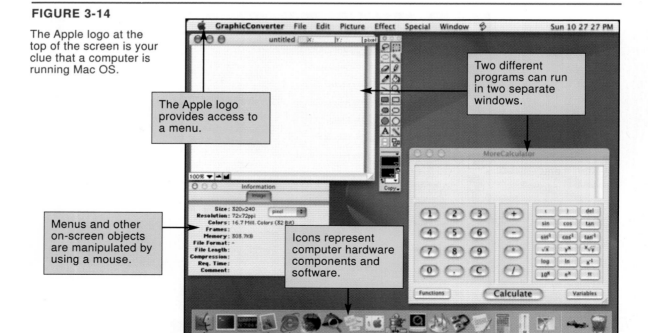

The Apple logo provides access to a menu.

Two different programs can run in two separate windows.

Menus and other on-screen objects are manipulated by using a mouse.

Icons represent computer hardware components and software.

COMPUTER SOFTWARE   **125**

Are UNIX and Linux the same? The **UNIX** operating system was developed in 1969 at AT&T's Bell Labs. It gained a good reputation for its dependability in multiuser environments, and many versions of it became available for mainframes and microcomputers. In 1991, a young Finnish student named Linus Torvalds developed the **Linux** (pronounced LIH nucks) operating system, based on a version of the UNIX kernel called Minix. Linux is rather unique because it is distributed along with its source code under the terms of a General Public License (GPL), which allows everyone to make copies for their own use, to give to others, or to sell. This licensing policy has encouraged programmers to develop Linux utilities, software, and enhancements. Linux is primarily distributed over the Web.

If you're interested in exploring the world of "open source" operating systems, start your journey at the Linux InfoWeb.

└click ◗ ▓

Although Linux is designed for microcomputers, it shares several technical features with UNIX, such as multitasking, virtual memory, TCP/IP drivers, and multiuser capabilities. These features make Linux a popular operating system for e-mail and Web servers, as well as for local area networks. Linux has been gaining popularity as a desktop operating system, and some new personal computers now come configured with Linux instead of Windows or Mac OS. Linux typically requires a bit more tinkering than the Windows and Mac desktop operating systems. The comparatively limited number of programs that run under Linux also discourages many nontechnical PC users from selecting it as the OS for their desktop and notebook computers.

Several Web sites offer a Linux "distribution," which is a package that contains the Linux kernel, system utilities, applications, and an installation routine. The most popular Linux distributions include Red Hat Linux, Caldera OpenLinux, and Debian GNU/Linux. Most of these distributions include a GUI module that provides a user interface similar to the one pictured in Figure 3-15.

FIGURE 3-15

Linux users can choose from several graphical interfaces. Pictured here is the popular KDE graphical desktop.

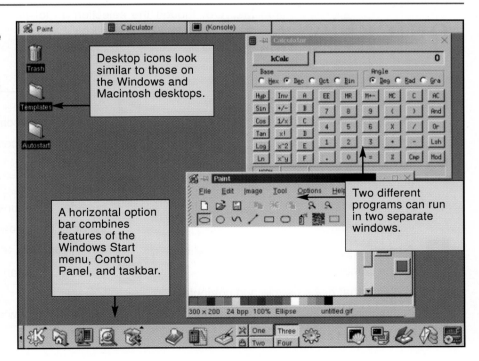

Desktop icons look similar to those on the Windows and Macintosh desktops.

Two different programs can run in two separate windows.

A horizontal option bar combines features of the Windows Start menu, Control Panel, and taskbar.

Why do I keep hearing about DOS? Old-timers in the computer industry sometimes reminisce about DOS. It was the first operating system that many of them used, and its cryptic command-line user interface left an indelible impression. **DOS** (which rhymes with "toss") stands for Disk Operating System. It was developed by Microsoft—the same company that later produced Windows—and introduced on the original IBM PC in 1982. Although IBM called this operating system PC-DOS, Microsoft marketed it to other companies under the name MS-DOS.

DOS is not all that bad, so if you want to find out more about it, connect to the **DOS** InfoWeb.

└click ◄▉

After more than 20 years, the remnants of DOS still linger in the world of personal computers because it provides part of the operating system kernel for Windows versions 3.1, 95, 98, and Me. Users rarely interact with DOS, however, because it is well hidden by the Windows graphical user interface.

During the peak of its popularity, thousands of software programs were produced for computers running DOS. You can occasionally find some of these programs on the Internet, and run them using the MS-DOS Prompt option (Windows 98, Me, NT, and 2000) or the Command Prompt option (Windows XP) on the Windows Start menu. DOS programs look rather unsophisticated by today's standards; so, for most of us, DOS and DOS software are nothing more than footnotes in the history of the computer industry.

QUICK Check B
Section

1 Every cycle of a computer's microprocessor is a(n) ⬚ for accomplishing tasks.

2 To run more than one program at a time, the operating system must allocate specific areas of ⬚ for each program.

3 A user ⬚ can be defined as the combination of hardware and software that helps people and computers communicate.

4 The core part of an operating system is called its ⬚ .

5 A(n) ⬚ operating system allows a single computer to deal with input, output, and processing requests from many users.

6 A(n) ⬚ operating system provides communications and routing services that allow computers to share data, programs, and peripheral devices.

7 Windows 2000 and Linux are classified as ⬚ operating systems, whereas Windows XP and Mac OS are classified as ⬚ operating systems.

check answers ◄▉

LAB 3-B
USING THE WINDOWS INTERFACE

In this lab, you'll learn:

■ Why the standard Windows controls make it easy to learn new Windows software

■ What happens when you use the mouse pointer to click, double-click, and right-click an object

■ How ToolTips or ScreenTips help you identify icons and toolbar buttons

■ How to use the Maximize, Minimize, Restore, and Close buttons

■ How to use scroll bars

■ How to navigate through a series of menus

■ Which menus are common to most Windows applications

■ The meaning of menu conventions, such as the ellipsis and triangle

■ How to use standard dialog box controls, such as option buttons, spin boxes, tabs, check boxes, and lists

■ How to use toolbar buttons

■ How to adjust toolbars

■ How to take a screenshot and print it

LAB Assignments

1 Start the interactive part of the lab. Insert your Tracking Disk if you want to save your QuickCheck results. Perform each of the lab steps as directed, and answer all of the lab QuickCheck questions. When you exit the lab, your answers are automatically graded and your results are displayed.

2 Draw a sketch or print a screenshot of the Windows desktop on any computer that you use. Use ToolTips (or ScreenTips) to identify all of the icons on the desktop and the taskbar.

3 Use the Start button and Accessories menu to start an application program called Paint. (If Paint is not installed on your computer, you can use any application software, such as a word processing program.) Draw a sketch or print a screenshot of the Paint (or other application) window and label the following components: window title, title bar, Maximize/Restore button, Minimize button, Close button, menu bar, toolbar, and scroll bar.

4 Look at each of the menu options provided by the Paint software (or other application). Make a list of those that seem to be standard Windows menu options.

5 Draw a sketch of Paint's Print dialog box (or other application's Print dialog box). Label the following parts: buttons, spin bar, pull-down list, option button, and check boxes.

Section **C**

APPLICATION SOFTWARE

Most computers include some basic word processing, e-mail, and Internet-access software, but computer owners invariably want additional software to increase their computers' repertory of productivity, business, learning, or entertainment activities. Section C provides an overview of the vast array of application software that's available for personal computers.

DOCUMENT PRODUCTION SOFTWARE

How can my computer help me with my writing? Whether you are writing a 10-page paper, writing software documentation, designing a brochure for your new startup company, or laying out the school newspaper, you will probably use some form of **document production software**. This software assists you with composing, editing, designing, printing, and electronically publishing documents. The three most popular types of document production software are word processing, desktop publishing, and Web authoring.

This InfoWeb is your guide to today's best-selling **Document Production Software**.

—click ▶❋—

Word processing software, such as Microsoft Word, has replaced type-writers for producing documents such as reports, letters, memos, papers, and manuscripts. Word processing software gives you the ability to create, spell-check, edit, and format a document on the screen before you commit it to paper.

Desktop publishing software (abbreviated DTP) takes word processing software one step further by helping you use graphic design techniques to enhance the format and appearance of a document. Although today's word processing software offers many page layout and design features, DTP software, such as QuarkXPress and Adobe PageMaker, provides sophisticated features to help you produce professional-quality output for newspapers, newsletters, brochures, magazines, and books.

Web authoring software helps you design and develop customized Web pages that you can publish electronically on the Internet. Only a few years ago, creating Web pages was a fairly technical task that required authors to insert special formatting HTML tags, such as <A HREF = "contents.htm">. Now, Web authoring software, such as Microsoft FrontPage and Macromedia Dreamweaver, helps nontechnical Web authors by providing easy-to-use tools for composing the text for a Web page, assembling graphical elements, and automatically generating HTML tags.

How does document production software help me turn my ideas into sentences and paragraphs? Document production software makes it easy to let your ideas flow because it automatically handles many tasks that might otherwise distract you. For example, you don't need to worry about fitting words within the margins. A feature called "word wrap" determines how your text will flow from line to line by automatically moving words down to the next line as you reach the right margin. Imagine that the sentences in your document are ribbons of text; word wrap bends the ribbons. Changing the margin size just means bending the ribbon in different places. Even after you type an entire document, adjusting the size of your right, left, top, and bottom margins is simple (see Figure 3-16 on the next page).

FIGURE 3-16

Document production software makes it easy to get your ideas down on your screen-based "paper." Start the video to see word wrap and the spelling checker in action.

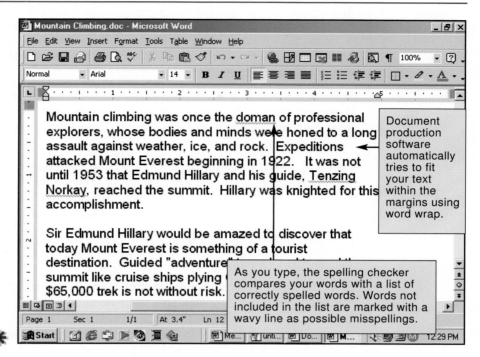

click to start ►

What if I'm a bad speller? Most document production software includes a **spelling checker** that marks misspelled words in a document. You can easily correct a misspelled word as you type, or you can run the spelling checker when you finish entering all of the text. Some software even has an autocorrecting capability that automatically changes a typo, such as "teh," to the correct spelling ("the").

Although your software's spelling checker helps you correct misspellings, it cannot guarantee an error-free document. A spelling checker works by comparing each word from your document to a list of correctly spelled words that is stored in a data module called a **spelling dictionary**. If the word from your document is in the dictionary, the spelling checker considers the word correctly spelled. If the word is not in the dictionary, the word is counted as misspelled. Sounds OK, right? But, suppose your document contains a reference to the city of "Negaunee." This word is not in the dictionary, so the spelling checker considers it misspelled, even though it is spelled correctly. Proper nouns and scientific, medical, and technical words are likely to be flagged as misspelled, even if you spell them correctly, because they do not appear in the spelling checker's dictionary. Now suppose that your document contains the phrase "a pear of shoes." Although you meant to use "pair" rather than "pear," the spelling checker will not catch your mistake because "pear" is a valid word in the dictionary. Your spelling checker won't help if you have trouble deciding whether to use "there" or "their," "its" or "it's," or "too" or "to." Remember, then, that a spelling checker cannot substitute for a thorough proofread.

Will document production software help improve my writing? Because word processing software tends to focus on the writing process, it offers several features that can improve the quality of your writing. These features may not be available in desktop publishing software or Web authoring software, which put more focus on the format, rather than the content, of a document.

Your word processing software is likely to include a **thesaurus**, which can help you find a synonym for a word so that you can make your writing more varied and interesting. A **grammar checker** "reads" through your document and points out potential grammatical trouble spots, such as incomplete sentences, run-on sentences, and verbs that don't agree with nouns.

Your word processing software might also be able to analyze the reading level of your document using a standard **readability formula**, such as the Flesch-Kincaid reading level. You can use this analysis to find out if your writing matches your target audience, based on sentence length and vocabulary.

Can document production software help me break bad writing habits? Most word processing, DTP, and Web authoring software includes a **Search and Replace** feature. You can use this feature to hunt down mistakes that you typically make in your writing. For example, you might know from experience that you tend to overuse the word "typically." You can use Search and Replace to find each occurrence of "typically," and then you can decide whether you should substitute a different word, such as "usually" or "ordinarily."

How do I get my documents to look good? The **format** for a document refers to the way that all of the elements of a document—text, pictures, titles, and page numbers—are arranged on the page. The final format of your document depends on how and where you intend to use it. A school paper, for example, simply needs to be printed in standard paragraph format—perhaps double spaced and with numbered pages. Your word processing software has all of the features you need for this formatting task. A brochure, newsletter, or corporate report, on the other hand, might require more ambitious formatting, such as columns that continue on noncontiguous pages and text labels that overlay graphics. You might consider transferring your document from your word processing software to your desktop publishing software for access to more sophisticated formatting tools. For documents that you plan to publish on the Web, Web authoring software usually provides the most useful set of formatting tools.

www.InfoWebLinks.com

You can add to your font collection by downloading font files from the **Font** InfoWeb.

└click ►▓ ─

The "look" of your final document depends on several formatting factors, such as font style, paragraph style, and page layout. A **font** is a set of letters that share a unified design. Font size is measured as **point size**, abbreviated pt. (one point is about 1/72 of an inch). Figure 3-17 illustrates several popular fonts that are included with document production software.

FIGURE 3-17

You can vary the font style by selecting character formatting attributes such as bold, italics, underline, superscript, and subscript. You can also select a color and size for a font. The font size for the text in a typical paragraph is set at 8, 10, or 12 pt. Titles can be as large as 72 pt.

Times New Roman Font	8 pt.
Times New Roman Font	10 pt.
Times New Roman Font	12 pt.
Times New Roman Font	16 pt.
Times New Roman Font	**16 pt. Bold**
Times New Roman Font	16 pt. Green
Arial Font	16 pt.
Comic Sans MS	16 pt.
Georgia Font	16 pt. Bold Gold
Serpentine Font 16 pt. Orange	

Paragraph style includes the alignment of text within the margins, and the space between each line of text. **Paragraph alignment** refers to the horizontal position of text—whether it is aligned at the left margin, aligned at the right margin, or fully justified so that the text is aligned evenly on both the right and left margins. Your document will look more formal if it is **fully justified**, like the text in this paragraph, rather than if it has an uneven or "ragged" right margin. **Line spacing** (also called **leading**, pronounced "LED ing") refers to the vertical spacing between lines. Documents are typically single spaced or double spaced, but word processing and DTP software allow you to adjust line spacing in 1 pt. increments.

Instead of individually selecting font and paragraph style elements, document production software typically allows you to define a **style** that lets you apply several font and paragraph elements with a single click. (See Figure 3-18.) For example, instead of applying bold to a title, changing its font to Times New Roman, and then adjusting the font size to 24 pt., you can simply define a Title style as 24 pt., Times New Roman, bold. You can then apply all three style elements at once simply by selecting the Title style.

FIGURE 3-18

By defining a style, you can apply multiple font attributes with a single click.

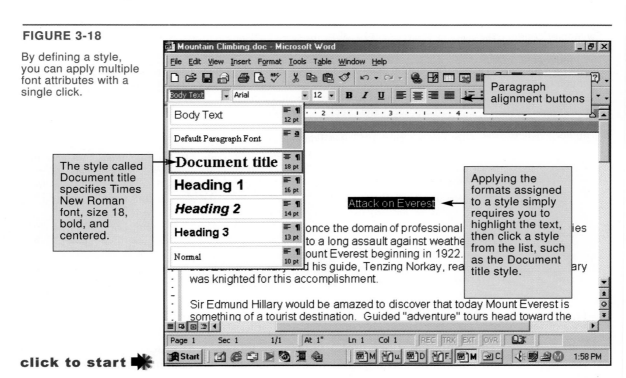

The style called Document title specifies Times New Roman font, size 18, bold, and centered.

Applying the formats assigned to a style simply requires you to highlight the text, then click a style from the list, such as the Document title style.

click to start ✳▶

Page layout refers to the physical position of each element on a page. In addition to paragraphs of text, these elements might include:

- **Headers and footers.** A **header** is text that you specify to automatically appear in the top margin of every page. A **footer** is text that you specify to automatically appear in the bottom margin of every page. You might put your name and the document title in the header or footer of a document so that its printed pages won't get mixed up with those of another printed document.

- **Page numbers.** Word processing and DTP software automatically number the pages of a document according to your specifications, usually placing the page number either within a header or footer. A Web page, no matter what its length, is all a single page, so page numbering is not typically provided by Web authoring software.

- **Graphical elements.** Photos, diagrams, graphs, and charts can be incorporated in your documents. **Clip art**—a collection of drawings and photos designed to be inserted in documents—is a popular source of graphical elements.

- **Tables.** A **table** is a grid-like structure that can hold text or pictures. For printed documents, tables are a popular way to provide easy-to-read columns of data, and to position graphics. It may sound surprising, but for Web pages, tables provide one of the few ways to precisely position text and pictures. As a result, Web page designers make extensive and very creative use of tables.

Most word processing is page-oriented, because it treats each page as a rectangle that can be filled with text and graphics. Text automatically flows from one page to the next. In contrast most DTP software is frame-oriented because it allows you to divide each page into several rectangular-shaped **frames** that you can fill with either text or graphics. Text flows from one frame to the next, rather than from page to page. (See Figure 3-19.)

FIGURE 3-19

Frames provide you with finer control over the position of elements on a page, such as a figure and a caption on top of it.

One frame holds the centered title and author's byline. This text is linked to the text in subsequent frames.

Wrapping text around a frame adds interest to the layout.

Text can link to frames on the next page, or any page of the document.

Attack on Everest
by Janell Chalmers

Mountain climbing was once the domain of professional explorers, whose bodies and minds were honed to a long assault against weather, ice, and rock. Expeditions attacked Mount Everest beginning in 1922. It was not until 1953 that Edmund Hillary and his guide, Tenzing Norkay, reached the summit. Hillary was knighted for this accomplishment.

Sir Edmund Hillary would be amazed to discover that today Mount Everest has become something of a tourist destination. Guided "adventure" tours head toward the

"Because it's there."
George Mallory

summit like cruise ships plying Caribbean ports. This $65,000 trek is not without risk. In 1996 a sudden storm killed eight climbers.

Back in 1923, British mountaineer, George Mallory was asked, why climb Everest? His reply, "Because it's there." A new answer to this question, "Because we can" may be largely attributable to new high Nyl Gor ligh fron Ultraviolet lenses protect eyes from dangerous "snow-blindness."

click to start ▶✳

Does document production software increase productivity? Word processing software, in particular, provides several features that automate tasks and allow you to work more productively. For example, suppose that you want to send prospective employers a letter and your resume. Rather than composing and addressing each letter individually, your software can perform a **mail merge** that automatically creates personalized letters by combining the information in a mailing list with a form letter. Some of the additional capabilities of word processing software include:

- Automatically generating a table of contents and index for a document

- Automatically numbering footnotes and positioning each footnote on the page where it is referenced

- Providing document templates and document wizards that show you the correct content and format for a variety of documents, such as business letters, fax cover sheets, and memos

- Exporting a document into HTML format

SPREADSHEET SOFTWARE

What is a spreadsheet? A **spreadsheet** uses rows and columns of numbers to create a model or representation of a real situation. For example, your checkbook register is a type of spreadsheet because it is a numerical representation of the cash flowing in and out of your bank account. Today, **spreadsheet software**, such as Microsoft Excel, provides tools to create electronic spreadsheets. It is similar to a "smart" piece of paper that automatically adds up the columns of numbers that you write on it. You can use it to make other calculations too, based on simple equations that you write or more complex, built-in formulas. As an added bonus, spreadsheet software helps you turn your data into a variety of colorful graphs and charts.

www.InfoWebLinks.com

For links to today's best-selling spreadsheet software, connect to the <u>Spreadsheet</u> InfoWeb.

►click ➡

Spreadsheet software was initially popular with accountants and financial managers who dealt with paper-based spreadsheets, but found the electronic version far easier to use and less prone to errors than manual calculations. Other people soon discovered the benefits of spreadsheets for projects that require repetitive calculations—budgeting, maintaining a grade book, balancing a checkbook, tracking investments, calculating loan payments, and estimating project costs. Because it is so easy to experiment with different numbers, spreadsheet software is particularly useful for **what-if analysis**. You can use what-if analyses to answer questions such as, "What if I get an A on my next two Economics exams? But what if I get only Bs?" "What if I invest $100 a month in my retirement plan? But what if I invest $200 a month?" "Is it better to take out a 30-year mortgage at 6.75% interest or a 15-year mortgage at 6.25% interest?"

What does a computerized spreadsheet look like? You use spreadsheet software to create an on-screen **worksheet**. A worksheet is based on a grid of columns and rows. Each **cell** in the grid can contain a value, label, or formula. A **value** is a number that you want to use in a calculation. A **label** is any text used to describe data. For example, suppose that your worksheet contains the value $486,000. You could use a label to identify this number as "Income." (See Figure 3-20.)

3

FIGURE 3-20

In a worksheet, each column is lettered and each row is numbered. The intersection of a column and row is called a cell. Each cell has a unique cell reference, or "address," derived from its column and row location. For example, A1 is the cell reference for the upper-left cell in a worksheet because it is in column A and row 1. You can select any cell and make it the active cell by clicking it. Once a cell is active, you can enter data into it.

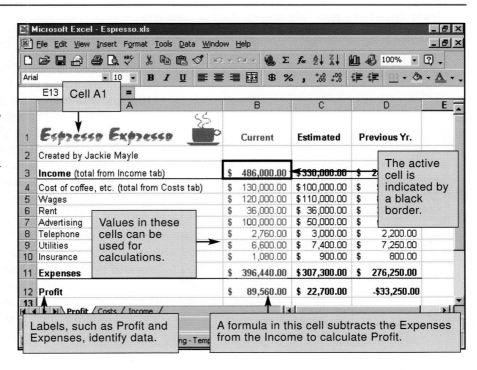

Cell A1

The active cell is indicated by a black border.

Values in these cells can be used for calculations.

Labels, such as Profit and Expenses, identify data.

A formula in this cell subtracts the Expenses from the Income to calculate Profit.

You can format the labels and values on a worksheet in much the same way as you would format text in a word processing document. You can change fonts and font size, select a font color, and select font styles, such as bold, italics, and underlines.

How does spreadsheet software work? The values contained in a cell can be manipulated by formulas that are placed in other cells. A **formula** works behind the scenes to tell the computer how to use the contents of cells in calculations. You can enter a simple formula in a cell to add, subtract, multiply, or divide numbers. More complex formulas can be designed to perform just about any calculation you can imagine. Figure 3-21 illustrates how a formula might be used in a simple spreadsheet to calculate savings.

FIGURE 3-21

When a cell contains a formula, it displays the *result* of the formula, rather than the formula itself. To view and edit the formula, you use the Formula bar.

You can think of the formula as working "behind the scenes" to perform calculations and then display the result.

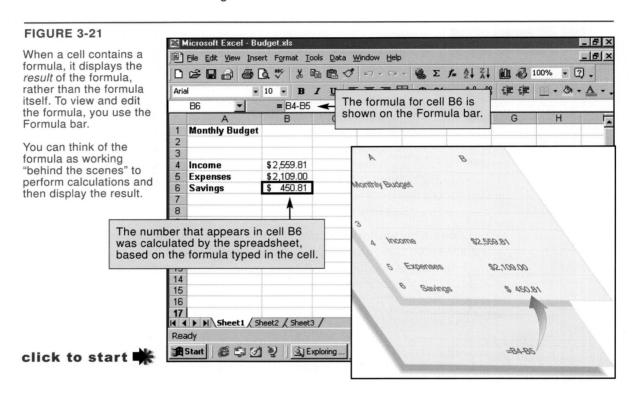

click to start ➡✳

The formula for cell B6 is shown on the Formula bar.

The number that appears in cell B6 was calculated by the spreadsheet, based on the formula typed in the cell.

FIGURE 3-22

Functions are special formulas provided by spreadsheet software.

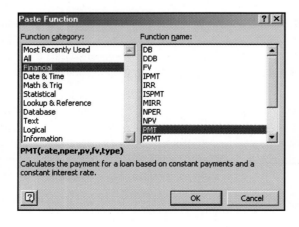

A formula, such as =D4-D5+((D8/B2)*110), can contain **cell references** (like D4 and D5), numbers (like 110), and **mathematical operators**, such as the multiplication symbol (*), the division symbol (/), the addition symbol, and the subtraction symbol. Parts of a formula can be enclosed in parentheses to indicate the order in which the mathematical operations should be performed. The operation in the innermost set of parentheses—in this case, (D8/B2)—should be performed first.

You can enter a formula "from scratch" by typing it into a cell, or you can use a built-in **function** provided by the spreadsheet software. To use a function, you simply select one from a list, as shown in Figure 3-22, and then indicate the cell references of any values that you want to include in the calculation.

What happens when I modify a worksheet? When you change the contents of any cell in a worksheet, all of the formulas are recalculated. This **automatic recalculation** feature assures you that the results in every cell are accurate with regard to the information currently entered in the worksheet.

Your worksheet is also automatically updated to reflect any rows or columns that you add, delete, or copy within the worksheet. Unless you specify otherwise, a cell reference is a **relative reference**—that is, a reference that can change from B4 to B3, for example, if row 3 is deleted and all the data moves up one row. See Figure 3-23.

If you don't want a cell reference to change, you can use an absolute reference. An **absolute reference** never changes when you insert rows or copy or move formulas. Understanding when to use absolute references is one of the key aspects to developing spreadsheet design expertise. Figure 3-23 and its associated tour provide additional information about relative and absolute references.

FIGURE 3-23

As shown in the examples, relative references within a formula can change when you change the sequence of a worksheet's rows and columns.

An absolute reference is "anchored" so that it always refers to a specific cell.

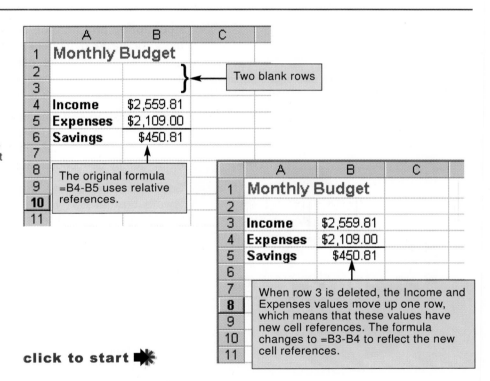

3

click to start ➡✳

How will I know which formulas and functions to use when I create a worksheet? In order to create an effective and accurate worksheet, you typically must understand the calculations and formulas that are involved. If, for example, you want to create a worksheet that will help you calculate your final grade in a course, you need to know the grading scale, and understand how your instructor plans to weight each assignment and test.

Most spreadsheet software includes a few templates or wizards for predesigned worksheets, such as invoices, income-expense reports, balance sheets, and loan payment schedules. Additional templates are available on the Web. These templates are typically designed by professionals and contain all of the necessary labels and formulas. To use a template, you simply plug in the values for your calculation.

ACCOUNTING AND FINANCE, MATHEMATICAL MODELING, AND STATISTICAL SOFTWARE

Aside from spreadsheets, what other "number crunching" software is available? Spreadsheet software provides a sort of "blank canvas" on which you can create numeric models by simply "painting" values, labels, and formulas. The advantage of spreadsheet software is the flexibility that it provides—flexibility to create customized calculations according to your exact specifications. The disadvantage of spreadsheet software is that—aside from a few predesigned templates—you are responsible for entering formulas and selecting functions for calculations. If you don't know the formulas, or don't understand the functions, you're out of luck.

In contrast to the "blank canvas" approach provided by spreadsheet software, other "number crunching" software works more like "paint by numbers." It provides a structured environment dedicated to a particular number crunching task, such as money management, mathematical modeling, or statistical analysis.

FIGURE 3-24

Personal finance software helps you keep track of bank accounts, investments, credit card balances, and bills. Some packages also support online banking—a way to use your computer and modem to download transactions directly from your bank, transfer funds between accounts, and pay bills.

Accounting and finance software offers a variety of tools for tracking monetary transactions and investments. In this software category, **personal finance software**, such as Microsoft Money and Intuit Quicken, is geared toward individual finances (Figure 3-24).

Tax preparation software, such as Intuit TurboTax, is a specialized type of personal finance software designed to help you gather your annual income and expense data, identify deductions, and calculate tax payments.

Some accounting and finance software is geared toward business. If you're an entrepreneur—even if you have a part-time business while you're in college—**small business accounting software** can be a real asset. Easy-to-use programs, such as Intuit QuickBooks, don't require more than a basic understanding of accounting and finance principles. This type of software helps you invoice customers and keep track of what they owe. It stores additional customer data, such as contact information and purchasing history. Inventory functions keep track of the products that you carry. Payroll capabilities automatically calculate wages and deduct federal, state, and local taxes.

Statistical software, such as SPSS and Statsoft STATISTICA, helps you analyze large sets of data to discover relationships and patterns. It is a helpful tool for summarizing survey results, test scores, experiment results, or population data. Most statistical software includes graphing capability so that you can display and explore your data visually.

Mathematical modeling software, such as Mathcad and Mathematica, provides tools for solving a wide range of math, science, and engineering problems. Students, teachers, mathematicians, and engineers, in particular, appreciate how this software helps them recognize patterns that can be difficult to identify in columns of numbers.

For more information about popular "number crunching" software, check out the <u>Numeric Software</u> InfoWeb.

click

DATA MANAGEMENT SOFTWARE

What is data management software? **Data management software** helps you to store, find, organize, update, and report information. Some data management software is tailored to special applications. A **personal information manager**, for example, is a specialized data management application that keeps track of daily appointments, addresses, and To Do lists. Other data management software allows you to work with any type of data you like. Two main types of data management software exist: file management software and database management software.

What's the difference between file management software and database management software? To better understand the difference between file and database management software, you'll need a little background on flat files and databases.

Within the context of computing, a file can contain many different types of data, arranged in a variety of ways. You are familiar with files that contain word processing documents. The data in these documents is typically arranged in a free-form manner. For example, a document about African-American literature might contain a reference to Alex Haley' s novel, *Roots*, but this reference would be embedded within a paragraph and could be difficult to find.

In contrast to free-form files, structured files contain data that is organized in much the same way as an old-fashioned library card file. A **structured file** is a collection of records, which are composed of fields that can hold data. A **record** holds data for a single entity—a person, place, thing, or event. A **field** holds one item of data relevant to a record. Figure 3-25 illustrates records and fields in a structured file.

3

FIGURE 3-25

In a file of library books, data for each book is stored as a record in the file. The record for each book contains a standard set of fields, filled with data that pertains to the book.

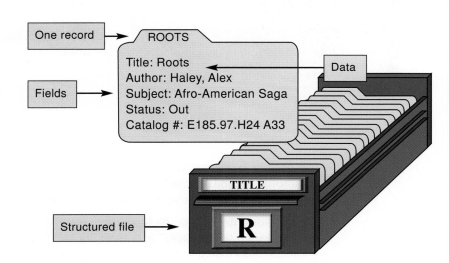

A structured file in which all of the records conform to the same set of fields is called a **flat file**. Flat files can be a useful repository for simple lists of information, such as e-mail addresses, holiday card addresses, doctor visits, appointments, or household valuables. **File management software** is designed to help you create, modify, search, sort, and print the data in flat files.

It might seem odd, but spreadsheet software provides quite an adequate set of file management tools. It includes special data handling features that allow you to enter data, sort data, search for data that meets specific criteria, and print reports. As a rule of thumb, spreadsheet software can handle any data that you could put on a set of index cards or in a Rolodex.

Although the term **database** can be used to refer to a flat file, it also encompasses a collection of data in which records may have different fields. For example, MTV might maintain a database of information pertaining to musicians and rock videos. One series of records might contain biographical data about the musicians, including name, birth date, and home town. The other series of records might contain data about the videos, including title, artist, and release date. A database allows you to store these diverse records in a single file and establish relationships between them. In the MTV database, for example, it would be possible to establish relationships between biographical data about the musicians and data about their videos, as shown in Figure 3-26.

FIGURE 3-26

A database allows you to work with different types of records and establish relationships between them.

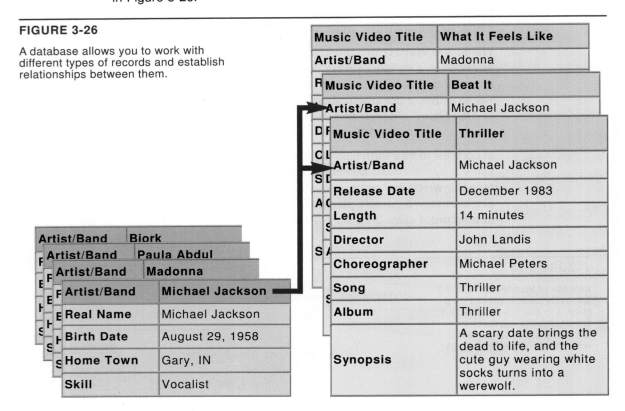

Most of today's databases are based on a relational model or an object-oriented model. A **relational database** structures records into tables in which each column is a field, and each row is a record. Relationships can be established between tables.

An **object-oriented database** treats each record as an object, which can be manipulated using program instructions called methods. For example, a university database containing information about its students might include an object called "Course Grades" and a method called "Calculate GPA."

For more information about file and database management software, connect to the Data Management Software InfoWeb.

Database management software (DBMS) is designed for creating and manipulating the records that form a database. It is an important tool for business, government, and educational institutions. Individuals, who have much less data to manipulate, tend to use file management software, rather than DBMS. Most of today's database management software, such as Microsoft Access, is designed for creating and manipulating relational databases. Object-oriented database management software is required for creating and manipulating object-oriented databases.

How do I use data management software? Whether you are using file management software or database management software, you must have a file of data to work with—such as a collection of information about jazz recordings. You might obtain a file with the data you need from a reference CD or from a Web site. More typically, you would create your own file by first defining the record structure, then entering the data. A **record structure** defines a list of fields and their data types. Simple tools like the form in Figure 3-27 help you to define the record structure for a database.

FIGURE 3-27

Your data management software provides the tools that you need to create the record structure for your data.

The *Jazz Recordings* file, shown at right, contains fields for Song Title, Performing Artist, Composer, Date, Record Label, and Length.

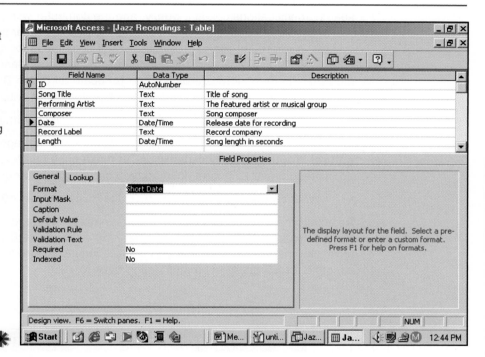

3

click to start ►►

When you define a field, you can specify its data type as either character, numeric, date, logical, hyperlink, or memo. For example, if you're creating a file to hold personal data about your friends, you might define the Name field as character data, the Birthday field as date data, and the E-mail Address field as hyperlink data. Different data types are treated in different ways. For example, numeric data can be used in calculations, whereas character data cannot. The table in Figure 3-28 provides more information about how you might use data types.

FIGURE 3-28	**Using Data Types**	
Data Type	**Uses**	**Examples**
Character	Use for fields that contain text-based data and will not be used for calculations	Names, addresses, social security numbers, phone numbers, products
Numeric	Use for fields that contain numeric data that might be used in calculations	Price, quantity, tax rate, test scores, miles per gallon
Date	Use for fields that contain dates	Birth date, date hired, current year
Logical	Use for fields that can have one of two values	True/false, yes/no, 0/1
Hyperlink	Use for fields that contain a URL that you would like to link to by clicking the field	www.cnn.com, www.excite.com
Memo	Use for fields that contain long sections of text	Descriptions, evaluations, diagnoses, notes
Currency	Use for fields that contain monetary amounts	Hourly wage, price, rental fee

After I design the record structure, what next? Once you create a record structure, you can enter the data for each of your records. With the data in place, you can modify the data in individual records to keep it up to date. You can also sort the records in a variety of ways, using any field as the **sort key**—that is, the field that is used to alphabetize or otherwise sort the records.

How do I locate specific data? Many flat files and databases contain hundreds or thousands of records. If you want to find a particular record or a group of records, scrolling through every record is much too cumbersome. Instead, you can enter search specifications called a **query**, and the computer will quickly locate the records you seek. Most data management software provides one or more methods for making queries. A **query language** provides a set of commands for locating and manipulating data. **SQL** (Structured Query Language) is a popular query language used by numerous data management software packages. To locate all of the Duke Ellington recordings made after 1958 from a *Jazz Recordings* file, you might enter an SQL query such as:

Select * from JazzRecordings where Artist = 'Ellington' and Date => '1958'

In addition to a formal query language, some data management software provides **natural language query** capabilities. To make such queries, you don't have to learn an esoteric query language. Instead, you can simply enter questions, such as:

What recordings were made by Duke Ellington from 1958 to the present?

As an alternative to a query language or a natural language query, your data management software might allow you to **query by example** (QBE), simply by filling out a form with the type of data that you want to locate. Figure 3-29 illustrates a query by example for Ellington recordings dating back to 1958.

FIGURE 3-29

When you query by example, your data management software displays a blank form on the screen, and you enter examples of the data that you want to find.

As you might guess from this example, QBE requires you to learn a few "tricks." The asterisk is used as a "wild card" so that the software will locate recordings made by anyone with a last name of Ellington: Duke Ellington, D. Ellington, and so on. The dash following 1958 means include any subsequent dates.

How can I use search results? Your data management software will typically help you print reports, export data to other programs (such as to a spreadsheet where you can graph the data), convert the data to other formats (such as HTML so that you can post the data on the Web), and transmit data to other computers.

Whether you print, import, copy, save, or transmit the data you find in databases, it is your responsibility to use it appropriately. Never introduce inaccurate information into a database. Respect copyrights, giving credit to the person or organization that compiled the data. You should also respect the privacy of the people who are the subject of the data. Unless you have permission to do so, do not divulge names, social security numbers, or other identifying information that may compromise someone's privacy.

GRAPHICS SOFTWARE

What kind of software do I need to work with drawings, photos, and other pictures? In computer lingo, the term **graphics** refers to any picture, drawing, sketch, photograph, image, or icon that appears on your computer screen. **Graphics software** is designed to help you create, display, modify, manipulate, and print graphics. Some graphics software packages specialize in a particular type of graphic, while others allow you to work with multiple graphics formats. If you are really interested in working with graphics, you will undoubtedly end up using more than one graphics software package.

Paint software (sometimes called "image editing software") provides a set of electronic pens, brushes, and paints for painting images on the screen. Graphic artists, Web page designers, and illustrators use paint software as their primary computer-based graphics tool.

Photo editing software includes features specially designed to fix poor-quality photos by modifying contrast and brightness, cropping out unwanted objects, and removing "red eye." Photos can also be edited using paint software, but photo editing software typically provides tools and wizards that simplify common photo editing tasks.

Drawing software provides a set of lines, shapes, and colors that can be assembled into diagrams, corporate logos, and schematics. The drawings created with this type of software tend to have a "flat" cartoon-like quality, but they are very easy to modify, and look good at just about any size. Figure 3-30 provides more information on paint, photo editing, and drawing software.

FIGURE 3-30

Paint software works well with realistic art and photos.

Photo editing software includes special features for touching up photographs.

Drawing software tends to create two-dimensional "cartoon-like" images.

3-D graphics software provides a set of tools for creating "wireframes" that represent three-dimensional objects. A wireframe acts much like the framework for a pop-up tent. Just as you would construct the framework for the tent, then cover it with a nylon tent cover, 3-D graphics software can cover a wireframe object with surface texture and color to create a graphic of a 3-D object. (See Figure 3-31).

FIGURE 3-31

3-D graphics software provides tools for creating a wireframe that represents a three-dimensional object.

Some 3-D software specializes in engineering-style graphics, while other 3-D software specializes in figures.

For links to information about specific graphics software packages, visit the Graphics Software InfoWeb.

click ➡✴

CAD software (computer-aided design software) is a special type of 3-D graphics software designed for architects and engineers who use computers to create blueprints and product specifications. Scaled-down versions of professional CAD software provide simplified tools for home-owners who want to redesign their kitchens, examine new landscaping options, or experiment with floor plans.

Presentation software provides the tools you need for combining text, photos, clip-art, graphs, animations, and sound into a series of electronic **slides**. You can display the electronic slides on a color monitor for a one-on-one presentation, or use a computer projection device, like the one shown in Figure 3-32, for group presentations. You can also output the presentation as overhead transparencies, paper copies, or 35 mm slides.

FIGURE 3-32

A computer-based presentation consists of a series of slides, created with presentation software. A presentation can be displayed for a group by using a projection device like the one pictured.

Clip-art

1st and 2nd Quarter Sales

- The Northern region continues to lead in overall sales

Bulleted list

- Eastern sales grew significantly in the 2nd quarter

East
West
North

1st Qtr   2nd Qtr

Graph

click to start ➡✴

MUSIC SOFTWARE

Why would I need music software? You don't have to be a musician or composer to have a use for music software. Many types of music software are available. You might be surprised to find how many of them come in handy.

It is possible—and easy—to make your own digital voice and music recordings, which you store on your computer's hard disk. Windows and Mac OS operating system utilities typically supply the necessary **audio editing software**—Sound Recorder on PCs (Figure 3-33), and iTunes on Macs.

FIGURE 3-33

Audio editing software, such as Sound Recorder, provides controls much like those on a tape recorder. Menus provide additional digital editing features, such as speed control, volume adjustments, clipping, and mixing.

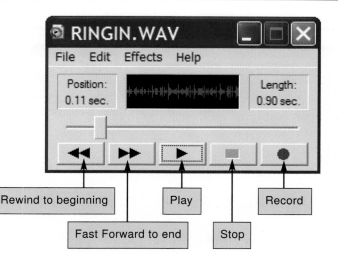

Rewind to beginning

Play

Record

Fast Forward to end

Stop

Audio editing software typically includes playback as well as recording capabilities. A specialized version of this software called Karaoke software integrates music files and on-screen lyrics—everything you need to sing along with your favorite tunes.

MP3 is a music compression file format that stores digitized music in such a way that the sound quality is excellent, but the file size remains relatively small—small enough to be easily downloaded from the Web. To listen to MP3 music on your computer, you need an **MP3 player**. Versions of MP3 player software are available for many handheld computers, and for personal computers running Windows, Mac OS, and Linux. With two additional types of MP3 software (sometimes combined into a single package), you can convert the tracks from standard audio CDs into MP3 format. To do so, you first use software called a **CD ripper** to pull the track off of the CD and store it in "raw" digital format on your computer's hard disk. Next, you use **MP3 encoding software** to convert the file into MP3 format. Once the file is in MP3 format, you can listen to it on your computer, or you can transfer it to a portable MP3 player.

At the **Music Software** InfoWeb, you'll find detailed information on popular software in this category.

─click ➧ ─

Ear training software targets musicians and music students who want to learn to play by ear, develop tuning skills, recognize notes and keys, and develop other musical skills. **Notation software** is the musician's equivalent of a word processor. It helps musicians compose, edit, and print the notes for their compositions. For non-musicians, **computer-aided music software** is designed to generate unique musical compositions simply by selecting the musical style, instruments, key, and tempo. **MIDI sequencing software** and software synthesizers are an important part of the studio musician's toolbox. They're great for sound effects, and for controlling keyboards and other digital instruments.

VIDEO EDITING SOFTWARE

Learn more about Apple
iMovie and Adobe
Premiere at the Video
Editing Software
InfoWeb.

click ◢

Is video editing software difficult to use? The growing popularity of computer-based video editing can be attributed to video editing software, such as Windows Movie Maker and Apple iMovie, now included with Windows computers and Macs. **Video editing software** provides a set of tools for transferring video footage from a camcorder to a computer, clipping out unwanted footage, assembling video segments in any sequence, adding special visual effects, and adding a sound track. Despite an impressive array of features, video editing software is relatively easy to use, as explained in Figure 3-34.

FIGURE 3-34

Video editing software, such as Adobe Premiere, helps you import a series of video clips from a camera or VCR, arrange the clips in the order of your choice, add transitions between clips, and add an audio track.

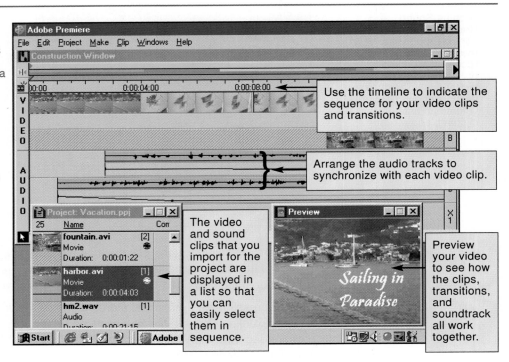

Use the timeline to indicate the sequence for your video clips and transitions.

Arrange the audio tracks to synchronize with each video clip.

The video and sound clips that you import for the project are displayed in a list so that you can easily select them in sequence.

Preview your video to see how the clips, transitions, and soundtrack all work together.

EDUCATIONAL AND REFERENCE SOFTWARE

How can I use my computer to learn new things? **Educational software** helps you learn and practice new skills. For the youngest students, educational software, such as MindTwister Math and 3-D Froggy Phonics, teaches basic arithmetic and reading skills. Instruction is presented in game format, and the levels of play are adapted to the player's age and ability.

What can you learn on
your computer? Check
out the Educational and
Reference Software
InfoWeb.

click ◢

For older students and adults, software is available for such diverse educational endeavors as learning languages, training yourself to use new software, learning how to play the piano or guitar, preparing for standardized tests, improving keyboarding skills, and even learning managerial skills for a diverse workplace. Exam preparation software is available for standardized tests such as the SAT, GMAT, and LSAT. Although little research is available on the effectiveness of this software, experts believe that the results should be similar to those of in-person coaching courses that improve composite SAT scores by about 100 points.

What's reference software? Reference software provides you with a collection of information and a way to access that information. This type of software includes massive amounts of data—unlike data management software, which is shipped without any data. The reference software category spans a wide range of applications—from encyclopedias to medical references, from map software to trip planners, and from cookbooks to telephone books. The options are as broad as the full range of human interests.

Reference software is generally shipped on a CD-ROM because of the quantity of data it includes. Many of these products provide links to Web sites that contain updates for the information on the CD-ROM. Other software publishers have eliminated the CD-ROM entirely and have placed all of their reference materials on the Web. Access to that information often requires a fee or a subscription.

The most popular software packages in this category—encyclopedias—contain text, graphics, audio, and video on a full range of topics from apples to zenophobia. Best-sellers include Microsoft's Encarta, Grolier's encyclopedia, Compton's encyclopedia, IBM's World Book encyclopedia, and Britannica's CD. All of these titles contain the standard information you would expect in an encyclopedia, such as articles written by experts on various topics, maps, photographs, and timelines. An encyclopedia on CD-ROM or the Web has several advantages over its printed counterpart. Finding information is easier, for example. Also, electronic formats take up less space on your bookshelf, and include interesting video and audio clips. A single CD is cheaper to produce than a shelf full of hard-bound printed books. These lower production costs translate to more affordable products, and allow an average person to own a comprehensive encyclopedia.

ENTERTAINMENT SOFTWARE

What's the best-selling entertainment software? Although some people might get a kick out of watching an animated screen saver, computer games are the most popular type of entertainment software. Over $6 billion of computer and video games, like those in Figure 3-35, are sold each year in the U.S. alone. Contrary to popular belief, teenage boys are not the only computer game enthusiasts. According to the Interactive Digital Software Association, 90 percent of all computer games are purchased by people 18 and older. Thirteen percent of gamers are over 50, and about 43 percent are women.

FIGURE 3-35

Computer games provide many different challenges. Some require fast reflexes, while others require careful planning and good problem-solving ability.

Computer games are generally classified into subcategories, such as role-playing, action, adventure, puzzles, simulations, and strategy/war games. **Role-playing games** are based on a detailed story line—often one that takes place in a medieval world populated with dastardly villains and evil monsters. The goal is to build a character into a powerful entity that can conquer the bad guys and accumulate treasure.

The Entertainment Software InfoWeb is your link to the best game sites on the Internet.

click ❋

Some of the most popular role-playing games include Diablo, EverQuest, Icewind Dale, and Planescape.

Action games, like arcade games, require fast reflexes as you maneuver a character through a maze or dungeon. Popular action games include Quake, Unreal Tournament, Half-life, Doom, and Tomb Raider.

Adventure games are similar to role-playing games except that the focus is on solving problems, rather than building a character into a powerful wizard or fighter. Popular games in this category include Myst, The Longest Journey, and Return to Monkey Island.

Puzzle games include computerized versions of traditional board games, such as Monopoly or cards, and Rubick's cube-like challenges, such as the classic Tetrus, and the wildly popular Lemmings.

Simulation games provide a realistic setting, such as the cockpit of an airplane. A player must learn to manipulate controls using the keyboard, a joystick, or a special-purpose input device. These games are great for people who want to learn to fly an airplane or drive a race car without the associated expenses or risks.

Sports games place participants in the midst of action-packed sports events, such as a football game, baseball game, hockey final, soccer match, or golf tournament. Most sports games offer arcade-like action and require quick reflexes.

Who rates software and how do they do it? Find out at the Software Ratings InfoWeb.

click ❋

Strategy games, such as Age of Empires and the Sims, have their roots in chess. Players (one player might be the computer) take turns moving characters, armies, and other resources in a quest to capture territory.

Are computer games rated like movies and music? Since it was established in 1994, the Entertainment Software Rating Board (ESRB) has rated more than 7,000 video and computer games. Rating symbols, shown in Figure 3-36, can usually be found in the lower-right corner of the game box. In past years, about 70 percent of the top 20 computer games received an "Everyone" rating. About 20 percent received a "Teen" rating, and about 10 percent received a "Mature" rating.

FIGURE 3-36	ESRB Software Ratings and Symbols		
	**TEEN** Suitable for 13 and older. May contain violent content, mild or strong language, and/or suggestive themes.		**MATURE** Suitable for 17 and older. May contain mature sexual themes or more intense violence or language.
	EARLY CHILDHOOD Suitable for ages 3 and older. Contains no material that parents would find inappropriate.		**EVERYONE** Suitable for ages 6 and older. May contains minimal violence, some comic mischief, or crude language.
	ADULTS ONLY Content suitable only for adults. May include graphic depictions of sex and/or violence.		**RATING PENDING** Product has been submitted, but a rating has not yet been assigned.

BUSINESS SOFTWARE

Do businesses use specialized software? The term "business software" provides a broad umbrella for several types of software, which are designed to help businesses and organizations accomplish routine or specialized tasks. **Vertical market software** is designed to automate specialized tasks in a specific market or business. Examples include patient management and billing software that is specially designed for hospitals, job estimating software for construction businesses, and student record management software for schools. Today, almost every business has access to some type of specialized vertical market software designed to automate, streamline, or computerize key business activities.

Horizontal market software is generic software that can be used by just about any kind of business. **Payroll software** is a good example of horizontal market software. Almost every business has employees and must maintain payroll records. No matter what type of business uses it, payroll software must collect similar data and make similar calculations in order to produce payroll checks and W-2 forms. Accounting software and project management software are additional examples of horizontal market software. **Accounting software** helps a business keep track of the money flowing in and out of various accounts. **Project management software** is an important tool for planning large projects, scheduling project tasks, and tracking project costs.

"Groupware" is another umbrella term in the world of business software. **Groupware** is designed to help several people collaborate on a single project using network or Internet connections. It usually provides the capability to: maintain schedules for all of the group members, automatically select meeting times for the group, facilitate communication by e-mail or other channels, distribute documents according to a prearranged schedule or sequence, and allow multiple people to contribute to a single document.

3

QUICK Check Section C

1 Various kinds of document _____ software provide tools for creating and formatting printed and Web-based documents.

2 _____ software provides a sort of "blank canvas" on which you can create numeric models by simply "painting" values, labels, and formulas.

3 _____ management software is useful for working with flat files, whereas _____ management software works well if you want to establish relationships between different types of records.

4 _____ software helps you work with wireframes, CAD drawings, photos, and slide presentations.

5 Audio editing software allows you to make _____ voice and music recordings, which you store on your computer's hard disk.

6 _____ market software is designed to automate specialized tasks in a specific market or business.

check answers

Section D

SOFTWARE INSTALLATION AND COPYRIGHTS

Software is sold in some surprising places. You might find graphics software at your local art supply store. Your favorite beauty salon might carry *Cosmopolitan's* makeup and hairstyle makeover software. You might even find homeopathic medicine software on sale at a health food store. Of course, software is also available from traditional sources, including office stores, computer superstores, electronics superstores, and discount stores, as well as local computer stores. You can buy software from mail-order catalogs, the software publisher's Web site, and software download sites.

However you obtain a new software package, you must install it on your computer before you can use it. That is the first topic in Section D. From time to time, you might want to eliminate some of the software that exists on your computer. The procedure for uninstalling software is the second topic in this section. The section ends with a discussion of software copyrights—important information that will help you understand the difference between legal and illegal software copying.

INSTALLATION BASICS

What's included in a typical software package? The key "ingredients" necessary to install new software are the files that contain the programs and data. These files might be supplied on **distribution disks**—one or more CDs or a series of floppy disks—that are packaged in a box, along with an instruction manual. Software downloaded over the Internet typically arrives as one huge file that contains the program modules and the text of the instruction manual.

How do I know if a software program will work on my computer? Tucked away at the software publisher's Web site or printed on the software package (as shown in Figure 3-37), you'll find **system requirements**, which specify the operating system and minimum hardware capacities necessary for a software product to work correctly.

FIGURE 3-37

System requirements typically can be found on the software box, or posted on the software download site.

System Requirements:
- Operating Systems: Windows® 95/98/2000, Me & NT® 4.0
- Processor: Pentium class computer
- Memory: 16 MB or more
- Hard Drive Space: 10 MB free
- Network Protocol: TCP/IP
- Network Connection: 10/100 Ethernet LAN/WAN, cable modem, DSL router, ISDN router, or dial-up modem

BLACKICE™ Defender 2.1
©2000 Network ICE Corporation. All rights reserved.
©2000 Macmillan USA, Inc. and its licensors. All rights reserved. Network ICE and BlackICE Defender are trademarks of Network ICE. All other companies and products listed herein are trademarks or registered trademarks of their respective holders.

Distributed by:
Macmillan USA, Inc.
201 West 103rd Street
Indianapolis, IN 46290

www.networkice.com   www.macmillansoftware.com

COMPUTER SOFTWARE   **149**

Why is it necessary to install most software? When you **install** software, the new software files are placed in the appropriate folders on your computer's hard disk, and then your computer performs any software or hardware configurations that are necessary to make sure that the program is ready to run. During the installation process your computer usually performs the following activities:

- Copies files from distribution disks or CDs to specified folders on the hard disk

- Uncompresses files if they have been distributed in a compressed format

- Analyzes the computer's resources, such as processor speed, RAM capacity, and hard disk capacity, to verify that they meet or exceed the minimum system requirements

- Analyzes hardware components and peripheral devices to select appropriate device drivers

- Looks for any system files and players, such as Internet Explorer or Windows Media Player, which are required to run the program, but not supplied on the distribution disk

- Updates necessary system files, such as the Windows Registry and the Windows Program menu, with information about the new software

Are all of the files for the software provided on the distribution disks? With Windows and other operating systems, application software programs share some common files. These files are often supplied by the operating system and perform routine tasks, such as displaying the Print dialog box, which allows you to select a printer and specify how many copies of a file you want to print. These "shared" files are not typically provided on the distribution disks for a new software program because the files should already exist on your computer. The installation routine attempts to locate these files, and will notify you if any of them are missing.

Are all of the files for the new software installed in the same folder? The main executable files and data files for the software are placed in the folder that you specify. Some support programs for the software, however, might be stored in other folders, such as Windows/System. The location for these files is determined by the software installation routine. Figure 3-38 maps out the location of files for a typical Windows software installation.

3

FIGURE 3-38

When you install software, its files might end up in different folders.

Distribution CD

Windows/System

Filename	Size	Type
Vidmdbg.dll	20 KB	Support Program
Vidodec32.dll	92 KB	Support Program
Vidwave.dll	37 KB	Support Program
Version.dll	24 KB	Support Program
Vidpodbc.dll	955 KB	Support Program
Vidgain.dll	116 KB	Support Program
Vgateway.ocx	42 KB	Support Program

Programs/VidEdit

Filename	Size	Type
Videdit.exe	5,500 KB	Main Executable Program
Vidfact.hlp	275 KB	Help File
Vidcore.hlp	99 KB	Help File
Vidcore.dll	1,425 KB	Support Program
Vidfact.dll	1,517 KB	Support Program
Readme.doc	65 KB	Data File
Vdplugin.dll	813 KB	Support Program
vdtrans.dll	921 KB	Support Program

INSTALLING FROM DISTRIBUTION DISKS OR CDS

How do I install software from distribution disks or CDs? Installation procedures vary, depending on a computer's operating system. Let's take a look at the installation process on a computer running Windows.

Windows software typically contains a **setup program** that guides you through the installation process. Figure 3-39 shows you what to expect when you use a setup program.

FIGURE 3-39 Using the setup program to install video capture software from distribution CDs.

1 Insert the first distribution disk, CD, or DVD. The setup program should start automatically. If it does not, look for a file called *Setup.exe* and then run it.

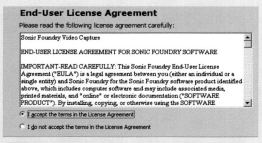

2 Read the license agreement, if one is presented on the screen. By agreeing to the terms of the license, you can proceed with the installation.

◉ Full Installation
○ Custom Installation

3 Select the installation option that best meets your needs. If you select a full installation, the setup program copies all files and data from the distribution medium to the hard disk of your computer system. A full installation provides you with access to all features of the software.

If you select a custom installation, the setup program displays a list of software features for your selection. After you select the features you want, the setup program copies only the selected program and data files to your hard disk. A custom installation can save space on your hard disk.

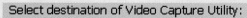
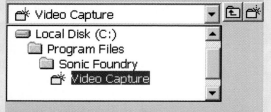

4 Follow the prompts provided by the setup program to specify a folder to hold the new software program. You can typically create a new folder during the setup process, if you did not prepare a folder ahead of time.

5 If the software includes multiple distribution disks, insert each one in the specified drive when the setup program tells you to do so.

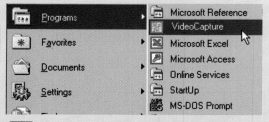

6 When the setup is complete, start the program that you just installed to make sure it works.

INSTALLING DOWNLOADED SOFTWARE

Is the installation process different for downloaded software? The installation process is slightly different for Windows software that you download. Usually all of the files needed for the new software are **zipped** to consolidate them into one large file, which is compressed to decrease its size and reduce the download time. As a first step in the installation process, this large, downloaded file must be reconstituted, or **unzipped**, into the original collection of files. Depending on the software, one or more parts of the installation process might be automated. You could encounter any of the following compressed file types for downloaded software:

- **Self-installing executable file.** Under the most automated installation system, the process of downloading the new software automatically initiates the entire installation process. The software download is packaged as one large file with an .exe extension. This **self-installing executable file** automatically unzips itself and starts the setup program. You simply have to follow the setup program prompts to acknowledge the license agreement, indicate the folder for the software files, and complete the installation.

- **Self-executing zip file.** Downloaded files with .exe extensions do not always install themselves. Some are simply **self-executing zip files**, which automatically unzip the software's files, but do not automatically start the setup program. Under this installation system, you start the executable file to unzip the files for the new software. One of these files will be the *Setup.exe* program. Next, you manually start the setup program and follow its prompts to complete the installation.

- **Manual download and install.** If you download the software and it arrives as one huge file with a .zip extension, you must locate this file on your hard disk and then use a program such as WinZip to unzip it. You then must run the setup program to acknowledge the license agreement, indicate the folder for the software files, and complete the installation. Windows XP includes built-in support for .zip files, so a third-party program like WinZip is not required, but you must still locate the .zip file and run it to initiate the installation process.

Is installing a software upgrade different from installing a full version? Installing a software upgrade, either from a distribution CD or from a download, is very similar to installing a full version of the software. The update usually provides a setup program that checks to make sure your computer contains a valid version of the program that you want to upgrade, then it guides you through the rest of the upgrade process.

UNINSTALLING SOFTWARE

How do I get rid of software? With some operating systems, such as DOS, you can remove software simply by deleting its files. Other operating systems, such as Windows and Mac OS, provide access to an **uninstall routine**, which deletes the software's files from various directories on your computer's hard disk. The uninstall routine also removes references to the program from the desktop and from operating system files, such as the file system and, in the case of Windows, from the Windows Registry.

With Windows software, you can typically find the uninstall routine on the same menu as the program (see Figure 3-40). If an uninstall routine is not provided by the software, you can use the one provided by the operating system. In Windows, the Add/Remove Programs icon is located in the Control Panel, accessible from the Start menu.

FIGURE 3-40

To uninstall any Windows application software, first look for an Uninstall option listed on the same menu that you use to start the program (top). If that option is not available, use the Add/Remove Programs option from the Control Panel (bottom).

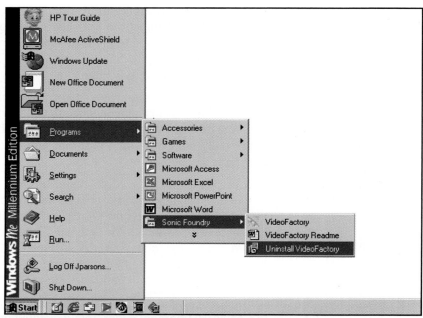

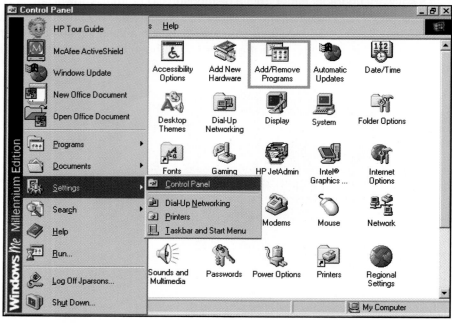

SOFTWARE COPYRIGHTS

To read the actual text of software copyright laws, connect to the **Software Copyright** InfoWeb.

click ➤

Is it legal to copy software? Once you purchase a software package, you might assume that you can install it and use it in any way that you like. In fact, your "purchase" entitles you to use the software only in certain pre-scribed ways. In most countries, computer software, like a book or movie, is protected by a copyright. A **copyright** is a form of legal protection that grants the author of an original "work" an exclusive right to copy, distribute, sell, and modify that work, except under special circumstances described by copyright laws. These exceptions include:

1 The purchaser has the right to copy software from a distribution disk or Web site to a computer's hard disk in order to install it.

2 The purchaser can make an extra, or backup, copy of the software in case the original copy becomes erased or damaged.

3 The purchaser is allowed to copy and distribute sections of a software program for use in critical reviews and teaching.

Most software displays a **copyright notice**, such as "© 2001 eCourseWare," on one of its screens. This notice is not required by law, however, so programs without a copyright notice are still protected by copyright law. People who circumvent copyright law and illegally copy, distribute, or modify software are sometimes called software pirates, and their illegal copies are referred to as pirated software.

3

FIGURE 3-41

When software has a shrink-wrap license, you agree to the terms of the software license by opening the package. If you do not agree with the terms, you should return the software in its unopened package.

SOFTWARE LICENSES

What is a software license? In addition to copyright protection, computer software is often protected by the terms of a software license. A **software license**, or "license agreement," is a legal contract that defines the ways in which you may use a computer program. For personal computer software, you will find the license on the outside of the package, on a separate card inside the package, on the CD packaging, or in one of the program files.

Most legal contracts require signatures before the terms of the contract take effect. This requirement becomes unwieldy with software—imagine having to sign a license agreement and return it before you can use a new software package. To circumvent the signature requirement, software publishers typically use two techniques to validate a software license: shrink-wrap licenses and installation agreements.

When you purchase computer software, the distribution disks, CDs, or DVDs are usually sealed in an envelope, plastic box, or shrink wrapping. A **shrink-wrap license** goes into effect as soon as you open the packaging. Figure 3-41 explains more about the mechanics of a shrink-wrap license.

An **installation agreement** is displayed on the screen when you first install the software. After reading the software license on the screen, you can indicate that you accept the terms of the license by clicking a designated button—usually labeled "OK," "I agree," or "I accept."

Software licenses are often lengthy and written in "legalese," but your legal right to use the software continues only as long as you abide by the terms of the software license. Therefore, you should understand the software license for any software you use. To become familiar with a typical license agreement, you can read through the one in Figure 3-42.

FIGURE 3-42

When you read a software license agreement, look for answers to the following questions:

Am I buying the software or licensing it?

When does the license go into effect?

Under what circumstances can I make copies?

Can I rent the software?

Can I sell the software?

What if the software includes a distribution CD and a set of distribution disks?

Does the software publisher provide a warranty?

Can I loan the software to a friend?

> ### Software License Agreement
> **Important - READ CAREFULLY:** This License Agreement ("Agreement") is a legal agreement between you and eCourseWare Corporation for the software product, eCourse GraphWare ("The SOFTWARE"). By installing, copying, or otherwise using the SOFTWARE, you agree to be bound by the terms of this Agreement. The SOFTWARE is protected by copyright laws and international copyright treaties. The SOFTWARE is licensed, not sold.
> **GRANT OF LICENSE.** This Agreement gives you the right to install and use one copy of the SOFTWARE on a single computer. The primary user of the computer on which the SOFTWARE is installed may make a second copy for his or her exclusive use on a portable computer.
> **OTHER RIGHTS AND LIMITATIONS.** You may not reverse engineer, decompile, or disassemble the SOFTWARE except and only to the extent that such activity is expressly permitted by applicable law.
> The SOFTWARE is licensed as a single product; its components may not be separated for use on more than one computer. You may not rent, lease, or lend the SOFTWARE. You may permanently transfer all of your rights under this Agreement, provided you retain no copies, you transfer all of the SOFTWARE, and the recipient agrees to the terms of this Agreement. If the software product is an upgrade, any transfer must include all prior versions of the SOFTWARE.
> You may receive the SOFTWARE in more than one medium. Regardless of the type of medium you receive, you may use only one medium that is appropriate for your single computer. You may not use or install the other medium on another computer.
> **WARRANTY.** eCourseWare warrants that the SOFTWARE will perform substantially in accordance with the accompanying written documentation for a period of ninety (90) days from the date of receipt. TO THE MAXIMUM EXTENT PERMITTED BY APPLICABLE LAW, eCourseWare AND ITS SUPPLIERS DISCLAIM ALL OTHER WARRANTIES AND CONDITIONS EITHER EXPRESS OR IMPLIED, INCLUDING, BUT NOT LIMITED TO, IMPLIED WARRANTIES OF MERCHANTABILITY, FITNESS FOR A PARTICULAR PURPOSE, TITLE, AND NON-INFRINGEMENT, WITH REGARD TO THE SOFTWARE PRODUCT.

Are all software licenses similar? Copyright laws provide fairly severe restrictions on copying, distributing, and reselling software; however, a license agreement may offer additional rights to consumers. The licenses for commercial software, shareware, freeware, open source, and public domain software provide different levels of permission for software use, copying, and distribution.

Commercial software is typically sold in computer stores or at Web sites. Although you "buy" this software, you actually purchase only the right to use it under the terms of the software license. A license for commercial software typically adheres closely to the limitations provided by copyright law, although it might give you permission to install the software on a computer at work and on a computer at home, provided that you use only one of them at a time.

Shareware is copyrighted software marketed under a "try before you buy" policy. It typically includes a license that permits you to use the software for a trial period. To use it beyond the trial period, you must pay a registration fee. A shareware license usually allows you to make copies of the software and distribute them to others. If they choose to use the software, they must pay a registration fee as well. These shared copies provide a low-cost marketing and distribution channel. Registration fee payment relies on the honor system, so unfortunately many shareware authors collect only a fraction of the money they deserve for their programming efforts. Thousands of shareware programs are available, encompassing just about as many applications as commercial software.

Freeware is copyrighted software that—as you might expect—is available for free. Because the software is protected by copyright, you cannot do anything with it that is not expressly allowed by copyright law or by the author. Typically, the license for freeware permits you to use the software, copy it, and give it away; but does not permit you to alter it or sell it. Many utility programs, device drivers, and some games are available as freeware.

Open source software makes the uncompiled program instructions—the source code—available to programmers who want to modify and improve the software. Open source software may be sold or distributed free of charge, but it must, in every case, include the source code. Linux is an example of open source software, as is FreeBSD—a version of UNIX designed for personal computers.

Public domain software is not protected by copyright because the copyright has expired, or the author has placed the program in the public domain, making it available without restriction. Public domain software may be freely copied, distributed, and even resold. The primary restriction on public domain software is that you are not allowed to apply for a copyright on it.

3

QUICK Check Section D

1 A(n) [＿＿＿＿＿] program typically handles the process of copying files from a distribution disk or CD to the hard disk.

2 Software that you download is usually [＿＿＿＿＿] into a single, compressed file, so it must be reconstituted to its original files as part of the installation process.

3 You should [＿＿＿＿＿] unwanted software, instead of simply deleting the folder that contains the software files.

4 [＿＿＿＿＿] laws provide software authors with the exclusive right to copy, distribute, sell, and modify their work, except under special circumstances.

5 [＿＿＿＿＿] is copyrighted software that is marketed with a "try before you buy" policy.

6 Linux is an example of open [＿＿＿＿＿] software.

7 Public [＿＿＿＿＿] software is not copyrighted, making it available for use without restriction, except that you cannot apply for a copyright on it.

check answers

LAB 3-D
INSTALLING AND
UNINSTALLING SOFTWARE

Interactive **LAB**
Installing Software

└click to start ►✳

In this lab, you'll learn:

- How to use a setup program to install Windows application software from a distribution CD

- What to do if the setup program doesn't automatically start

- The difference between typical, compact, and custom installation options

- How to specify a folder for a new software installation

- How to install downloaded software

- How to install an upgrade

- How to uninstall a Windows application

- What happens in addition to deleting files when you uninstall a software application

- How to locate the program that will uninstall a software application

- Why you might not want to delete all of the files associated with an application

⚙ **LAB**Assignments

1   Start the interactive part of the lab. Insert your Tracking Disk if you want to save your QuickCheck results. Perform each of the lab steps as directed, and answer all of the lab QuickCheck questions. When you exit the lab, your answers are automatically graded and your results are displayed.

2   Browse the Web and locate a software application that you might like to download. Use information supplied by the Web site to answer the following questions:

   a. What is the name of the program and the URL of the download site?

   b. What is the size of the download file?

   c. According to the instructions, does the download file appear to require manual installation, is it a self-executing zip file, or is it a self-installing executable file?

3   On the computer that you typically use, look through the list of programs (click Start, then select Programs to see a list of them). List the names of any programs that include their own uninstall routines.

4   On the computer that you typically use, open the Control Panel and then open the Add/Remove Programs dialog box. List the first 10 programs that are currently installed on the computer.

TECHTALK
THE WINDOWS REGISTRY

To many computer owners, the Windows Registry is simply a mysterious "black box" that is mentioned occasionally in articles about computer troubleshooting. Certainly, it is possible to use a computer without intimate knowledge of the Registry; however, the Registry is the "glue" that binds together many of the most important components of a PC—the computer hardware, peripheral devices, application software, and system software. After reading this TechTalk section, you should have a basic understanding of the Registry and its role in the operation of a computer system.

Why does a PC need the Registry? Let's reflect back for moment on what you know so far about how a computer works. You know that you use menus, dialog boxes, and other controls provided by application software to direct the operations that a computer carries out. For some operations—particularly those that involve hardware—the application software communicates with the operating system. The operating system might communicate with device drivers or, in some cases, it can directly communicate with a peripheral device.

In order to act as an intermediary between software and peripheral devices, your operating system needs information about these components—where they are located, what's been installed, how they are configured, and how you want to use them. CMOS memory holds the most essential data about your computer's processing and storage hardware, but the **Windows Registry** keeps track of your computer's peripheral devices and software so that the operating system can access the information it needs to coordinate the activities in a computer system. Some examples of specific data that the Registry tracks include your preferences for desktop colors, icons, pointers, shortcuts, and display resolution; the sounds that are assigned to various system events, such as clicking and shutting down; the capability of your CD-ROM drive for playing audio CDs and autorunning computer CDs; the options that appear on a shortcut menu when you right-click an object; your computer's network card settings and protocols; and the location of the uninstall routines for all installed software.

Where can I find the Registry? The contents of the Registry are stored in multiple files in the Windows/System folder of your computer's hard disk, and combined into a single database when Windows starts. Although each version of Windows uses a slightly different storage scheme, the basic organization and function of the Registry are similar in all versions.

FIGURE 3-43

The Windows Registry is organized as a hierarchy of folders and files.

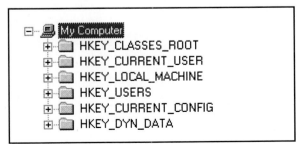

Windows stores the entire contents of the Registry in two files: *System.dat* and *User.dat*. *System.dat* includes configuration data for all the hardware and software installed on a computer. *User.dat* contains user-specific information, sometimes called a "user profile," which includes software settings and desktop settings.

What does the Registry look like? The Registry has a logical structure that appears as a hierarchy of folders, similar to the directory structure of your hard disk, as shown in Figure 3-43.

3

There are six main folders in the Registry, and their names begin with HKEY. Each folder contains data that pertains to a particular part of a computer system, as described in Figure 3-44.

FIGURE 3-44	Registry Folder Contents
Folder	**Contents**
HKEY_CLASSES_ROOT	This folder contains data that associates file extensions with a particular application, and it contains a list of desktop shortcuts to programs.
HKEY_CURRENT_USER	Information for the current user is transferred here from the HKEY_USERS folder.
HKEY_LOCAL_MACHINE	This folder contains computer-specific information about hardware configuration and software preferences. This information is used for all users who log onto this computer.
HKEY_USERS	This folder contains individual preferences for each person who uses the computer.
HKEY_CURRENT_CONFIG	This folder links to the section of HKEY_LOCAL_MACHINE appropriate for the current hardware configuration.
HKEY_DYN_DATA	This folder points to the part of HKEY_LOCAL_MACHINE that maintains data for Plug and Play devices. This data is dynamic and can change as devices are added and removed from the system.

What does the Registry data look like? The Registry contains thousands of esoteric-looking data entries, as shown in Figure 3-45.

FIGURE 3-45

The Registry entries for Display Settings specify such settings as DPI, display fonts, and resolution.

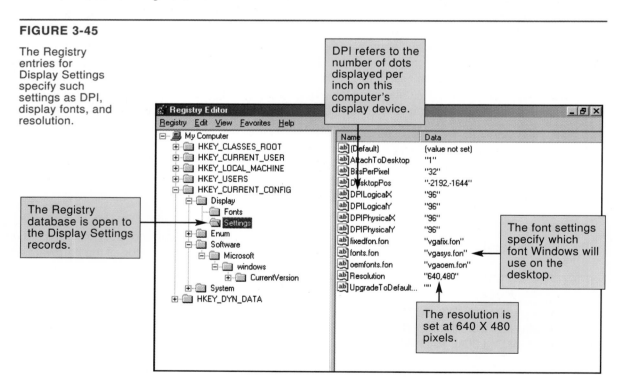

DPI refers to the number of dots displayed per inch on this computer's display device.

The Registry database is open to the Display Settings records.

The font settings specify which font Windows will use on the desktop.

The resolution is set at 640 X 480 pixels.

Can I make changes to the Registry? You indirectly change the Registry whenever you install or remove software or hardware. The setup program for your software automatically updates the Registry with essential information about the program's location and configuration. Device drivers and the Windows Plug and Play feature provide similar update services for hardware.

You can also make changes to the Windows Registry by using the dialog boxes for various configuration routines provided by the operating system and application software. For example, if you want to change the desktop colors for your user profile, you can do so by selecting the Settings option from the Start menu, clicking Control Panel, and then selecting the Display option. Any changes that you make to the settings in the Display Properties dialog box (Figure 3-46) will be recorded in the Windows Registry.

FIGURE 3-46

Changes that you make when using the Display Properties dialog box will automatically update the corresponding entries in the HKEY_CURRENT_CONFIG folder of the Registry.

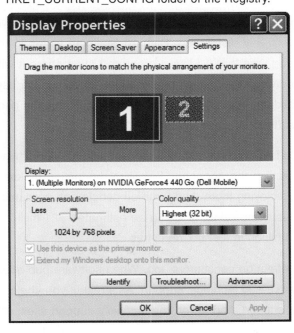

Windows provides a tool called the **Registry Editor** to manually edit the data that is in the Registry files. Before you use the Registry Editor, however, be aware that introducing an error into the Registry can result in a computer that just won't boot, requiring the help of an experienced technician. As one expert warns: "Mucking around with the Windows Registry is a lot like handling dynamite. You wouldn't try to defuse a bomb without special training and a detailed backup plan. You should adopt the same attitude when editing the Windows Registry: Don't even start unless you know what you're doing and have taken the necessary precautions."

That being said, if you must edit the Registry, make sure that you take the following minimal precautions:

- Back up the Registry with a tool specifically designed for that purpose before you use the Registry Editor.

- Change only one setting at a time.

- Check and double-check your typing to make sure that you didn't make an error.

QUICK Check
TechTalk

1 The Windows Registry contains settings and preferences for the peripheral devices and software that are installed on a computer. True or false? [＿＿＿＿＿]

2 The Registry is stored in the Windows/[＿＿＿＿＿] folder.

3 Registry data is stored in two files, *System.dat* and [＿＿＿＿＿] .dat.

4 Windows provides a utility called the Registry [＿＿＿＿＿], which can be used to manually change the contents of the Registry; however, it is not recommended that you use this utility unless you know what you are doing and have taken the necessary precautions.

check answers ✳

3

ISSUE

IS PIRACY A PROBLEM?

Software is easy to steal. You don't have to walk out of a Best Buy store with a Microsoft Office XP box under your shirt. You can simply borrow your friend's CD-ROM and install a copy of the program on your computer's hard disk. It seems so simple that it couldn't be illegal. But it is.

In many countries, including the United States, software pirates are subject to criminal prosecution. And yet, piracy continues to grow. According to the Software and Information Industry Association (SIIA), a leading anti-piracy watchdog, revenue losses from business software piracy typically exceed $2 billion per year. This figure reveals only a part of the piracy problem—it does not include losses from rampant game and educational software piracy.

A small, but vocal, minority of software users, such as members of GNU (which stands for "Gnu's Not UNIX"), believes that data and software should be freely distributed. Richard Stallman writes in the GNU Manifesto, "I consider that the golden rule requires that if I like a program I must share it with other people who like it. Software sellers want to divide users and conquer them, making each user agree not to share with others. I refuse to break solidarity with other users in this way. I cannot in good conscience sign a nondisclosure agreement or a software license agreement."

Is software piracy really damaging? Who cares if you use Microsoft Office without paying for it? Software piracy is damaging because it has a negative effect on the economy. Software production makes a major contribution to the United States economy, employing more than 2 million people and accounting for billions of dollars in corporate revenue. This industry, however, is losing an estimated $21 million a day, which translates to 118,000 lost jobs and $1.5 billion in lost tax revenues.

Decreases in software revenues can have a direct effect on consumers, too. When software publishers must cut corners, they tend to reduce customer service and technical support. As a result, you, the consumer, get put on hold when you call for technical support, find fewer free technical support sites, and encounter customer support personnel who are only moderately knowledgeable about their products. The bottom line—software piracy negatively affects customer service.

As an alternative to cutting support costs, some software publishers might build the cost of software piracy into the price of the software. The unfortunate result is that those who legitimately license and purchase software pay an inflated price.

Software piracy is a global problem. Although the United States accounts for the highest dollar amount of software piracy, approximately two-thirds of the piracy occurs outside the United States. The countries with the highest piracy rates are China, Japan, Korea, Germany, France, Brazil, Italy, Canada, and the United Kingdom. But piracy is also a problem in other countries. By some estimates, more than 90 percent of all business software used in Bulgaria, Indonesia, Russia, and Vietnam is pirated.

As a justification of high piracy rates, some observers point out that people in many countries simply might not be able to afford software that is priced for the U.S. market. This argument would make sense in China, where the average annual income is equivalent to about $3,500, and in North Korea, where the average income is only $900. A Korean who legitimately purchases Microsoft Office for $250 would be spending more than one-quarter of his or her annual income. Most of the countries with a high incidence of software piracy, however, have strong economies and respectable per capita incomes. To further discredit the theory that piracy stems from poverty, India—which has a fairly large computer-user community, but a per capita income of only $1,600—is not among the top 10 countries with high rates of software piracy.

You can read the GNU Manifesto and other thought-provoking articles about software piracy at the <u>Copyright and Piracy</u> InfoWeb.

click ➡✳

If economic factors do not account for the pervasiveness of software piracy, what does? Some analysts suggest that people need more education about software copyrights and the economic implications of piracy. Other analysts believe that copyright enforcement must be increased by supporting and implementing more vigorous efforts to identify and prosecute pirates.

3

┌─ WHAT DO YOU THINK?

1. Do you believe that software piracy is a serious issue? ⭕Yes ⭕ No ⭕ Not sure

2. Do you know of any instances of software piracy? ⭕Yes ⭕ No ⭕ Not sure

3. Do you think that most software pirates understand that they are doing something illegal? ⭕Yes ⭕ No ⭕ Not sure

4. Should software publishers try to adjust software pricing for local markets? ⭕Yes ⭕ No ⭕ Not sure

click to save your responses➡

INTERACTIVE SUMMARY

The Interactive Summary helps you to select and remember important concepts from this chapter. Fill in the blanks to best complete each sentence. When using the NP6 BookOnCD, you can click the Check Answers buttons to automatically score your answers. Place your Tracking Disk in the floppy disk drive if you want to save your scores.

[_____] consists of computer programs and data files that work together to provide a computer with the instructions and data necessary for carrying out a specific type of task, such as document production, video editing, graphic design, or Web browsing. Computer [_____] write the instructions for the programs that become the components of a computer software product. To understand how software is installed and uninstalled, it is important for computer owners to recognize that today's software typically consists of many files.

To create a software environment, a programmer must define the [_____] for each element in the environment, such as where an object appears, its shape, its color, and its behavior. A computer [_____] provides the tools that a programmer uses to create software. Most programmers today prefer to use [_____] languages, such as C++, Java, COBOL, and Visual Basic. A computer's microprocessor only understands [_____] language, however, so a program that is written in a high-level language must be compiled or interpreted before it can be processed. A [_____] translates all of the instructions in a program as a single batch, and the resulting machine language instructions, called [_____] code, are placed in a new file. An alternative method of translation uses an [_____] to translate instructions one at a time while the program runs.

check answers ◗❊

A computer's software is like the chain of command in an army. [_____] software tells the operating system what to do. The operating system tells the device drivers, device drivers tell the hardware, and the hardware actually does the work. The operating system interacts with application software, device drivers, and hardware to manage a computer's [_____]. In addition, many operating systems also influence the "look and feel" of your software, or what's known as the user [_____].

The core part of an operating system is called the [_____]. In addition to this core, many operating systems provide helpful tools, called [_____], which you can use to control and customize your computer equipment and work environment. Operating systems are informally categorized and characterized using one or more of the following terms: A [_____] operating system expects to deal with one set of input devices—those that can be controlled by one person at a time. A [_____] operating system is designed to deal with input, output, and processing requests from many users. A [_____] operating system provides process and memory management services that allow two or more programs to run simultaneously. A [_____] operating system is one that's designed for a personal computer—either a desktop or notebook computer. Popular desktop operating systems include Windows 95/98/Me/XP and Mac OS. Popular [_____] operating systems include Windows NT/2000, Linux, and UNIX.

check answers

Document [_____] software assists you with composing, editing, designing, printing, and electronically publishing documents. The three most popular types of document production software include word processing, desktop publishing, and Web authoring. [_____] software is similar to a "smart" piece of paper that automatically adds up the columns of numbers that you write on it. You can use it to make other calculations too, based on simple equations that you write or more complex, built-in formulas. Because it is so easy to experiment with different numbers, this type of software is particularly useful for [_____] analyses. Data [_____] software helps you to store, find, organize, update, and report information. File management software is designed to help you create, modify, search, sort, and print simple lists stored in a [_____] file. Database management software (DBMS) is designed for creating and manipulating multiple types of records that form a database. Many of today's databases are based on the [_____] model, which structures data as a table of columns (fields) and rows (records). Relationships can be established between tables to join the tables together so that they can be treated as one. [_____] software, including paint, photo editing, drawing, CAD, 3-D, and presentation software, is designed to help you to create, display, modify, manipulate, and print images. Music and video editing software, educational and reference software, and entertainment software round out the most popular categories for personal computer software. For businesses, [_____] market software is designed to automate specialized tasks in a specific market or business. [_____] market software is generic software that can be used by just about any kind of business.

check answers ✳

When you [_____] software, the new software files are placed in the appropriate folders on your computer's hard disk, and then your computer performs any software or hardware configurations that are necessary to make sure that the program is ready to run. The main [_____] files and data modules for the software are placed in the folder that you specify. Some [_____] modules for the software, however, might be stored in different directories. Windows software typically contains a [_____] program that guides you through the installation process.

To install application software from a [_____] CD, you simply place the CD in the drive and wait for the setup program to begin. The installation process is slightly different for application software that you download. Usually all of the files needed for the new software are consolidated into one large file, which is [_____] to decrease its size and reduce the download time. This large, downloaded file must be reconstituted, or [_____], into the original collection of files as a first step in the installation process. A self-installing [_____] file automatically unzips the downloaded file and starts the setup program. A self-executing [_____] file automatically unzips the software's files, but does not automatically start the setup program.

A [_____] is a form of legal protection that grants the author of an original "work" an exclusive right to copy, distribute, sell, and modify that work, except under special circumstances described by copyright laws. A software [_____] is a legal contract that defines the ways in which you may use a computer program. Licenses for commercial, shareware, freeware, open source, and public domain software provide consumers with different sets of rights pertaining to copying and distribution.

check answers ✳

3

INTERACTIVE
KEY TERMS

Make sure that you understand all of the boldfaced key terms presented in this chapter. If you're using the NP6 BookOnCD, you can use this list of terms as an interactive study activity. First, try to define a term in your own words, then click the term to compare your definition with the definition that is presented in the chapter.

Absolute reference, 135
Action games, 146
Adventure games, 146
Application software, 117
Automatic recalculation, 135
Bootstrap program, 121
CD ripper, 143
Cell, 133
Cell references, 134
Clip art, 132
Command-line interface, 120
Commercial software, 154
Compiler, 115
Computer program, 112
Computer programmers, 114
Copyright notice, 153
Copyright, 153
Database, 138
Desktop operating system, 122
Distribution disk, 148
DOS, 126
Field, 137
Flat file, 137
Font, 130
Footer, 131
Format, 130
Formula, 134
Frames, 132
Freeware, 155
Fully justified, 131
Function, 134
Grammar checker, 130
Graphical user interface, 120
Graphics, 141
Groupware, 147
Header, 131
High-level languages, 115
Install, 149
Installation agreement, 154
Interpreter, 116

Kernel, 121
Label, 133
Leading, 131
Line spacing, 131
Linux, 125
Mac OS, 124
Machine language, 115
Mail merge, 132
Mathematical operators, 134
Microsoft Windows, 122
MP3, 143
MP3 Player, 143
Multitasking operating system, 122
Multiuser operating system, 122
Natural language query, 140
Network operating system, 122
Object code, 115
Object-oriented database, 138
Open source software, 155
Operating system, 118
Page layout, 131
Paragraph alignment, 131
Paragraph style, 131
Point size, 130
Programming language, 115
Properties, 114
Public domain software, 155
Puzzle games, 146
Query, 140
Query by example, 140
Query language, 140
Readability formula, 130
Record, 137
Record structure, 139
Registry Editor, 159
Relational database, 138
Relative reference, 135
Resource, 119
Role-playing games, 146
Scripts, 116

Search and Replace, 130
Self-executing zip files, 151
Self-installing executable file, 151
Setup program, 150
Shareware, 155
Shrink-wrap license, 153
Simulation games, 146
Single-user operating system, 122
Slides, 142
Software, 112
Software license, 153
Software publishers, 114
Sort key, 140
Source code, 115
Spelling checker, 129
Spelling dictionary, 129
Sports games, 146
Spreadsheet, 133
SQL, 140
Strategy games, 146
Structured file, 137
Style, 131
System requirements, 148
System software, 117
Table, 132
Thesaurus, 130
Uninstall routine, 152
UNIX, 125
Unzipped, 151
User interface, 120
Utilities, 121
Value, 133
What-if analysis, 133
Windows Registry, 157
Worksheet, 133
Zipped, 151

TIP Additional software categories that are boldfaced in this chapter are listed separately on page 165.

SOFTWARE KEY TERMS

3-D graphics software, 142
Accounting and finance software, 136
Accounting software, 147
Audio editing software, 143
CAD software, 142
Computer-aided music software, 143
Data management software, 137
Database management software, 138
Desktop publishing software, 128
Document production software, 128
Drawing software, 141
Ear training software, 143

Educational software, 144
File management software, 137
Graphics software, 141
Horizontal market software, 147
Mathematical modeling software, 136
MIDI sequencing software, 143
MP3 encoding software, 143
Notation software, 143
Paint software, 141
Payroll software, 147
Personal finance software, 136
Personal information manager, 137
Photo editing software, 141

Presentation software, 142
Project management software, 147
Reference software, 145
Small business accounting software, 136
Spreadsheet software, 133
Statistical software, 136
Tax preparation software, 136
Vertical market software, 147
Video editing software, 144
Web authoring software, 128
Word processing software, 128

INTERACTIVE
SITUATION QUESTIONS

3

Apply what you've learned to some typical computing situations. When using the NP6 BookOnCD, you can type your answers, then use the Check Answers button to automatically score your responses. Place your Tracking Disk in the floppy disk drive if you want to save your scores.

1 Suppose that you are trying to connect to a Web site, but your browser is displaying a "JavaScript error" message. You can assume that the Java _____ has encountered an instruction that it could not translate into machine language.

2 If your goal is to produce a printed brochure that contains numerous graphics and looks professionally typeset, you should use DTP software that provides _____-oriented layout, instead of a word processor that provides page-oriented layout.

3 Suppose that you want to use one software package to enter the data for a flat file, make some calculations based on the data, and produce some graphs of the data. Your best choice for this task would be _____ software.

4 Suppose that you've been hired to organize a professional skateboard competition. When you consider how you'll need to use computers, you realize that you must collect information on each competitor and keep track of every competitive event. With at least two types of related records, you'll probably need database _____ software.

5 You just purchased a new software package. You insert the distribution CD, but nothing happens. No problem, you can manually run the _____ program, which will start the install routine.

6 You downloaded a new software program from the Web. It arrives as one huge file with an .exe extension. You recognize this as a self-_____ executable file that will automatically unzip the downloaded file and start the installation routine.

7 You download an open source software program from the Web. You assume that the download includes the uncompiled _____ code for the program, as well as the _____ version.

check answers

INTERACTIVE PRACTICE TESTS

When you use the NP6 BookOnCD, you can take Practice Tests that consist of 10 multiple-choice, true/false, and fill-in-the-blank questions. The questions are selected at random from a large test bank, so each time you take a test, you'll receive a different set of questions. Your tests are scored immediately, and you can print study guides that help you find the correct answers for any questions that you missed. If you are using a Tracking Disk, insert it in the floppy disk drive to save your test scores. **click to start** ➧

STUDY TIPS

Study Tips help you to organize and consolidate the information in a chapter by making lists, outlines, charts, and sketches. You can use paper and pencil or word processing software to complete most of the Study Tips activities.

1 Make sure that you can use your own words to answer each of the green focus questions that appear throughout the chapter.

2 Make sure that you can list and describe the three types of files that are typically supplied on a software distribution disk.

3 Provide some examples of objects for which a programmer must specify properties when creating a program.

4 Explain the difference between a compiler and an interpreter.

5 List three types of system software, and at least five categories of application software.

6 Make sure that you can list and describe the four main resources that an operating system manages.

7 Explain the term "memory leak," and describe what you can do if one occurs on your PC.

8 Describe the difference between a graphical user interface and a command-line user interface.

9 Describe five tasks for which you must interact directly with the operating system.

10 Create a table with the column headings single-user, multiuser, network, multitasking, and desktop operating system across the top. List Linux, UNIX, Mac OS, and each version of Windows down the side of the table. Use a check mark to indicate which characteristics fit each operating system.

11 Study the figures of Windows, Mac OS, and Linux in Section B. If you started an unfamiliar computer, describe how you would identify its operating system.

12 Discuss the pros and cons of using Linux as a desktop operating system.

13 Describe the strengths of word processing, DTP, and Web authoring software.

14 Explain how a spelling checker works and why it is not a substitute for proofreading.

15 Describe the features of the word processing software that you use most often.

16 Draw a sketch of a simple worksheet and label the following: columns, rows, cell, active cell, values, labels, formulas, and Formula bar.

17 Explain the difference between an absolute reference and a relative reference, giving an example of each.

18 List five types of "number crunching" software that you can use instead of spreadsheet software.

19 Describe how you would use each of the six types of graphics software described in this chapter.

20 Describe the process of installing software from a distribution CD, and contrast it with the process of installing downloaded software.

21 Explain the differences between commercial software, shareware, open source software, freeware, and public domain software.

PROJECTS

An NP6 Project is an open-ended activity that will help you apply the concepts you have learned. Many projects require resources in addition to your textbook, such as current magazines, library materials, or Web access. When you tackle a project, be prepared to use your critical thinking skills, logical analysis skills, and creativity.

1 **Issue Research: Software Piracy** The Issue section of this chapter focused on copyrights and software piracy. For this project, you will write a two–five page paper about this issue based on information that you gather from the Internet. To begin this project, consult the Copyright and Piracy InfoWeb (see page 161), and link to the recommended Web pages to get an in-depth overview of the issue. Armed with this background, select one of the following viewpoints and statements and argue for or against it:

a. Free software advocates: As an enabling technology, software should be freely distributed, along with its modifiable source code.

b. Librarians: Copyright laws, especially the Digital Millennium Copyright Act, minimize the needs of the public, and go too far in their efforts to protect the rights of software authors.

c. Software Publishers Association: Strong copyright laws and enforcement are essential in order for companies to publish and support high-quality software.

Whatever viewpoint you decide to present, make sure that you back it up with facts and references to authoritative articles and Web pages. You can place citations to these pages (including the author's name, article title, date of publication, and URL) at the end of your paper as endnotes, on each page as footnotes, or along with the appropriate paragraphs using parentheses. Follow your professor's instructions for submitting your paper via e-mail or as a printed document.

2 **Legal Beagle: Analyzing a License Agreement** When you use a software package, it is important to understand the legal restrictions on its use. For this project, make a photocopy of the license agreement for any software package. Read the license agreement, then answer these questions:

a. Is this a shrink-wrap license? Why or why not?

b. After you pay your computer dealer for the program covered by this license, who owns the program?

c. Can you legally have one copy of the program on your computer at work and another copy of the program on your computer at home if you use the software only in one place at a time?

d. Can you legally sell the software? Why or why not?

e. Under what conditions can you legally transfer possession of the program to someone else?

f. If you were the owner of a software store, could you legally rent the program to customers if you were sure they did not keep a copy after the rental period was over?

g. Can you legally install this software on one computer, but give more than one user access to it?

h. If you use this program for an important business decision and later find out that a mistake in the program caused you to lose $500,000, what legal recourse is provided by the license agreement?

ADDITIONAL
PROJECTS

 TIP

Click ➨ to access the Web for additional projects.

3

4

FILE MANAGEMENT, VIRUS PROTECTION, AND BACKUP

CONTENTS

➤ **SECTION A: FILE BASICS**
Filenames, Extensions, and
  Formats
File Locations, Folders, and
  Paths
File Sizes and Dates

➤ **SECTION B: FILE MANAGEMENT**
Application-based File
  Management
File Management Utilities
File Management Metaphors
Windows Explorer
Physical File Storage

➤ **SECTION C: COMPUTER VIRUSES**
Viruses, Trojan Horses, and
  Worms
Antivirus Software
Virus Hoaxes

➤ **SECTION D: DATA BACKUP**
Backup and Restore Procedures
Backup Equipment
Backup Software

➤ **TECHTALK: FILE FORMATS**

➤ **ISSUE: IS IT A CRIME?**

➤ **REVIEW ACTIVITIES**
Interactive Summary
Interactive Key Terms
Interactive Situation Questions
Interactive Practice Tests
Study Tips
Projects

LABS
➤ Working with Windows
  Explorer
➤ Backing Up Your Computer

InfoWebLinks

The InfoWebLinks, located in the margins of this chapter, show the way to a variety of Web sites that contain additional information and updates to the chapter topics. Your computer needs an Internet connection to access these links. You can connect to the Web links for this chapter by:

- clicking the InfoWeb links in the margins
- clicking this <u>underlined link</u>
- starting your browser and entering the URL
  www.infoweblinks.com/np6/chapter4.htm

 TIP

When using the **BookOnCD**, the ➤ symbols are "clickable."

CHAPTER PREVIEW

What do you associate with the word "retro"? Maybe it conjures up images of fashionably nostalgic styles from the past—curvatious diners and chrome-laden automobiles, peace symbols and bell bottoms, or disco lights and leisure suits. For the troops on the front lines of the computer virus battlefield, "retro" means a nightmare—a virus that disables antivirus software and leaves computer files open to attack. The topics in Chapter 4 target computer files from several angles, including what they are, how you can keep them organized, and how you can protect them.

Section A launches the chapter with a general introduction to computer files—the storage bins for all of the "stuff" on your computer. It begins with some very practical information about filenames, helps you understand the importance of filename extensions in the Windows environment, and guides you through the tricky maze of devices, folders, and filenames that form a path to a file.

Section B explains techniques for organizing computer files so that they are easy to access, update, and back up. It also explains how an operating system stores, deletes, and tracks files—good background for understanding when and why to use a file shredder or defragmentation utility.

Section C delves into the fascinating world of computer viruses. You'll discover why you shouldn't open e-mail attachments like LOVE-LETTER-FOR-YOU, and where you might expect the Ping of Death to strike. This section also helps you distinguish between real virus alerts and hoaxes—a skill that can help you avoid the embarrassment of sending your friends panicky e-mails about a non-existent virus.

Section D focuses on one of the most important aspects of computing—backup. You'll learn how to evaluate different backup options, such as tapes, CDs, a network, or a Web site. You'll also discover the pitfalls of depending on the Restore CD provided with your computer.

When you complete this chapter you should be able to:

- Create valid names for files and folders, plus demonstrate that you can construct and trace file paths

- Demonstrate how to use file management features of application software and operating system utilities

- Describe how a computer physically stores data on disks, but represents this storage system with a logical model

- Explain how file viruses, boot sector viruses, macro viruses, Trojan horses, worms, and Denial of Service attacks affect files and disrupt computer operations

- Describe how a computer owner can use antivirus software to avoid, find, and remove viruses

- Demonstrate that you can implement a viable backup and restore plan

- Compare the advantages and disadvantages of using tapes, floppy disks, a second hard disk, CDs, Zip disks, networks, and Web sites for backups

4

TIP Click to access the Web for a complete list of learning objectives for Chapter 4.

Section

FILE BASICS

The term "file" was used for filing cabinets and collections of papers long before it became part of the personal computer lexicon. Today, a **computer file**—or simply "a file"— is defined as a named collection of data that exists on a storage medium, such as a hard disk, floppy disk, CD, DVD, or tape. A file can contain a group of records, a document, a photo, music, a video, an e-mail message, or a computer program.

Computer files have several characteristics, such as a name, format, location, size, and date. To make effective use of computer files, you'll need a good understanding of these file basics, and that is the focus of Section A.

FILENAMES, EXTENSIONS, AND FORMATS

What are the rules for naming files? Every file has a name and might also have a filename extension. When you save a file, you must provide it with a valid filename that adheres to specific rules, referred to as **file-naming conventions**. Each operating system has a unique set of file-naming conventions. You can use Figure 4-1 to determine whether filenames, such as *Nul*, *My File.doc*, *Report:2002*, and *Bud01/02.txt*, are valid under the operating system that you use.

FIGURE 4-1	File-Naming Conventions			
	DOS and Windows 3.1	**Windows 95/98/ME/XP/NT/2000**	**Mac OS (Classic)**	**UNIX/Linux**
Maximum length of filename	8-character filename plus an extension of 3 characters or less	Filename and extension cannot exceed 255 characters	1-31 characters	14-256 characters (depending on UNIX/Linux version) including an extension of any length
Spaces allowed	No	Yes	Yes	No
Numbers allowed	Yes	Yes	Yes	Yes
Characters not allowed	✳ / [ ] ; '' = \ : , | ?	✳ \ : < > | '' / ?	:	✳ ! @ # $ % ^ & ( ) { } [ ] '' \ ? ; < >
Filenames not allowed	Aux, Com1, Com2, Com3, Com4, Con, Lpt1, Lpt2, Lpt3, Prn, Nul	Aux, Com1, Com2, Com3, Com4, Con, Lpt1, Lpt2, Lpt3, Prn, Nul	Any filename is allowed	Depends on the version of UNIX or Linux
Case sensitive	No	No	No	Yes (use lowercase)

Why are certain characters and words not allowed in a filename? If an operating system attaches special significance to a symbol, you might not be able to use it in a filename. For example, DOS and Windows use the colon (:) character to separate the device letter from a filename or folder, as in *C:Music*. A filename such as *Report:2002* is not valid because the operating system would become confused about how to interpret the colon.

Some operating systems also contain a list of **reserved words** that are used as commands or special identifiers. You cannot use these words alone as a filename. You can, however, use these words as part of a longer filename. For example, under Windows XP, the filename *Nul* would not be valid, but you could name a file something like *Nul Committee Notes.doc* or *Null Set.exe*.

Are filename extensions important? A **filename extension** (or "file extension") is an optional file identifier that is separated from the main filename by a period, as in *Paint.exe*. With some operating systems, such as Windows and DOS, filename extensions work like tickets that admit people to different plays, movies, or concerts. If you have the right ticket, you get in. If a file has the right extension for a particular application program, you'll see it in the list of files that you can open with that software. For example, files with a .doc extension appear in the Open and Save As lists when you're working with Microsoft Word software.

A filename extension is usually related to the **file format**, which is defined as the arrangement of data in a file and the coding scheme that is used to represent the data. Files that contain graphics are usually stored using a different file format than files containing text. Hundreds of file formats exist, and you'll encounter many of them as you use a variety of software. Most software programs have what's called a **native file format** that is used to store files. For example, Microsoft Word stores files in DOC format, whereas Adobe Illustrator stores graphics files in AI format. When using a software application such as Microsoft Word to open a file, the program displays any files that have the filename extension for its native file format, as shown in Figure 4-2.

4

FIGURE 4-2

The next time that you use a software application, take note of the filename extensions that appear when you look at the list of files in the Open dialog box. If you don't see any filename extensions, you've discovered the results of a Windows setting that can hide (but not erase) filename extensions.

If Windows is set to hide file extensions, you can view them by selecting the Tools menu in Windows Explorer, selecting Folder Options, then changing the "Hide file extensions" option.

click to start

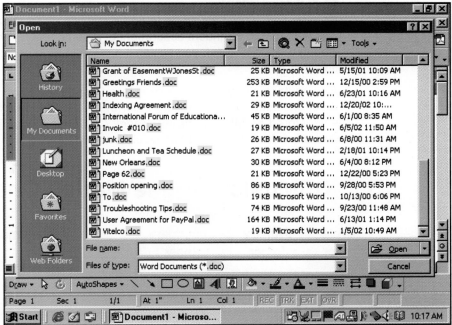

FILE LOCATIONS, FOLDERS, AND PATHS

How do I designate a file's location? To designate a file's location, you must first specify where the file is stored. Each of a PC's storage devices is identified by a device letter—a convention that is specific to DOS and Windows. The floppy disk drive is usually assigned device letter A and is referred to as "drive A." A device letter is usually followed by a colon, so drive A could be designated as A: or as 3½" Floppy (A:). The main hard disk drive is usually referred to as "drive C." Additional storage devices can be assigned letters from D through Z. Although most PCs stick to the standard of drive A for the floppy disk drive and drive C for the hard disk drive, the device letters for CD, Zip, and DVD drives are not standardized. For example, the CD-writer on your computer might be assigned device letter E, whereas the CD-writer on another computer might be assigned device letter R.

What's the purpose of folders? An operating system maintains a list of files called a **directory** for each storage disk, tape, CD, or DVD. The main directory of a disk is referred to as the **root directory**. On a PC, the root directory is typically identified by the device letter followed by a backslash. For example, the root directory of the hard disk drive would be C:\. You should try to avoid storing your data files in the root directory of your hard disk, and instead store them in a subdirectory.

A root directory can be subdivided into smaller lists, called **subdirectories**. When you use Windows, Mac OS, or a Linux graphical file manager, these subdirectories are depicted as **folders** because they work like the folders in a filing cabinet to store an assortment of related items. Each folder has a name, so you can easily create a folder called *Documents* to hold reports, letters, and so on. You can create another folder called *Music* to hold your MP3 files. Folders can be created within other folders. You might, for example, create a folder within your *Music* folder to hold your jazz collection, and another folder to hold your reggae collection.

A folder name is separated from a drive letter and other folder names by a special symbol. In DOS and Microsoft Windows, this symbol is the backslash (\ ). For example, the folder for your reggae music (within the *Music* folder on drive C) would be written as *C:\Music\Reggae*.

Imagine how hard it would be to find a specific piece of paper in a filing cabinet that was stuffed with a random assortment of reports, letters, and newspaper clippings. By storing a file in a folder, you assign it a place in an organized hierarchy of folders and files.

A computer file's location is defined by a **file specification** (sometimes called a **path**), which includes the drive letter, folder(s), filename, and extension. Suppose that you have stored an MP3 file called *Marley One Love* in the *Reggae* folder on your hard disk drive. Its file specification would be as follows:

C:\Music\Reggae\Marley One Love.mp3

| Drive letter | Primary folder | Secondary folder | Filename | Filename extension |

FILE SIZES AND DATES

What's the significance of a file's size? A file contains data, stored as a group of bits. The more bits, the larger the file. **File size** is usually measured in bytes, kilobytes, or megabytes. Knowing the size of a file can be important. Compared to small files, large files fill up storage space more quickly, require longer transmission times, and are more likely to be stripped off of e-mail attachments by a mail server. Your computer's operating system keeps track of file sizes and provides that information to you when you request a listing of files.

Is the file date important? Your computer keeps track of the date that a file was created or last modified. The **file date** is useful if you have created several versions of a file and want to make sure that you know which version is the most recent. It can also come in handy if you have downloaded several updates of a software package, such as an MP3 player, and you want to make sure that you install the latest version.

FIGURE 4-3

File sizes and dates can provide information that is useful when working with files.

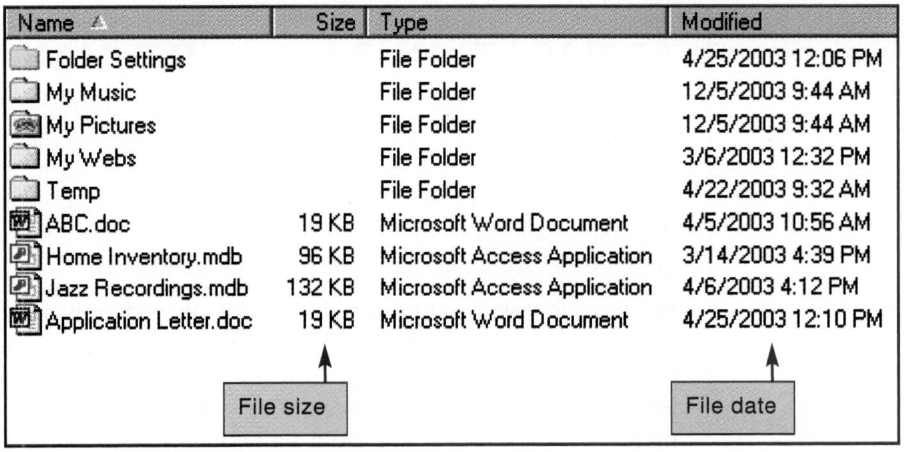

Name △	Size	Type	Modified
Folder Settings		File Folder	4/25/2003 12:06 PM
My Music		File Folder	12/5/2003 9:44 AM
My Pictures		File Folder	12/5/2003 9:44 AM
My Webs		File Folder	3/6/2003 12:32 PM
Temp		File Folder	4/22/2003 9:32 AM
ABC.doc	19 KB	Microsoft Word Document	4/5/2003 10:56 AM
Home Inventory.mdb	96 KB	Microsoft Access Application	3/14/2003 4:39 PM
Jazz Recordings.mdb	132 KB	Microsoft Access Application	4/6/2003 4:12 PM
Application Letter.doc	19 KB	Microsoft Word Document	4/25/2003 12:10 PM

File size   File date

4

QUICKCheck Section A

1 An operating system's file-naming [＿＿＿＿＿] provide a set of rules for naming files.

2 Most operating systems do not allow you to use [＿＿＿＿＿] words as filenames.

3 A file [＿＿＿＿＿] refers to the arrangement of data in a file, and the coding scheme that is used to represent the data.

4 The main directory of a disk is sometimes referred to as the [＿＿＿＿＿] directory.

5 A file's location is defined by a file [＿＿＿＿＿], which includes the drive letter, folder(s), filename, and extension.

6 A file's [＿＿＿＿＿] can be important information when you've created several versions of a file and you want to know which version is the most recent.

check answers ✻

Section

FILE MANAGEMENT

File management encompasses any procedure that helps you organize your computer-based files so that you can find and use them more efficiently. Depending on your computer's operating system, you may be able to organize and manipulate your files from within an application program, or by using a special file management utility provided by the operating system. Section B provides an overview of application-based and operating system-based file management.

APPLICATION-BASED FILE MANAGEMENT

How does a software application help me manage files? Applications, such as word processing software or graphics software, typically provide a way to open files and save them in a specific folder on a designated storage device. An application might also provide additional file management capabilities, such as deleting and renaming files. Let's look at an example of the file management capabilities provided by a typical Windows application—Microsoft Word.

Suppose that you want to write a letter to the editor of your local newspaper about the rising tide of graffiti in your neighborhood. Typically, you would open your word processing software and type the document. As you type, the document is held in RAM. At some point, you'll want to save the document. To do so, you click File on the menu bar, then select the Save As option. The Save As dialog box, shown in Figure 4-4, appears and allows you to specify a name for the file, and its location on one of your computer's storage devices.

FIGURE 4-4

Using the Save As dialog box to name a file and specify its storage location

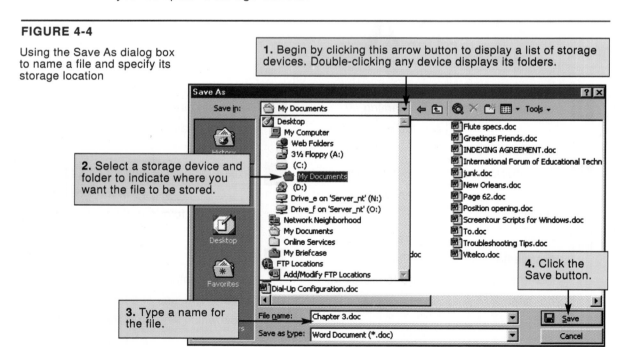

1. Begin by clicking this arrow button to display a list of storage devices. Double-clicking any device displays its folders.

2. Select a storage device and folder to indicate where you want the file to be stored.

3. Type a name for the file.

4. Click the Save button.

FIGURE 4-5

Should I use the Save or Save As command?

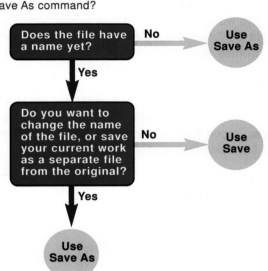

What's the difference between the Save option and the Save As option? Most Windows applications provide a curious set of options on the File menu. In addition to the Save As option, the menu also contains a Save option. The difference between the two options is subtle, but useful. The Save As option allows you to select a name and storage device for a file, whereas the Save option simply saves the latest version of a file under its current name and at its current location.

A potentially confusing aspect of these options occurs when you try to use the Save option for a file that doesn't yet have a name. Because you can't save a file without a name, your application displays the Save As dialog box, even though you selected the Save option. The flowchart in Figure 4-5 will help you decide whether to use the Save or Save As command.

What other options does the Save As dialog box provide? The Save As dialog box that is displayed by Windows applications allows you to do more than just save a file. You can use it to rename a file, delete a file, or create a folder, as shown in Figure 4-6.

4

FIGURE 4-6

The Save As dialog box not only helps you select a name and destination drive for a file, it also allows you to rename files, delete files, create folders, and rename them.

Use this icon to create a new folder.

To rename or delete a folder, right-click it and then use one of the options on the pop-up menu.

To rename or delete a file, right-click the filename, then select a command from the pop-up menu that appears. In addition to the Rename and Delete options, this menu might also include options to print the file, e-mail it, or scan it for viruses.

click to start

Save As

Save in: My Documents ▼ ← 🔁 🔍 ✕ 📁 ▦ ▾ Tools ▾

- Electronic Reference Fo...
- MLA ONLINE_files
- Music
- My Pictures
- My Webs
- Three Pigs
- Tour_files
- BOW fonts.doc
- Canada.doc
- CBT Development Article
- Comments on 1.5.doc
- Comments on Practical E
- Computer Desk order.do
- Dial up.doc
- Dial-Up Configuration.doc

Save
Add to Zip
Add to Chapter 3.zip
Zip and E-Mail Chapter 3.zi

Send To

Cut
Copy

Create Shortcut
Delete
Rename

Properties

...specs.doc
...tings Friends.doc
...XING AGREEMENT.doc

History
...cuments
Desktop
Favorites
Web Folders

File name: Dial-Up Configuration.doc ▼   💾 Save

Save as type: Word Document (*.doc) ▼   Cancel

FILE MANAGEMENT UTILITIES

How does the operating system help me manage files? Although most application software provides access to commands that you can use to save, open, rename, and delete individual files, you might want to work with groups of files, or perform other file operations that are inconvenient within the Open or Save dialog boxes. Most operating systems provide **file management utilities** that give you the "big picture" of the files you have stored on your disks and help you work with them. For example, Windows provides a file management utility that can be accessed from the My Computer icon, or from the Windows Explorer option on the Start menu. On computers with Mac OS, the file management utility is called the "Finder." These utilities, shown in Figure 4-7, help you view a list of files, find files, move files from one place to another, make copies of files, delete files, discover file properties, and rename files.

FIGURE 4-7

The Windows File Manager utility can be tailored to show files as icons (top) or as a list (middle). Mac OS provides a file management utility called the Finder (bottom).

FIGURE 4-8

You can visualize the directory of a disk as a tree on its side. The trunk corresponds to the root directory, the branches to folders, and the leaves to files.

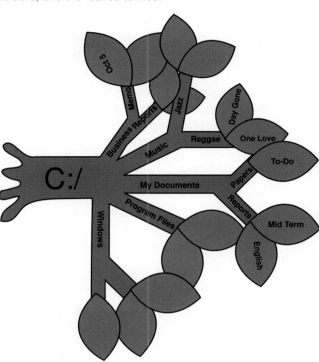

FIGURE 4-9

Windows Explorer borrows the folders from the filing cabinet metaphor, and places them in a hierarchical structure similar to a tree on its side.

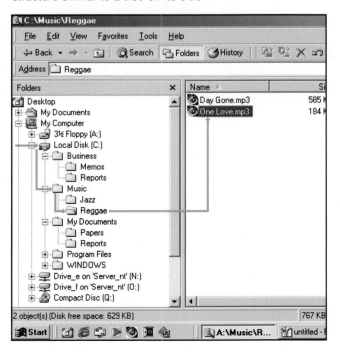

FILE MANAGEMENT METAPHORS

How does a metaphor help me visualize the "big picture" for my file storage? File management utilities often use some sort of **storage metaphor** to help you visualize and mentally organize the files on your disks and other storage devices. These metaphors are also called **logical storage models** because they are supposed to help you form a mental (logical) picture of the way in which your files are stored.

What storage metaphors are typically used for personal computers? After hearing so much about files and folders, you might have guessed that the filing cabinet is a popular metaphor for computer storage. In this metaphor, each storage device of a computer corresponds to one of the drawers in a filing cabinet. The drawers hold folders and the folders hold files.

Another storage metaphor is based on a hierarchical diagram that is sometimes referred to as a "tree structure." In this metaphor, a tree represents a storage device. The trunk of the tree corresponds to the root directory. The branches of the tree represent folders. These branches can split into small branches representing folders within folders. The leaves at the end of a branch represent the files in a particular folder. Figure 4-8 illustrates the tree lying on its side so that you can see the relationship to the metaphor shown in the next figure, Figure 4-9.

The tree structure metaphor provides a useful mental image of the way in which files and folders are organized. It is not, however, particularly practical as a user interface. Imagine the complexity of the tree diagram from Figure 4-8 if it were expanded to depict branches for hundreds of folders and leaves for thousands of files.

For practicality, storage metaphors are translated into more mundane screen displays. Figure 4-9 shows how Microsoft programmers combined the filing cabinet metaphor with the tree structure metaphor within the Windows Explorer file management utility.

4

WINDOWS EXPLORER

How do I use a file management utility? As an example of a file management utility, let's take a closer look at **Windows Explorer**, a utility program that is bundled with the Windows operating system, and is designed to help you organize and manipulate the files stored on your computer. Most file management operations begin with locating a particular file or folder. A file management utility should make it easy to find what you're looking for by drilling down through your computer's hierarchy of folders and files.

The Windows Explorer window is divided into two "window panes." The pane on the left side of the window lists each of the storage devices connected to your computer, plus several important system objects, such as My Computer, Network Neighborhood, and the Desktop. An icon for a storage device or other system object can be "expanded" by clicking its corresponding plus-sign icon. Opening an icon displays the next level of the storage hierarchy—usually a collection of folders. Any of these folders that contain subfolders can be further expanded by clicking their plus-sign icons.

A device icon or folder can be "opened" by clicking directly on the icon, rather than on the plus sign. Once an icon is opened, its contents appear in the pane on the right side of the Windows Explorer window. Figure 4-10 illustrates how to manipulate the directory display.

FIGURE 4-10

Windows Explorer makes it easy to drill down through the levels of the directory hierarchy to locate a folder or file.

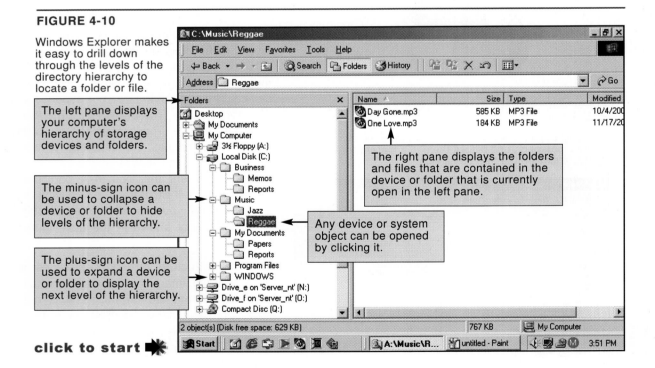

The left pane displays your computer's hierarchy of storage devices and folders.

The minus-sign icon can be used to collapse a device or folder to hide levels of the hierarchy.

The plus-sign icon can be used to expand a device or folder to display the next level of the hierarchy.

The right pane displays the folders and files that are contained in the device or folder that is currently open in the left pane.

Any device or system object can be opened by clicking it.

click to start ➤

What can I do with the folders and files that are listed in Windows Explorer?
In addition to locating files and folders, Windows Explorer provides a set of tools that
will help you manipulate files and folders in the following ways:

- **Rename.** You might want to change the name of a file or folder to better describe
  its contents. When renaming a file, you should be careful to keep the same filename
  extension so that you can open it with the correct application software.

- **Copy.** You can copy a file or folder—for example, you can copy a file from your hard
  disk to a floppy disk if you want to send it to a friend or colleague. You might also
  want to make a copy of a document so that you can revise the copy and leave the
  original intact. Remember to adhere to copyright and license restrictions when you
  copy files.

- **Move.** You can move a file from one folder to another, or from one storage device
  to another. When you move a file, it is erased from its original location, so make
  sure that you remember the new location of the file. You can also move folders from
  one storage device to another, or move them to a different folder.

- **Delete.** You can delete a file when you no longer need it. You can also delete a
  folder. Be careful when you delete a folder, because most file management utilities
  also delete all the files that a folder contains.

FIGURE 4-11

Windows Explorer
helps you to delete,
copy, move, and
rename files.

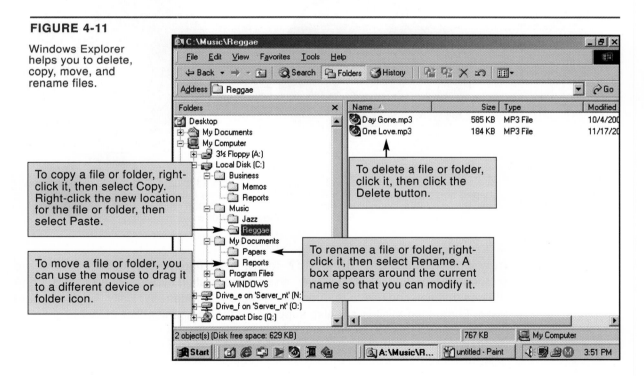

How can I work with more than one file at a time? To work with a group of files
or folders, you must first select them. You can accomplish this task in several ways.
You can hold down the Ctrl key as you click each item. This method works well if you
are selecting files or folders that are not listed consecutively. As an alternative, you
can hold down the Shift key while you click the first item and the last item that you
want to select. By using this method, you select the two items that you clicked, and all
the items in between. Windows Explorer displays all of the items that you selected by
highlighting them. Once a group of items is highlighted, you can use the same copy,
move, or delete procedure that you would use for a single item.

PHYSICAL FILE STORAGE

Is data stored in specific places on a disk? So far, you've seen how an operating system like Windows can help you visualize computer storage as files and folders. This pretty picture, however, has little to do with what actually happens on your disk. The structure of files and folders that you see in Windows Explorer is what's called a "logical" model—logical because it is supposed to help you create a mental picture. The **physical storage model** describes what actually happens on the disks and in the circuits. As you will see, the physical model is quite different from the logical model.

Before a computer can store a file on a disk, CD, or DVD, the storage medium must be formatted. The **formatting** process creates the equivalent of electronic storage bins by dividing a disk into **tracks**, and then further dividing each track into **sectors**. Tracks and sectors are numbered to provide addresses for each data storage bin. The numbering scheme depends on the storage device and the operating system. On CDs and DVDs, one or more tracks spiral out from the center of the disk; on floppy, Zip, and hard disks, tracks are arranged as concentric circles (Figure 4-12).

FIGURE 4-12

A process called formatting prepares the surface of a disk to hold data.

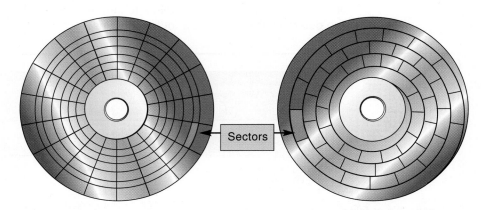

Disks are divided into tracks and wedge-shaped sectors—each side of a floppy disk typically has 80 tracks divided into 18 sectors. Each sector holds 512 bytes of data.

On a typical CD, a single track is about three miles long and is divided into 336,000 sectors. Each sector holds 2,048 bytes of data.

How does a disk get formatted? Today, most floppy, Zip, and hard disks are preformatted at the factory; however, computer operating systems provide **formatting utilities** that you can use to reformat some storage devices—typically floppy and hard disks. Formatting utilities are also supplied by the companies that manufacture hard disk drives, writable CD drives, and writable DVD drives.

When you use a formatting utility, it erases any data that happens to be on the disk, then prepares the tracks and sectors necessary to hold data. You might consider reformatting some of your old floppy disks (instead of just deleting the files that they contain) if you really want to make them blank before you reuse them. The screen tour associated with Figure 4-13 demonstrates how to use Windows to format a floppy disk.

FIGURE 4-13

Windows includes a floppy disk formatting utility, which can be accessed from the A: (Floppy disk) icon in the My Computer window or Windows Explorer.

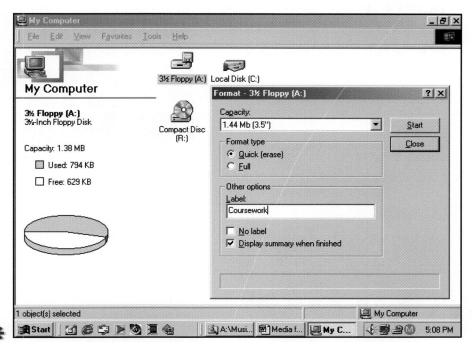

click to start ▶

How does the operating system keep track of a file's location? The operating system uses a **file system** to keep track of the names and locations of files that reside on a storage medium, such as a hard disk. Different operating systems use different file systems. Most versions of Mac OS use the Macintosh Hierarchical File System (HFS). Ext2fs (extended 2 file system) is the native file system for Linux. Windows NT, Windows 2000, and Windows XP use a file system called New Technology File System (NTFS). The file system for Windows 3.1 was called FAT16. Windows versions 95, 98, and Me use a file system called FAT32.

To speed up the process of storing and retrieving data, a disk drive usually works with a group of sectors called a **cluster** or a "block." The number of sectors that form a cluster varies, depending on the capacity of the disk and the way that the operating system works with files. A file system's primary task is to maintain a list of clusters and keep track of which are empty and which hold data. This information is stored in a special file. If your computer uses the FAT32 file system, for example, this special file is called the **File Allocation Table** (FAT). Each of your disks contains its own FAT, so that information about its contents is always available when the disk is in use. Unfortunately, storing this crucial file on disk also presents a risk because if the FAT is damaged by a hard disk head crash or scratch, you'll generally lose access to all of the data stored on the disk. FATs become damaged all too frequently, so it is important to back up your data.

When you save a file, your PC's operating system looks at the FAT to see which clusters are empty. It will select one of these clusters, record the file data there, and then revise the FAT to include the filename and its location.

A file that does not fit into a single cluster spills over into the next contiguous (meaning adjacent) cluster unless that cluster already contains data. When contiguous clusters are not available, the operating system stores parts of a file in noncontiguous (nonadjacent) clusters. Figure 4-14 helps you visualize how the FAT keeps track of filenames and locations.

FIGURE 4-14

Each colored cluster on the disk contains part of a file. Clusters 3 and 4 (blue) contain the Bio.txt file. Cluster 9 (aqua) contains the Pick.wps file. Clusters 7, 8, and 10 contain the Jordan.wks file.

A computer locates and displays the Jordan.wks file by looking for its name in the File Allocation Table. By following the pointers listed in the Status column, the computer sees that the file is continued in clusters 8 and 10.

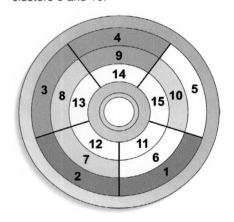

File Allocation Table		
Cluster	Status	Comment
1	1	Reserved for operating system
2	1	Reserved for operating system
3	4	First cluster of Bio.txt. Points to cluster 4, which holds more data for Bio.txt
4	999	Last cluster for Bio.txt
5	0	Empty
6	0	Empty
7	8	First cluster for Jordan.wks. Points to cluster 8, which holds more data for the Jordan.wks file
8	10	Second cluster for Jordan.wks. Points to cluster 10, which holds more data for the Jordan.wks file
9	999	First and ony cluster containing Pick.wps
10	999	Last cluster of Jordan.wks

When you want to retrieve a file, the OS looks through the FAT for the filename and its location. It moves the disk drive's read-write head to the first cluster that contains the file data. Using additional data from the FAT, the operating system can move the read-write heads to each of the clusters that contain the remaining parts of the file.

What happens when a file is deleted? When you click a file's icon and then select the delete option, you might have visions of the read-write head somehow scrubbing out the clusters that contain data. That doesn't happen. Instead, the operating system simply changes the status of the file's clusters to "empty" and removes the filename from the FAT. The filename no longer appears in a directory listing, but the file's data remains in the clusters until a new file is stored there. You might think that this data is as good as erased, but it is possible to purchase utilities that recover a lot of this "deleted" data—law enforcement agents, for example, use these utilities to gather evidence from "deleted" files on the computer disks of suspected criminals.

To delete data from a disk in such a way that no one can ever read it, you can use special **file shredder software** that overwrites "empty" sectors with random 1s and 0s. You might find this software handy if you plan to donate your computer to an organization, and you want to make sure that your personal data no longer remains on the hard disk.

FILE MANAGEMENT, VIRUS PROTECTION, AND BACKUP   **183**

How does the Recycle Bin affect file deletions? The Windows Recycle Bin and similar utilities in other operating systems are designed to protect you from accidentally deleting hard disk files that you actually need. Instead of marking a file's FAT clusters as available, the operating system moves the file to the Recycle Bin folder. The "deleted" file still takes up space on the disk, but does not appear in the usual directory listing. The file does, however, appear in the directory listing for the Recycle Bin folder, and you can undelete any files in this listing.

How does a disk become fragmented? As a computer writes files on a disk, parts of files tend to become scattered all over the disk. These **fragmented files** are stored in noncontiguous clusters. Drive performance generally declines as the read-write heads move back and forth to locate the clusters that contain the parts of a file. To regain peak performance, you can use a **defragmentation utility** to rearrange the files on a disk so that they are stored in contiguous clusters. (See Figure 4-15.)

FIGURE 4-15

Defragmenting a disk helps your computer operate more efficiently. Consider using a defragmentation utility at least once a month to keep your computer running in top form.

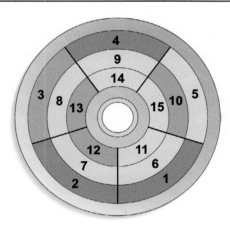

On this fragmented disk, the purple, yellow, and blue files are stored in noncontiguous clusters.

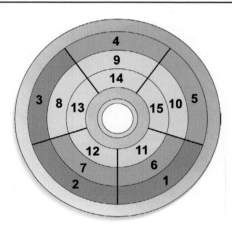

When the disk is defragmented, the sectors of data for each file are moved to contiguous clusters.

4

QUICK Check
Section B

1 The [＿＿＿＿＿＿] option on an application's File menu allows you to name a file and specify its storage location.

2 A(n) [＿＿＿＿＿＿] storage model helps you form a mental picture of how your files are arranged on a disk.

3 On a floppy disk or hard disk, data is stored in concentric circles called [＿＿＿＿＿＿], which are divided into wedge-shaped [＿＿＿＿＿＿].

4 An operating system uses a [＿＿＿＿＿＿] system to keep track of the names and locations of files that reside on a storage medium.

5 Windows maintains a file [＿＿＿＿＿＿] table, which contains the name and location of every file on a disk.

check answers ➤

PRACTICE   TRACKING

LAB 4-B
WORKING WITH WINDOWS EXPLORER

Interactive **LAB**
Working with Explorer

My Documents

Chopsticks.bmp
BMP File

Modified: 4/27/2002 4:16

Size: 452 KB

click to start ➤

In this lab, you'll learn:

■ How to access Windows Explorer

■ How to expand and collapse the directory structure to locate folders and files

■ How to rename or delete a file or folder

■ The basic principles for creating an efficient directory structure for your files

■ How to create a folder

■ How to select a single file or a group of files

■ How to move files from one folder to another

LAB Assignments

1   Start the interactive part of the lab. Insert your Tracking Disk if you want to save your QuickCheck results. Perform each of the lab steps as directed, and answer all of the lab QuickCheck questions. When you exit the lab, your answers are automatically graded and your results are displayed.

2   Use Windows Explorer to look at the directory of the hard disk or floppy disk that currently contains most of your files. Draw a diagram showing the hierarchy of folders. Write a paragraph explaining how you could improve this hierarchy, and draw a diagram to illustrate your plan.

3   Use a new floppy disk or format an old disk that doesn't contain important data. Create three folders on the disk: *Music*, *Web Graphics*, and *Articles*. Within the *Music* folder, create four additional folders: *Jazz*, *Reggae*, *Rock*, and *Classical*. Within the *Classical* folder, create two more folders: *Classical MIDI* and *Classical MP3*. If you have Internet access, go on to #4.

4   Use your browser software to connect to the Internet, then go to a Web site, such as *www.zdnet.com* or *www.cnet.com*. Look for a small graphic (remember, you only have 1.44 MB of space on your floppy disk!) and download it to your Web Graphics folder. Next, use a search engine like *www.google.com* or *www.yahoo.com* to search for "classical MIDI music." Download one of the compositions to the *Music\Classical\Classical MIDI* folder. Open Windows Explorer and expand all of the directories for drive A. Open the *Music\Classical\Classical MIDI* folder and make sure that your music download appears. Capture a screenshot. Follow your instructor's directions to submit this screenshot as a printout or e-mail attachment.

Section **C**

COMPUTER VIRUSES

Computer viruses cause sensational headlines. They also cause an estimated $1.6 billion in lost productivity every year. Last year, in North America alone, businesses lost more than 7,000 person-years of productivity while responding to viruses, Denial-of-Service glitches, and other cyber attacks.

Viruses are one of the biggest threats to the security of your computer files. The number of computer viruses is increasing at an unprecedented rate. In 1986, there was one known computer virus. By 1990, the total had jumped to 80. Today, the count exceeds 58,000, and between 10 and 15 new viruses appear every day. Viruses are spreading more rapidly than ever. The Michelangelo virus took seven months to reach 75,000 people; the Melissa virus took 10 hours to reach 3.5 million people; and a virus called I-love-you took only three hours to reach 72 million.

Computer viruses invade all types of computers, including mainframes, servers, personal computers, and even handheld computers. Spreading a virus is a crime in the U.S. and in many other countries, but a battery of laws has not prevented viruses from "accidentally" escaping from a hacker's computer, or from being intentionally released. Although technically, the term virus refers to a type of program that behaves in a specific way, it has become a generic term that refers to a variety of destructive programs. To defend your computer against viruses, you should understand what they are, how they work, and how to use antivirus software.

VIRUSES, TROJAN HORSES, AND WORMS

What's the technical definition of a virus? A **computer virus** is a set of program instructions that attaches itself to a file, reproduces itself, and spreads to other files. It can corrupt files, destroy data, display an irritating message, or otherwise disrupt computer operations. A common misconception is that viruses spread themselves from one computer to another. They can only replicate themselves on the host computer. Viruses spread because people distribute infected files by exchanging disks and CDs, sending e-mail attachments, and downloading software from the Web.

A computer virus generally infects the files executed by your computer—files with extensions such as .exe, .com, or .vbs. When your computer executes an infected program, it also executes the attached virus instructions. These instructions then remain in RAM, waiting to infect the next program that your computer runs, or the next disk that it accesses. In addition to replicating itself, a virus might perform a **trigger event**, sometimes referred to as a "payload," which could be as harmless as displaying an annoying message, or as devastating as corrupting the data on your computer's hard disk. Trigger events are often keyed to a specific date. For example, the Michelangelo virus is designed to damage hard disk files on March 6, the birthday of artist Michelangelo.

A key characteristic of viruses is their ability to "lurk" in a computer for days or months, quietly replicating themselves. While this replication takes place, you might not even know that your computer has contracted a virus; therefore it is easy to inadvertently spread infected files to other people's computers.

4

Viruses can be classified by the types of files they infect. A virus that attaches to an application program, such as a game, is known as a **file virus**. One of the most notorious file viruses, called Chernobyl, can infect just about any EXE files, including games and productivity software. Its payload can overwrite sections of your hard disk.

A **boot sector virus** infects the system files that your computer uses every time you turn it on. These viruses can cause widespread damage and reoccurring problems. The old, but persistent, Stoned virus infects the boot sector of floppy and hard disks, for example. In various versions of this virus, the payload can display a message, such as "Your computer is now stoned!" or it can corrupt some of the data on your computer's hard disk.

A **macro virus** infects a set of instructions called a "macro." A **macro** is essentially a miniature program that usually contains legitimate instructions to automate document and worksheet production. A hacker can create a destructive macro, attach it to a document or worksheet, and then distribute it on a floppy disk or over the Internet—often as an e-mail attachment. When anyone views the document, the macro virus duplicates itself into the general macro pool, where it is picked up by other documents. The two most common macro viruses are the Melissa virus, which attaches itself to Microsoft Word documents, and Codemas, which attaches itself to Microsoft Excel spreadsheets.

How is a Trojan horse different from a virus? A **Trojan horse** is a computer program that seems to perform one function while actually doing something else. Technically, it is not the same as a virus because, unlike a virus, a Trojan horse is not designed to make copies of itself. Trojan horses are notorious for stealing passwords. For example, a Trojan horse called PictureNote.Trojan (alias Trojan Horse, Backdoor.Note, Picture.exe, and URLSnoop) usually arrives as an e-mail attachment named Picture.exe, which leads you to believe that you've received some type of graphics software. If you open this file, however, it searches for America Online (AOL) user information, and tries to steal your login and e-mail passwords.

Some Trojan horses delete files and cause other trouble. Although a Trojan horse is not defined as a program that replicates itself, some Trojan horses do contain a virus or a worm, which can replicate and spread.

What's a worm? With the proliferation of network traffic and e-mail, worms have become a major concern in the computing community. Unlike a virus, which is designed to spread from file to file, a **worm** is designed to spread from computer to computer. Most worms take advantage of communications networks—especially the Internet—to travel within e-mail and TCP/IP packets, jumping from one computer to another. Some worms are happy simply to spread throughout a network. Others also deliver payloads that vary from harmless messages to malicious file deletions.

The old saying "know thy enemy" applies to viruses. To learn more details about the viruses that are high on the list of current threats, visit the Virus Descriptions InfoWeb.

click ■✳

Klez, for example, is a mass-mailing worm that sends itself to every address in the address book of an infected computer. To make the virus difficult to track, the "From" line of the infected message contains the e-mail address of a randomly selected person from the address book, rather than the address of the computer that actually sent the mail. The infected e-mail message typically claims to contain an attachment that can be used to protect your computer against Klez, but it actually contains the worm, which can infect your computer when the message—not the attachment—is opened or previewed.

Another notorious worm known as "Love Bug" arrives as an e-mail attachment called LOVE-LETTER-FOR-YOU.TXT.vbs. Once you open the attachment, the worm overwrites most of the music, graphics, document, spreadsheet, and Web files on your disk. After trashing your files, the worm automatically mails itself to everyone in your e-mail address book, looking for other victims.

Notice that the attachment LOVE-LETTER-FOR-YOU.TXT.vbs appears to have two filename extensions. That's a clue that should arouse your suspicions. The second extension, .vbs, is the real filename extension and it means that the file contains an executable program—potentially a virus. Remember that you can set Windows to hide filename extensions. If you do so, the worm-harboring attachment appears simply as LOVE-LETTER-FOR-YOU.TXT. It looks like the attachment has an innocent .txt extension. You might increase your chances of identifying "bad" e-mail attachments if you make sure that Windows is set to display all filename extensions.

Some worms are designed to generate a lot of activity on a network by flooding it with useless traffic—enough traffic to overwhelm the network's processing capability and essentially bring all communications to a halt. These **Denial of Service attacks** have colorful names like Ping of Death, Smurf, and Teardrop, but network users cut off from e-mail and Web browsing have other names for them, like disruptive and obnoxious.

How are viruses spread? Viruses can slip into your computer from a variety of sources. Be cautious of floppy disks, homemade CDs, and Web sites that contain games and other supposedly fun stuff. They are a common source of file viruses, boot sector viruses, and Trojan horses. Figure 4-16 illustrates how a single disk can easily infect many computers.

FIGURE 4-16

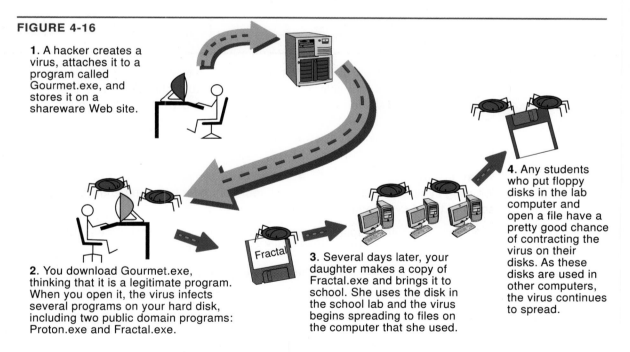

1. A hacker creates a virus, attaches it to a program called Gourmet.exe, and stores it on a shareware Web site.

2. You download Gourmet.exe, thinking that it is a legitimate program. When you open it, the virus infects several programs on your hard disk, including two public domain programs: Proton.exe and Fractal.exe.

3. Several days later, your daughter makes a copy of Fractal.exe and brings it to school. She uses the disk in the school lab and the virus begins spreading to files on the computer that she used.

4. Any students who put floppy disks in the lab computer and open a file have a pretty good chance of contracting the virus on their disks. As these disks are used in other computers, the virus continues to spread.

A common misconception is that write-protecting your floppy disks by opening the small hole in the corner of the disk prevents virus infection. Although a virus cannot "jump" onto your disk when it is write-protected, you must remove the write protection each time you save a file on the disk. With the write protection removed, your disk is open to a virus attack.

E-mail attachments are another common source of viruses. A seemingly innocent attachment could harbor a file virus or a boot sector virus. Typically, infected attachments look like executable files, usually with .exe filename extensions, although in some cases they can have .sys, .drv, .com, .bin, .vbs, .scr, or .ovl extensions. These files cannot infect your computer unless you open them, thereby executing the virus code that they contain. You should follow the experts' advice about e-mail attachments. Never open a suspicious attachment without first checking it with antivirus software (discussed on the next page).

Macro viruses tend to hang out in documents created with Microsoft Word and spreadsheets created with Microsoft Excel. You might receive files infected with macro viruses on a disk, as a Web download, or as an e-mail attachment. The infected files display the usual .doc or .xls extensions—there are no outward clues to the virus lurking within the file. Today, most software that executes macros includes security features that help protect your computer from macro viruses. As shown in Figure 4-17, Microsoft Word allows you to disable macros.

FIGURE 4-17

Macro security features may allow you to disable macros, or warn you if a document contains a macro. Macro security warnings do not necessarily mean that a document contains a macro infected with a virus. Scanning the macro with antivirus software, however, can detect the presence of a virus.

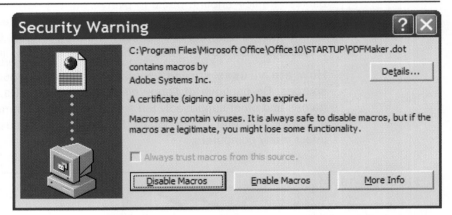

Chapter 1 explained that you can set your e-mail software to use HTML format, which provides a variety of font colors, types, and sizes for your messages. Unfortunately, e-mail that's in HTML format can harbor viruses and worms hidden in program-like "scripts" that are embedded in the HTML tags. These viruses are difficult to detect—even for antivirus software. As a result, many people stick with plain text, non-HTML e-mail.

What are the symptoms of a virus? The symptoms depend on the virus. The following symptoms might indicate that your computer has contracted a virus, though some of these symptoms can have other causes:

- Your computer displays vulgar, embarrassing, or annoying messages, such as "Gotcha! Arf Arf," "You're stoned!," or "I want a cookie."

- Your computer develops unusual visual or sound effects.

- You have difficulty saving files, or files mysteriously disappear.

- Your computer suddenly seems to work very slowly.

- Your computer reboots unexpectedly.

- Your executable files unaccountably increase in size.

- Your computer starts sending out lots of e-mail messages on its own.

It is important to remember, however, that some viruses, worms, and Trojan horses have no recognizable symptoms. Your computer can contract a worm, for example, that never displays an irritating message or attempts to delete your files, but which merrily replicates itself through your e-mail until it eventually arrives at a server where it can do some real damage to a network communication system. To avoid being a pawn in some hacker's destructive plot, you should use antivirus software to evict any viruses, worms, or Trojan horses that try to take up residence in your computer.

ANTIVIRUS SOFTWARE

What should I do if my computer gets a virus? If you suspect that your computer has a virus, you should immediately turn to resources provided by antivirus software. **Antivirus software** is a set of utility programs that looks for and eradicates viruses, Trojan horses, and worms. This essential software is available for handheld computers, personal computers, and servers.

If you don't have antivirus software for your computer, you should get it. Use the **Antivirus Software** InfoWeb to link to Web sites where you can purchase and download antivirus software.

└click ■■

How does antivirus software work? Antivirus software uses several techniques to find viruses. As you know, a virus attaches itself to an existing program. Its presence often increases the length of the original program. The earliest antivirus software simply examined the programs on a computer and recorded their length. A change in the length of a program from one computing session to the next indicated the possible presence of a virus. This method of virus detection requires that you start with a virus-free copy of the program.

To counter early antivirus software, hackers became more cunning. They created viruses that insert themselves into unused portions of a program file without changing its length. Of course, the people who designed antivirus software fought back. They designed software that examines the bytes in an uninfected application program and calculates a checksum. A **checksum** is a number that is calculated by combining the binary values of all bytes in a file. Each time you run an application program, the antivirus software calculates the checksum and compares it with the previous checksum. If any byte in the application program has changed, the checksum will be different, and the antivirus software assumes that a virus is present. The checksum approach also requires that you start with a copy of the program that is not infected with a virus. If the original copy is infected, the virus is included in the original checksum, and the antivirus software never detects it.

Antivirus software can identify viruses, Trojan horses, and worms by searching files for virus signatures. A **virus signature** is usually a section of the virus program, such as a unique series of instructions, that can be used to identify a known virus, much as a fingerprint is used to identify an individual. Most of today's antivirus software scans for virus signatures; for this reason, it is sometimes referred to as "virus scanning software."

The signature search technique is fairly quick, but it identifies only those viruses with a known signature. To detect new viruses—and new viruses seem to appear at an alarming rate—virus detection software must be updated regularly.

When should I use antivirus software? The short answer is "all the time." Most antivirus software allows you to specify what to check and when to check it. You can, for example, fire it up only when you receive a suspicious e-mail attachment. Or, you can set it to look through all of the files on your computer once a week. The best practice, however, is to keep your antivirus software running full-time in the background so that it scans all files the moment they are accessed, and checks every e-mail message as it arrives. The scanning process requires a short amount of time, which creates a slight delay in downloading e-mail and opening files. The wait is worth it, however, when you can feel confident that the files you open have been scanned for viruses.

Keeping viruses, Trojan horses, and worms out of your computer is preferable to trying to eliminate these pesky programs after they have taken up residence. Once they infiltrate your computer, they can be difficult to eradicate, even with antivirus software. Certain viruses, for example, are particularly tenacious—just the process of booting up your computer can trigger their replication sequence, or send them into hiding.

4

How often should I get an update? The information that your antivirus software uses to identify and eradicate viruses, Trojan horses, and worms is stored in one or more files usually referred to as "virus definitions." New viruses and variations of old viruses are unleashed just about every day. To keep up with these newly identified pests, antivirus software publishers provide virus definition updates, which are usually available as Web downloads. You should check your antivirus publisher's Web site for the latest updates of antivirus software every few weeks, or if you hear of a new virus making headlines (Figure 4-18).

FIGURE 4-18

You can purchase antivirus software on a CD or download it from the Web. Regardless of the source, it is important to get regular updates—provided at the publisher's Web site.

Some antivirus vendors feature an electronic update service that periodically reminds you to check for updates. When you provide the go-ahead, your computer connects to your antivirus vendor's Web site, downloads updated virus definitions and installs them.

How reliable is antivirus software? Considering the sheer number of viruses that exists and the number of new viruses that debuts every week, antivirus software is surprisingly reliable at identifying and eradicating viruses, Trojan horses, and worms. Viruses try to escape detection in many ways. **Multi-partite viruses** (pronounced multi PAR tite, which rhymes with "kite") are able to infect multiple types of targets. For example, a multi-partite virus might combine the characteristics of a file virus (which hides in .exe files) and a boot sector virus (which hides in the boot sector). If your antivirus software looks for that particular virus only in .exe files, the virus could escape detection by hiding in the boot sector as well. **Polymorphic viruses** mutate to escape detection by changing their signatures. **Stealth viruses** remove their signatures from a disk-based file and temporarily conceal themselves in memory. Antivirus software can only find stealth viruses by scanning memory.

Some viruses—called **retro viruses**—are designed to attack antivirus software by deleting the files that contain virus descriptions, or corrupting the main executable virus program. One antivirus vendor calls them "anti-antivirus viruses."

Unfortunately, antivirus software is not 100% reliable. On rare occasions, it might not identify a virus, or it might think that your computer has a virus when one does not actually exist. Despite these rare mistakes, the protection you get is worth the required investment of time and money. Remember that without antivirus software, your computer is susceptible to all of the nasty little programs that can cause damage to your files and irritate the friends whose files you infect.

VIRUS HOAXES

What's a virus hoax? Some viruses are very real, but you're likely to get e-mail about "viruses" that don't really exist. A **virus hoax** usually arrives as an e-mail message containing dire warnings about a supposedly new virus that is on the loose. The message typically suggests some strategy for avoiding the virus, and recommends that you forward the e-mail warning to all of your friends and colleagues. In many cases, however, the alleged virus does not exist, and the e-mail message is a prank designed to send unwary people into a panic.

How do I recognize a hoax? Back in the days when the online community was small, e-mail was one of the few sources for legitimate news of virus attacks. Today, virus attacks have the potential to affect so many computers that the real threats make headlines on the evening news.

Bogus virus e-mail messages usually contain a long list of people in the To: and Cc: boxes. They have been forwarded many times. Some "authority," such as the Centers for Disease Control, is usually cited to make you think that the alert is official. Most hoaxes include a recommended procedure for eradicating the virus, such as reformatting your computer's hard disk drive—a process that could cause more damage than the virus itself! Fake viruses are often characterized as doing bizarre deeds. For example, check out the message about a phony virus called GoodTimes in Figure 4-19.

FIGURE 4-19

The notorious GoodTimes hoax described a totally unrealistic virus.

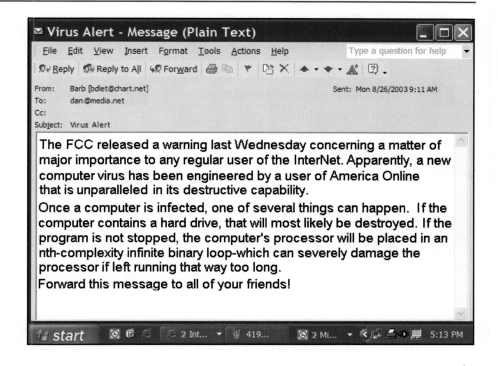

4

Are any virus e-mail warnings real? You might receive several types of legitimate virus warnings. Your LAN administrator might send e-mail messages alerting network users to a newly active virus. You might also receive legitimate virus warnings from your e-mail correspondents. For example, a friend might write something like, "I got a message from you with a virus attached to it." You might also receive messages like, "I discovered virus X on my computer and I might have sent it to you. Sorry." A person experienced in dealing with viruses might also send you the Web links to an antivirus site where you could find more information about the virus.

Some Web sites specialize in tracking hoaxes. For links to these sites, visit the Hoax InfoWeb.

└click ➡✳

What should I do about virus hoaxes? When you receive an e-mail message about a virus, don't panic. Virtually all of them are hoaxes. If you are uncertain, check one of the many antivirus Web sites. There you can look up the alleged virus by name to see if it is a hoax or a real threat. Under no circumstances should you forward virus hoax messages to other people. If the virus is a real threat, the antivirus Web site will provide the information that you need to check your computer and download an update to your antivirus software.

QUICKCheck C
Section

1 Viruses often attach themselves to a program file with a(n) [_____] extension so that when you run the program, you also run the virus code.

2 A boot [_____] virus infects the system files that your computer uses every time you turn it on.

3 Unlike a virus, which is designed to spread from file to file, a(n) [_____] is designed to spread from computer to computer.

4 Write-protecting your floppy disks is an effective technique for preventing virus infection. True or false? [_____]

5 A virus can enter a computer as an e-mail attachment or as a script in an e-mail message formatted as HTML. True or false? [_____]

6 Antivirus software calculates a(n) [_____] to make sure that the bytes in an executable file have not changed from one computing session to another.

7 [_____] viruses remove their signatures from a disk in order to temporarily conceal themselves in memory and avoid detection by antivirus software.

8 A virus that doesn't really exist is referred to as a virus [_____].

check answers ➡✳

Section **D**

DATA BACKUP

Have you ever mistakenly copied an old version of a document over a new version? Has your computer's hard disk drive gone on the fritz? Did a virus wipe out your files before you discovered that it had taken up residence in your computer? Has lightning "fried" your computer system? These kinds of data disasters are not rare; they happen to everyone. You can't always prevent them, so you need a backup plan that helps you recover data that's been wiped out by operator error, viruses, or hardware failures.

Computer experts universally recommend that you make backups of your data. It sounds pretty basic, right? Unfortunately, this advice tells you what to do, not how to do it. It fails to address some key questions, such as: Do I need special backup equipment and software? How often should I make a backup? How many of my files should I back up? What should I do with the backups?

In this last section of Chapter 4, you'll find the answers to your questions about backing up data that's stored on a personal computer. We'll begin by looking at how to devise a backup plan that's right for you, then we'll discuss your equipment and software options. Along the way, you should pick up lots of practical tips that will help you keep your data safe.

4

BACKUP AND RESTORE PROCEDURES

How do I make a backup? A **backup** is a copy of one or more files that has been made in case the original files become damaged. A backup is usually stored on a different storage medium from the original files. For example, you can back up files from your hard disk to a different hard disk, a writable CD or DVD, tape, floppy disk, or Web site. The exact steps that you follow to make a backup depend on your backup equipment, the software you use to make backups, and your personal backup plan. That said, the list in Figure 4-20 should give you a general idea of the steps that are involved in a typical backup session.

FIGURE 4-20 The steps in a typical backup session

1. Insert the disk, CD, or tape on which you'll store the backup.
2. Start the software you're using for the backup.
3. Select the folders and files that you want to back up.
4. Give the "go ahead" to start copying data.
5. Feed in additional disks, CDs, or tapes if prompted to do so.
6. Clearly label each disk, CD, or tape that you use.
7. Test your backup.

click to start ✴

FIGURE 4-21

The steps in a typical restore session

1. Start the software you used to make the backup.
2. Select the file or files that you want to restore.
3. Insert the appropriate backup tape or disk.
4. Wait for the files to be copied from the backup to the hard disk.

How do I restore data? In technical jargon, you **restore** data by copying files from a backup to the original storage medium or its replacement. As with the procedures for backing up data, the process that you use to restore data to your hard disk varies, depending on your backup equipment and software. It also depends on exactly what you need to restore.

After a hard disk crash, for example, you'll probably need to restore all of your backup data to a new hard disk. On the other hand, if you inadvertently delete a file, or mistakenly copy one file over another, you might need to restore only a single file from the backup. Most software designed to back up and restore data allows you to select which files you want to restore. A typical session to restore data would follow the steps in Figure 4-21.

What's the best backup plan? A good backup plan allows you to restore your computing environment to its pre-disaster state with a minimum of fuss. Unfortunately, no single backup plan fits everyone's computing style or budget. You must devise your own backup plan that's tailored to your particular computing needs.

The checklist in Figure 4-22 outlines the factors you should consider as you formulate your own backup plan.

FIGURE 4-22

Backup tips

☑ Decide how much of your data you want, need, and can afford to back up.

☑ Create a realistic schedule for making backups.

☑ Make sure that you have a way to avoid backing up files that contain viruses.

☑ Find out what kind of boot disks you might need to get your computer up and running after a hard disk failure or boot sector virus attack.

☑ Make sure that you have a procedure for testing your restore procedure so that you can successfully retrieve the data that you've backed up.

☑ Find a safe place to store your backups.

☑ Decide what kind of storage device you'll use to make backups.

☑ Select software to handle backup needs.

Do I have to back up every file? A **full-system backup** contains a copy of every program, data, and system file on a computer. The advantage of a full system backup is that you can easily restore everything to its pre-disaster state simply by copying the backup files to a new hard disk. A full-system backup takes a lot of time, however, and fully automating the process requires a large-capacity tape backup device.

A pretty good alternative to a full system backup is a "selective" backup that contains only your most important data files. A backup of your important data files ensures that your computer-based documents and projects are protected from many data disasters. You can back up these files on floppy disks, Zip disks, removable hard disks, external hard disk, CDs, or DVDs. The disadvantage of this backup strategy is that because you backed up only data files, you must manually reinstall all of your software, in addition to restoring your data files.

If your strategy is to back up your important data files, the procedure can be simplified if you've stored all of these files in one folder or its subfolders. For example, Windows users might store their data files in folders contained in the *My Documents* folder. A folder called *My Documents\Music* might hold MP3 files, a *My Documents\Reports* folder can hold reports, a *My Documents\Art* folder can hold various graphics files, and so on. With your data files organized under the umbrella of a single folder, you will be less likely to omit an important file when you make backups.

Some applications, such as financial software, create files and update them without your direct intervention. If you have the option during setup, make sure that these files end up under the *My Documents* umbrella. Otherwise, you must discover the location of the files and make sure that they are backed up with the rest of your data.

In addition to data files that you create, a few other types of data files might be important to you. Consider making backups of the following files:

- **Internet connection information.** Your ISP's phone number and TCP/IP address, your user ID, and your password are often stored in an encrypted file somewhere in the *Windows\System* folder. Your ISP can usually help you find this file.

- **E-mail folders.** If you're using POP e-mail software, your e-mail folder contains all of the e-mail messages that you've sent and received, but not deleted. Check the Help menu on your e-mail program to discover the location of these files.

- **E-mail address book.** Your e-mail address book might be stored separately from your e-mail messages. To find the file on a Windows computer, use the Search or Find option on the Start menu to search for "Address Book."

- **Favorite URLs.** If you're attached to the URLs that you've collected in your Favorites or Bookmarks list, you might want to back up the file that contains this list. To find the file, search your hard disk for "Favorites."

- **Downloads.** If you paid to download any files, you might want to back them up so that you don't have to pay for them again. These files include software, which usually arrives in the form of a compressed .exe file that expands into several separate files as you install it. For backup purposes, the compressed .exe file should be all that you need.

What about the Windows Registry? Windows users typically hear a variety of rumors about backing up the Windows Registry. The Registry, as it is usually called, is an important group of files used by the Windows operating system to store configuration information about all of the devices and software installed on a computer system. If the Registry becomes damaged, your computer might not be able to boot up, launch programs, or communicate with peripheral devices. It is a good idea to have an extra copy of the Registry in case the original file is damaged.

www. InfoWebLinks. com

For more detailed information on backup techniques, such as backing up the Registry, check out the **Backup Techniques** InfoWeb.

click ➹

As simple as it sounds, backing up the Registry can present a bit of a problem because the Registry is always open while your computer is on. Some software that you might use for backups cannot copy open files. If you use such software, the Registry will never make its way onto a backup. Windows users whose backup plans encompass all of the files on the hard disk must make sure that their backup software provides an option for including the Windows Registry. Even if a full-system backup is not planned, many experts recommend that you at least copy the Registry to a separate folder on the hard disk or to a floppy disk. If you do so, you should remember to update this copy whenever you install new software or hardware.

4

How do I avoid backing up files that contain viruses? Viruses can damage files to the point that your computer can't access any data on its hard disk. In such a case, it is really frustrating when you restore data from a backup only to discover that the restored files contain the same virus that wiped out your data. If your antivirus software is not set to constantly scan for viruses on your computer system, you should run an up-to-date virus check as the first step in your backup routine.

How often should I back up my data? Your backup schedule depends on how much data you can afford to lose. If you're working on an important project, you might want to back up the project files several times a day. Under normal use, however, most people schedule a once-a-week backup. If you work with a To Do list, use it to remind yourself when it is time to make a backup.

How many sets of backups do I need? One backup is good, but in case your backup gets corrupted, you should maintain a rotating set of backups. For example, if you are backing up to tape, you can use one tape for your first backup, then use a different tape for your next backup. Use even another tape for your third backup. For your fourth backup, you can overwrite the data on your first backup tape; for your fifth backup, you can overwrite the data on the second tape, and so on. So that you know which backup is the most recent, write the date of the backup on the tape label.

FIGURE 4-23

Full, incremental, and differential backups each take a slightly different approach to backing up files.

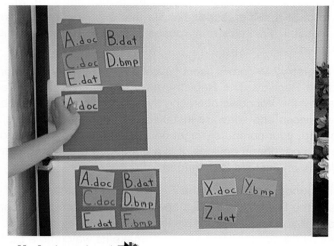

click to start ➡✳

Will all of my backups contain the same files? A **full backup** makes a fresh copy of every file that exists in the folders that you've specified for the backup. In contrast to a *full-system* backup, a full backup does not necessarily contain every file on your computer. A full backup can refer to a backup that contains all of your data files, for example, if those are the files that you wish to regularly back up.

It is not necessary to make a full backup on every backup date, especially if most of your files don't change from one backup session to another. Instead of making a full backup every time, you can make differential or incremental backups.

A **differential backup** makes a backup of only those files that were added or changed since your last full backup session. After making a full backup of your important files, you will make differential backups at regular intervals. If you need to restore all of your files after a hard disk crash, first restore the files from your full backup, then restore the files from your latest differential backup.

An **incremental backup** makes a backup of the files that were added or changed since the last backup—not necessarily the files that changed from the last *full* backup, but the files that changed since *any* full or incremental backup. After making a full backup of your important files, you will make your first incremental backup containing the files that changed since the full backup. When you make your second incremental backup, it will contain only the files that changed since the first incremental backup. To restore files from an incremental backup, first files from a full backup are restored, followed by files from each incremental backup, starting with the oldest and ending with the most recent. The video associated with Figure 4-23 describes the difference between full, differential, and incremental backups.

How can I be sure that my backups will work? If your computer's hard disk crashes, you do not want to discover that your backups were blank! To prevent such a disastrous situation, it is important to enable the "read after write" or "compare" option provided by backup software. These options force the software to check the data in each sector as it is written to make sure that it is copied without error. You should also test your backup by trying to restore one file. Try it with one of your least important data files, just in case your backup is faulty.

Do I need a boot disk? If your computer's hard disk is out of commission, you might wonder how it can access the operating system files that are needed to carry out the boot process. If your hard disk failed, or a virus wiped out the boot sector files on your hard disk, you will not be able to use your normal procedures to boot your computer.

A **boot disk** (sometimes called an "emergency boot disk") is a floppy disk or CD that contains the operating system files needed to boot your computer without accessing the hard disk. Several types of boot disks exist, including recovery CDs, Windows Startup Disks, and rescue disks. It is a good idea to have one of each.

Most of today's computer manufacturers supply a type of boot disk with new computer systems called a **recovery CD**. It contains the operating system files needed to boot the computer, plus all of the Windows and application software files needed to restore your computer to the state it was in when you bought it. A recovery CD is a valuable part of your backup arsenal when used in conjunction with a backup of your data files.

Another type of boot disk, called the **Windows Startup Disk**, is valuable to Windows users because it loads not only the operating system, but also the CD-ROM drivers necessary for your computer to access files on the CD-ROM. You can create a startup disk for Windows 95, 98, and Me by following the steps in Figure 4-24. Instructions for creating a Windows XP startup disk are available at the Microsoft Web site.

4

FIGURE 4-24

To create a Windows Startup Disk, you need a formatted floppy disk.

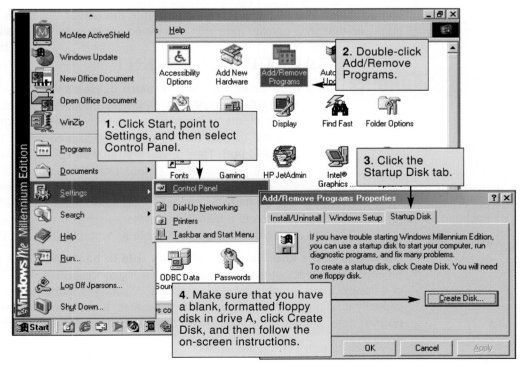

Your antivirus software company probably advises you to create another version of a boot disk, called a **rescue disk**, which contains operating system files, plus a special version of the antivirus software that can perform the first wave of virus cleanup in RAM and on the hard disk.

Where should I store my backups? Store your backups in a safe place. Don't keep them at your computer desk because a fire or flood that damages your computer could also wipe out your backups. In addition, a thief who steals your computer might also scoop up nearby equipment and media. Storing your backups at a different location is the best idea, but at least store them in a room apart from your computer.

Can I store my backups on the Internet? Several Web sites offer fee-based back-up storage space. When needed, you can simply download backup files from the Web site to your hard disk. These sites are practical for backups of your data files. When Web-based backups are used in conjunction with a recovery CD, you can usually restore your computer into functional condition after a data disaster. Experts suggest, however, that you do not rely on a Web site as your only method of backup. If a site goes out of business or is the target of a DoS attack, your backup data may not be accessible.

Interested in using a Web site for your backup? You can evaluate several of these sites by following the links from the **Web-based Backup** InfoWeb.

◀click ◼❈

Although suitable for data files, Web-based backup might not be feasible for storing a full-system backup for two reasons. First, without a recovery CD it would be difficult to restore the system files necessary to get your computer connected to the Internet in order to access your Web-based backup. Second, the transfer time for several gigabytes of files could take days.

Can I store my files on a network server? If your computer is connected to a local area network, you might be able to use the network server as a backup device. Before entrusting your data to a server, check with the network administrator to make sure that you are allowed to store a large amount of data on the server. Because you might not want strangers to access your data, you should store it in a password-protected, non-shared folder. You also should make sure that the server is backed up on a regular basis, so that your backup data won't be wiped out by a server crash.

BACKUP EQUIPMENT

Tape backup technology is constantly changing to keep up with hard disk drives that are getting increasingly larger. For the latest specs and prices, visit the **Tape Backup** InfoWeb.

◀click ◼❈

Is a tape drive the best backup device? Even with the proliferation of writable CDs and DVDs, tape drives remain the best backup device for personal computers. Internal models can be installed in an open drive bay. External models can be connected to a computer's SCSI, parallel, serial, or USB port. Tape drives are fairly inexpensive and fast enough to back up an entire hard disk in less than two hours. Make sure that you purchase a tape drive with the capacity to hold the entire contents of your hard disk so that you can leave the tape unattended during a full-system backup. Tape is a fairly reliable storage medium—similar to floppy disks and Zip disks—but not as durable as writable CDs and DVDs.

Do floppy disks and Zip disks play any role in backups? Floppy disks are inexpensive and just about every computer has a floppy disk drive. The 1.44 MB capacity of a floppy disk is suitable for storing several documents, but does not provide enough capacity for digital photos or most MP3 music files. If you have no other means to back up your data, at least copy your e-mail address book and important data files to floppy disks.

Zip disks with 100 MB or 250 MB capacity are sufficient for backups of documents and most digital graphics files. Several 750 MB Zip disks might be sufficient for backing up all of your data files, and could be feasible for a full-system backup if you have not installed lots of application software.

What about writable CDs and DVDs? Writable optical technologies provide good storage capacity, and blank disks are fairly inexpensive. You can typically use them to back up all of your data files. It might also be feasible to back up your entire system on a series of CDs or DVDs. You would, however, have to monitor the backup process and switch disks occasionally. The major disadvantage of writable CDs and DVDs is that the writing process is slow—slower than writing data to tape or a removable hard disk.

How about a second hard disk drive? A second hard disk drive is a good backup option—especially if it has equivalent capacity to your main hard disk. This capacity allows the backup process to proceed unattended, because you won't have to swap disks or CDs. Speed-wise, a hard disk is even faster than many tape drives. Unfortunately, like your main hard disk, your backup hard disk is susceptible to head crashes, making it one of the least reliable storage options. Another disadvantage: unless your second hard disk drive uses removable storage cartridges that you can store in a safe place, your backups will also be susceptible to electrical damage and any other catastrophe that besets your computer.

How do I choose a backup device? The backup device that you select depends on the value of your data, your current equipment, and your budget. If you can afford a tape drive, buy one, install it, and use it. Otherwise, use what you have—your writable CD drive, Zip drive, or floppy disk drive. If you have several backup options available, use the table in Figure 4-25 to evaluate the strengths and weaknesses of each one.

4

FIGURE 4-25	Storage Capacities of Backup Media			
	Device Cost	Media Cost	Capacity	Comments
Floppy disk	$40-99	25¢	1.44 MB	Low capacity means that you have to wait around to feed in disks
Zip disk	$200 (average)	$15	750 MB	Holds much more than a floppy but a backup still requires multiple disks
External hard disk	$200 (average)	-NA-	80 GB (average)	Fast and convenient, but may hold only one backup
Removable hard disk	$149 (average)	$100.00	2 GB (average)	Fast, limited capacity, but disks can be removed and locked in a secure location
CD-R	$200	50¢	680 MB	Limited capacity, can't be re-used, long shelf life
CD-RW	$100-200	$1.25	680 MB	Limited capacity, reusable, very slow
Writable DVD	$400 (average)	$8.00	4.7 GB	Good capacity, not yet standardized
Tape	$300 (average)	$50.00	40 GB (average)	Great capacity, reasonable media cost, convenient—you can let backups run overnight
Web site		$5.95 per month		Transfer rate depends on your Internet connection; security and privacy of your data may be a concern

BACKUP SOFTWARE

www.InfoWebLinks.com

For current links to backup software information, reviews, and manufacturers, visit the **Backup Software** InfoWeb.

└click ▪❋──

Do I need special software to make a backup? The software that you use to create your backups depends on your backup plan. If you are simply copying one or more data files to a floppy or Zip disk, you can use the Copy command that is provided by your operating system or a file management utility, such as Windows Explorer. For complex backup operations, you should use backup software. **Backup software** is a set of utility programs designed to back up and restore files. It usually provides options that make it easy to schedule periodic backups, define a set of files that you want to regularly back up, and automate the restoration process for incremental and differential backups. Backup software differs from most copy routines because it typically compresses all of the files for a backup and places them in one large file. The file is indexed so that individual files can be located, uncompressed, and restored, if necessary.

What's the easiest way to make a copy of a floppy disk? Students who work in school computer labs often save and transport their files on floppy disks. Many personal computer operating systems provide a **Copy Disk utility** that makes an exact copy of one floppy disk onto another disk of the same size and capacity. (See Figure 4-26.) This utility does not typically make copies of hard disks or CDs—only floppy disks—so its use for backups is limited to those occasions when you need a backup of a floppy disk.

FIGURE 4-26

The Copy Disk utility copies the contents of one floppy disk onto another floppy disk.

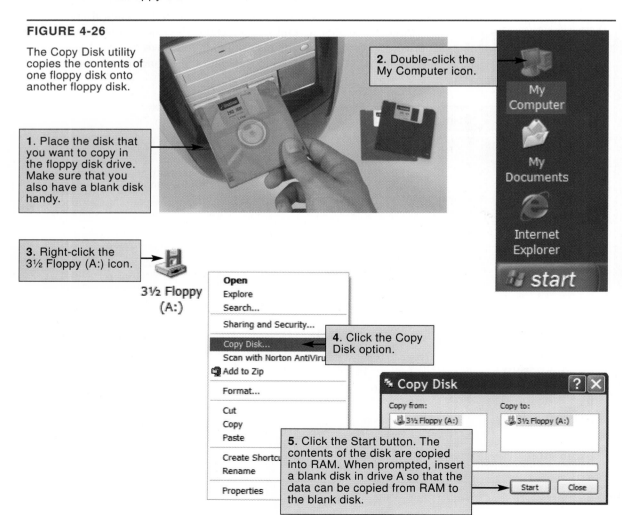

2. Double-click the My Computer icon.

1. Place the disk that you want to copy in the floppy disk drive. Make sure that you also have a blank disk handy.

3. Right-click the 3½ Floppy (A:) icon.

3½ Floppy (A:)

Open
Explore
Search...

Sharing and Security...

Copy Disk...
Scan with Norton AntiViru[s]
Add to Zip

Format...

Cut
Copy
Paste

Create Shortc[ut]
Rename

Properties

4. Click the Copy Disk option.

Copy Disk ? X

Copy from: Copy to:
3½ Floppy (A:)   3½ Floppy (A:)

5. Click the Start button. The contents of the disk are copied into RAM. When prompted, insert a blank disk in drive A so that the data can be copied from RAM to the blank disk.

Start   Close

Where can I get "real" backup software? "Real" backup software gives you great flexibility in selecting the series of files and folders that you want to back up. It might even allow you to schedule automated backups. Your operating system is likely to include backup software. For example, some versions of Windows include Microsoft Backup software, which you can usually find by using the Start button, then selecting Accessories and System Tools.

Backup software is supplied with many backup devices, particularly tape drives. You can also download and purchase backup software from companies that specialize in data protection software. Look for useful features such as the following:

☑ The ability to restore all of your programs and data files without manually reinstalling Windows or any other applications

☑ An option to schedule unattended backups

☑ Support for a variety of backup devices, including tape drives, CD-R and CD-RW, DVD-RAM, Zip, Jaz, SuperDisk, and floppy disks

Whatever backup software you use, remember that it needs to be accessible when it comes time to restore your data. If the only copy of your backup software exists on your backup disks, you will be in a "Catch-22" situation. You won't be able to access your backup software until you restore the files from your backup, but you won't be able to restore your files until your backup software is running! Make sure that you keep the original distribution CD for your backup software, or that you have a separate backup that contains any backup software that you downloaded from the Web. Also be sure to make the required recovery disks so that you can restore Windows and get your backup program running.

4

QUICKCheck Section D

1 It is important to test your [_____] and restore procedures to make sure that you can successfully recover your data.

2 Some full-system backups miss the Windows [_____] because its files are always open while the computer is on.

3 A(n) [_____] disk is a floppy disk or CD that contains the operating system files needed to start your computer without accessing the hard disk.

4 Many personal computer operating systems provide a(n) [_____] utility that makes an exact copy of a floppy disk.

5 The backup process is simplified if you store all of your important data files in the [_____] folder.

check answers ►✳

LAB 4-D
BACKING UP YOUR COMPUTER

Interactive **LAB**
Backing Up Your Computer

click to start ►✳

In this lab, you'll learn:

- How to start the Windows Backup utility
- How to use the Backup Wizard
- How to create a backup job
- Which files to select for a backup job
- The difference between the "selected file" and the "new and changed files" options
- How to back up the Windows Registry
- The advantages and disadvantages of using a password to protect your backup data
- The implications of compressing your backup data
- How to restore data from an entire backup job
- How to restore a single file from a backup

LAB Assignments

1 Start the interactive part of the lab. Insert your Tracking Disk if you want to save your QuickCheck results. Perform each of the lab steps as directed, and answer all of the lab QuickCheck questions. When you exit the lab, your answers are automatically graded and your results are displayed.

2 Describe where most of your data files are stored, and estimate how many megabytes of data (not programs) you have in all of these files. Next, take a close look at these files and estimate how much data (in megabytes) you cannot afford to lose. Finally, explain what you think would be the best hardware device for backing up this amount of data.

3 Draw a sketch or capture a screenshot of the Microsoft Backup window's toolbar. Use ToolTips, ScreenTips, or the window's status bar to find the name of each toolbar button. Use this information to label the buttons on your sketch or screenshot.

4 Assume that you will use Microsoft Backup to make a backup of your data files. Describe the backup job that you would create—specify the folders that you must include. It is not necessary to list individual files unless they are not within one of the folders that you would back up. Make sure that you indicate whether or not you would use password protection, the type of compression that you would select, and how you would handle the Windows Registry.

TECHTALK

FILE FORMATS

As you learned earlier in the chapter, the way that data is stored in a file is referred to as its file format (or file type), and is indicated by its filename extension. Most computer users quickly catch on to the idea that a filename extension provides a clue as to which application software is needed to open the file. For example, when you see that a file has a .doc extension, you immediately conclude that it can be opened using Microsoft Word.

Some operating systems do a fairly good job of shielding users from the intricacies of file formats. For example, Windows uses a file association list to link a filename extension to its corresponding application software. This handy feature allows you to open a data file without first opening an application, simply by double-clicking the file from within Windows Explorer, or selecting it from the Documents list that's accessible from the Start menu.

Of course, your application software also shields you from the messy task of searching through directories to find the files that it will open. When you use the Open dialog box, most applications automatically comb through the files on a specified device and in a specified folder to display only those that have the "right" filename extensions.

With all of this help from the operating system and your application software, it might seem that knowing about file formats is unimportant. While a vague understanding of file formats might be sufficient for computer "newbies," a more in-depth understanding can come in handy. This TechTalk is designed to take your current knowledge of file formats in the Windows environment and "kick it up a notch" so that you'll be able to do the following:

- Figure out the right format for e-mail attachments that you send to friends or colleagues
- Find the right player software for music and media files that you download from the Web
- Discover how to work with a file that doesn't seem to open
- Convert files from one format to another

What determines a file's format? Although a filename extension is a good indicator of a file's format, it does not really define the format. You could use the Rename command to change a QuickTime movie called *Balloons.mov* to *Balloons.doc*. Despite the .doc extension, the file is still in QuickTime format because the data elements within the file are arranged in a specific configuration unique to QuickTime.

The format of a file may include a header, data, and possibly an end-of-file marker. You might recall that file headers were defined in Chapter 2 on page 61. A file header is a section of data at the beginning of a file that contains information about a file—typically the date it was created, the date it was last updated, its size, and its file type. A file header should not be confused with the headers that appear at the top of each page in a document created with a word processor. Instead, envision a file header as a hidden "Post-it" note that's attached to the beginning of a file. Although it is hidden to users, computers can read the information in a file header to determine the file's format.

The remaining contents of a file depend on whether it contains text, graphics, audio, or multimedia data. A text file, for example, might contain sentences and paragraphs interspersed with codes for centering, boldfacing, and margin settings. A graphics file might contain color data for each pixel, followed by a description of the color palette. The arrangement of this data is dictated by the file format. Figure 4-27 illustrates the layout for a Windows bitmap file, and contrasts it with the layout of a GIF file.

FIGURE 4-27

Although both contain graphics, the format for a Windows bitmap file is different from the format for a GIF file.

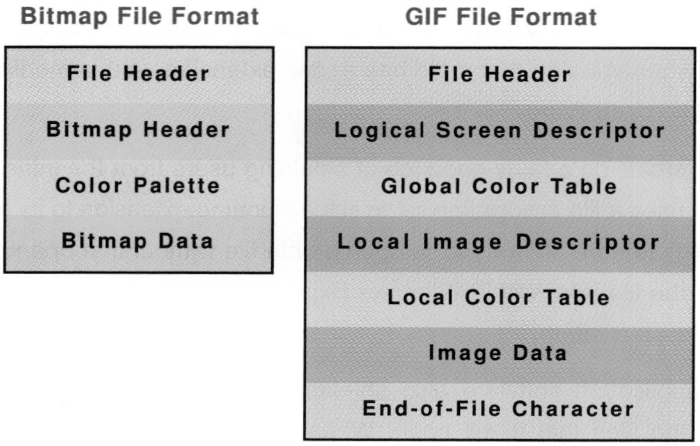

Bitmap File Format	GIF File Format
File Header	File Header
Bitmap Header	Logical Screen Descriptor
Color Palette	Global Color Table
Bitmap Data	Local Image Descriptor
	Local Color Table
	Image Data
	End-of-File Character

Which file formats am I most likely to encounter? A software program typically consists of at least one executable file with an .exe filename extension. It might also include a number of support modules with extensions such as .dll, .vbx, and .ocx. Configuration and startup files usually have .bat, .sys, .ini, and .bin extensions. In addition, you'll find files with .hlp and .tmp extensions. Files with .hlp extensions hold the information for a program's Help utility. Files with .tmp extensions are temporary files. When you open a file with some software, including word processing, spreadsheet, and graphics applications, your operating system makes a copy of the original file and stores this copy on disk as a temporary file. It is this temporary file that you work with as you view and revise a file.

To the uninitiated, the filename extensions that are associated with programs and the operating system might seem "odd." Nevertheless, these files—even the so-called "temporary" files—are crucial for the correct operation of your computer system, so it is important that you do not delete them. The table in Figure 4-28 lists the files that are typically associated with the operating system and executable files.

FIGURE 4-28	Filename Extensions Associated with the OS and Executables	
Type of File	**Description**	**Extension**
Batch File	A sequence of operating system commands that is executed automatically when the computer boots	.bat
Configuration File	Information about programs that the computer uses to allocate the resources necessary to run them	.cfg .sys .mif .bin .ini
Help	The information that is displayed by online Help	.hlp
Temporary File	A sort of "scratch pad" that contains data while a file is open, but that is discarded when you close the file	.tmp
Program Modules	The main executable files for a computer program	.exe .com
Support Modules	Program instructions that are executed in conjunction with the main .exe file for a program	.ocx .vbx .vbs .dll

The list of data file formats is long, but it is useful to become familiar with the most popular formats and the type of data they contain. Figure 4-29 provides this information in a convenient table. Where noted, a file format is associated with a particular software program.

FIGURE 4-29	Data Filename Extensions
Type of File	**Extension**
Text	.txt .dat .rtf .doc (Microsoft Word and WordPad) .wpd (WordPerfect)
Sound	.wav .mid .mp3 .au .ra (RealAudio)
Graphics	.bmp .pcx .tif .wmf .gif .jpg .png .eps .ai (Adobe Illustrator)
Animation/Video	.flc .fli .avi .mpg .mov (QuickTime) .rm (RealMedia)
Web Pages	.htm .html .asp .vrml
Spreadsheets	.xls (Microsoft Excel) .wks (Lotus 1-2-3) .dif
Database	.mdb (Microsoft Access)
Miscellaneous	.pdf (Adobe Acrobat) .ppt (Microsoft PowerPoint) .zip (WinZip) .pub (Microsoft Publisher) .qxd (QuarkExpress)

The **File Formats** InfoWeb provides a list of filename extensions and their corresponding software.

click ➡✳

How do I know which files a program will open? A software application can typically open files that exist in its "native" file format, plus several additional file formats. For example, Microsoft Word opens files in its native DOC format, plus files in formats such as HTML (.htm or .html), Text (.txt), and Rich Text Format (.rtf). Within the Windows environment, you can discover which formats a particular software program can open by looking at the *Files of type* list in the Open dialog box, as shown in Figure 4-30.

4

FIGURE 4-30

An application's *Files of type* list usually displays the file formats that a program can open. You can also look for an Import option on the File menu.

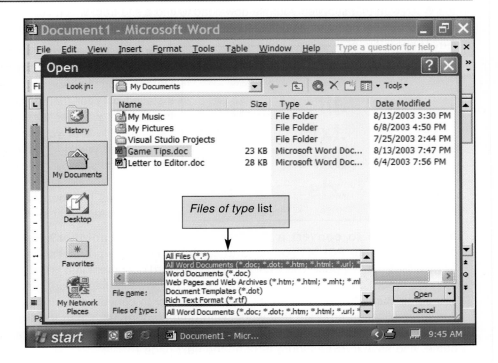

Files of type list

Why can't I open some files? Suppose that you receive an e-mail attachment called *Cool.tif*. "Aha!" you say to yourself, "My PhotoShop software ought to open that file." You try—several times—but all you get is an error message. When a file doesn't open, one of three things probably went wrong:

☑ The file might have been damaged—a techie would call it "corrupted"—by a transmission or disk error. Although you might be able to use special file recovery software to repair the damage, it is usually easier to obtain an undamaged copy of the file from its original source.

☑ Someone might have inadvertently changed the filename extension. While renaming the *Cool* file, perhaps the original .bmp extension was changed to .tif. If you have a little time, you can change the filename extension and try to open the file. If a file contains a graphic, chances are that it should have the extension for one of the popular graphics formats, such as .bmp, .gif, .jpg, .tif, or .pcx. Otherwise, you should contact the source of the file to get accurate information about its real format.

☑ Some file formats exist in several variations and your software might not have the capability to open a particular variation of the format. You might be able to open the file if you use different application software. For example, Photoshop might not be able to open a particular file with a .tif filename extension, but CorelDraw might open it.

What if none of my software works with a particular file format? Although a computer might be able to discover a file's format, it might not necessarily know how to work with it. Just as you might be able to identify a helicopter, you can't necessarily fly it without some instructions. Your computer also requires a set of instructions to use most file formats. These instructions are provided by software. To use a particular file format, you must make sure that your computer has the corresponding software.

Suppose that you download a file with a .rm extension. The header in this file identifies it as RealMedia format, but none of your current software will work with this file format. Several Web sites provide lists of filename extensions and their corresponding software. By looking up a filename extension in one of these lists, you can find out what application software you'll need to find, buy, download, and install.

Many files that you download from the Web require special "player" or "reader" software. For example, PDF text files require software called Acrobat Reader; MP3 music files require software called an MP3 Player; and RM video files require the RealMedia Player software. Typically, you can follow a link from the Web page that supplied your file download to find a site from which you can download the necessary player or reader software—usually for free.

FIGURE 4-31 Extensions for common file formats

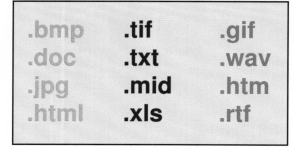

.bmp	.tif	.gif
.doc	.txt	.wav
.jpg	.mid	.htm
.html	.xls	.rtf

How do I know what kinds of file formats I can send to my friends, colleagues, and instructor? Unless you know what application software is installed on your friends' computers, you'll not know for certain whether they will be able to open a particular file that you send. There's a pretty good chance that your friends will be able to open many files that you save with the extensions listed in Figure 4-31. You should check with the recipient before sending files in proprietary formats, such as Adobe Illustrator's AI format and RealMedia's RA format.

Is it possible to convert a file from one format to another? Perhaps you created a Word document on your PC, but you need to convert it into a format that's usable by your colleague who owns a Mac. Or, suppose you want to convert a Word document into HTML format so that you can post it on the Web. You might also want to convert a Windows bitmap (.bmp) graphic into GIF format so that you can include it on a Web page. The easiest way to convert a file from one format to another is to find an application program that works with both file formats. Open the file using that software, then use the Export option, or the Save As dialog box, to select a new file format, assign the file a new name, and save it. (See Figure 4-32 on the next page.)

FIGURE 4-32

An easy way to convert a file from one format to another is to open it with an application that supports both file formats, then use the Save As dialog box to select an alternative file format.

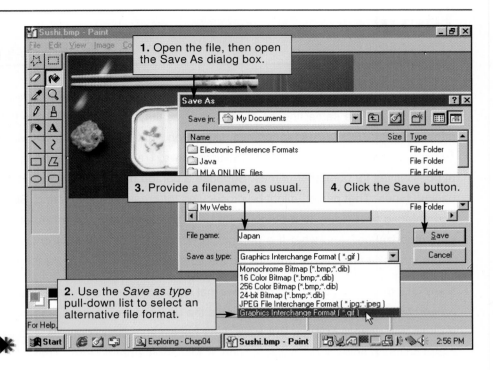

1. Open the file, then open the Save As dialog box.

3. Provide a filename, as usual.

4. Click the Save button.

2. Use the *Save as type* pull-down list to select an alternative file format.

click to start ➡

www.InfoWebLinks.com

Conversion software runs the gamut from simple shareware to "industrial-strength" commercial packages. The **Conversion Software** InfoWeb will help you compare what's available.

└click ➡

When you need a conversion routine for an obscure file format, or if you need to convert between many different file formats, consider specialized conversion software, available through commercial or shareware outlets. A typical conversion program tends to focus on a single category of files, so you need one program to convert music files, but a different program to convert document files, and yet another program to convert graphics files.

Many file formats convert easily to another format, and the resulting file is virtually indistinguishable from the original. Some conversions, however, do not retain all of the characteristics of the original file. When you convert a DOC file into HTML format, for example, the HTML page does not contain any of the headers, footers, superscripts, page numbers, special characters, or page breaks that existed in the original DOC file.

4

QUICK Check
TechTalk

1 A file [＿＿＿＿＿＿] is a section of data at the beginning of the file that contains information about the file type.

2 Filename extensions, such as .ocx, .vbs, and .dll, typically indicate [＿＿＿＿＿＿] modules.

3 The [＿＿＿＿＿＿] file format for Microsoft Word is DOC.

4 [＿＿＿＿＿＿] software can help you transform one file type into a different file type.

check answers ➡

ISSUE

IS IT A CRIME?

It doesn't take any special digital expertise to mastermind every computer crime. Setting fire to a computer doesn't require the same finesse as writing a stealthy virus, but both can have the same disastrous effect on data. "Old-fashioned" crimes, like arson, that take a high-tech twist because they involve a computer, can be prosecuted using traditional laws. Traditional laws do not, however, cover the range of possibilities for computer crimes. Suppose a person unlawfully enters a computer facility and steals backup tapes. That person might be prosecuted for breaking and entering. But would common breaking and entering laws apply to a person who uses an off-site terminal to "enter" a computer system without authorization? And what if a person copies a data file without authorization? Has that file really been "stolen" if the original remains on the computer?

Many countries have computer crime laws that specifically define computer data and software as personal property. These laws also define as crimes the unauthorized access, use, modification, or disabling of a computer system or data. But laws don't necessarily stop criminals. If they did, we wouldn't have heard so much news about hackers such as Mafiaboy, Robert Morris, Cap'n Crunch, and Kevin Mitnick.

In a 1995 case that still echos in the halls of justice, a computer hacker named Kevin Mitnick was accused of breaking into dozens of corporate, university, government, and personal computers. Before being arrested, Mitnick reportedly stole thousands of data files and more than 20,000 credit card numbers. U.S. attorney Kent Walker commented, "He was clearly the most wanted computer hacker in the world." Mitnick's unauthorized access and use of computer data are explicitly defined as criminal acts by computer crime laws in most countries.

Denying many, but not all, of the accusations against him, Mitnick claimed, "No way, no how, did I break into NORAD. That's a complete myth. And I never attempted to access anything considered to be classified government systems." Although vilified in the media, Mitnick had the support of many hackers and other people who believed that the prosecution grossly exaggerated the extent of his crimes. Nonetheless, Mitnick was sentenced to 46 months in prison, and ordered to pay restitution in the amount of $4,125 during his three-year period of supervised release. The prosecution was horrified by such a paltry sum—an amount that was much less than its request for $1.5 million in restitution.

Forbes reporter Adam L. Penenberg took issue with the 46-month sentence imposed by Judge Marianne Pfaelzer, and wrote, "This in a country where the average prison term for manslaughter is three years. Mitnick's crimes were curiously innocuous. He broke into corporate computers, but no evidence indicates that he destroyed data. Or sold anything he copied. Yes, he pilfered software—but in doing so left it behind. This world of bits is a strange one, in which you can take something and still leave it for its rightful owner. The theft laws designed for payroll sacks and motor vehicles just don't apply to a hacker."

Unfortunately for Mitnick, the jail term and $4,125 fine were, perhaps, the most lenient part of his sentence. Mitnick, who had served most of his jail term while awaiting trial, was scheduled for a supervised release soon after sentencing. The additional conditions of Mitnick's supervised release included a ban on access to computer hardware, software, and any form of wireless communication. He was prohibited from possessing any kind of passwords, cellular phone codes, or data encryption devices. And just to make sure that he didn't get into any trouble with technologies that are not specifically mentioned in the terms of his supervised release, Mitnick was prohibited from using any new or future technology that performs as a computer or provides access to one. Perhaps worst of all, he could not work for a company with computers or computer access on its premises.

The Mitnick case illustrates our culture's ambivalent attitude toward hackers. On the one hand, they are viewed as evil cyberterrorists who are set on destroying the glue that binds together the Information Age. From this perspective, hackers are criminals who must be hunted down, forced to make restitution for damages, and prevented from creating further havoc.

From another perspective, hackers are viewed more as Casper, the friendly ghost, in our complex cybermachines—as moderately bothersome entities whose pranks are tolerated by the computer community, along with software bugs and hardware glitches. Seen from this perspective, a hacker's pranks are part of the normal course of study that leads to the highest echelons of computer expertise. "Everyone has done it," claim devotees, "even Bill Gates (founder of Microsoft) and Steve Jobs (founder of Apple Computer)."

Which perspective is right? Are hackers dangerous cyberterrorists or harmless pranksters? Before you make up your mind about computer hacking and cracking, you might want to further investigate the Mitnick case and similar cases by following the Computer Crime InfoWeb links.

Who's in cybercrime news? What happened to Mafiaboy? Where is Kevin Mitnick today? How are cybercriminals caught? The **Computer Crime** InfoWeb provides answers to these questions and more.

click ➡❋

4

WHAT DO YOU THINK?

1. Should it be a crime to steal a copy of computer data while leaving the original data in place and unaltered?　　　　　○Yes ○ No ○ Not sure

2. Was Mitnick's sentence fair?　　　　　○Yes ○ No ○ Not sure

3. Should hackers be sent to jail if they cannot pay restitution to companies and individuals who lost money as the result of a prank?　　　　　○Yes ○ No ○ Not sure

4. Do you think that a hacker would make a good consultant on computer security?　　　　　○Yes ○ No ○ Not sure

click to save your responses ❋

INTERACTIVE SUMMARY

The Interactive Summary helps you to select and remember important concepts from this chapter. Fill in the blanks to best complete each sentence. When using the NP6 BookOnCD, you can click the Check Answers buttons to automatically score your answers. Place your Tracking Disk in the floppy disk drive if you want to save your scores.

A computer _____ is a named collection of data that exists on a storage medium, such as a hard disk, floppy disk, CD, DVD, or tape. Every file has a name and might also have a filename extension. The rules for naming a file are called file-naming _____. These rules typically do not allow you to use certain characters or _____ words in a filename. A filename _____ is usually related to a file format, which is defined as the arrangement of data in a file and the coding scheme that is used to represent the data. A software program's _____ file format is the default format that is used for storing the files created with that program.

A file's location is defined by a file _____ (sometimes called a "path"), which includes the storage device, folder(s), filename, and extension. In Windows, storage devices are identified by a drive letter, followed by a _____. An operating system maintains a list of files called a directory for each storage disk, tape, CD, or DVD. The main directory of a disk is sometimes referred to as the _____ directory, which can be subdivided into several smaller lists called subdirectories. Subdirectories often are depicted as _____.   **check answers** ➤✳

File _____ encompasses any procedure that helps you organize your computer-based files so that you can find and use them more effectively. _____-based file management uses tools provided from within a software program to open and save files. Additional tools might also allow you to create new folders, rename files, and delete files. The Save and Save As dialog boxes are examples of application-based file management tools.

Most operating systems provide file management _____ that give you the "big picture" of the files that you have stored on your disks. The structure of folders that you envision on your disk is a logical model, which is often represented by a storage _____, such as a tree structure or filing cabinet. Windows Explorer is an example of a file management utility that is provided by an operating system. Windows Explorer allows you to find, rename, copy, move, and delete files and folders. In addition, it allows you to perform these file management activities with more than one file at a time.

The way that data is actually stored is referred to as the _____ storage model. Before a computer stores data on a disk, CD, or DVD, it creates the equivalent of electronic storage bins by dividing the disk into _____, and then further dividing each track into _____. The process of creating tracks and sectors is called _____. Each sector of a disk is numbered, providing a storage address that can be tracked by the operating system. Many computers work with a group of sectors, called a _____, to increase the efficiency of file storage operations. An operating system uses a file system to carry out your computer's actual storage activities and maintain a file, such as the File Allocation Table (FAT), which keeps track of every file's physical location.   **check answers** ➤✳

FILE MANAGEMENT, VIRUS PROTECTION, AND BACKUP   **211**

A computer virus is a set of program instructions that attaches itself to a file, reproduces itself, and spreads to other files. You may encounter several types of viruses. A virus that attaches itself to an application program, such as a game, is known as a _____ virus. A boot _____ virus infects the system files that your computer uses every time you turn it on. A _____ virus infects a set of instructions that automates document and worksheet production.

A Trojan horse is a computer program that seems to perform one function while actually doing something else. Such programs are notorious for stealing _____, though some delete files and cause other problems. A _____ is a program that is designed to spread from computer to computer. Most take advantage of communications networks—especially the Internet—to travel within e-mail and TCP/IP packets, jumping from one computer to another.

Viruses can slip into your computer from a variety of sources, such as floppy disks, homemade CDs, and Web sites that contain games and other supposedly fun stuff. E-mail _____ are another common source of viruses. HTML-formatted e-mail is susceptible to viruses and worms hidden in program-like "scripts" that are embedded in the HTML tags. _____ software can help prevent viruses from invading your computer system, and can root out viruses that take up residence.   **check answers** ➧

A backup is a copy of one or more files that has been made in case the original files become damaged. For safety, a backup is usually stored on a different storage medium from the original files. A good backup plan allows you to _____ your computing environment to its pre-disaster state with a minimum of fuss. Unfortunately, no single backup plan fits everyone's computing style or budget. Your personal backup plan depends on the files that you need to back up, the hardware that you have available to make backups, and your backup software. In any case, it is a good idea to back up the Windows _____ and make a _____ disk that contains the operating system files needed to start your computer without accessing the hard disk.

Before backing up your data, make sure that it is free of _____. Part of your backup routine should be to _____ your backup to make sure that you can successfully restore data from the backup to your hard disk. Backups can be recorded on tape, floppy disks, a second hard disk, a CD-R, a CD-RW, or a writable DVD. Backups should be stored in a safe place, away from the computer. Online backup, provided by a Web site, might be part of your backup strategy.   **check answers** ➧

4

INTERACTIVE
KEY TERMS

Make sure that you understand all of the boldfaced key terms presented in this chapter. If you're using the NP6 BookOnCD, you can use this list of terms as an interactive study activity. First, try to define a term in your own words, then click the term to compare your definition with the definition that is presented in the chapter.

Antivirus software, 189
Backup, 193
Backup software, 200
Boot disk, 197
Boot sector virus, 186
Checksum, 189
Cluster, 181
Computer file, 170
Computer virus, 185
Copy Disk utility, 200
Defragmentation utility, 183
Denial of Service attacks, 187
Differential backup 196
Directory, 172
File Allocation Table (FAT), 181
File date, 173
File format, 171
File management utilities, 176
Filename extension, 171
File management, 174

File-naming conventions, 170
File shredder software, 182
File size, 173
File specification, 172
File system, 181
File virus, 186
Folders, 172
Formatting, 180
Formatting utilities, 180
Fragmented files, 183
Full backup, 196
Full-system backup, 194
Incremental backup, 196
Logical storage models, 177
Macro, 186
Macro virus, 186
Multi-partite viruses, 190
Native file format, 171
Path, 172
Physical storage model, 180

Polymorphic viruses, 190
Recovery CD, 197
Rescue disk, 198
Reserved words, 171
Restore, 194
Retro viruses, 190
Root directory, 172
Sectors, 180
Stealth viruses, 190
Storage metaphor, 177
Subdirectories, 172
Tracks, 180
Trigger event, 185
Trojan horse, 186
Virus hoax, 191
Virus signature, 189
Windows Explorer, 178
Windows Startup Disk, 197
Worm, 186

INTERACTIVE
SITUATION QUESTIONS

Apply what you've learned to some typical computing situations. When using the NP6 BookOnCD, you can type your answers, then use the Check Answers button to automatically score your responses. Place your Tracking Disk in the floppy disk drive if you want to save your scores.

1 Suppose you are using Microsoft Word and you want to open a file. When your software lists the documents that you can open, you can expect them to be in Word's [   ] file format, which is DOC.

2 Can you use a Windows application, create a document, and store it using the filename *I L*ve NY* ? (Yes or No) [   ]

3 When you want to work with a group of your files—to move them to different folders, for example—it would be most efficient to use an operating system utility, such as Windows [   ].

4 When specifying a location for a data file on your hard disk, you should avoid saving it in the [   ] directory.

5 Suppose that you have a floppy disk that contains data you no longer need. You can use a(n) [   ] utility to erase the data on the disk and re-create all of the tracks and sectors on the disk.

6 You have an old computer that you will donate to a school, but you want to make sure that its hard disk contains no trace of your data. To do so, you should use file [   ] software that overwrites "empty" sectors with random 1s and 0s.

7 You receive an e-mail attachment called *Read this.txt.vbs*. Because it appears to have two filename[   ], you should assume that this file harbors a virus.

8 You receive an e-mail message from a friend that says, "My antivirus software says that an attachment I received from you contains the Klez virus." Would you assume that this message from your friend is a hoax? Yes or no? [   ]

9 You just bought a tape drive and you make a full-system backup. Before you depend on this backup, you should [   ] it to make sure that you can successfully restore the data in the event of a hard disk crash.

10 Your hard disk crashed for some unknown reason. Now when you switch on the computer power all you get is an "Error reading drive C:" message. Your first reaction should be to reach for a(n) [   ] disk that contains the operating system files needed to start your computer without accessing the hard disk.   **check answers** ➧

4

INTERACTIVE
PRACTICE TESTS

When you use the NP6 BookOnCD, you can take Practice Tests that consist of 10 multiple-choice, true/false, and fill-in-the-blank questions. The questions are selected at random from a large test bank, so each time you take a test, you'll receive a different set of questions. Your tests are scored immediately, and you can print study guides that help you find the correct answers for any questions that you missed. If you are using a Tracking Disk, insert it in the floppy disk drive to save your test scores.

click to start ➡

STUDY
TIPS

Study Tips help you to organize and consolidate the information in a chapter by making lists, outlines, charts, and sketches. You can use paper and pencil or word processing software to complete most of the Study Tips activities.

1 Make sure that you can use your own words to answer each of the green focus questions that appear throughout the chapter.

2 Make a list of five filenames that are valid under the file-naming conventions for your operating system. Also create a list of five filenames that are not valid, and explain the problem with each one.

3 Pick any five files on the computer that you typically use, and write out the full path for each one.

4 Describe the difference between the Save and the Save As options provided by an application.

5 In your own words, describe the difference between a logical storage model and a physical storage model.

6 Explain the kinds of file management tasks that might best be accomplished using a file management utility such as Windows Explorer, instead of the Save As or Open dialog box provided by a software application.

7 Explain the differences between an operating system and a file system.

8 Describe the difference between a sector and a cluster.

9 Make sure that you can describe what happens in the FAT when a file is stored or deleted.

10 Describe the characteristics of viruses, Trojan horses, worms, and Denial of Service attacks.

11 List the filename extensions of files that might typically harbor a virus.

12 Explain how multi-partite, stealth, polymorphic, and retro viruses work.

13 Explain how anitvirus software works, and how it is able to catch new viruses that are created after the software is installed on your computer.

14 Describe the various types of boot disks that might help you recover from a hard disk crash.

15 Discuss the pros and cons of each type of backup hardware.

16 Make a list of backup tips that you think would help people devise a solid backup plan.

PROJECTS

An NP6 Project is an open-ended activity that will help you apply the concepts you have learned. Many projects require resources in addition to your textbook, such as current magazines, library materials, or Web access. When you tackle a project, be prepared to use your critical thinking skills, logical analysis skills, and your creativity.

1 **Issue Research: Computer Crime** The Issue section of this chapter focused on cybercrime. For this project, write a two–five page opinion paper about the "right to hack," based on information that you gather from the Internet. To begin this project, consult the Computer Crime InfoWeb (see page 209), and link to the recommended Web pages to get an in-depth overview of the issue. Armed with this background, select one of the following statements and argue for or against it:

a. People have the "right" to hone their computing skills by breaking into computers. As a computer scientist once said, "The right to hack is held higher than the right of someone to tell you not to. It's an inalienable right."

b. If problems in computer security exist, it is acceptable to use any means to point them out. A person who creates a virus is perfectly justified in releasing it if the purpose is to make everyone aware of these security breaches.

c. Computer crimes are no different than other crimes, and computer criminals should be held responsible for the damage that they cause.

Whatever viewpoint you decide to present, make sure that you back it up with facts and references to authoritative articles and Web pages. You can place citations to these pages (including the author's name, article title, date of publication, and URL) at the end of your paper as endnotes, on each page as footnotes, or along with the appropriate paragraphs using parentheses. Follow your professor's instructions for submitting your paper via e-mail or as a printed document.

2 **Hoax!** Suppose that you work as a reporter for a local television station. Your boss wants the station to run a 90-second story about virus hoaxes, and gives you the responsibility for writing the script. The basic objectives of the story are: (1) to remind people not to panic when they receive e-mail about viruses and (2) to provide a set of concrete steps that a person could take to discover whether a virus threat is real or a hoax. Of course, your boss wants the story to be interesting, so you have to include a human-interest angle. Write the script for the story, including notes about the visuals that will appear. Follow your professor's instructions for submitting your paper as an e-mail attachment or as a printed document.

3 **Backup on the Web** For this project, investigate a Web site that provides storage for data backups. Find out the cost of using the site and investigate the site's terms and conditions for use. Try to discover if data stored at the site would be secure and private. Also try to determine if the backup and restore procedures seem feasible. You might also try to determine if a plan exists for notifying customers if the site is about to go out of business. You might also look for a review of the backup provider at sites such as *www.zdnet.com* or *www.cnet.com*. After completing your research, organize your notes into a two-page paper that explains whether or not you would use the site for storing your backups. Follow your professor's instructions for submitting your paper as an e-mail attachment or as a printed document.

4

ADDITIONAL
PROJECTS

Click ➡✳ to access the Web for additional projects.

QUICK CHECK ANSWERS

CHAPTER 1

QuickCheck A
1. central
2. stored
3. system
4. False
5. False
6. operating

QuickCheck B
1. backbone
2. TCP, Transmission Control Protocol
3. servers
4. voice
5. False
6. False
7. national, dial-up
8. False
9. logging in, logging on
10. False

QuickCheck C
1. URL, Uniform Resource Locator
2. case
3. HTML, Hypertext Markup Language
4. home
5. True
6. False
7. query
8. directory, index

QuickCheck D
1. header
2. MIME, Multipurpose Internet Mail Extension
3. True
4. server
5. POP, Post Office Protocol; SMTP, Simple Mail Transfer Protocol
6. inbox; outbox

QuickCheck TechTalk
1. operating system
2. POST, power-on self-test
3. safe
4. True

CHAPTER 2

QuickCheck A
1. digital; analog
2. binary base 2
3. True
4. extended ASCII
5. ASCII; binary
6. True
7. integrated circuit, IC, microprocessor

QuickCheck B
1. ALU, Arithmetic Logic Unit
2. control unit
3. True
4. clock, system clock
5. megabytes, MB
6. capacitors
7. ROM, read-only memory
8. CMOS, complementary metal oxide semiconductor

QuickCheck C
1. pits
2. access
3. random; sequential
4. density
5. False
6. controller
7. False
8. DVD, DVD-ROM

QuickCheck D
1. expansion
2. slots
3. driver
4. resolution
5. depth
6. False
7. ink jet, ink jet printers

QuickCheck TechTalk
1. machine
2. op, operation
3. pointer
4. register

ANSWERS

CHAPTER 3

QuickCheck A
1. executable
2. properties
3. high;
   machine
4. compiler
5. system

QuickCheck B
1. resource
2. memory, RAM
3. interface
4. kernel
5. multiuser
6. network, server
7. server;
   desktop

QuickCheck C
1. production
2. spreadsheet
3. file;
   database
4. graphics
5. digital
6. vertical

QuickCheck D
1. setup
2. zipped, compressed
3. uninstall
4. copyright
5. shareware
6. source
7. domain

QuickCheck TechTalk
1. True
2. system
3. user
4. editor

CHAPTER 4

QuickCheck A
1. conventions
2. reserved
3. format
4. root
5. specification, path
6. date

QuickCheck B
1. save as
2. logical
3. tracks;
   sectors
4. file
5. allocation

QuickCheck C
1. .exe
2. sector
3. worm
4. False
5. True
6. checksum
7. stealth
8. hoax

QuickCheck D
1. backup
2. Registry
3. boot
4. copy disk, disk copy
5. My Documents

QuickCheck TechTalk
1. header
2. support
3. native
4. conversion

CREDITS

Cover
   Photo courtesy of NASA

Chapter 1
   Figure 1-4: Courtesy of IBM Corporation

Chapter 2
   Chapter opener: Courtesy of NASA
   Figure 2-5: Courtesy of Motorola Semiconductor Products Sector ©1999 SEMATECH, INC
   Figure 2-14: Courtesy of IBM Corporation
   Figure 2-19: Courtesy of Western Digital Corporation

Chapter 3
   Figure 3-24: Courtesy of Intuit Inc.
   Figure 3-30: Courtesy of NASA

All other media elements copyright 2002 by MediaTechnics Corporation

GLOSSARY

3-D graphics software The software used to create three-dimensional wireframe objects, then render them into images. 142

Absolute reference In a worksheet formula, cell references (usually preceded by a $ symbol) that cannot change as a result of a move or copy operation. 135

Access time The estimated time for a storage device to locate data on a disk, usually measured in milliseconds. 79

Accounting and finance software A category of application software that includes accounting, money management, and tax preparation software. 136

Accounting software Software designed specifically for managing monetary transactions and investments. 147

Action games Entertainment software, similar to arcade games, in which the user maneuvers through a 3-D world such as Unreal or Quake 3. 146

Active matrix screen A type of LCD technology that produces a clear, sharp image because each pixel is controlled by its own transistor. 94

Adventure games Entertainment software, similar to role-playing games, where the focus is on solving problems. 146

AGP Short for accelerated graphics port. An AGP is a type of interface, or slot, that provides a high-speed pathway for advanced graphics. 89

ALU (arithmetic logic unit) The part of the CPU that performs arithmetic and logical operations on the numbers stored in its registers. 67

Always-on connection A permanent connection, as opposed to a connection that is established and dropped as needed. 19

Analog device A device that operates on continuously varying data, such as a dimmer switch, or a watch with a sweep second hand. 58

Antivirus software A computer program used to scan a computer's memory and disks to identify, isolate, and eliminate viruses. 189

Application software Computer programs that help you perform a specific task such as word processing. Also called application programs, applications, or programs. 12, 117

Archiving The process of moving infrequently used data from a primary storage device to a storage medium such as a CD-ROM. 86

ASCII (American Standard Code for Information Interchange) A code that represents characters as a series of 1s and 0s. Most computers use ASCII code to represent text, making it possible to transfer data between computers. 60

Audio editing software A program that enables users to create and edit digital voice and music recordings. 143

Automatic recalculation A feature found in spreadsheet software that automatically recalculates every formula after a user makes a change to any cell. 135

Backup A duplicate copy of a file, disk, or tape. Also refers to a Windows utility that allows you to create and restore backups. 193

Backup software A set of utility programs that performs a variety of backup related tasks, such as helping users select files for backup. 200

Beep code A series of audible beeps used to announce diagnostic test results during the boot process. 45

Benchmarks A set of tests used to measure computer hardware or software performance. 68

Binary digits Series of 1s and 0s representing data. 58

Binary number system A method for representing numbers using only two digits, 0 and 1. Contrast to the decimal number system, which uses ten digits: 0, 1, 2, 3, 4, 5, 6, 7, 8, and 9. 59

Bit The smallest unit of information handled by a computer. A bit is one of two values, either a 0 or a 1. Eight bits comprise a byte, which can represent a letter or number. 11

Boot disk A floppy disk or CD that contains the files needed for the boot process. 197

Boot process The sequence of events that occurs within a computer system between the time the user starts the computer and the time it is ready to process commands. 44

Boot sector virus A computer virus that infects the sectors on a disk that contain the data a computer uses during the boot process. The virus spreads every time the infected disk is in the computer when it boots. 186

Bootstrap program A program stored in ROM that loads and initializes the operating system on a computer. 121

Broken link A non-functioning Web link. 296

Browser A program that communicates with a Web server and displays Web pages. 28

Byte An 8-bit unit of information that represents a single character. 11

Cable modem A communications device that can be used to connect a computer to the Internet via the cable TV infrastructure. 19

Cache Special high-speed memory that gives the CPU rapid access to data that would otherwise be accessed from disk. Also called RAM cache or cache memory. 68

CAD software (Computer-Aided Design software) A program designed to draw 3-D graphics for architecture and engineering tasks. 142

Capacitors Electronic circuit components that store an electrical charge; in RAM, a charged capacitor represents an "on" bit, and a discharged one represents an "off" bit. 71

Case sensitive A condition in which uppercase letters are not equivalent to their lowercase counterparts. 23

CD ripper Software that converts the music on an audio CD to a WAV file. 143

CD-R An acronym for compact disc-recordable. CD-R is a type of optical disk technology that allows the user to create CD-ROMs and audio CDs. 85

CD-ROM drive A storage device that uses laser technology to read data from a CD-ROM. 10

CD-RW An acronym for compact disc-rewritable. CD-RW is a type of optical disk technology that allows the user to write data onto a CD, then change that data much like on a floppy or hard disk. 86

CD-writer A general term for recordable CD technologies such as CD-R and CD-RW. 10

Cell In spreadsheet terminology, the intersection of a column and a row. In cellular communications, a limited geographical area surrounding a cellular phone tower. 133

Cell references The column letter and row number that designate the location of a worksheet cell. For example, the cell reference C5 refers to a cell in column C, row 5. 134

Central processing unit (CPU) The main processing unit in a computer, consisting of circuitry that executes instructions to process data. 4

Character data Letters, symbols, or numerals that will not be used in arithmetic operations (name, social security number, etc.). 59

Chat group A discussion in which a group of people communicates online simultaneously. 17

Checksum A value, calculated by combining all the bytes in a file, that is used by virus detection programs to identify whether any bytes have been altered. 189

CISC A general-purpose microprocessor chip designed to handle a wider array of instructions than a RISC chip. CISC stands for complex instruction set computer. 68

Client A computer or software that requests information from another computer or server. 8

Clip art Graphics designed to be inserted into documents, Web pages, and worksheets, usually available in CD-ROM or Web-based collections. 132

Cluster A group of sectors on a storage medium. A group of two or more devices connected together to share processing, storage, input, or output workloads. 181

CMOS memory A type of battery-powered integrated circuit that holds semi-permanent configuration data (acronym for complementary metal oxide semiconductor). 73

Color depth The number of bits that determines the range of possible colors that can be assigned to each pixel. For example, an 8-bit color depth can create 256 colors. 94

Command-line interface A style of user interface which requires users to type commands, rather than use a mouse to manipulate graphics. 120

Commercial software Copyrighted computer applications sold to consumers for profit. 154

Compiler Software that translates a program written in a high-level language into low-level instructions before the program is executed. 11

Computer A device that accepts input, processes data, stores data, and produces output. 4

Computer-aided music software Software used to generate unique musical compositions with a simplified set of tools, such as tempo, key, and style. 143

Computer file A single collection of data stored on a storage medium. 170

Computer network A collection of computers and related devices, connected in a way that allows them to share data, hardware, and software. 7

Computer program A set of detailed, step-by-step instructions that tells a computer how to solve a problem or carry out a task. 4, 112

Computer programmers People who code or write computer programs. 114

Computer virus A program designed to attach itself to a file, reproduce, and spread from one file to another, destroying data, displaying an irritating message, or otherwise disrupting computer operations. 185

Control unit The part of the ALU that directs and coordinates processing. 67

Controller A circuit board in a hard drive that positions the disk and read-write heads to locate data. 82

Copy Disk utility A utility program that duplicates the contents of an entire floppy disk. 200

Copyright A form of legal protection that grants certain exclusive rights to the author of a program or the owner of the copyright. 153

Copyright notice A line such as "Copyright 2002 ACME Co." that identifies a copyright holder. 153

CRT (cathode ray tube) A display technology that uses a large vacuum tube, similar to that used in television sets. 92

Data In the context of computing and data management, data refers to the symbols that a computer uses to represent facts and ideas. 4, 11

Data bus An electronic pathway or circuit that connects the electronic components (such as the processor and RAM) on a computer's motherboard. 88

Data file A file containing words, numbers, and/or pictures that the user can view, edit, save, send, and/or print. 11

Data management software Software designed for tasks associated with maintaining and accessing data stored in structured files and databases. 137

Data representation The use of electrical signals, marks, or binary digits to represent character, numeric, visual, or audio data. 58

Data transfer rate The amount of data that a storage device can move from a storage medium to computer memory in one second. 79

Database A collection of information that may be stored in more than one file or in more than one record type. 138

Database management software Software developed for the task of manipulating data that has been stored as a database. 138

Defragmentation utility A software tool used to rearrange the files on a disk so that they are stored in contiguous clusters. 183

Denial of Service attacks An attack that is designed to overwhelm a network's processing capabilities, shutting it down. 187

Desktop computers Computers small enough to fit on a desk and built around a single microprocessor chip. 6

Desktop operating system An operating system such as Windows Me or Mac OSX that is specifically designed for personal computers. 122

Desktop publishing software Software used to create high-quality output suitable for commercial printing. DTP software provides precise control over layout. 128

Device driver The software that provides the computer with the means to control a peripheral device. 92

Dial-up connection A connection that uses a phone line to establish a temporary Internet connection. 18

Differential backup A copy of all the files that changed since the last full backup of a disk. 196

Digital Any system that works with discrete data, such as 0s and 1s, in contrast to analog. 11

Digital device A device that works with discrete (distinct or separate) numbers or digits. 58

Digital electronics Circuitry that's designed to work with digital signals. 58

Digitize To convert non-digital information or media to a digital format through the use of a scanner, sampler, or other input device. 61

DIMM Short for dual in-line memory module, a DIMM is a small circuit board that holds RAM chips. A DIMM has a 64-bit path to the memory chips. 63

DIP (dual in-line package) A chip configuration characterized by a rectangular body with numerous plugs along its edge. 63

Directory A list of files contained on a computer storage device. 172

Disk density The closeness of the particles on a disk surface. As density increases, the particles are packed more tightly together and are usually smaller. 80

Distribution disks One or more floppy disks or CDs that contain programs and data, which can be installed to a hard disk. 148

DMA Short for direct memory access, DMA refers to specialized circuitry that transfers data between drives and RAM, bypassing the CPU. 82

Document production software Computer programs that assist the user in composing, editing, designing, and printing documents. 128

DOS (disk operating system) The operating system software shipped with the first IBM PCs, and used on millions of computers until the introduction of Microsoft Windows. 126

Dot matrix printer A printer that creates characters and graphics by striking an inked ribbon with small wires called "pins," generating a fine pattern of dots. 96

Dot pitch The diagonal distance between colored dots on a display screen. Measured in millimeters, dot pitch helps to determine the quality of an image displayed on a monitor. 93

Downloading The process of transferring a copy of a file from a remote computer to a local computer's disk drive. 17

Drawing software Programs that are used to create images with lines, shapes, and colors, such as logos or diagrams. 141

Drive bays Areas within a computer system unit that can accommodate additional storage devices. 78

DSL (Digital Subscriber Line) A high-speed Internet connection that uses existing telephone lines, requiring close proximity to a switching station. 20

DSS (Digital Satellite System) A type of Internet connection that uses a network of satellites to transmit data. 20

DVD (Digital Video Disc) An optical storage medium similar in appearance and technology to a CD-ROM but with higher storage capacity. The acronym stands for "digital video disc" or "digital versatile disc." 86

DVD drive An optical storage device that reads data from CD-ROM and DVD disks. 10

DVD-RAM A technology that allows users to record data on a DVD disk. 87

DVD-ROM A DVD disk that contains data that has been permanently stamped on the disk surface. 86

DVD-RW A technology that allows users to record data on a DVD disk. 87

DVD+RW A DVD technology that allows users to record and change data on DVD disks. 87

DVD-Video DVD disks that contain digital movies. 86

Dye sublimation printer An expensive, color-precise printer that heats ribbons containing color to produce consistent, photograph-quality images. 95

Ear training software Software used by musicians to develop tuning skills, recognize keys, and develop musical skills. 143

EBCDIC (Extended Binary-Coded Decimal Interchange Code) A method by which digital computers, usually mainframes, represent character data. 60

E-commerce Short for electronic commerce, it is the business of buying and selling products online. 16

Educational software Software used to develop and practice skills. 144

EIDE Short for enhanced integrated drive (or device) electronics, EIDE is a disk drive technology formally known as ATA. 82

Electronic mail (E-mail) A single electronic message or the entire system of computers and software that handles electronic messages. 36

E-mail Messages that are transmitted between computers over a communications network. Short for electronic mail. 16

E-mail account A service that provides an e-mail address, and mailbox. 36

E-mail attachment A separate file that is transmitted along with an e-mail message. 37

E-mail client software Software that is installed on a client computer and has access to e-mail servers on a network. This software is used to compose, send, and read e-mail messages. 41

E-mail message A computer file containing a letter or memo that is transmitted electronically via a communications network. 36

E-mail servers A computer that uses special software to store, and send, e-mail messages over the Internet. 40

E-mail system The collection of computers and software that works together to provide e-mail services. 40

Exa- Prefix for a quintillion. 61

Executable file A file, usually with an .exe extension, containing instructions that tell a computer how to perform a specific task. 11

Expansion bus The segment of the data bus that transports data between RAM and peripheral devices. 88

Expansion card A circuit board that is plugged into a slot on a PC motherboard to add extra functions, devices, or ports. 88

Expansion port A socket into which the user plugs a cable from a peripheral device, allowing data to pass between the computer and the peripheral device. 90

Expansion slot A socket or "slot" on a PC motherboard designed to hold a circuit board called an expansion card. 88

Extended ASCII Similar to ASCII but with 8-bit character representation instead of 7-bit, allowing for an additional 128 characters. 60

Field The smallest meaningful unit of information contained in a data file. 137

File A named collection of data (such as a computer program, document, or graphic) that exists on a storage medium, such as a hard disk, floppy disk, or CD-ROM. 11

File allocation table (FAT) A special file that is used by some operating systems to store the physical location of all the files on a storage medium, such as a hard disk or floppy disk. 181

File date The date that a file was created or last modified. 173

File format The method of organization used to encode and store data in a computer. Text formats include DOC and TXT. Graphics formats include BMP, TIFF, GIF, and PCX. 171

File header Hidden information inserted at the beginning of a file to identify its properties, such as the software that can open it. 61

File management Any procedure that is used to organize computer-based file systems. 174

File management software Computer programs that help the user organize records, find records that match specific criteria, and print lists based on the information contained in records. 137

File management utilities Software, such as Windows Explorer, that helps users locate, rename, move, copy, and delete files. 176

File shredder software Software that overwrites sectors of a disk with random 1s and 0s to ensure that deleted data cannot be recovered. 182

File size The physical size of a file on a storage medium, usually measured in kilobytes (KB). 173

File specification A combination of the drive letter, subdirectory, filename, and extension that identifies a file (for example, A:\word\filename.doc). Also called a "path." 172

File system A system that is used by an operating system to keep files organized. 181

File virus A computer virus that infects executable files, such as programs with .exe filename extensions. 186

Filename extension A set of letters and/or numbers added to the end of a filename that helps to identify the file contents or file type. 11, 171

File-naming conventions A set of rules, established by the operating system, that must be followed to create a valid filename. 170

Flat file A single file that is the electronic version of a box of index cards, in which all records use the same record format. 137

Floppy disk A removable magnetic storage medium, typically 3½" in size, with a capacity of 1.44 MB. 79

Floppy disk drive A storage device that writes data on, and reads data from, floppy disks. 9

Folders The subdirectories, or subdivisions, of a directory that can contain files or other folders. 172

Font A typeface or style of lettering, such as Arial, Times New Roman, and Gothic. 130

Footer Text that appears in the bottom margin of each page of a document. 131

Format Specified properties for setting a document's appearance. 130

Formatting The process of dividing a disk into sectors so that it can be used to store information. 180

Formatting utilities Software usually included in an operating system that assists with formatting disks. 180

Formula In spreadsheet terminology, a combination of numbers and symbols that tells the computer how to use the contents of cells in calculations. 134

Fragmented files Files stored in scattered, noncontiguous clusters on a disk. 183

Frames An outline or boundary, frequently defining a box. For document production software, a pre-defined area into which text or graphics may be placed. 132

Freeware Copyrighted software that is given away by the author or owner. 155

Full backup A copy of all the files for a specified backup job. 196

Full-system backup A backup, or copy, of all of the files stored on a computer. 194

Fully justified The horizontal alignment of text where the text terminates exactly at both margins of the document. 131

Function In worksheets, a built-in formula for making a calculation. In programming, a section of code that manipulates data, but is not included in the main sequential execution path of a program. 134

Giga- Prefix for a billion. 61

Gigahertz (GHz) A measure of frequency equivalent to one billion cycles per second. 67

Grammar checker A feature of word processing software that coaches the user on correct sentence structure and word usage. 130

Graphical user interface (GUI) A type of user interface that features on-screen objects, such as menus and icons, manipulated by a mouse. Abbreviated GUI (pronounced "gooey"). 120

Graphics Any picture, photograph, or image that can be manipulated or viewed on a computer. 141

Graphics card A circuit board inserted into a computer to handle the display of text, graphics, animation, and videos. Also called a "video card." 92

Graphics software Computer programs for creating, editing, and manipulating images. 141

Groupware Software that enables multiple users to collaborate on a project, usually through a pool of data that can be shared by members of the workgroup. 147

Handheld computer A small, pocket-sized computer that is designed to run on its own power supply and provide users with basic applications. 7

Hard disk drive A computer storage device that contains a large-capacity "hard disk" sealed inside the drive case. A hard disk is NOT the same as a 3½" floppy disk that has a rigid plastic case. 9

Hard disk platter The component of a hard disk drive on which data is stored. It is a flat, rigid disk made of aluminum or glass and coated with a magnetic oxide. 81

Head crash A collision between the read-write head and the surface of the hard disk platter, resulting in damage to some of the data on the disk. 83

Header Text that is placed in the top margin of each page of a document. 131

High-level language A computer language that allows a programmer to write instructions using human-like language. 115

Home page (1) A document that is the starting, or entry, page at a Web site. (2) The Web page that a browser displays each time it is started. 30

Horizontal market software Any computer program that can be used by many different kinds of businesses (for example, an accounting program). 147

HTML (Hypertext Markup Language) A standardized format used to specify the format for Web page documents. 27

HTML tags A set of instructions, such as <B>, inserted into an HTML document to provide formatting and display information to a Web browser. 29

HTTP (Hypertext Transfer Protocol) The communications protocol used to transmit Web pages. HTTP:// is an identifier that appears at the beginning of most Web page URLs (for example, http://www.fooyong.com). 27

Hypertext A way of organizing an information database by linking information through the use of text and multimedia. Helped the development of the WWW. 26

IMAP (Internet Messaging Access Protocol) A protocol similar to POP that is used to retrieve e-mail messages from an e-mail server, but offers additional features, such as choosing which e-mails to download from the server. 40

Incremental backup A copy of the files that changed since the last backup. 196

Information The words, numbers, and graphics used as the basis for human actions and decisions. 11

Ink jet printer A non-impact printer that creates characters or graphics by spraying liquid ink onto paper or other media. 94

Input As a noun, "input" means the information that is conveyed to a computer. As a verb, "input" means to enter data into a computer. 4

Install The process by which programs and data are copied to the hard disk of a computer system and otherwise prepared for access and use. 149

Installation agreement A version of the license agreement that appears on the computer screen when software is being installed, and prompts the user to accept or decline. 154

Instant messaging A private chat in which users can communicate with each other. 17

Instruction cycle The steps followed by a computer to process a single instruction; fetch, interpret, execute, then increment the instruction pointer. 99

Instruction set The collection of instructions that a CPU is designed to process. 67

Integrated circuit (IC) A thin slice of silicon crystal containing microscopic circuit elements, such as transistors, wires, capacitors, and resistors; also called chips and microchips. 62

Internet The worldwide communication infrastructure that links computer networks using TCP/IP protocol. 15

Internet backbone The major communications links that form the core of the Internet. 15

Internet telephony A set of hardware and software that allows users to make phone-style calls over the Internet, usually without a long-distance charge. 17

Interpreter A program that converts high-level instructions in a computer program into machine language instructions, one instruction at a time. 116

IP address A unique, identifying number assigned to each computer connected to the Internet. 16

ISA (Industry Standard Architecture) A standard for moving data on the expansion bus. Can refer to a type of slot, a bus, or a peripheral device. An older technology, it is rapidly being replaced by PCI architecture. 89

ISDN (Integrated Services Digital Network) A telephone company service that transports data digitally over dial-up or dedicated lines. 20

ISP (Internet Service Provider) A company that provides Internet access to businesses, organizations, and individuals. 20

Kernel The core module of an operating system that typically manages memory, processes, tasks, and disks. 121

Keyword 1) A word or term used as the basis for a database or Web-page search. 2) A command word supplied by a programming language. 32

Kilobit (Kbit or Kb) 1,024 bits. 61

Kilobyte (KB) Approximately 1,000 bytes; exactly 1,024 bytes. 61

Label In the context of spreadsheets, any text used to describe data. 133

LAN (local area network) An interconnected group of computers and peripherals located within a relatively limited area, such as a building or campus. 7

Lands Non-pitted surface areas on a CD that represent digital data. (See also Pits.) 78

Laser printer A printer that uses laser-based technology, similar to that used by photocopiers, to produce text and graphics. 95

LCD (liquid crystal display) A type of flat panel computer screen, typically found on notebook computers. 9, 92

LCD screen (See LCD.)

Leading Also called line spacing, the vertical spacing between lines of text. 131

Level 1 cache (L1 cache) Cache memory built into a microprocessor chip. L1 cache typically can be read in one clock cycle. 68

Level 2 cache (L2 cache) Cache memory that is located in a chip separate from the microprocessor chip. 68

Line spacing (See Leading.)

Links Underlined text that allow users to jump between Web pages. 26

Linux A server operating system that is a derivative of UNIX and available as freeware. 125

Logical storage models Also referred to as metaphors, any visual aid that helps a computer user visualize a file system. 177

Mac OS The operating system software designed for use on Apple Macintosh and iMac computers. 124

Machine code Program instructions written in binary code that the computer can execute directly. 98

Machine language A low-level language written in binary code that the computer can execute directly. 115

Macro A small set of instructions that automates a task. Typically, a macro is created by performing the task once and recording the steps. Whenever the macro is played back, the steps are repeated. 186

Macro virus A computer virus that infects the macros that are attached to documents and spreadsheets. (See Macro.) 186

Macs (Macintosh computers) A personal computer platform designed and manufactured by Apple Computer. 13

Magnetic storage The recording of data onto disks or tape by magnetizing particles of an oxide-based surface coating. 77

Mail merge A feature of document production software that automates the process of producing customized documents, such as form letters and advertising flyers. 132

Mailing list server Any computer and software that maintains a list of people who are interested in a topic, and facilitates message exchanges among all members of the list. 16

Mainframe computer A large, fast, and expensive computer generally used by businesses or government agencies to provide centralized storage processing and management for large amounts of data. 8

Mathematical modeling software Software for visualizing and solving a wide range of math, science, and engineering problems. 136

Mathematical operators Symbols such as + / * -, that represent specific mathematical functions in a formula. 134

Megabit (Mb or Mbit) 1,048,576 bits. 61

Megabyte (MB) Approximately 1 million bytes; exactly 1,048,576 bytes. 61

Megahertz (MHz) A measure of frequency equivalent to 1 million cycles per second. 67

Memory The computer circuitry that holds data waiting to be processed. 5

Message header The section of an e-mail document that contains the address, subject, and file attachment information. 36

Microcomputer A category of computer that is built around a single microprocessor chip. 6

Microprocessor An integrated circuit that contains the circuitry for processing data. It is a single-chip version of the central processing unit (CPU) found in all computers. 6, 66

Microprocessor clock A device on the motherboard of a computer responsible for setting the pace of executing instructions. 67

Microsoft Windows An operating system, developed by Microsoft Corporation, that provides a graphical interface. Versions include Windows 3.1, Windows 95, Windows 98, Windows Me, Windows XP, Windows NT, and Windows 2000. 122

MIDI sequencing software Software that uses a standardized way of transmitting encoded music or sounds for controlling musical devices, such as a keyboard or sound card. 143

MIME (Multipurpose Internet Mail Extension) A conversion process used for formatting non-ASCII messages so that they can be sent over the Internet. 37

Minicomputer A mid-range computer, somewhat larger than a microcomputer, that can carry out processing tasks for many simultaneous users. 6

Modem A device that sends and receives data to and from computers. (See voice band modem, cable modem.) 10

Monitor A display device that forms an image by converting electrical signals from the computer into points of colored light on the screen. 9

Motherboard The main circuit board in a computer that houses chips and other electronic components. 63

Mouse An input device, located on the surface of a desk, that allows the user to manipulate objects on the screen by clicking, dragging, and dropping. 9

MP3 A file format that provides highly compressed audio files with very little loss of sound quality. 143

MP3 encoding software Software that compresses a WAV file into an MP3 file. 143

MP3 player Software that plays MP3 music files. 143

Multi-partite viruses A computer virus that is able to infect many types of targets by hiding itself in numerous locations on a computer. 190

Multitasking operating system An operating system that runs two or more programs at the same time. 122

Multiuser operating system An operating system that allows a single computer to deal simultaneously with processing requests from multiple users. 122

Nanometer A unit of length that is one billionth of a meter. (A meter is about 39 inches.) 66

Nanosecond A unit of time representing 1 billionth of a second. 72

Native file format A file format that is unique to a program or group of programs and has a unique file extension. 171

Natural language query A query using language spoken by human beings, as opposed to an artificially constructed language such as machine language. 140

Netiquette Internet etiquette or a set of guidelines for posting messages and e-mails in a civil, concise way. 39

Network card An expansion board mounted inside a computer to allow access to a local area network. Also called a network interface card (NIC). 19

Network operating system Programs designed to control the flow of data, maintain security, and keep track of accounts on a network. 122

Newsgroup An online discussion group that centers around a specific topic. 16

Notation software Software used to help musicians compose, edit, and print their compositions. 143

Notebook computers Small, lightweight, portable computers that usually run on batteries. Sometimes called laptops. 6

Numeric data Numbers that represent quantities and can be used in arithmetic operations. 59

Object-oriented database A database model that organizes data into classes of objects that can be manipulated by programmer-defined methods. 138

Op code Short for operation code, an op code is an assembly language command word that designates an operation, such as add (ADD), compare (CMP), or jump (JMP). 98

Open source software Software, such as Linux, that includes its uncompiled source code, which can be modified and distributed by programmers. 155

Operand The part of an instruction that specifies the data, or the address of the data, on which the operation is to be performed. 98

Operating system (OS) The software that controls the computer's use of its hardware resources, such as memory and disk storage space. 12, 118

Optical storage A means of recording data as light and dark spots on a CD, DVD, or other optical media. 78

Output The results produced by a computer (for example, reports, graphs, and music). 5

Packet A small unit of data transmitted over a network or the Internet. 16

Page layout The physical positions of elements on a document page, such as headers, footers, page numbers, and graphics. 131

Paint software The software required to create and manipulate bitmap graphics. 141

Paragraph alignment The horizontal position (left, right, justified, centered, for example) of the text in a document. 131

Paragraph style A specification for the format of a paragraph, which includes the alignment of text within margins and line spacing. 131

Parallel processing A technique by which two or more processors in a computer perform processing tasks simultaneously. 68

Passive matrix screen A display found on older notebook computers that relies on timing to ensure that the liquid crystal cells are illuminated. 94

Password A special set of symbols used to restrict access to a user's computer or network. 22

Path A file's location in a file structure. (See File specification.) 172

Payroll software A type of horizontal market software used to maintain payroll records. 147

PC card (PCMCIA card) A credit card-sized circuit board used to connect a modem, memory, network card, or storage device to a notebook computer. 90

PCI (Peripheral Component Interconnect) A method for transporting data on the expansion bus. Can refer to type of data bus, expansion slot, or transport method used by a peripheral device. 89

PCMCIA slot A PCMCIA (Personal Computer Memory Card International Association) slot is an external expansion slot typically found on notebook computers. 90

PCs Microcomputers that use Windows software and contain Intel-compatible microprocessors. 13

PDA (personal digital assistant) A computer that is smaller and more portable than a notebook computer (also called a palmtop computer). 7

Peer-to-peer The process by which one workstation/server shares resources with another workstation/server. Refers to the capability of a network computer to act as both a file server and workstation. 18

Peripheral device A component or equipment, such as a printer or scanner, that expands a computer's input, output, or storage capabilities. 11

Personal computer A microcomputer designed for use by an individual user for applications such as Internet browsing and word processing. 6

Personal finance software Software geared toward individual finances that helps track bank account balances, credit card payments, investments, and bills. 136

Personal information manager Software that specializes in keeping track of personal data, such as appointments or addresses. 137

PGAs (pin-grid arrays) A common chip design used for microprocessors. 63

Phase change technology A writable CD and DVD technology that uses disks with a modifiable crystal structure, and allows users to add, modify, and delete data. 86

Photo editing software The software used to edit, enhance, retouch, and manipulate digital photographs. 141

Physical storage model A representation of data as it is physically stored. 180

Pipelining A technology that allows a processor to begin executing an instruction before completing the previous instruction. 68

Pits Spots on a CD that are "burned," representing part of a data unit. 78

Pixels Short for picture element, a pixel is the smallest unit in a graphic image. Computer display devices use a matrix of pixels to display text and graphics. 93

Platform A "family" or category of computers based on the same underlying software and hardware. 13

Plug and Play The ability of a computer to automatically recognize and adjust the system configuration for a newly added device. 92

Point size A unit of measure (1/72 of an inch) used to describe the height of characters. 130

Polymorphic viruses Viruses that can escape detection from antivirus software by changing their signatures. 190

POP (Post Office Protocol) A protocol that is used to retrieve e-mail messages from an e-mail server. 40

POP server A computer that receives and stores e-mail data until retrieved by the e-mail account holder. 41

PostScript A printer language, developed by Adobe Systems, which uses a special set of commands to control page layout, fonts, and graphics. 96

Power-on self-test (POST) A diagnostic process that runs during startup to check components of the computer, such as the graphics card, RAM, keyboard, and disk drives. 44

Presentation software Software that provides tools to combine text, graphics, graphs, animation, and sound into a series of electronic "slides" that can be output on a projector, or as overhead transparencies, paper copies, or 35-millimeter slides. 142

Printer Control Language (PCL) A standard language used to send page formatting instructions from a computer to a laser or ink jet printer. 96

Processing The manipulation of data using a systematic series of actions. 4

Programming language A set of keywords and grammar rules (syntax) that allows a programmer to write instructions that a computer can execute. 115

Project management software Software specifically designed as a tool for planning, scheduling, and tracking projects and their costs. 147

Properties The characteristics of an object in programs. 114

Proprietary services Services specific to or offered by one company. 22

Public domain software Software that is available for use by the public without restriction except that it cannot be copyrighted. 155

Puzzle games Entertainment software that often is a computerized version of a popular board game focused on solving a puzzle. 146

Query A search specification that prompts the computer to look for particular records in a file. 32, 140

Query by example (QBE) A type of database interface in which the user fills in a field with an example of the type of information that she is seeking. 140

Query language A set of command words that can be used to direct the computer to create databases, locate information, sort records, and change the data in those records. 140

RAID (Redundant Array of Independent Disks) Disks used by mainframes and microcomputers, in which many disk platters are used to provide data redundancy for faster data access and increased protection from media failure. 83

RAM (random access memory) A type of computer memory circuit that holds data, program instructions, and the operating system while the computer is on. 70

Random access The ability of a storage device (such as a disk drive) to go directly to a specific storage location without having to search sequentially from a beginning location. 79

RDRAM (Rambus dynamic RAM) A fast (up to 600 MHz) type of memory used in newer personal computers. 72

Readability formula A feature found in some word processing software that can estimate the reading level of a written document. 130

Read-write head The mechanism in a disk drive that magnetizes particles on the storage disk surface to write data, or senses the bits that are present to read data. 77

Record In the context of database management, a record is the fields of data that pertain to a single entity in a database. 137

Record structure The list of fields, data types, and relationships that form a template for the records in a file or database. 139

Recovery CD A CD that contains all the operating system files and application software files necessary to restore a computer to its original state. 197

Reference software Software that contains a large database of information with tools for sorting, viewing, and accessing specific topics. 145

Registers A sort of "scratch pad" area of the ALU and control unit where data or instructions are moved so that they can be processed. 67

Registry Editor A tool provided by Windows that allows users to manually edit

Registry files. 159

Relational database A database structure that incorporates the use of tables that can establish relationships with other similar tables. 138

Relative reference In a worksheet, cell references that can change if cells change position as a result of a move or copy operation. 135

Rescue disk A boot disk that contains operating system files plus antivirus software. 198

Reserved words Special words used as commands in some operating systems that may not be used in filenames. 171

Resolution The density of the grid used to display or print text and graphics. The greater the horizontal and vertical density, the higher the resolution. 93

Resource A component, either hardware or software, that is available for use by a computer's processor. 119

Restore The act of moving data from a backup storage medium to a hard disk in the event original data has been lost. 194

Retro viruses Viruses designed to corrupt antivirus software. 190

RIMM (Rambus in-line memory module) A memory module using RDRAM. 72

RISC (Reduced Instruction Set Computer) A microprocessor chip designed for rapid and efficient processing of a small set of simple instructions. 68

Role-playing games Entertainment software that is based on a story line in which the user plays a character role. 146

ROM (read-only memory) One or more integrated circuits that contain permanent instructions that the computer uses during the boot process. 72

ROM BIOS A small set of basic input/output system instructions stored in ROM, which causes the computer system to load critical operating files when the user turns on the computer. 72

Root directory The main directory of a disk. 172

Router A device found at each intersection on the Internet backbone that examines the IP address of incoming data, and forwards the data towards its destination. 16

Safe Mode A menu option that appears when Windows is unable to complete the boot sequence. By entering Safe Mode, a user can gracefully shut down the computer, then try to reboot it. 46

Script A program containing a list of commands that are automatically executed as needed. 116

SCSI (Small Computer System Interface) An interface standard used for attaching peripheral devices, such as disk drives. Pronounced "scuzzy." 82

SDRAM Short for synchronous dynamic RAM, it is a type of RAM that synchronizes itself with the CPU, thus enabling it to run at much higher clock speeds than conventional RAM. 72

Search and Replace A feature of document production software that allows the user to automatically locate all instances of a particular word or phrase and substitute another word or phrase. 130

Search engine A program that uses keywords to find information on the Internet, and returns a list of relevant documents. 16, 31

Search operator A word or symbol that has a specific function within a search, such as "AND" or "+". 32

SEC cartridges (single edge contact) A common, cassette-like chip design for microprocessors. 63

Sectors Subdivisions of the tracks on a storage medium that provide a storage area for data. 180

Self-executing zip file A type of file that can be run to unzip the file or files contained within it. 151

Self-installing executable file A program that automatically unzips and then initiates and runs its setup program. 151

Semiconducting materials (semiconductors) Substances, such as silicon or germanium, that can act either as a conductor or insulator. Used in the manufacture of computer chips. 62

Sequential access A form of data storage, usually on computer tape, that requires a device to read or write data one record after another, starting at the beginning of the medium. 79

Serial processing Processing of data one instruction at a time, completing one instruction before beginning another. 68

Server A computer or software on a network that supplies the network with data and storage. 8

Setup program A program module supplied with a software package for the purpose of installing the software. 150

Shareware Copyrighted software marketed under a license that allows users to use the software for a trial period and then send in a registration fee if they wish to continue to use it. 155

Shrink-wrap license A legal agreement printed on computer software packaging, which goes into effect when the package is opened. 153

Simulation games Entertainment software that provides a realistic setting for emulating real-world skills, such as flying an airplane. 146

Single-user operating system A type of operating system that is designed for one user at a time with one set of input and output devices. 122

Slides The output frames from presentation software, which can be displayed on a computer monitor. 142

Small business accounting software Software that is specifically designed to assist with basic small business accounting needs. 136

Smileys Text-based symbols used to express emotion. 39

SMTP server (Simple Mail Transfer Protocol server) A computer used to send e-mail across a network or the Internet. 41

Software The instructions that prepare a computer to do a task, indicate how to interact with a user, and specify how to process data. 4, 112

Software license A legal contract that defines the ways in which a user may use a computer program. 153

Software publishers Companies that produce computer software. 114

Solid ink printer A printer that uses a stick of solid ink, which is melted, sprayed onto, and fused to the paper, resulting in photograph-quality images without the use of special paper. 95

SO-RIMM (small outline Rambus in-line memory) A small memory module that contains RDRAM, used primarily in notebook computers. 72

Sort key A field used to arrange records in order. 140

Sound card A circuit board that gives the computer the ability to accept audio input from a microphone, play sound files stored on disks and CD-ROMs, and produce audio output through speakers or headphones. 10

Source code Computer instructions written in a high-level language. 115

Spelling checker A feature of document production software that checks each word in a document against an electronic dictionary of correctly spelled words, then presents a list of alternatives for possible misspellings. 129

Spelling dictionary A data module that is used by a spelling checker as a list of correctly spelled words. 129

Sports games A type of entertainment software that simulates playing in sporting events. 146

Spreadsheet A numerical model or representation of a real situation, presented in the form of a table. 133

Spreadsheet software Software for creating electronic worksheets that hold data in cells and perform calculations based on that data. 133

SQL (Structured Query Language) A popular query language used by mainframes and microcomputers. 140

Statistical software Software for analyzing large sets of data to discover patterns and relationships within them. 136

Stealth viruses Viruses that can escape detection from antivirus software by removing their signatures and hiding in memory. 190

Storage The area in a computer where data is retained on a permanent basis. 5

Storage device A mechanical apparatus that records data to and retrieves data from a storage medium. 76

Storage medium The physical material used to store computer data, such as a floppy disk, a hard disk, or a CD-ROM. 76

Storage metaphor A likeness or analogy that helps people visualize the way that computers store files. 177

Store-and-forward technology A technology used by communications networks in which an e-mail message is temporarily held in storage on a server until it is requested by a client computer. 40

Stored program A set of instructions that resides on a storage device, such as a hard drive, and can be loaded into memory and executed. 5

Strategy games A type of entertainment software that allows one or more players to participate in a strategy-oriented game. 146

Structured file A file that consists of a collection of records, each with the same set of fields. 137

Style A feature in many desktop publishing and word processing programs that allows the user to apply numerous format settings in a single command. 131

Subdirectories Directories found under the root directory. 172

Supercomputer The fastest and most expensive type of computer, capable of processing more than 1 trillion instructions per second. 8

SVGA (Super Video Graphics Array) SVGA typically refers to 800 x 600 resolution. 93

SXGA (Super eXtended Graphics Array) A screen resolution of 1280 x 1024. 93

System requirements (1) Specifications for the operating system and hardware configuration necessary for a software product to work correctly. (2) The criteria that must be met for a new computer system or software product to be a success. 148

System software Computer programs that help the computer carry out essential operating tasks. 12, 117

System unit The case or box that contains the computer's power supply, storage devices, main circuit board, processor, and memory. 9

Table An arrangement of data in a grid of rows and columns. In a relational database, a collection of record types with their data. 132

Tape backup A copy of data from a comput- er's hard disk, stored on magnetic tape and used to restore lost data. 83

Tax preparation software Personal finance software that is specifically designed to assist with tax preparation. 136

TCP/IP (Transmission Control Protocol/Internet Protocol) A standard set of communication rules used by every computer that connects to the Internet. 15

Telenet A common way to remotely control another computer or server on a network or the Internet. 18

Tera- Prefix for a trillion. 61

Thermal transfer printer An expensive, color-precise printer that uses wax containing color to produce numerous dots of color on plain paper. 95

Thesaurus A feature of documentation soft- ware that provides synonyms. 130

Topic directory A list of topics and subtopics arranged in a hierarchy from general to specific. 33

Tracks A series of concentric or spiral stor- age areas created on a storage medium during the formatting process. 180

Trigger event An event that activates a task often associated with a computer virus. 185

Trojan horse A computer program that appears to perform one function while actually doing something else, such as inserting a virus into a computer system, or stealing a password. 186

UDMA (Ultra DMA) A faster version of DMA technology. 82

Ultra ATA A disk drive technology that is an enhanced version of EIDE. Also referred to as Ultra DMA or Ultra IDE. 82

Unicode A 16-bit character representation code that can represent more than

65,000 characters. 60

Uninstall routine A program that removes software files, references, and Registry entries from a computer's hard disk. 152

UNIX A multiuser, multitasking server oper- ating system developed by AT&T's Bell Laboratories in 1969. 125

Unzipped Refers to files that have been uncompressed. 151

Uploading The process of sending a copy of a file from a local computer to a remote computer. 17

URL (Uniform Resource Locator) The address of a Web page. 27

Usenet A worldwide Internet bulletin board system of newsgroups that share common topics. 16

User ID A combination of letters and numbers that serves as a user's "call sign" or identification. Also referred to as a user name. 22

User interface The software and hard- ware that enable people to interact with computers. 120

Utilities A subcategory of system software designed to augment the operating system by providing ways for a computer user to control the allocation and use of hardware resources. 121

UXGA (Ultra eXtended Graphics Array) A screen resolution of 1600 x 1200. 93

Value A number used in a calculation. 133

Vertical market software Computer pro- grams designed to meet the needs of a specific market segment or industry, such as medical record-keeping software for use in hospitals. 147

VGA (Video Graphics Array) A screen resolution of 640 x 480. 93

Video editing software Software that pro- vides tools for capturing and editing video from a camcorder. 144

Videogame console A computer specifically designed for playing games using a television screen and game controllers. 7

Viewable image size (vis) A measurement of the maximum image size that can be displayed on a monitor screen. 93

Virtual memory A computer's use of hard disk storage to simulate RAM. 71

Virus hoax A message, usually e-mail, that makes claims about a virus problem that doesn't actually exist. 191

Virus signature The unique computer code contained in a virus that helps with its identification. Antivirus software searches for known virus signatures to identify a virus. 189

Voice band modem The type of modem that

would typically be used to connect a computer to a telephone line. (See Modem.) 18

Volatile A term that describes data (usually in RAM), which can exist only with a constant supply of power. 71

Web Short for World Wide Web. An Internet service that links documents and information from computers distributed all over the world, using the HTTP protocol. 26

Web authoring software Computer programs for designing and developing customized Web pages that can be published electronically on the Internet. 128

Web pages Documents on the World Wide Web that consist of a specially coded HTML file with associated text, audio, video, and graphics files. A Web page often contains links to other Web pages. 26

Web servers Computers that use special software to transmit Web pages over the Internet. 27

Web site Usually a group of Web pages identified by a similar domain name, such as www.cnn.com. 16, 27

Web-based e-mail An e-mail account that stores, sends, and receives e-mail on a Web site rather than a user's computer. 40

What-if analysis The process of setting up a model in a spreadsheet and experimenting to see what happens when different values are entered. 133

Windows Explorer A file management utility included with most Windows operating systems that helps users manage their files. 178

Windows Registry A crucial set of data files maintained by the operating system that contains the settings needed by a computer to correctly use any hardware and software that has been installed on the system. 157

Windows Startup Disk A disk that is created by the user to load the operating system and the CD-ROM drivers, allowing for system restoration. 197

Word processing software Computer programs that assist the user in producing documents, such as reports, letters, papers, and manuscripts. 128

Word size The number of bits a CPU can manipulate at one time, which is dependent on the size of the registers in the CPU, and the number of data lines in the bus. 67

Worksheet A computerized, or electronic, spreadsheet. 133

Workstation (1) A computer connected to a local area network. (2) A powerful desktop computer designed for specific tasks. 7

Worm A software program designed to enter a computer system, usually a network, through security "holes" and then replicate itself. 186

Write-protect window A small hole and sliding cover on a floppy disk that restricts writing to the disk. 81

XGA (Extended Graphics Array) XGA usually refers to 1,024 x 768 resolution. 93

Zipped Refers to one or more files that have been compressed. 151

INDEX

ABC News, 27
access. *See also* access
time, 18
   e-mail, 42
   transmission speed
      expression, 61
access time, 79
   sequential access, 79
   storage medium, 79
accounting and finance software. *See also* software
   discussed, 136, 147
      mathematical modeling
         software, 136
      personal finance soft-
         ware, 136
      statistical software, 136
      tax preparation software,
         136
Adobe Acrobat, 205, 206
Adobe Illustrator, 171
Adobe PageMaker, 128
Adobe Photoshop, 206
Age of Empires, 146
.ai filename extension, 205,
   206
ALU. *See* arithmetic logic
   unit
always-on connection, cable
   modem, 19
AMD, 69
America Online (AOL), 20,
   186
   proprietary services, 20, 22
American Management
   Association, 48
American Standard Code for
   Information Interchange
   (ASCII)
   discussed, 60
      Extended ASCII, 60
      numeric data representa-
         tion, 61
   e-mail text, 37
analog device, 58
antivirus software, 188. *See*
   also virus
   discussed, 189-190
      checksum, 189
      updates, 190
      virus signature, 189
AOL. *See* America Online
Apple, 13, 103, 120. *See*
   also Mac
application software. *See*
   also software
   defined, 12
   discussed, 116-117
      document production soft-
         ware, 128-132
      e-mail client software, 41,
         42

operating systems and,
   12-13
archiving, 86. *See also*
   backup; storage
arithmetic logic unit (ALU).
   See also microprocessor
   discussed, 67, 100
      control unit, 67, 100
      registers, 67
ASCII. *See* American
   Standard Code for
   Information Interchange
.asp filename extension, 205
asterisk (*), as wildcard, 32
AT&T WorldNet, 20
ATM machine, 22
attachment. *See also* e-mail
   e-mail, 37, 39
.au filename extension, 205
audio editing software, 143
audio file, format, 204
AutoCad, 148
.avi filename extension, 205

backslash (\), folder names,
   172
backup. *See also* backup
   software
   archiving, 86
   boot disk, 197
      recovery CD, 197
      rescue disk, 198
      Windows Startup Disk,
         197
   defined, 193
   procedures, 193-198
      data restoration, 194
      differential backup, 196
      full backup, 196
      full-system backup, 194
      incremental backup, 196
      selective backup, 194
      storage, 198, 199
         CD-ROM/DVD, 199
         floppy disk/Zip disk, 198-
            199
         hard disk, 83, 199
         tape backup, 83, 198
      verifying, 197
      virus infection, 196
backup software
   defined, 200
   discussed, 200-201
      Copy Disk utility, 200
"base 2". *See* binary number
   system
basic input/output system
   (BIOS). *See also*
   NetBIOS
   ROM BIOS, 72
      compared to CD-ROM,
         85

.bat filename extension, 204
beep code. *See also* boot
   process
   POST, 45
benchmark, microprocessor,
   68
binary digits, 58. *See also*
   bit; digital data
   computer use of, 61
binary number system, 59
.bin filename extension, 187,
   204

BIOS. *See* basic input/out-
   put system
bit, 58, 59. *See also* binary
   digits; byte
   compared to byte, 61
      nibble, 61
   defined, 11
      kilobit, 61
      megabit, 61
bitmap file
   layout, 204
Blair Witch Project, 12
.bmp filename extension, 11,
   112, 205, 206
bookmarks, browser, 31
boot disk. *See also* boot
   process
   backup, 197
   rescue disk, 198
   Windows Startup Disk, 197
boot process. *See also* installation; setup program
   bootstrap program, 121
   discussed, 44-47
      rebooting, 47
   order of events, 45
      completion of boot
         process, 46
      problems with OS, 46
      screen information, 46
   power-on self-test, 44, 45
      beep code, 45
      problem identification, 45
   ROM BIOS, 72
   Safe Mode, 46
   Windows Startup Disk, 197
Britannica, 145
browser. *See also* World
   Wide Web
   defined, 28
   discussed, 28-31
      copy option, 30
      favorites/bookmarks, 31
      find option, 31
      history list, 31
      home button, 30
      HTML tags, 29
      navigation buttons, 30
      print option, 30

save option, 30
stop button, 31
URL box, 30
buffer, 120
bulletin board, Usenet, 16
business software. *See also*
software
discussed, 147
accounting software, 147
groupware, 147
horizontal market soft-
ware, 147
payroll software, 147
project management
software, 147
vertical market software,
147
byte. *See also* bit
compared to bit, 61
nibble, 61
defined, 11
kilobyte, 61
megabyte, 61
terabyte, 61

cable. *See also* cable
modem; hardware
expansion cable, 90
cable modem
discussed, 19
always-on connection, 19
.ca domain, 236
cache. *See also* cache size;
memory; storage
Level 1 cache, 68
Level 2 cache, 68
cache size, 67
performance factors, 68
CAD software, 142
CalTech, 49
capacitor, 71
Cap'n Crunch, 208
Carnivore technology, 48
case sensitivity
password, 23
CD-ROM, 76
for backups, 199
capacity and speed, 85
CD ripper, 143, 367
CD-writer, 10
comparison
to DVD, 86, 87
to hard disk, 84, 86
to ROM BIOS, 85
creating
CD-R, 85-86
CD-RW, 85-86
phase-change technology,
86
discussed, 10, 84-86
drive bay, 78
as optical storage, 78
for software, 81
technology, 84-86
Celeron chip, 69. *See also*
chip; microprocessor
cell, worksheet, 133
cell references, 134

central processing unit
(CPU), 6, 8, 66. *See also*
microprocessor
defined, 4
.cfg filename extension, 204
character data, 59-60. *See
also* data
codes
ASCII, 60, 61
EBCDIC, 60
Extended ASCII, 60
Unicode, 60
character data type, 139
chat group, 17
Chernobyl virus, 186
China, 161
chip. *See also* digital
electronics
discussed, 62-63
DIMMs, 63
DIPs, 63
PGAs, 63
SEC cartridge, 63
on motherboard, 63
CISC. *See* complex instruction set computer
client, defined, 8
clip art, 132. *See also*
graphics
clock, microprocessor
clock, 67
clock speed, 67
CMOS. *See* complementary
metal oxide semiconductor
CNN, 27
code
object code, 115
source code, 115
Codemas virus, 186
coding. *See also* computer
programming
color
CMYK color, 94
"True Color," 94
.com filename extension,
185, 187
compiler, 115
complementary metal oxide
semiconductor (CMOS).
See also memory
discussed, 73-74
storage in, 44
complex instruction set computer (CISC), compared
to RISC, 68
compression
backup software, 200
Compton, 145
computer. *See also* Mac; personal computer; software
categories, 6-8
desktop computer, 6
handheld computer, 7
IBM PC, 6
mainframe, 6, 8
microcomputer, 6
microprocessor, 6, 63
minicomputer, 6

personal computer, 6
PlayStation, 7-8
server, 8
supercomputer, 8
central processing unit, 4
data, 4
function, digital electronics,
62-64
in general, 4-5
defined, 4
origin of term, 4
input, 4
memory, 5
stored program, 5
output, 5
platform, 13
processing, 4
recycling, 102-103
remote access, 18
workstation, 7
computer crime. *See also*
hacker
discussed, 208-209
computer network. *See also*
network
defined, 7
computer program. *See also*
software
computer program, 4
defined, 4, 112
stored program, 5
utilities, 121
computer programmer, 114.
computer programmer, 114
discussed, 114
computer programming.
See also programming
language
modular programming, 113
Computer Recycle Center,
102
conversion software, 207.
See also file format
Copy Disk utility, 200
copying
Copy Disk utility, 200
file, 179
software, 153
Web page, 30
copyright
defined, 153
software, 153
CorelDraw, 206
CPU. *See* central processing unit
crash, hard disk, 83, 194
currency data type, 139
customer service, ISPs, 22
cyberterrorist, 209. *See also*
hacker
cycle, instruction cycle, 99

data. *See also*
character data, 59
compared to information, 11
compared to software, 113
defined, 4, 11
numeric data, 59

packets, 16
restoring, 194
"writing data," 76
data compression. *See* compression
data file, 11. *See also* file
filename extension, 11
data management software. *See also* software
discussed, 137-141
file management software, 137
personal information manager, 137
query, 140
query by example, 140
query language, 140
record structure, 139, 140
search process, 141
data representation, 58
data storage. *See also* storage
format, 11
bit, 11
on Internet, 16
data transfer rate, 79
data types
currency, 139
database
character data type, 139
date data type, 139
logical data type, 139
memo data type, 139
numeric data type, 139
hyperlink, 139
database. *See also* record
break-in, 314
defined, 138
object-oriented database, 138
relational database, 138
database design. *See also* field; record
database management software, 138
.dat filename extension, 205
date
changing, 73
file, 173
date data type, 139
defragmentation, hard drive, 183
deleting
file, 179, 182
file shredder software, 182
Recycle Bin, 183
Dell, 13, 103
Denial of Service attack, 187
desktop publishing software, 128
Diablo, 146
dictionary, spell checker, 129
.dif filename extension, 205
digital camera, 11
discussed, 58-61
binary digits, 58
binary number system, 59

bit, 58, 59
character data, 59-60
numeric data, 59
digital device, 58
digital electronics, 58
discussed, 62-64
computer chip, 62-63
integrated circuit, 62
motherboard, 63-64
semiconductors, 62
digital format, 11
binary digits, 58
Digital Satellite Service (DSS), 20
Digital Software Association, 145
Digital Subscriber Line (DSL), 20
DIMMs, 63.
DIPs, 63.
directory
files, 172
root directory, 172
subdirectory, 172
display
"freeze up", troubleshooting, 45
notebook computer, LCD screen, 94
recycling, 102
display devices. *See also* display; *specific devices*
CRT, compared to LCD, 92-93
discussed, 92-94
dot pitch, 93
graphics card, 92, 93
image size and quality, 93
LCD, 9, 92-93
resolution, 93-94
color depth, 94
SVGA, 93, 94
SXGA, 93, 94
UXGA, 93, 94
VGA, 93
XGA, 94
division symbol (/), 134
.dll filename extension, 204
.doc filename extension, 188, 203, 205
document production software. *See also* application software
discussed, 128-132
desktop publishing software, 128
dictionary, 129
font, 130
format, 130
frames, 132
justification, 131
line spacing, 131
paragraph alignment, 131
paragraph style, 131
point size, 130
readability, 130
Search and Replace, 130
spell checker, 129

style, 131
thesaurus, 130
Web authoring software, 128
word processing software, 128
word wrap, 128
orientation
frame orientation, 132
page-orientation, 132
page layout
graphical elements, 132
headers and footers, 131
page numbers, 131
table, 132
productivity enhancement, mail merge, 132
Doom, 146
DOS, 126. *See also* operating system
filename naming conventions, 170
dot pitch, 93. *See also* display
Dow Chemical, 48
downloading, Internet, 17
drawing software, 141
drive bay, 78
driver
device driver, 92
Plug and Play, 92
printer driver, 97
.drv filename extension, 187
DSL. *See* Digital Subscriber Line
DSS. *See* Digital Satellite Service
DVD, 76
for backups, 199
comparison, to CD-ROM, 86, 87
creating
DVD-RAM, 87
DVD-RW, 87
DVDR+W, 87
discussed, 10, 86-87
DVD-ROM, 86
DVD-Video, 86
drive bay, 78
as optical storage, 78
for software, 81
DVD player, 7-8
computer, compared to video player, 87

e-commerce, 16
e-mail. *See also* e-mail system
address book, 195
attachment
virus infection, 186, 187-188
backups, 195
discussed, 16, 38
mailing list server, 16
HTML format, 38, 188
netiquette, 39
smileys, 39
overview, 36-39

advanced e-mail, 38
attachments, 37
basic e-mail, 37
e-mail account, 36
e-mail message, 36
forwarding messages, 37
message header, 36
MIME, 37
store-and-forward
  technology, 40
privacy, 48-49
e-mail server, 40
e-mail system
defined, 40
IMAP, 40
discussed, 41
POP, 40
compared to Web-based
  e-mail, 42
discussed, 41
Web-based e-mail, 40
ear training software, 143
EBCDIC. *See* Extended
  Binary-Coded Decimal
  Interchange Code
editing
audio editing software, 143
video editing software, 144
educational and reference
  software
discussed, 144-145
  educational software, 144
  reference software, 145
Electronic Communications
  Act of 2000, 48
Electronic Communications
  Privacy Act of 1986, 48
electronics
digital electronics, 58
discussed, 62-64
employer, e-mail monitoring,
  48-49
encyclopedia, 145
entertainment software. *See
  also* games; software
discussed, 145-146
  action games, 146
  adventure games, 146
  game ratings, 146
  puzzle games, 146
  role-play games, 146
  simulation games, 146
  sports games, 146
  strategy games, 146
Entertainment Software
  Rating Board, 146
.eps filename extension, 205
error. *See also* testing
General Protection Fault,
  119
"soft error," 47
EverQuest, 146
exabyte, 61
exam preparation software,
  144
executable file. *See also* file
defined, 11
discussed, 11, 112, 113

self-installing executable
  file, 151
virus infection, 185, 186
.exe filename extension, 11,
  112, 185
expansion cable. *See also*
  cable; hardware
discussed, 90-91
  IEEE 1394, 91
  parallel DB-25M, 91
  SCSI C-50F, 91
  serial DB-9, 91
  USB, 90, 91
  VGA HDB-15, 91
expansion card
defined, 88-89
graphics card, 92, 93
network interface card, 19,
  223
expansion port. *See also*
  expansion slot; port
discussed, 90
  USB port, 90, 91, 97
for peripheral device, 91
expansion slot. *See also*
  expansion port
discussed, 88-89
  AGP, 89, 92
  ISA, 89
  PCI, 89, 92
for notebook computer, 90
  PC card, 90
  PCMCIA slot, 90
Extended Binary-Coded
  Decimal Interchange
  Code (EBCDIC), 60

FAT. *See* File Allocation
  Table
favorites, browser, 31
FBI, Carnivore technology, 48
field
file management software,
  137
file. *See also* file format; file
  management; folder
computer file, 170
copying, 179
corrupted file, 206
date, 173
defined, 11, 170
  data file, 11
deleting, 179, 182
  Recycle Bin, 183
executable file, 11, 112, 113
  self-installing, 151
flat file, 137
folders and, 149, 172
fragmented file, 183
locating, 172
opening, 205-206
  files that won't open, 206
saving, 76, 181-182
size, 173
software, 113
structured file, 137
temporary file, 204
  in Windows Explorer, 179

File Allocation Table (FAT),
  181-182
file format, 171
compatibility, 206
converting, 206-207
discussed, 203-207
  files that won't open, 206
  software requirements,
    206
native file format, 171, 205
file header, 61, 203
file management, 121. *See
  also* file management
  software
defined, 174
discussed, 174-175
  logical storage model, 177
  Save, compared to Save
    As, 175
  storage metaphor, 177
utilities, 176
file management software.
  See also data manage-
  ment software
discussed, 137
  field, 137
  flat file, 137
  record, 137
  structured file, 137
file shredder software, 182
file specification, 172
file system
function, 181
cluster, 181
filename. *See also* filename
  extension
naming conventions,
  170-171
  reserved characters and
    words, 171
renaming file, 179
filename extension, 11
discussed, 171
  file format, 171, 206
for OS and executables,
  204
flat file, 137
.flc filename extension, 205
.fli filename extension, 205
floppy disk, 76. *See also*
  hard disk; storage
advantages and disadvan-
  tages, 80-81
  write-protect window, 81
for backup, 198
copying, 200
defined, 9, 79
digital camera adapter, 335
discussed, 79-81
  capacity, 80
  disk density, 80
  HD DS, 80
  Superdisk, 80
  virus infection, 187
  Zip disk, 80, 81
folder. *See also* file
files and, 149, 172
  directory, 172

root directory, 172
  subdirectory, 172
  in Windows Explorer, 179
folder name, 172
font, 130
footer. *See also* header
  document, 131
form
  for search engine, 33
format. *See also* formatting
  document production
    software, 130
  worksheet, 134
formatting
  hard disk, 180-181
formula
  spreadsheet, 134
  worksheet, 134
FreeBSD, 155
function
  worksheet, 134

games, 84. *See also* enter-
    tainment software
  action games, 146
  adventure games, 146
  game ratings, 146
  puzzle games, 146
  role-play games, 146
  simulation games, 146
  sports games, 146
  strategy games, 146
Gates, Bill, 209
Gateway, 13, 103
GHz. *See* gigahertz
.gif filename extension,
    205, 206
  file format, 204
gigabyte, 61
gigahertz (GHz), 67
GoodTimes virus, 191
graphic. *See also* graphics
    software
  clip art, 132
  defined, 141
  digitizing, 61
  e-mailing, 38
  graphical elements, 132
  3D graphics
    software, 142
graphical user interface
    (GUI), 120
graphics card, 92, 93. *See*
    also display devices;
    expansion card
graphics file
  format, 204, 206
graphics software
  discussed, 141-142
    CAD software, 142
    drawing software, 141
    paint software, 141
    photo editing software,
      141
    presentation software,
      142
    3D graphics software,
      142
graphics tablet, 11

GreenDisk, 102
Grolier, 145
groupware, 147
GUI. *See* graphical user
    interface

hackers, 208-209
Half-life, 146
handheld computer
  defined, 7
  PDA, 7
hard disk, 76. *See also* floppy
    disk; storage
  as backup, 83, 199
  compared to CD-ROM,
    84, 86
  compared to RAM, 70
  defragmentation, 183
  disadvantages, head
    crash, 83
  discussed, 9, 11, 81-83
    cylinder, 82
    platter, 81
  formatting, 180-181
    sectors, 180
    tracks, 180
  formatting utilities, 180
  how it works, 81-82
  technology
    controller, 82
    DMA, 82
    EIDE, 82
    RAID, 83
    SCSI, 82
    UDMA, 82
    Ultra ATA, 82
header
  document, 131
  e-mail message header, 36
  file header, 61, 203
  tape drive "header labels,"
    83
Hewlett-Packard, 13, 103
high-level language, 115
history list, browser, 31
.hlp filename extension, 112,
    204
home page. *See also* Web
    page
  defined, 30
.htm filename extension, 11,
    27, 205
HTML. *See* Hypertext
    Markup Language
HTML tags, 128
  defined, 29
  discussed, 29
.html filename extension, 27
HTTP. *See* Hypertext
    Transfer Protocol
hyperlink data type, 139.
    See also linking
hypertext. *See also*
    Hypertext Transfer
    Protocol
  development, 26
Hypertext Markup Language
    (HTML)
  defined, 27

Hypertext Transfer Protocol
    (HTTP)
  defined, 27

I-love-you virus, 185
IBM, 13, 69
  PC Recycling Service, 103
IC. *See* integrated circuit
ICANN. *See* Internet
    Corporation for Assigned
    Names and Numbers
Icewind Dale, 146
icons, 12, 112, 178
IMAP. *See* Internet
    Messaging Access
    Protocol
Imation, 80
iMovie, 144
India, 161
information
  compared to data, 11
  defined, 11
  personal information man-
    ager, 137
.ini filename extension, 204
ink jet printer. *See also*
    printer
  discussed, 94-95
input. *See also* output
  buffer, 120
  CD-ROM, 10
  defined, 4
  handwriting, 7
  keyboard, 9
  mouse, 9
  queues, 120
  touch-sensitive screen, 7
installation. *See also* boot
    process; software
    installation
  ISP equipment, 21
  peripheral device, 92
  printer, 97
instant messaging, 17
instruction set, 67, 70. *See*
    also microprocessor
  how instructions are exe-
    cuted, 98-101, 115-116
    ALU, 100
    control unit role, 100
    instruction cycle, 99
    op code, 98
    operands, 98
  parallel processing, 68
  RISC, compared to CISC,
    68
  serial processing, 68
integrated circuit (IC), 62
Integrated Services Digital
    Network (ISDN)
  discussed, 20
Intel, 69, 98
interface
  application programming
    interface, 60
  command-line interface,
    120
  graphical user interface,
    120

user interface, 120, 121
Internet. *See also* Internet access; Internet service provider; World Wide Web
  data storage, 16
    backups, 195, 198
  data transmission, 16
  in general, 15-18
    Internet backbone, 15
    TCP/IP, 15
  IDs an passwords, 22-24
  "logging on," 22
  resources
    broadcasting, 17
    bulletin boards, 16
    chat groups, 17
    downloads/uploads, 17
    e-commerce, 16
    e-mail, 16
    instant messaging, 17
    Internet telephony, 17
    newsgroups, 16
    P2P, 18
    remote access, 18
    search engines, 16
    Telnet, 18
    Web sites, 16
  Web authoring software, 128
Internet access, 18-20
  cable modem, 19
  dial-up connection, 18-19
  DSL, 20
  DSS, 20
  ISDN, 20
  options, 18
    school/business networks, 20
Internet Messaging Access Protocol (IMAP)
  e-mail, 40
  discussed, 41
Internet service provider (ISP)
  defined, 20
  discussed, 20-22
  local ISP, compared to national ISP, 20-21
  selecting, 21-22
interpreter, 116
Intuit Quicken, 136
Intuit TurboTax, 136
Iomega, 80
IP address. *See also* uniform resource locator
  defined, 16
iPAQ, 7
ISDN. *See* Integrated Services Digital Network
ISP. *See* Internet service provider
iTunes, 143

JavaScript, 116. *See also* script
Jobs, Steve, 209

joystick, 11
.jpg filename extension, 205, 206

kernal, 121. *See also* operating system
key
  sort key, 140
keyboard, 9
  buffer, 120
keyword
  defined, 32
kilobit, 61. *See also* bit
kilobyte, 61. *See also* byte
Klez worm, 186

label, worksheet, 133
LAN. *See* local area network
laptop. *See* notebook computer
laser printer. *See also* printer
  discussed, 95-96
  Printer Control Language, 96
LCD. *See* liquid crystal display
leading, 131
Lemmings, 146
letters, 132
license. *See* software license
line spacing, 131
linking
  handheld and personal computer, 7
  Web pages, 26
Linux, 12, 13, 122, 155
  compared to UNIX, 125
  distribution, 125
liquid crystal display (LCD), 9. *See also* display
  active matrix, 94
  advantages, 92-93
  compared to CRT, 92
  native resolution, 94
  passive matrix, 94
  TFT, 94
list server, 16. *See also* e-mail
local area network (LAN). *See also* network
  defined, 7
logical data type, 139
Longest Journey, 146
Lotus 1-2-3, 205
Love Bug worm, 186
LOVE-LETTER-FOR-YOU.TXT.vbs, 186-187

Mac OS, 12, 13, 122, 152. *See also* Apple; Macintosh; operating system
  compared to Windows, 124
  file system, 181
  filename naming conventions, 170
  utilities, 176

machine language, 115
Macintosh (Mac), 280. *See also* Apple
  discussed, 13
  iMac, 13
macro, disabling, 188
macro virus, 186, 188. *See also* virus
Macromedia Dreamweaver, 128
Mafiaboy, 208
mail merge, 132
mainframe. *See also* computer
  defined, 6
  discussed, 8
margin
  changing, 128
  justified, 131
MasterCard, 313
Mathcad, 136
Mathematica, 136
mathematical operators, 134
.mdb filename extension, 205
megabit, 61. *See also* bit
megabyte, 61. *See also* byte
megahertz (MHz), 67, 72
megapixel, 335
Melissa virus, 185, 186
memo data type, 139
memory. *See also* cache; complementary metal oxide semiconductor; random-access memory; read-only memory; storage
  cache memory, 68
  defined, 5
  descriptions of, 74
  OS management, 119-120
  virtual memory, 71
  volatility, 71, 72
MHz. *See* megahertz
Michelangelo virus, 185
microchip, 62
microcomputer, 6. *See also* computer
microprocessor, 6, 63. *See also* computer; instruction set
  comparing, benchmarks, 68
  contemporary
    AMD, 69
    Intel, 69
    Pentium, 69
  control unit, 100
  defined, 66
  discussed, 66-67
    ALU, 67, 100
    control unit, 67
    instruction set, 67
    nanometer, 66
    registers, 67
  how instructions are executed, 98-101, 115-116
  multiprocessor architecture, 627

performance factors, 67-68
  cache size, 68
  CISC and RISC, 68
  cycle, 67
  gigahertz, 67
  megahertz, 67
  microprocessor clock, 67
  parallel processing, 68
  resources management,
    119
  serial processing, 68
  word size, 67
  upgrades, 69
Microsoft Access, 138, 205
Microsoft Backup, 201
Microsoft Encarta, 145
Microsoft Excel, 133, 186,
  188, 205
Microsoft FrontPage, 128
Microsoft Internet Explorer,
  28
Microsoft Money, 136
Microsoft Movie Maker, 144
Microsoft Office, 160
Microsoft PowerPoint, 205
Microsoft Publisher, 205
Microsoft Windows, 12, 122.
  See also Windows
  Registry
  discussed, 122-124
  features, 12
  file systems, 181
  filename naming conven-
    tions, 170
  OS, compared to applica-
    tion software, 13
  upgrades, 124
  Windows 3.1, 120, 123
  Windows 95, 124
  Windows 98, 124
  Windows 2000, 123, 124
  Windows CE, 12
  Windows Me, 124
  Windows NT, 124
  Windows XP, 123, 124,
    151, 171
Microsoft Word, 128, 171,
  174, 203
  virus infection, 186, 188
Microsoft XBox, 7
MIDI software, 143
.mid filename extension, 11,
  205
.mif filename extension, 204
millisecond, 79
MIME. See multi-purpose
  Internet mail extension
MindTwister Math, 144
minicomputer, 6. See also
  computer
Minix, 125
Mitnick, Kevin, 208-209
modem, 88. See also
  telephone
  cable modem, 19
  defined, 10
  transmission speed, 61

voice band modem, 18
monitor, 9. See also com-
  puter; display; personal
  computer
  LCD, 9, 92-93
  resolution, 93-94
monitoring
  e-mail monitoring, 48-49
Moore, Gordon, 98
Moore's Law, 98
Morris, Robert, 208
motherboard, 63-64. See
  also digital electronics
mouse, 9, 12, 124
.mov filename extension,
  205
MP3, 143
.mp3 filename extension,
  205
MPEG file format, 87
.mpg filename extension,
  205
multi-purpose Internet mail
  extension (MIME),
  defined, 37
multimedia file, format, 204
multiplication symbol (*),
  134
multitasking operating system, 122, 123. See also
  operating system
music software
  discussed, 143
    audio editing software,
      143
    CD ripper, 143, 367
    ear training software, 143
    MIDI software, 143
    MP3, 143
    notation software, 143
Myst, 146

nanometer, 66
nanosecond, 72
National Safety Council, 102
near, search operator, 32
Nelson, Ted, 26
netiquette. See also e-mail
  guidelines for, 39
  smileys, 39
Netscape Navigator, 28
network
  workstation, 7
network interface card
  (NIC), 19
networking
  Windows OS, 124
New York Times, 22, 48
newsgroups, 16
nibble, 61
NIC. See network interface
  card
Nintendo GameCube, 7
Nokia, 103
North Korea, 161
NOT operator, 32
notation software, 143

notebook computer. See
  also computer; personal
  computer
  defined, 6
  display, LCD, 94
  expansion access, 62
  expansion slot, 90
    PC card, 90
    PCMCIA slot, 90
Novell Netware, 122
numeric data, 59. See also
  data
  ASCII, 61
numeric data type, 139

object code, 115
object-oriented database,
  138. See also database
.ocx filename extension, 204
Omnibus Crime Control
  and Safe Streets Act of
  1968, 48
op code, 98
operands, 98
operating system (OS). See
  also specific operating
  systems
  application software and,
    12-13
  compatibility, 13, 122
  defined, 12
    desktop OS, 122
    multi-user OS, 122
    multitasking OS, 122
    network OS, 122
    single-user OS, 122
    as system software, 12
  devices management, 120
  discussed, 118-122
  DOS, 126
  file management utilities,
    176
  file system and, 181-182
  loading
    in boot process, 44-47, 70
    bootstrap program, 121
    kernal, 121
    utilities, 121
  memory management,
    119-120
  Microsoft Windows, 12
    compared to application
      software, 13
  network OS, 257
  platform, 13
  popular systems
    Linux, 12
    Mac OS, 12
    Microsoft Windows, 12
    Microsoft Windows CE, 12
    Palm OS, 12
    UNIX, 12
  storage management, 120
  UNIX and Linux, com-
    pared, 125
  what it does, 118-119
    resources, 119

OR operator, 32
OS. *See* operating system
output. *See also* input; printer
  CD-writer, 10
  defined, 5
.ovl filename extension, 187

P2P. *See* peer-to-peer
packet
  defined, 16
page layout
  graphical elements, 132
  headers and footers, 131
  page numbers, 131
paint software, 141
Palm, 7
Palm OS, 12
paragraph alignment, 131
paragraph style, 131
parallel processing, 68
password. *See also* security;
  user ID
  case sensitive, 23
  defined, 22
  Internet, 22-24
    choosing, 23-24
    remembering, 23
  theft, 186
path, file, 172
payroll software, 147
PC, 6, 13, 69. *See also* personal computer
PC card, 90
PCMCIA slot, 90
.pcx filename extension, 205
PDA. *See* Personal Digital
  Assistant
.pdf filename extension,
  205, 206
peer-to-peer (P2P)
  discussed, 18
Penenberg, Adam L., 208
Pentium chip, 69, 98. *See
  also* chip; microprocessor
peripheral device. *See also
  specific devices*
  connecting, 91
  defined, 11
  identifying, 45, 46
  installing, 92
    device driver, 92
    Plug and Play, 92
  OS management, 120
personal computer. *See also*
  computer
  computer system, 9
    CD-ROM, 10
    CD-writer, 10
    display, 9
    DVD, 10
    floppy disk drive, 9
    hard disk drive, 9, 11
    keyboard, 9
    modem, 10
    mouse, 9
    peripheral device, 11
    printer, 10

    sound card, 10
    system unit, 9
  defined, 6
    desktop computer, 6, 62
    notebook computer, 6, 62
  discussed, 6, 9-11, 13
  drive bay, 78
Personal Digital Assistant
  (PDA). *See also* computer
  defined, 7
personal identification number (PIN), 22
personal information
  manager, 137
PGAs, 63
PGP. *See* Pretty Good
  Privacy
photo editing software, 141
Picture.exe, 186
PictureNote.Trojan, 186
PIN. *See* personal identification number
Ping of Death, 187
Planescape, 146
platform, defined, 13
PlayStation. *See also*
  computer
  discussed, 7-8
  videogame console, 7
.png filename extension, 205
PocketPC, 7
POP. *See* Post Office
  Protocol
port. *See also* expansion
  port
  defined, 90
Post Office Protocol (POP),
  40. *See also* e-mail
  compared to Web-based
    e-mail, 42
  discussed, 41
    e-mail client software, 41,
      42
  POP server, 41
  SMTP server, 41
POST. *See* power-on self-test
power-on self-test (POST).
  See also boot process
  beep code, 45
  defined, 44
  laser printer, Printer
    Control Language, 96
  problem identification, 45
.ppt filename extension, 205
presentation software, 142
printer, 11. *See also* output
  defined, 10
  discussed, 94-97
    resolution, 94, 95
    speed, 94
  dot-matrix printer, 96
  drivers and software, 97
  dye sublimation printer, 95
  ink jet printer, 94-95
  installing, 97
  laser printer, 95-96
  solid ink printer, 95

  thermal transfer printer, 95
printing
  from browser, 30
privacy. *See also* security
  e-mail, 48-49
processing. *See also* microprocessor
  defined, 4
  parallel processing, 68
  serial processing, 68
productivity
  enhancing, 132
  virus affecting, 185
program. *See* computer
  program
programmer. *See* computer
  programmer
programming. *See* computer
  programming
programming language, 115
  high-level language, 115
  machine language, 115
project management
  software, 147
public domain software, 155
.pub filename extension, 205

QBE. *See* query by example
Quake, 146
QuarkXPress, 128, 205
query. *See also* search
  engines
  defined, 32
  natural language query, 34
  searching with, 140
query by example (QBE),
  140
query language, 140
  natural query language, 140
  Structured Query Language,
    140
queue, 120
QuickBooks, 136
quotation marks, search
  operator, 32
.qxd filename extension, 205

radio, Internet broadcasting,
  17
RAID. *See* redundant array
  of independent disks
RAM. *See* random-access
  memory
random-access memory
  (RAM), 76. *See also* memory; read-only memory
  compared to hard-disk
    storage, 70
  compared to ROM, 72
  defined, 44, 70
  discussed, 70-72
    capacitors, 71
    volatility, 71
  how much do you need?,
    71
  virtual memory, 71
  loading OS into, 44

types
  RAM speed, 72
  RDRAM, 72
  RIMM, 72
  SDRAM, 72
  SO-RIMM, 72
.ra filename extension, 205
read-only memory (ROM).
  See also memory; ran-
  dom-access memory
  compared to RAM, 72
  defined, 44
  discussed, 72
  ROM BIOS, 72
readability formula, 130
RealMedia, 206
record, 137, 138. *See also*
  database; record structure
record structure
  creating, 139, 140
  sort key, 140
Recycle Bin, 183
reduced instruction set computer (RISC), compared
  to CISC, 68
redundant array of independent disks (RAID). *See also*
  hard disk; storage
  discussed, 83
registry. *See* Windows
  Registry
relational database, 138
reliability, magnetic storage,
  77
remote access, e-mail, 42
rescue disk, 198
reserved word, filename, 171
resolution
  LCD, 94
  native resolution, 94
  printer, 94, 95
resources, managing, 119
Return to Monkey Island, 146
RISC. *See* reduced instruction set computer
.rm filename extension, 205,
  206
ROM. *See* read-only memory
root directory, 172
router
  defined, 16
.rtf filename extension, 205

Safe Mode, boot process,
  46-47
satellite
  Digital Satellite Service, 20
saving
  file, 76, 181-182
  from browser, 30
  Save, compared to Save
    As, 175
scanner, 11
school, e-mail policy, 49
script, 116. *See also*
  JavaScript; VBScript
.scr filename extension, 187
search engines

defined, 16, 31
discussed, 31-34
  field search, 32
  keyword, 32
  natural language query, 34
  query, 32
  search operators, 32
  topic directory, 33
  using a form, 33
Search and Replace, 130
SEC cartridge, 63
sector, 180
  clusters, 181
security. *See also* password;
  privacy
  e-mail, 42
semiconductors, 62
server. *See also* computer
  backup storage on, 198
  defined, 8
  discussed, 8
  client, 8
  e-mail server, 40
  mailing list server, 16
  POP server, 41
  server OS, 122, 124
  SMTP server, 41
  Web server, 27
SET. *See* Secure Electronic
  Transaction
Setup program. *See also*
  boot process
  entering and exiting, 73
  software installation, 150
Setup.exe program, 151
shareware, 155
Simple Mail Transfer
  Protocol (SMTP)
Sims, 146
slides, 141. *See also* graphics software
smileys, 39. *See also* e-mail
SMTP. *See* Simple Mail
  Transfer Protocol
SMTP server, 41
Smurf, 187
software. *See also* accounting and finance software;
  application software; data
  management software;
  program; software installation; spreadsheet soft-
  ware; Web page authoring
  antivirus software, 188,
    189-190
  backup software, 200-201
  business software, 147
  commercial software, 154
  conversion software, 207
  copying, 153
  copyrights, 153
  creating, 114
    properties, 114
  data and, 113
  database management
    software, 138
  defined, 4, 112
  discussed, 112

drawing software, 141
educational and reference
  software, 144-145
entertainment software,
  145-146
file shredder software, 182
freeware, 155
full version, compared to
  upgrade, 151
graphics software, 141-142
how it works, 115-116
  compiler, 115
  interpreter, 116
  object code, 115
  scripts, 116
music software, 143
open source software, 155
"patch," 46
printer, 97
public domain software,
  155
recycling, 102
shareware, 155
support modules, 112
system software, 12,
  116-117
uninstalling, 152
video editing software, 144
Software and Information
  Industry Association, 160
software installation. *See*
  also installation
  downloaded software, 151
    self-installing executable
      file, 151
    Zip files, 151
  from distribution disk, 150
    setup program, 150
  full version, compared to
    upgrade, 151
  in general, 148-149
    distribution disk, 148,
      149, 150
    files and folders, 149
    system requirements, 148
software license
  defined, 153
  discussed, 153-155
    commercial license, 154
    freeware, 155
    installation agreement,
      154
    open source software,
      155
    public domain software,
      155
    shareware, 155
    shrink-wrap license, 153
software piracy, discussed,
  160
software publisher, 114
Sony, 103
Sony PlayStation, 7
sort key, 140
sound. *See also* audio
  digitizing, 61
sound card. *See also* audio
  discussed, 10

Sound Recorder, 143
source code, 115
speed. *See also* access time
  CD-ROM, 85
  data transfer rate, 79
  nanosecond, 72
  printer, 94
spell checker
  document production
    software, 129
  e-mail, 39
  spreadsheet, 133
spreadsheet software. *See also* software
  discussed, 133-136
    formula, 134
    what-if analysis, 133
    worksheet, 133
  worksheet, 133
    automatic recalculation, 134
    cell, 133
    cell references, 134
    cell references, absolute, 135
    defined, 133
    formula, 134, 135
    function, 134, 135
    label, 133
    mathematical operators, 134
    modifying worksheet, 135
    templates/wizards, 135
    value, 133
SPSS, 136
SQL. *See* Structured Query Language
SSL. *See* Secure Sockets Layer
Stallman, Richard, 160
Start button, 12
startup, Windows Startup Disk, 197
statistical software, 136
Statsoft STATISTICA, 136
Stoned virus, 186
storage. *See also* cache; data storage; floppy disk; hard disk; memory; storage technology
  archiving, 86
  backups, 198
  CD-ROM, 10
  defined, 5
  discussed, 76-79
    drive bay, 78
    storage device, 76
    storage medium, 76
  floppy disk drive, 9
  hard disk drive, 9
  logical storage model, 177
  magnetic storage, 77
    compared to optical, 77-78
    read-write head, 77
    reliability, 77
  optical storage
    compared to magnetic, 77-78

lands, 78
  pits, 78
  OS management, 120
  RAID, 83
  relation to computer system, 76
  storage devices, adding to computer, 78
  storage metaphor, tree structure, 177
  tape storage, 83-84
storage technology, 76
  advantages and disadvantages, 79
  access time, 79
  data transfer rate, 79
  random access, 79
  sequential access, 79
  file storage
    file system, 181
    formatting, 180
    formatting utilities, 180-181
  physical storage model, 180
structured file, 137. *See also* database; file
Structured Query Language (SQL), 140. *See also* database.
students, e-mail privacy, 49
style, 131
supercomputer. *See also* computer
  discussed, 8
Superdisk, 80
.sys filename extension, 187, 204
system software. *See also* software
  discussed, 12, 116-117
System.dat file, 157

table, 132
  database relationships, 138
tag *See* HTML tags
tape drive, 76. *See also* backup; storage
  advantages, 83
  discussed, 83-84, 198
  installation, 84
  operation, 83-84
  tape backup, 83
tax preparation software, 136
TCP/IP. *See* Transmission Control Protocol/Internet Protocol
Teardrop, 187
telephone. *See also* modem
  dial-up connection, 18-19
    connection speed, 19
  Internet telephony, 17
Telnet, 18
temporary file, 204
terabyte, 61
Tetrus, 146
text
  justified, 131

point size, 130
  style, 292
text file, format, 204
thesaurus, 130. *See also* spell checker
3D Froggy Phonics, 144
3D graphics software, 142. *See also* graphic
3M, 103
.tif filename extension, 11, 205, 206
.tmp filename extension, 204
Tomb Raider, 146
topic directory, 33
Torvalds, Linus, 125
Toshiba, 13
Transmission Control Protocol/Internet Protocol (TCP/IP)
  defined, 15
Trojan horse. *See also* virus
  compared to virus, 186
troubleshooting. *See also* Windows Registry
  display "freeze up," 45
.txt filename extension, 112, 205

Unicode, 60
uniform resource locator (URL). *See also* IP address
  discussed, 27
  rules for typing, 28
  URL box, 30
UNIX, 12, 155
  compared to Linux, 125
  filename naming conventions, 170
Unreal Tournament, 146
upgrade, microprocessor, 69
uploading, Internet, 17
USB port, 90, 91, 97. *See also* expansion port
Usenet, defined, 16
user ID. *See also* password
  defined, 22
  Internet, 22-24
  choosing, 23
user interface, 120, 121
User.dat file, 157
utilities, 121. *See also* operating system; program
  Copy Disk utility, 200
  defragmentation utility, 183
  file management utilities, 176
  formatting utilities, 180-181

value, worksheet, 133
VBScript, 116
.vbs filename extension, 185, 187
.vbx filename extension, 204
VDE. *See* visual development environment
video editing, 12. *See also* video editing software

video editing software, 144
  discussed, 144
VideoFactory, 112, 116
videogame console, 7. *See
  also* computer
virus
  in backup file, 196
  characteristics, 47
    trigger event, 185
  compared to Trojan horse,
    186
  compared to worm, 186-187
  defined, 185
    boot sector virus, 186
    file virus, 186
    macro virus, 186, 188
    multi-partite virus, 190
    polymorphic virus, 190
    retro virus, 190
    stealth virus, 190
  in e-mail, 39, 187-188
  hoaxes, 191-192
  sources, 187-188
Visor, 7
volatility, memory, 71, 72
.vrml filename extension, 205

Walker, Kent, 208
.wav filename extension, 205
Web. *See* World Wide Web
Web authoring software.
    See also Web page
  discussed, 128
Web browser. *See* browser
Web page, 26. *See also*
    Web authoring software
  copying, 30
  home page, 30
  printing, 30
  saving, 30
Web server, 27
Web site
  defined, 27
  discussed, 16
wildcards, search operator,
    32
Windows Explorer, 177. *See
    also* Microsoft Windows
  discussed, 178-179
    multiple files, 179
Windows Registry. *See also*
    Microsoft Windows
  backups, 195
  changes to, Registry
    Editor, 159
  discussed, 157-159
    Registry data, 158
  locating files for, 157-158
    six main folders, 158
WinZip, 151, 205. *See also*
    Zip file
wireframe, 142
.wks filename extension, 205
.wmf filename extension, 205
word processing software,
    128
word size, 67
word wrap, 128

worksheet. *See also*
    spreadsheet
  automatic recalculation, 134
  cell, 133
  cell references, 134
  cell references, absolute,
    135
  defined, 133
  formula, 134, 135
  function, 134, 135
  label, 133
  mathematical operators,
    134
  modifying worksheet, 135
  templates/wizards, 135
  value, 133
workstation. *See also*
    computer
  defined, 7
World Wide Web (Web). *See
    also* Internet
  browsers, 28-31
  discussed, 26-28
    HTML, 27
    HTTP, 27
    URL, 27, 28
  search engines, 31-34
worm, 286. *See also* virus
  defined, 186
  discussed, 186-187
writing. *See* document pro-
    duction software

Xerox, 103
Xerox PARC, 120, 124
.xls filename extension, 188,
    205

Zip disk, 80
  for backup, 198-199
Zip drive, 76, 81
Zip file
  self-executing, 151
  zip/unzip, 151
.zip filename extension, 205
zipping. *See* compression